JEFFERSON *and the* INDIANS

The Tragic Fate of the First Americans

Thomas Jefferson. Oil on canvas by Thomas Sully, 1821.
Courtesy of the American Philosophical Society.

JEFFERSON *and the* INDIANS

THE TRAGIC FATE
OF THE
FIRST AMERICANS

Anthony F. C. Wallace

THE BELKNAP PRESS of
HARVARD UNIVERSITY PRESS
Cambridge, Massachusetts
London, England

Printed in the United States of America

First Harvard University Press paperback edition, 2001

Library of Congress Cataloging-in-Publication Data

Wallace, Anthony F. C., 1923–
Jefferson and the Indians : the tragic fate of the first Americans /
Anthony F. C. Wallace.
p. cm.
ISBN 0-674-00066-8 (hc. : alk. paper)
ISBN 0-674-00548-1 (pbk. : alk. paper)
1. Indians of North America—Government relations—1789–1869.
2. Indians, Treatment of—North America.
3. Indians of North America—Social conditions.
4. Jefferson, Thomas, 1743–1826—Views on Indians.
5. Jefferson, Thomas, 1743–1826—Political and social views.
6. United States—Politics and government–1789–1815.
7. United States—Race relations. I. Title
E93.W18 1999
323.1′197073—dc21 99-21558

To Betty

my companion on the Jefferson journey

Cities, Towns, and Other Points of Interest, c. 1800

Preface

THOMAS JEFFERSON was an enigma in his own time, revered by some, reviled by others. Today, two hundred years later, he is an enigma with charisma, fascinating to the public and the scholarly world alike. His image looms over us from a cliff in the Black Hills and from the Memorial in Washington; visitors throng his house and gardens at Monticello, where he longed to live among his books, even though he perennially sought public office. His inspiring one-liners, most notably "all men are created equal" and "life, liberty, and the pursuit of happiness," have taken on a life of their own, attaining meanings far removed from what Jefferson himself likely intended. In our own time, Thomas Jefferson has become a culture-hero, the American Prometheus, our version of the universal Trickster, that morally ambiguous mythic being who steals fire from the gods and brings the arts, sciences, and social institutions to the world.

Joseph Ellis has called Jefferson the American Sphinx, and, along with other biographers, has noted his many inconsistencies. Jefferson's advocacy of national independence, minimal government, and maximal individual freedom has been hailed as the world's charter for democracy and also as the authority for isolationism, states' rights and nullification, and revolutionary militias. He has been praised as a critic of slavery and condemned as a hypocritical slave-owning racist. His relationship with a black slave, Sally Hemings, his wife's half-sister and the mother of one or more of his own children, has been characterized as a long-term union of mutual affection and respect, as an example of sexual exploitation by a master who refused to emancipate his concubine or her children while he lived, and as an unthinkable association for a gentleman of virtue. And, with respect to Native Americans, Jefferson appears both as the scholarly admirer of Indian character, archaeology, and language and as the planner of cultural genocide, the architect of the removal policy, the surveyor of the Trail of Tears.

The fascination with Jefferson has grown, perhaps, because he embodied some of the major dilemmas of American culture—fault-lines in the national character where differing views on how to share the spaces of the world grind together. He evokes an awareness of classic problems in a democracy: what to do about slavery; how to deal with ethnic differences; how to define the proper balance between freedom and governance; how to preserve agrarian values in an increasingly industrial world; how far to expand the nation's boundaries; how to manage an emerging commercial empire's foreign affairs, by defensive isolation or aggressive alliance building; how to decide on war and peace; how to balance the budget while promoting the national interest; how to respond to the conflicting claims of religion and science. On some of these issues, Jefferson was at times a shape-shifter, articulating one policy in public only to execute another in private, or later publicly. In no domain of his life as a philosopher-politician-official do such dilemmas appear more conspicuously than in his relations with Native Americans.

This is a book about Jefferson's attitudes, beliefs, and behavior toward the Indians. It does not pretend to be a survey of Native American cultures of his time or a compendium of tribal histories. I have tried to be fair in assessing Jefferson's conduct in Indian affairs, but viewed from the late twentieth century, some of his actions appear to be hypocritical, arbitrary, duplicitous, even harsh. Certainly some of the unintended consequences of his policies of civilization, removal, and protection of frontier populations against Indian retaliation for encroachments and atrocities were catastrophic for the Indians. Thomas Jefferson played a major role in one of the great tragedies of recent world history, a tragedy which he so elegantly mourned: the dispossession and decimation of the First Americans.

In the chapters that follow, we trace the development of Jefferson's ambivalent attitudes toward Indians and the hardening of these attitudes into presidential policy. The Introduction tells the story of Jefferson and John Logan, the Great Mingo, the eloquent Indian whose tragic fate symbolized for Jefferson, and for generations of readers, the coming doom of the red race. Chapter 1 describes the business world in which Jefferson grew up, a world of real estate speculators, including his father's friends, obsessed with obtaining Indian land. Chapter 2 examines Jefferson's political rhetoric toward Native Americans during the Revolution; his experiences as war governor led him to depict the Indians first as cruel enemies and then as friendly neighbors. Chapters 3, 4, and 5 deal with Jefferson's proposals for scholarly studies of Indian languages, cultures, and ancient origins. Chapter 6 takes up the Federalist program for "civilizing" the Indians, which Jefferson observed in the 1790s, adopted when he became President, and found difficult to implement. In Chapters 7, 8, and 9 we follow Jefferson's Indian policy as President: purchasing Indian lands, establishing peace and trade with the tribes of the Louisiana Territory, and encountering opposition to the civilization program from Native American religious and political reformers. The last chapter brings him back to his philosophical labors in the quiet study at Monticello, and the Conclusion considers the legacy of his dealings with the First Americans.

Throughout, we find the same theme recurring, the self-serving Jeffersonian conception of Native Americans that is revealed in the carefully edited story of Logan which he presented to the world in 1785 in *Notes on the State of Virginia*: the Indians as noble but doomed savages, tragically slaughtered in wars precipitated by a few murderous frontiersmen and a few vengeful warriors, a surviving remnant yearning to be civilized but fated to lose their land to a deserving white yeomanry.

Contents

Indian Nations, c. 1800

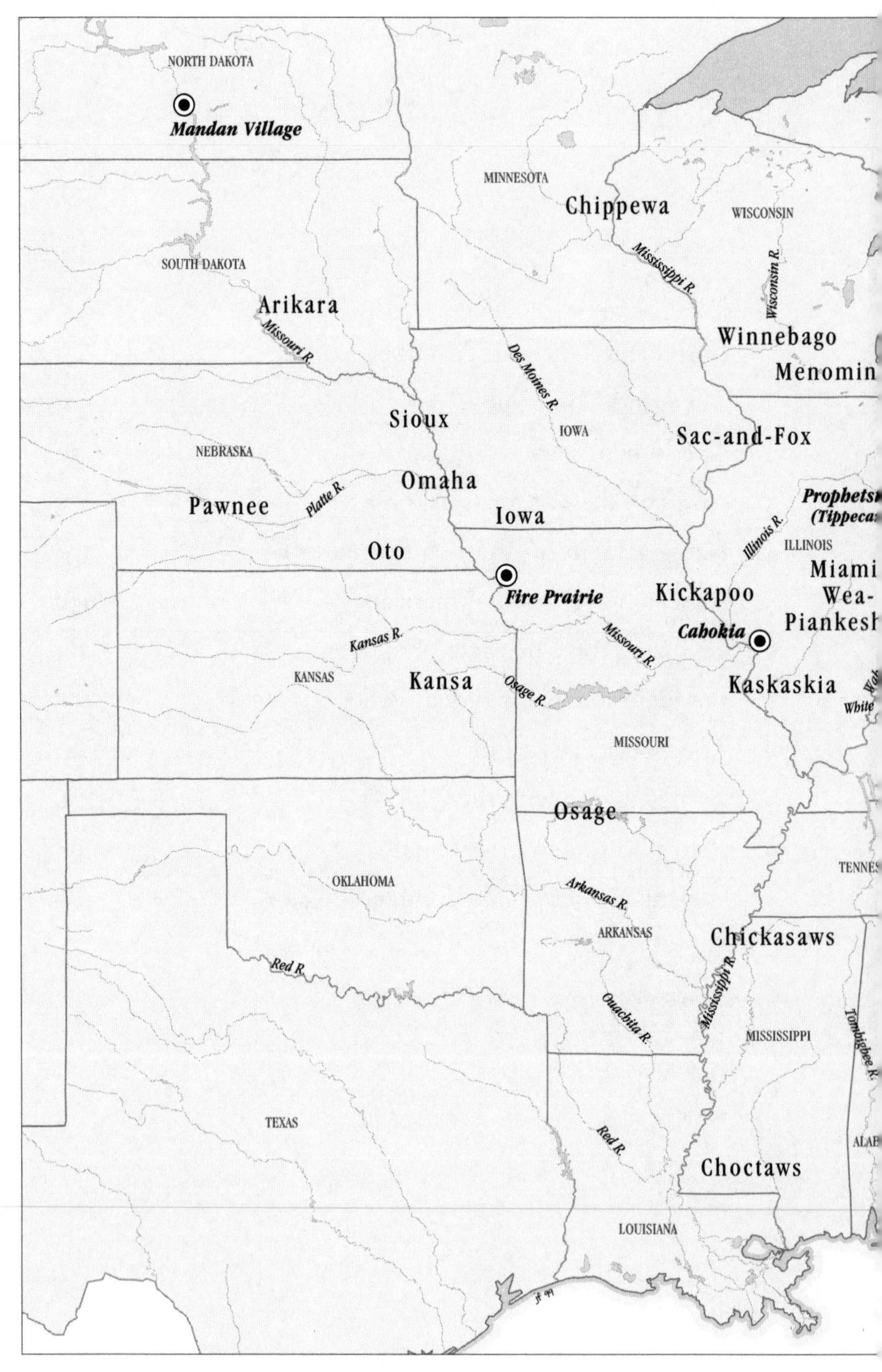

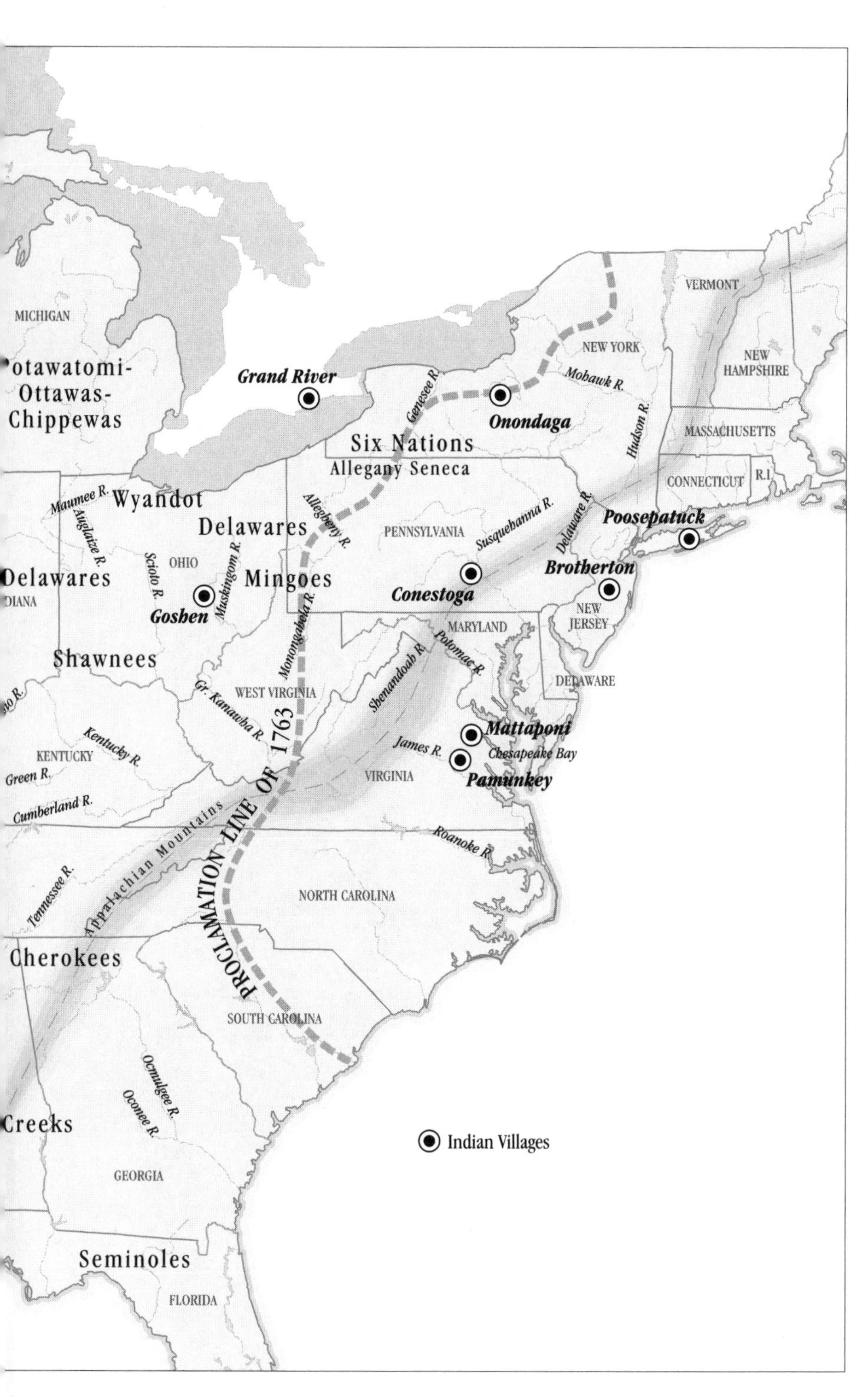

MICHIGAN
Potawatomi-
Ottawas-
Chippewas
Grand River
Six Nations
Allegany Seneca
Onondaga
NEW YORK
Mohawk R.
Genesee R.
Hudson R.
VERMONT
NEW
HAMPSHIRE
MASSACHUSETTS
CONNECTICUT
R.I.
Poosepatuck
Brotherton
NEW
JERSEY
Delaware R.
Susquehanna R.
PENNSYLVANIA
Conestoga
Allegheny R.
Maumee R.
Wyandot
Auglaize R.
Delawares
OHIO
Scioto R.
Muskingum R.
Mingoes
Delawares
DIANA
Goshen
Monongahela R.
MARYLAND
Potomac R.
Shenandoah R.
DELAWARE
Shawnees
WEST VIRGINIA
Gr. Kanawha R.
Kentucky R.
KENTUCKY
Green R.
Cumberland R.
Mattaponi
James R.
Chesapeake Bay
Pamunkey
VIRGINIA
PROCLAMATION LINE OF 1763
Appalachian Mountains
Roanoke R.
Tennessee R.
NORTH CAROLINA
Cherokees
SOUTH CAROLINA
Ocmulgee R.
Oconee R.
Creeks
GEORGIA
Seminoles
FLORIDA
Indian Villages

Indian Land Cessions during Thomas Jefferson's Presidency, 1801–1809

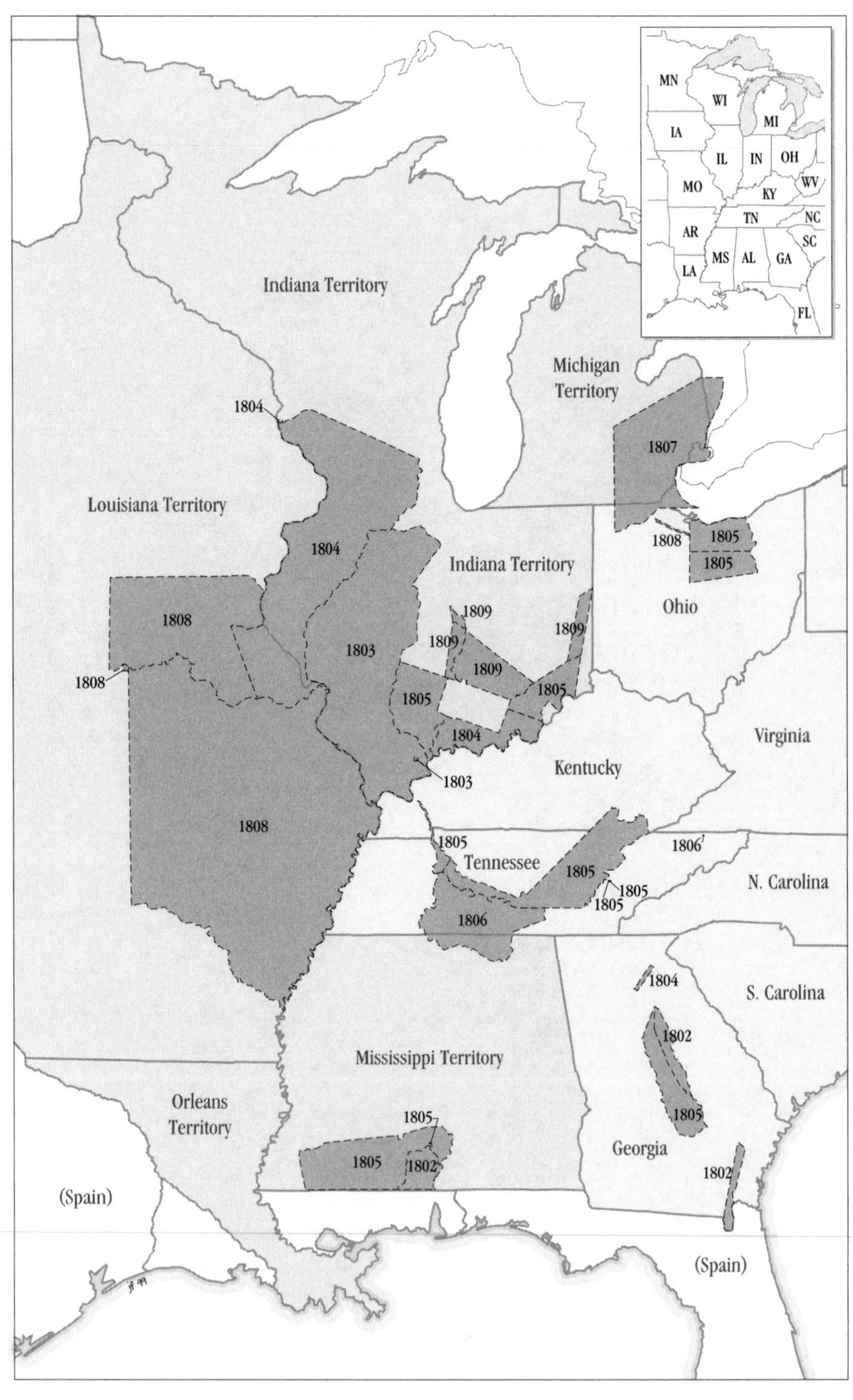

JEFFERSON *and the* INDIANS

The Tragic Fate of the First Americans

Logan's Lament

I appeal to any white man to say, if ever he entered Logan's cabin hungry, and he gave him not meat; if ever he came cold and naked, and he clothed him not. During the course of the last long and bloody war [the French and Indian War, 1755–1763], Logan remained idle in his cabin, an advocate for peace. Such was my love for the whites, that my countrymen pointed as they passed, and said, "Logan is the friend of white men." I had even thought to have lived with you, but for the injuries of one man. Col. Cresap, the last spring, in cold blood, and unprovoked, murdered all the relations of Logan, not sparing even my women and children. There runs not a drop of my blood in the veins of any living creature. This called on me for revenge. I have sought it: I have killed many: I have fully glutted my vengeance. For my country, I rejoice at the beams of peace. But do not harbour a thought that mine is the joy of fear. Logan never felt fear. He will not turn on his heel to save his life. Who is there to mourn for Logan?—Not one.

INTRODUCTION

Logan's Mourner

IN HIS *Notes on the State of Virginia,* which Thomas Jefferson began writing in 1781 and first published in 1785, he inserted an English rendering of a speech by the Indian leader Tachnedorus, or John Logan. The address had been delivered to the victorious Lord Dunmore, governor of Virginia, on the occasion of the signing of a peace treaty with the Shawnees in 1774. It was the valedictory address of a defeated warrior.[1]

Jefferson introduced Logan's Lament, as the speech came to be called (see opposite), ostensibly as part of his refutation of the claim of the famous French naturalist, the Comte de Buffon, that the American aborigines, like other products of the New World, were deficient in natural abilities in comparison with Europeans. An elegant writer but no speechmaker himself, Jefferson was an admirer of eloquence in any mode, and he declared that Logan's speech was in no way inferior to the best examples of classical rhetoric, including Demosthenes and Cicero.[2]

The impact on the public of Jefferson's story of Logan the Great Mingo and of the speech itself was extraordinary. Its popularity derived in part from its succinct expression of an apocalyptic view of Indian history that was becoming increasingly prevalent in Jefferson's time, helped along in various ways by Jefferson himself. Logan, the last of his line, was symbolically the last of a dying race, consumed in the holocaust brought by the European invaders, tragically destined to become extinct, yet facing annihilation without surrender. He had sought, too late, to join the white man's world. Now, a doomed but unrepentant savage, he must die alone.

Logan's Lament has been endlessly reprinted, beginning with Washington Irving's *Sketch Book* and later in the McGuffey *Readers,* and has been memorized and recited by millions of schoolchildren. It still endures as an example of rhetorical excellence; a few of my own colleagues and students report learning it in their youth. At a small park in Ohio, on the site of the treaty-signing, there stands a memorial monument with Logan's speech inscribed in bronze. And below, another bronze plaque was added in 1979, a tribute by a class of fifth-grade students, honoring the brave Logan, who fought to defend his people.[3] Even Jefferson's detractors, like the nineteenth-century historian Brantz Mayer, have conceded the power of Logan's words; in 1867 in a book devoted to questioning the veracity of Jefferson's account of the murder of Logan's family, Mayer admitted, "For ninety years 'Logan's speech' has been repeated by every school boy and admired by every cultivated person as a gem of masculine eloquence."[4] Scholarly interest in Logan continues to this day, and the general image of the Indian as noble savage conveyed in the story of Logan and in other sections of Jefferson's *Notes* has animated a long tradition of American novel and drama.[5]

The immediate historical context of Logan's Lament was sketched by Jefferson in a prefatory passage in the *Notes.* The events he narrated there, and the circumstances that he did not reveal and perhaps even concealed, make the story of Logan and Lord Dunmore's War a paradigm for Indian–white relations, not only in Jefferson's time but for later generations as well. The story of Logan embodies a tragic, self-fulfilling philosophy of history that describes the process by which the fall of the Indian nations and the acquisition of their land would be accomplished. These themes come up again and again in Jefferson's career, both public and private, and form the leitmotif of his Indian policy.

Thus Jefferson's story of Logan, and Logan's Lament, may be regarded as an epitomizing event, to use anthropologist Raymond Fogelson's apt phrase—a narrative that encapsulates, in an account of a single salient happening, the attitudes, values, feelings, and expectations of a community about important, complex, ongoing historical processes. It serves as a rationalization of the past and a vision of the future, a paradigm of destiny, a parable of fate. And the spin that Jefferson gave the affair reveals the leanings of a political mind.[6]

The Story of Logan

Jefferson's first account in the *Notes* of the incidents necessary for understanding Logan's speech was terse: "In the spring of the year 1774, a robbery and murder were committed on an inhabitant of the frontiers of Virginia, by two Indians of the Shawanee tribe. The neighbouring whites, according to their custom, undertook to punish this outrage in a summary way. Col. Cresap, a man infamous for the many murders he had committed on those much-injured people, collected a party, and proceeded down the Kanhaway in quest of vengeance. Unfortunately a canoe of women and children, with one man only, was seen coming from the opposite shore, unarmed, and unsuspecting an hostile attack from the whites. Cresap and his party concealed themselves on the bank of the river, and the moment the canoe reached the shore, singled out their objects, and, at one fire, killed every person in it."

Jefferson continues, "This happened to be the family of Logan, who had long been distinguished as a friend of the whites. This unworthy return provoked his vengeance. He accordingly signalized himself in the war which ensued. In the autumn of the same year, a decisive battle was fought at the mouth of the Great Kanawha, between the collected forces of the Shawanese, Mingoes, and Delawares, and a detachment of the Virginia militia. The Indians were defeated, and sued for peace. Logan however disdained to be seen among the suppliants. But, lest the sincerity of a treaty should be distrusted, from which so distinguished a chief absented himself, he sent by a messenger the following speech to be delivered to Lord Dunmore."[7]

A letter by Devereux Smith, a Pennsylvanian at Pittsburgh, written to the governor and Council of Pennsylvania a few weeks after the events, generally confirms Jefferson's account but adds important information. Smith conveyed the disturbing news of impending war in the Ohio valley and of the criminal provocations of the bellicose Virginians who were intruding on both Pennsylvanian and Indian territories. Smith reported that a party of Virginians led by Michael Cresap had attacked peaceable Shawnees, ostensibly in revenge for a previous murder, killing and scalping three and wounding two more. About the same time, a party led by Daniel Greathouse killed and scalped nine Indians, including Logan's kin, at Baker's Tavern, fifty-five miles down the river, across from the mouth of Yellow Creek (which enters the Ohio several miles above present Wheeling, West Virginia). It was these last murders and the mutilation of Logan's pregnant sister that spurred Logan to take revenge. According to Smith, Logan's attacks were directed particularly at settlements along the upper Monongahela River and in the neighborhood of Redstone Creek, whence Cresap's and Greathouse's men had come.[8]

While these events were taking place on the frontier, Jefferson was busy with the early politics of the Revolution. In late April 1774, when the murders of Logan's kin occurred, Jefferson was in Williamsburg preparing to attend the meeting of the House of Burgesses and helping to establish the Virginia Committee of Correspondence. The Virginia Assembly met in May, resolved on a general day of fasting and prayer to protest the closing of the port of Boston, and was promptly dissolved by Lord Dunmore. Jefferson returned to Albemarle County, where he prepared his instructions to the Virginia delegates to the First Continental Congress, later published as *A Summary View of the Rights of British America.* It was during this spring and summer that Logan and his war party collected their thirteen white scalps and one prisoner along the Monongahela, terrorizing the settlements and causing thousands of refugees to flee eastward. Illness prevented Jefferson from attending the first meeting of the Continental Congress in Philadelphia in the fall, but he was active during this time on patriotic business. In October the decisive battle of Point Pleasant was fought at the mouth of the Great Kanawha, and at the subsequent peace treaty the Shawnees relinquished their land claims in Kentucky.

How did Jefferson obtain the text of Logan's speech? It was first published in William Bradford's *Pennsylvania Journal* on January 20, 1775, from a copy sent Bradford by James Madison of Montpelier as "a specimen of Indian Eloquence and Mistaken Valour." Two weeks later Logan's speech, in less polished language, appeared in Dixon and Hunter's *Virginia Gazette.* Jefferson's text is almost identical to the Madison version. But in his *Appendix to the Notes on the State of Virginia,* which was published separately in 1800, Jefferson claimed that he had heard the speech at Lord Dunmore's in 1774 and had written it down in his memorandum book in the form published in the *Notes.* His informant, he said, was General John Gibson, to whom Logan had delivered his speech and who had translated it into English for Lord Dunmore—an assertion confirmed by Gibson.[9]

Despite certain inaccuracies in Jefferson's narrative, it was not publicly challenged until 1797, when a testy Federalist politician, Maryland Attorney General Luther Martin—Michael Cresap's son-in-law—published letters in the press claiming that Logan's speech was a fabrication and that the charge against Michael Cresap of murdering Logan's family was a calumny. Jefferson, now vice-president and future candidate for the presidency, felt it necessary to rebut this attack. He solicited depositions from surviving participants and observers of the affair and in 1800 published an amended version of the story of Logan. The speech remained the same in this *Appendix,* but Jefferson provided a new narrative of the preceding events.

The new version corrected a couple of errors. The initial Indian provocation was characterized as robbery only, not murder, of "certain land adventurers on the Ohio." Cresap, no longer described as "infamous" for many murders of Indians, was now a captain, not a colonel (his father, the famous frontiersman and Indian trader Thomas Cresap, was the colonel and was not involved in the massacre). The murder of Logan's family occurred across from Yellow Creek on the Ohio River, not the Great Kanawha, at Baker's Tavern, across from a Mingo town near Steubenville, Ohio. Jefferson failed to mention that the massacre had been perpetrated in Cresap's absence; however, some of Cresap's party, led by Daniel Greathouse, had taken part, and Cresap had participated in two other attacks that resulted in the death of some of Logan's other relatives.[10]

The *Appendix* also contained the text of a note tied to a war club left behind by Logan at the scene of one of his attacks, comparing the outrage at Baker's Tavern to the infamous massacre of twenty peaceable Conestoga Indians along the Susquehanna ten years before:

> Captain Cresap,
> What did you kill my people on Yellow Creek for? The white people killed my kin, at Conestoga, a great while ago; and I thought nothing of that. But you killed my kin again, on Yellow Creek, and took my cousin prisoner. Then I thought I must kill too; and I have been three times to war since; but the Indians are not angry; only myself.
> Captain John Logan[11]

Logan had in fact been born along the Susquehanna, about 1725, a son of the notable Cayuga chief Shikellamy, who served among the population of displaced Indian refugees along that river as a kind of viceroy from the Iroquois confederation known as the Six Nations. In the community where Logan grew up, Moravian missionaries were a familiar presence. After his father's death in 1748, Logan for a time took his place as Six Nations deputy, but after the French and Indian War and the murder of his Conestoga kin by the "Paxton boys," he, like many other Indian residents, moved to western Pennsylvania and then on to the Ohio River valley, where he and the other Iroquois became known as Mingoes. There he took a Shawnee woman as wife. He entertained white visitors with civility (according to the Moravian missionary John Heckewelder) and preferred to live close to white settlements.[12]

The modifications Jefferson inserted into the *Appendix* seem to have satisfied, or at least stifled, his critics. But in 1851 the historian Brantz Mayer published a book, *Tah-Gah-Jute; or, Logan and Cresap: An Historical Essay,* defending Cresap and attacking Jefferson. Mayer revealed that Jefferson had suppressed a letter from General George Rogers Clark, written in response to Jefferson's appeal for testimony, that exculpated Cresap from the murder at Baker's Tavern and blamed Greathouse, whose actions were "more barbarous" than Jefferson had described. According to Mayer, Logan's sister's unborn near-term child had been ripped from the womb and "stuck on a pole." And while granting the literary excellence of Logan's Lament as reported by Jefferson, Mayer also implied that the original speech, if ever there was one, was merely an "outburst" from a drunken "blood-stained savage."

Clark's letter was found among Jefferson's papers after his death, and historians have puzzled ever since over his motives in concealing it. Jefferson had accepted other testimony that partially exonerated Cresap; and Clark, an old friend of Jefferson's from Revolutionary War days and a companion of Cresap's in the spring of 1774, was probably the best-informed observer Jefferson could have consulted. Jefferson left no written explanation for his failure to print Clark's letter in the *Appendix,* though he did entrust a verbal message to Samuel Brown, who had forwarded Clark's letter to Jefferson, explaining "what was thought best as to General Clark's deposition." This cryptic remark in his thank-you note to Brown remains his only known comment on this episode of censorship.[13]

Clark's letter itself, however, suggests the reason for its suppression: Jefferson did not want to see his protégé Clark and other brave settlers portrayed as conspirators in a scheme to precipitate a general war against the Ohio Indians for the purpose of seizing their lands. Ever protective of his idealized yeomanry, Jefferson used Cresap and Greathouse as scapegoats for a horde of frontier speculators, surveyors, and settlers who were planning that summer to establish a permanent settlement in Kentucky and were prepared to make war on the Shawnees and any other Indians who claimed hunting rights in the region. Clark was a member of one well-armed, organized body of nearly a hundred men, and Michael Cresap joined it along the way. During the summers of 1773 and 1774, several other groups of thirty to forty armed men each were also roaming through

Kentucky and along the Ohio, surveying likely town sites for George Washington and other eastern speculators (of whom Jefferson was one) and provoking increasingly violent retaliation by the Shawnees and Cherokees.

Heckewelder, the Moravian missionary who visited the region in 1772–1773, recalled conditions on the frontier at the time: "The whole country on the Ohio river, had already drawn the attention of many persons from the neighbouring provinces; who generally forming themselves into parties, would rove through the country in search of land, either to settle on, or for speculation; and some, careless of watching over their conduct, or destitute of both honour and humanity, would join a rabble (a class of people generally met with on the frontiers) who maintained, that to kill an Indian, was the same as killing a bear or a buffalo, and would fire on Indians that came across them by the way;—nay, more, would decoy such as lived across the river, to come over, for the purpose of joining them in hilarity; and when these complied, they fell on them and murdered them. Unfortunately, some of the murdered were of the family of Logan, noted man among the Indians."[14]

Before the Logan massacre, John Connolly, Lord Dunmore's man in Pittsburgh, had circulated an inflammatory statement falsely accusing the Indians of planning a general war. Crucial passages of Clark's letter reveal that Connolly's circular prompted Cresap's "little army," already bent on attacking a Shawnee town, formally to declare war: "The War Post was planted, a Council Called and the Letter read and the Ceremonies used by the Indians on so important an Occasion acted, and War was formally declared."[15] It was after this declaration of war that the massacre of Logan's family occurred. Historians and contemporary observers have intimated that the massacre of Logan's family was planned by Lord Dunmore or other Virginians with the expectation that the inevitable retaliation by Indian kinsmen would so terrorize the frontiers that Virginia would be forced to conquer the Shawnees and Delawares and terminate the presence of these tribes in Kentucky and western Pennsylvania.[16]

Whether Jefferson was privy as early as 1774 and 1775 to the information contained in Clark's letter may be doubted. But his intimate correspondence with Clark in the conquest of the Ohio valley during the Revolution suggests that he might have been aware of Clark's information well before receiving the letter, perhaps even while he was writing his version of the events in the *Notes* in 1781. By 1797, when Jefferson was preparing his rebuttal to the charges of Cresap's son-in-law, the split between the eastern-based Federalists and the western-favoring Republicans was widening, and Jefferson's political ambitions were becoming more dependent on the support of voters west of the Appalachians. He would not have been eager to condemn the fathers of the voters of western Pennsylvania, Ohio, and western Virginia (including present West Virginia and Kentucky) as murderous Indian-haters or as irresponsible land-grabbing adventurers.

This reluctance would have been especially persuasive after Kentucky in 1792 became a state with its own electoral votes and after the Whiskey Rebellion of 1794—an uprising to protest a federal excise tax on whiskey producers. The whiskey tax, along with its heavy-handed military suppression by Washington and Alexander Hamilton, aroused Jefferson's anti Federalist ire. The "rebellion" itself (which amounted mostly to verbal protests, mass meetings, and the tar-and-feathering of a few well-to-do tax collectors) was centered among Scotch-Irish settlers in the valley of the Monongahela and especially the Redstone district, where Cresap's party had originated. This area had become one of the two principal routes of entry into Kentucky and the Ohio valley, the other being the Cumberland Gap at the southern edge of Virginia, and as such was important to Jefferson's own political aspirations. Under these circumstances, it would have been difficult for Jefferson to condemn a whole population as war mongers; and no doubt many honest, well-meaning farm families disapproved of the barbarous acts of Cresap's and Greathouse's men and their kind.

In reality, Lord Dunmore's War, though precipitated in 1774 by the massacre of Logan's family, was not about Cresap, or Logan's murdered family, or Logan's reprisals. It was about the taking of Indian land.[17] Jefferson's transformation of these events, and the economic and political maneuverings behind them, into an atrocity story full of drama and pathos tells much about Jefferson and his public-relations strategy in Indian affairs. Irving Brant, biographer of James Madison, has claimed that Clark's letter, in exonerating Cresap, was merely "an attempt to wash out blood with whitewash."[18] But Jefferson's presentation of the massacre of some inoffensive Indians on the upper Ohio as the cause of Lord Dunmore's War may be seen as an attempt to wipe out ink with blood. For by focusing intensely on a single atrocity perpetrated by a few violent white men, it distracted attention from a larger set of legal and political issues involving rights to the land west of the Appalachians—issues of which Jefferson was undoubtedly aware.

These included, foremost, the questionable validity of Virginia's purchases from the Iroquois Confederacy of land in Virginia, western Pennsylvania, West Virginia, Ohio, and Kentucky. But also at issue was the ongoing effort of the Shawnees and other local groups who used and occupied these lands to resolve their complaints by peaceful negotiation with British and Virginia authorities, even after the Logan massacre. Another sticking point was the mutually contending claims of large speculative land companies, of General Washington's regiment and of Washington himself, and of thousands of settlers pouring over the Allegheny Mountains through the Monongahela valley to the north and the Cumberland Gap to the south, not to mention the ongoing boundary dispute between Pennsylvania and Virginia over the Monongahela region.

Jefferson himself, in this period, had an interest in lands claimed by at least two of the well-known land companies, the Loyal Company and the Greenbrier Company, and had taken initial steps toward investing in a small independent speculation at the mouth of the Great Kanawha. There is no reason to suppose that he colored his account later to defend these claims. But these investments, and his connection with the principals in several companies and enterprises, suggest that he must have been well informed about the issues in dispute. Dr. Walker, chief agent of the Loyal Company, was his father's friend, one of Jefferson's guardians in his youth, and later one of his consultants on Indian affairs. Patrick Henry, soon to become Jefferson's predecessor as governor of revolutionary Virginia, was an associate of Jefferson in land speculations in the west. Jefferson knew George Washington as a fellow burgess in Williamsburg and as an ally in opposing the pretensions of the Grand Ohio Company to carve a new colony, Vandalia, out of Virginia's western marches. Jefferson was interested in buying up lands surveyed by Andrew Lewis, chief agent of the Greenbrier Company and commander of the Virginia force that defeated the Shawnees at Point Pleasant at the mouth of the Great Kanawha, where Washington as well as Jefferson had land interests. Jefferson would shortly delegate to his friend George Rogers Clark the task of wresting Virginia's western lands from British and Indian dominion. And finally, he was personally acquainted with several of Virginia's royal governors, including Lord Dunmore himself (who was a silent partner in the Vandalia scheme).

Thus, while Jefferson was composing *A Summary View of the Rights of British America* in the summer of 1774 and preparing to attend the First Continental Congress in Philadelphia in the fall, he was surely cognizant that the territory claimed by Virginia between the Allegheny Mountains and the Ohio River, from Pittsburgh down to the Kentucky River, was in chaos. The lands south of the Ohio River as far down as the Great Kanawha supposedly had been ceded to Virginia by the Iroquois at Fort Stanwix in 1768, in a treaty at which Thomas Walker was Virginia's representative; and lands from the Great Kanawha on down to the Kentucky or even Tennessee rivers had been ceded to Virginia by the Cherokees at treaties to which Virginia appointed Andrew Lewis as negotiator. But the title to these lands had been obtained at treaties negotiated by royal superintendents of Indian affairs—Sir William Johnson with the Iroquois and John Stuart with the Cherokees—and therefore were defined as Crown lands. As yet the Crown had not sold or granted any of this territory and was denying Virginia and the other colonies the right to dispose of it themselves because it lay west of the Proclamation Line of 1763, which restricted English settlement west of the Appalachians.

In *A Summary View of the Rights of British America,* after comparing the American taking of Indian land to the Saxon invasion of England, Jefferson accused King George III of falsely applying to America the feudal notion, so foreign to Saxon law, that the Crown held an underlying title to all lands. Under color of this claim, Jefferson said, the Crown was now making the settlers' acquisition of new lands for cultivation extremely difficult.[19] In defying the Crown, the emigrating settlers hoped to gain title by surveying and improving tracts that they could later purchase as squatters with pre-emption rights, from whoever eventually established ownership.

Thus, to Washington, Jefferson, Clark, and no doubt Cresap and many others, movement onto the western lands was not only a personal economic move but a patriotic act in defiance of illegitimate restrictions imposed by a distant authority. What appeared to later observers as atrocities against the Indians may have been perceived by many frontier families—remembering atrocities perpetrated on their own relatives and friends less than a decade earlier—as a necessary process of ethnic cleansing (to use a later generation's phrase), a displacement of inveterate enemies who refused to let God's people settle upon land they had recently bought from the Indians in fair and public treaty. By an ironic twist,

Logan, as an Iroquois, was a member of the confederacy that had sold these very lands.

But by 1781 and 1782, when Jefferson was writing his *Notes on the State of Virginia,* the Revolution against the British had been won. With the task ahead being the orderly acquisition and settlement of western lands, it was time for reconciliation. Lord Dunmore's War had been a minor skirmish compared with the campaigns of the Revolution. It was time to bury the disputes among land companies and between states; time to absolve the western populace generally of crimes against innocent Indians; and time to recognize the virtues of America's native peoples. In short, it was time to mourn for Logan, even as the new nation sought its destiny in the western world, where now—it would henceforth be claimed by Jefferson—the land had always been legitimately acquired by purchase, not by force of arms.

In addition to finding the necessary scapegoats for the bloody murder of Logan's family, Jefferson's story of Logan carries another, more subtle, and perhaps subconscious, message about the darkening prospects for civilizing the Indians. In the passage which introduced Logan's speech as an example of native eloquence, Jefferson praised the intelligence of the American Indians and asserted that their savage state, like that of his own Celtic and Anglo-Saxon ancestors, was merely a result of historical and environmental circumstance, and that they, like the northern Europeans, had the capacity to rise up the ladder of progress. Proposals to Christianize and educate Indians were not new in 1780, but the results were as yet equivocal. Without saying so explicitly, Jefferson, in presenting Logan as the apotheosis of Indianhood, was suggesting that the attainment of civilization might never be the Indians' fate, despite their aspirations to it. Just as the line of Logan, the friend of the white man, who had "thought to live with you," had been unfairly extinguished by white men, so the race itself was destined one day to become extinct. Ultimately, in Jefferson's view, the Indian nations would be either civilized and incorporated into mainstream American society or, failing this—as in the prototypical case of Logan's family—"exterminated." The Jeffersonian vision of the destiny of the Americas had no place for Indians as Indians.

Despite Jefferson's wish to put the bloody past into a kind of historical limbo, the massacre at Baker's Tavern and the ensuing conflict had a grisly sequel. In 1781, during the Revolution, Virginia militiamen from the Monongahela district, in revenge for Indian raids on their settlements, massacred a group of Delawares—"civilized" and pacifist Moravian converts, men, women, and children, ninety in all—at Gnadenhütten on the Tuscarawas River, a branch of the Muskingum. Starving in refugee camps farther north, the Indians had returned to their old town to scavenge for food. In circumstances of barbarity comparable to the Logan killings and to the slaughter of the peaceable Conestoga Indians by the "Paxton Boys," the militiamen, after a vote, imprisoned, then tomahawked, clubbed to death, scalped, and burned the victims in their own houses.

The following year Colonel William Crawford, Washington's land agent and surveyor, was captured while retreating from a failed mission against the Delawares, and as commander of a force that included veterans of the Gnadenhütten massacre, was burned at the stake in retribution. Those events were not reported by Jefferson in the *Appendix* in 1800, although he must have known of them, for the Gnadenhütten massacre gained great notoriety as the criminal action of "white savages." Even some white people believed that the commander at Gnadenhütten, Colonel Daniel Williamson, should have been brought to trial for murder.

Neither Logan nor Cresap long survived Lord Dunmore's War either, and they never knew of the fame, or infamy, they acquired from the pen of Thomas Jefferson. Cresap fought in the Point Pleasant campaign and died of illness in New York a year later after marching his company of Maryland riflemen to join Washington before Boston. Logan died about 1780. During the Revolution, he had allegedly collected additional American scalps and prisoners. But his rage turned to melancholy and, according to Heckewelder, he became increasingly intemperate and deranged and was murdered at last by an Indian kinsman. Jefferson was advised of Logan's death in January 1781.[20] Thus ended the tragic life of Captain John Logan in circumstances of which Jefferson was probably unaware while he was originally writing the *Notes,* circumstances which were communicated to him by Heckewelder and published in the *Appendix* in 1800.[21]

Logan's murderer was a nephew, chosen and deputized to execute his uncle because, as the victim's closest relative, he would be immune from obligatory revenge. Years later he told a white visitor on the Allegheny River why the council ordered the killing: "Because he was too great a man to live . . . he talked so strong that nothing could be carried contrary to his opinions, his eloquence always took all the young men with him . . . He was a very, very great man, and as I killed him, I am to fill his place and inherit all his greatness."[22] By a twist of fate, the eloquence that earned Logan immortality led also to his death.

Jefferson's Character

Thomas Jefferson's views of American Indians were formed not just in the peaceful study at Monticello and in the halls of the American Philosophical Society. They were also fashioned on horseback, in taverns, and in legislative chambers by a close observer of the almost endless war, diplomacy, and treaty-making that accompanied Virginia's, and later the United States', efforts to obtain the lands beyond the Appalachian Mountains, whose foothills lay in a hazy blue line in western Albemarle County, just visible from Monticello. As Jefferson assumed increasingly important legislative and executive duties in his public life, he was inevitably required to involve himself seriously in Indian affairs.

"Indian Affairs"—the relations between the colonies, states, and federal

Monticello. Watercolor on paper by Jane Braddock Peticolas, c. 1825.
Courtesy of Monticello/Thomas Jefferson Memorial Foundation, Inc.

government and Native Americans, who owned and occupied most of the eastern United States until their removal in the 1830s and 40s—were necessarily a major preoccupation of public servants in the early republic. Participants in public life were required to build, out of their own experience, practical policies toward the Indians and then craft philosophical views to rationalize these measures. Jefferson, the stiff, bookish country lawyer, the literary connoisseur with a flair for writing elegant prose—for saying "what oft was thought, but ne'er so well express'd"—was adept at putting a philosophical gloss on the violently partisan, but not necessarily original, opinions he held on practically every subject, including the Indians.

In my view, the central paradox in Thomas Jefferson's character, a paradox that helps to account for at least some of the apparent contradictions in his beliefs and behavior toward Native Americans, is that he, the apostle of liberty, had a deeply controlling temperament.[23] It was a trait that he abhorred in others but could not recognize in himself. "How I wish," he once said, "that I had the power of a despot!"—a power that political enemies accused him of exercising all too freely.[24] He insisted that everyone he knew, and by extension *everyone,* be willing members of his happy family. He was both patriarch and queen bee, surrounded by workers and drones. It was he who decided what the happy family was and how its members should enjoy life, liberty, and the pursuit of happiness.

At Monticello, the happy family was, centrally, his children and grandchildren, then the Hemings family of household slaves, and, by extension, his hundred or so other slaves, to whom also he applied the term "family." In Washington, the happy family was the circle of friends who joined him at dinner, where he carefully managed the flow of conversation, designating subject matter and seeing to it that each guest was given adequate time to speak. In his administration, he and his cabinet "were one family." On the national scene, the happy family was the citizenry, especially the virtuous farmers, devoted to his formulation of republican principles, capable of an orderly pursuit of happiness with minimal government because they had internalized his values.

Everyone in Jefferson's families had his proper place in the circle of happiness and had to know what that place was. Those who did not accept his definition of a happy family had to be coerced, just as one would force a wayward daughter to leave a religious school because she wanted to enter a nunnery, or flog a slave who persisted in running away. During his presidency, he was prepared to transport whole populations—blacks, Louisiana whites, Indians—across rivers, continents, and oceans to achieve a proper arrangement of the races. On the national scene during his administration, Federalists were purged from public service, even from the officers' corps in the military. And on the international scene, non-family members (particularly the monarchical, threatening Britishers) were banished beyond the pale, the despised objects of a virulent hate, suspected of plotting to dominate him and his. Indians in "the hunter state" who conspired with the British were also ineligible for the republican family. As Leonard Levy has pointed out, Jefferson was prepared to violate the Bill of Rights, shed blood, and give no quarter, in order to eliminate those who did not share his vision of "liberty."[25]

Jefferson's language when contemplating the presence of men who threatened his freedom and the freedom of other American yeomen exploded into images of violence. In his famous letter of January 3, 1793, to William Short, celebrating the success of the French Revolution, he extravagantly mourned the death of so many victims: "My own affections have been deeply wounded by some of the martyrs to this cause, but rather than it should have failed, I would have seen half the earth desolated. Were there but an Adam & an Eve left in every country, & left free, it would be better than it is now."[26] Such sentiments recall his comment on Shays' Rebellion of 1786–1787 in Massachusetts: "I like a little rebellion now and then . . . The tree of liberty must be refreshed from time to time with the blood of patriots and tyrants. It is its natural manure."[27]

Along with an intense desire to control and a willingness to trample on civil liberties and use force to achieve national goals, Jefferson displayed a relentless moralism. Robert Tucker and David Hendrickson, in evaluating Jefferson's statecraft, have remarked on "his almost inveterate propensity to convert issues of interest into matters in which great moral principles were held to be at stake . . . he identified the pursuit of self-interest with the vindication of sacred right."[28] This "propensity" characterized his conduct of foreign policy and was a conspicuous element in his handling of Indian affairs, where he always justified his actions by declarations of virtuous, benevolent intention.

Despite repeated protestations to the contrary, Jefferson sought power and exercised it forcefully, always of course in the name of the liberty of "the people." "The people" were his alter ego, a projection of his own self, and when he wrote feelingly about the injustice of the colonies being enslaved by Parliament or George III, of American seamen being impressed by British men-of-war or Barbary pirates, of frontiersmen being slaughtered, captured, and tortured by "merciless savages," he was expressing his own abiding, if perhaps only partly conscious, fear of similar persecution.

For the flip side of Jefferson's insistence on having control was the fear of being controlled. Jefferson was dominated by the fear of being dominated, or even of being challenged, publicly or privately. He could not bring himself to address an audience of senators and congressmen as President, or even fellow members of the Virginia Assembly in earlier years. He was extremely shy of debate even in committee meetings, and he could not abide outspoken disagreements at cabinet meetings or private dinner parties, where he could, however, play the genial patrician host. Jefferson was more dedicated to freedom than to union, and this commitment placed him on the side of Indian-hating, riotous, even secessionist western frontiersmen rather than orderly, centralist eastern governments.

Thus Jefferson's character can be seen as driven by a desire to fend off some threat to his own freedom of thought and action. But unlike some other independent-minded men and women, he identified with "the people" and projected his private drama onto a national, indeed a global, scene, demanding liberty for the downtrodden everywhere, to the point of being prepared to force freedom on the unwilling. He assumed personal responsibility for leading "the people," almost like a prophet of old, in the crusade to win back and defend the promised land of liberty from evil scheming monks and monarchists. This synthesis of his own ego with the world around him led to the familiar Jeffersonian contradictions between libertarian and authoritarian action—or inaction—and rhetoric.

Joseph Ellis has discussed these inconsistencies in *American Sphinx: The Character of Thomas Jefferson,* for the most part sympathetically, accepting in him a propensity for simultaneously traveling along parallel mental paths, speaking in multiple internal voices but hearing only one at a time. Such contradictions have been most conspicuous in his handling of the issue of slavery and in his disregard of constitutional restrictions on executive power, when Madison's carefully crafted checks and balances hampered Jefferson's freedom of action. But they are also apparent in his conduct of Indian affairs.

Jefferson's vision of the world entailed a system of choices between sharing spaces and acquiring (and defending) turf. First as a Virginian and then as President, he was deeply committed to the purchase and settlement of Indian lands in the Old West (between the Appalachian Mountains and the Mississippi) and to making the internal improvements—roads and canals—necessary to connect these settlements with coastal markets. But he brought to this almost sacred cause a geopolitical mind that viewed places and events around the world in the light of a particular vision of American destiny. His mind's eye hovered, as it were, in stationary orbit above the earth, high enough to see the shores of Europe and Asia and the beginning outlines of Central and South America. This was a geopolitical vision not so much of an empire that embraced a diversity of nations, races, and cultures as of an ethnic homeland, European in origin and spirit, agrarian in economy, governed by republican institutions derived from old Anglo-Saxon and even pre-imperial Roman models. People of Indian ancestry could "incorporate with us" if they chose to accept "civilization." Those who preferred the hunter's life and the old ways of their ancestors would have to withdraw to the west, beyond the Mississippi, as game was depleted and hunting grounds were sold in the east. Eventually they too would have to adopt civilization or perish, as the Louisiana Territory itself and the lands beyond were settled.

In 1801, a few months after taking office as President, Jefferson wrote to James Monroe, then governor of Virginia, outlining his American dream. White settlers, sturdy independent farmers, would increase in numbers and eventually would "cover the whole northern, if not southern continent, with a people speaking the same language, governed in similar forms, and by similar laws; nor can we contemplate with satisfaction either blot or mixture on that surface."[29]

The looseness of social control on the frontiers, implicit in Jefferson's ideology, went along with a certain vagueness about the role of ethnicity in a republic. The democratic philosophy that Jefferson and his fellow revolutionaries embraced was a contradiction of the monarchical theory of society and therefore was seemingly egalitarian. But egalitarian ideals do not necessarily encourage diversity. The monarchical idea of empire, on the other hand, saw the realm as a hierarchy that embraced all men and women, from the lowliest slave to the king (and above the king the Divinity himself). All were subjects of the king, unequally assigned rights and duties according to their stations and governed by a strict authoritarian rule that controlled speech, action, and belief. But the imperial mode of governance included a diversity of ethnic groups, whether defined by race, language, religion, historical experience, or national origin, over whom sovereignty had been extended by conquest, intimidation, or offer of protection from other enemies. The empire was hierarchical, authoritarian, and ethnically inclusive.

The ideal society of the Jeffersonians, of course, was neither hierarchical nor authoritarian (however authoritarian Jefferson might be in personal temperament). All men were created equal; they had inalienable rights. The best government was that which governed least; and its structure had to be a carefully designed system of checks and balances, so that no religion, party, faction, region, economic class, trade, profession, or lineage could establish a tyrannical dominance over others, and so that it faithfully represented the several interest groups in the whole community. Society was a congeries of free associations, a network of contracts freely entered. But on the matter of ethnicity, the theory of commonwealth was mute. Jeffersonians saw "the people" as a culturally homogeneous mass of equals, a national community sharing uniform political institutions and internalizing uniform moral values so thoroughly that no coercion would ever be required, all bound together by a republican social contract that required its participants to have achieved the state of civilization. Those residents who could not participate fully in the civilized republic, either because of gender (women were barred from voting or holding office), racial inferiority (in the case of black Africans and their slave descendants), or cultural incompatibility (as in the case of Native Americans who remained in "the hunter state"), were excluded or marginalized. Noncivilized Indians would remove themselves to hunting grounds west of the Mississippi, in the short run; whites to the west of the Mississippi would be relocated in the eastern states; blacks would be removed to some island in the Caribbean or even sent back to Africa. The Jeffersonian state was not an empire; it was egalitarian, democratic, and ethnically exclusive.

This world view led immediately to the position that the Indian "nations" still inhabiting the United States, and owning vast amounts of its territory, were to be dealt with as quasi-foreign states (or, as Justice Marshall later put it, as "domestic dependent nations").[30] They were the objects of foreign policy, and interactions with them were not constrained by the legal or ethical imperatives of internal governance. Transactions with them were by treaties, and superintendence was managed by the secretary of war. Minimal government meant minimal government effort to restrain frontier populations from committing those invasions and atrocities that led to Native American retaliation, then military retaliation by the United States, and resultant land cessions. The Native Americans fell outside the pale of the Jeffersonian republic but inside the arena of Jeffersonian geopolitics—which was conducted by different rules. Thus eventually evolved the dual policy of obtaining land ("voluntarily") and restricting the Indians to reservations administered by a Bureau of Indian Affairs, while at the same time attempting to civilize as many as possible in preparation for admission to the republican family.

But there was a darker side to Jefferson's geopolitical vision. Ever in his thoughts (and to a great degree in reality) there were enemies—always the British, at times the French and Spanish—just outside the expanding circle of the American nation, threatening to block that "final consolidation" of the American world he sought to achieve. And in this view, all too often allied with these spoilers of the American dream, were the Indians, the "merciless savages" who had fought throughout his lifetime to block the westward march of the American folk. This image of Indians as savage murderers of innocent frontier farm families undoubtedly was implanted in his youth and was responsible for the rage that periodically boiled up into belligerence whenever Indians resisted his plans or threatened to break the peace.

Thus there was a degree of ruthlessness in Jefferson's dealings with the native peoples, the ruthlessness of a benevolent zealot who would do virtually anything to ensure that his new, free American republic survived and grew. As President of an expanding nation and as one personally committed to the purchase of Indian land, he knew from the Iroquois example that the civilization of the Indians would follow, not precede, the sale of hunting grounds. These hunting grounds already provided the cash crop—skins and furs—with which the tribes could purchase necessary hardware and dry goods. So the Jeffersonian program for inducing the Indians to sell their lands in preparation for civilization actually consisted of four steps: (1) run the hunters into debt, then threaten to cut off their supplies unless the debts are paid out of the proceeds of a land cession; (2) bribe influential chiefs with money and private reservations; (3) select and invite friendly leaders to Washington to visit and negotiate with the President, after being overawed by the evident power of the United States; and (4) threaten trade embargo or war.

The threat-of-war tactic was itself a four-stage process: (1) white encroachment and atrocity against Indians; (2) bloody Indian retaliation; (3)

military invasion, or threat of invasion, of Indian country to protect innocent settlers and punish hostile savages; (4) and finally a peace treaty that required a cession of Indian land. The story of Logan and Lord Dunmore's War, precipitated in 1774 by the murder of Logan's family and followed by the Shawnee cession of trans-Appalachian land long coveted by the Virginians, epitomized the process by which Native Americans would be dispossessed of their land and white expansion across the continent would actually occur. It was a process now known as "ethnic cleansing." Jefferson was no doubt doing what he felt he had to do in the public interest: obtain lands by all means short of unprovoked wars of conquest, and his praise of Logan's Lament was his sentimental tribute to the noble red man and his dying way of life.

Perhaps "crocodile tears" is too harsh a metaphor for Jefferson's mourning for Logan. Perhaps "duplicity" is too strong a word to characterize the contrast between Jefferson's actual methods of obtaining lands and the apparent benevolence of the civilization policy, which every year he assured Congress was proceeding smoothly. Perhaps "hypocrisy" is unfairly critical of the contrast between the bellicose Jefferson threatening to "exterminate" unfriendly tribes and the gentle scholar celebrating Logan's rhetoric, praising Indian intelligence and egalitarianism, patiently collecting vocabularies, and nostalgically excavating Indian burial mounds. If Jefferson was guilty of insincerity, duplicity, and hypocrisy in Indian affairs, it must be conceded that this shiftiness, like his political ruthlessness, was a weapon in his struggle to ensure the survival of the United States as a republic governed by Anglo-Saxon yeomen.

Jefferson probably sincerely intended to carry out his civilization policy, even though it had been initiated by the Federalists, but it also functioned in his hand as a public relations device that provided a moral justification for land purchases, which were his primary interest. And the scholarly exercises displayed in *Notes on the State of Virginia* and supported at the American Philosophical Society, while they were certainly the product of genuine intellectual curiosity, also served a public relations function: to convince Europeans that America was already a civilized nation, whose white citizens were capable of a parting salute to a red race doomed to cultural, if not physical, extinction, a generous obituary from a compassionate American people. Logan, the Great Mingo, was their Vercingetorix, the Gallic warrior executed and then memorialized by Julius Caesar (whom Jefferson despised). "Who is there to mourn for Logan? Not one." But there was one—Thomas Jefferson.

CHAPTER ONE

The Land Companies

THOMAS JEFFERSON grew up in an eighteenth-century Virginia that was hot with the fever of speculation in Indian lands. Ambitious men formed numerous land companies, large and small, that schemed to acquire title to Virginia's western domain beyond the Appalachian mountains. Their efforts led directly to the French and Indian War, Lord Dunmore's War, and a bloody forty-year struggle between the "Long Knives" of Virginia and the Native Americans of Kentucky and the Northwest Territory, which culminated in the War of 1812. This world of intrigue and violence fostered Jefferson's lifelong sympathy for settlers on the frontier and his commitment as President to obtaining Indian lands for them, at almost any cost short of unprovoked wars of conquest.

Jefferson's personal involvement in western land speculation began in 1757 when he inherited, along with his brothers and sisters, their father's share in the Loyal Land Company. In the 1740s and 1750s this company sold tracts to settlers in the valleys of present-day West Virginia and the southwest corner of Virginia. Then in February 1769 Jefferson made the first of several investments of his own in western real estate.[1] Thus, by the time he discovered the elegance of Logan's Lament, Jefferson had acquired a financial interest in the lands Logan had fought to retain.

Being a lawyer as well as a landowner, Jefferson naturally was concerned about the legalities of land acquisition from Indian tribes. Before 1774 he seems to have held the traditional view that Indian lands had been properly acquired by Virginia through purchase under the authority of the Crown. But the approach of the Revolution, and perhaps also an awareness of the coming confrontation between Virginia and the Ohio Indians provoked by the murder of Logan's family, which would culminate in Lord Dunmore's War, distorted his perception of, or at least his public rhetoric about, these matters.

In *A Summary View of the Rights of British America,* written for the Virginia delegates to the First Continental Congress, he asserted that "America was conquered, and her settlements made, and firmly established, at the expence of individuals, and not of the British public. Their own blood was spilt in acquiring lands for their settlement, their own fortunes expended in making that settlement effectual; for themselves they

Jefferson's map from *Notes on the State of Virginia,* 1786–1787. Detail on page 32. Courtesy of the American Philosophical Society.

fought, for themselves they conquered, and for themselves they have right to hold."[2] He denied "the fictitious principle that all lands belong originally to the king" and declared that his majesty "has no right to grant lands of himself. From the nature and purpose of civil institutions, all the lands within the limits which any particular society has circumscribed around itself, are assumed by that society, and subject to their allotment only. This may be done by themselves, assembled collectively, or by legislature, to whom they have delegated sovereign authority; and if they are allotted in neither of these ways, each individual of the society may appropriate to himself such lands as he finds vacant, and occupancy will give him title."[3]

In addition to denying the legitimacy of the Crown's claim to a preemption right over Indian land, this passage would seem to sanction, by implication, the purchase by private citizens of "vacant" lands occupied by Indians, with title being subject to later confirmation by the state. Two years later, however, in his "Draft of a Constitution for Virginia," Jefferson stated explicitly that only the state held the right to purchase Indian land: "No lands shall be appropriated until purchased of the Indian native proprietors; nor shall any purchases be made of them but on behalf of the public, by authority of acts of the General assembly to be passed for every purchase specially."[4] Thus on the eve of the Declaration of Independence, Jefferson had firmly concluded that purchases of Indian land by private companies or individuals were as invalid as purchases by the Crown. The Virginia Constitution of that year adopted the Jeffersonian principle, which largely followed the traditional British practice of delegating the right to purchase exclusively to colonial authorities, who might then grant lands to private persons.

After the Revolution ended, Jefferson again asserted that Virginia's white settlers had acquired Indian lands primarily by peaceful purchase (although some areas in the Tidewater region had been acquired by conquest during the wars with the Powhatans in the seventeenth century). "That the lands of this country were taken from them by conquest, is not so general a truth as is supposed. I find in our historians and records, repeated proofs of purchase, which cover a considerable part of the lower country; and many more would doubtless be found on further search. The upper country we know has been acquired altogether by purchases made in the most unexceptionable form."[5] In the original manuscript of *Notes on the State of Virginia,* where this passage occurs, after the word "search" he had added, and then crossed out, the qualification, "It is true that these purchases were sometimes made with the price in one hand and the sword in the other."[6]

Later in the *Notes,* Jefferson elaborated on the process by which an individual or company could acquire title. In the first half of the seventeenth century, he wrote, lands were purchased from Indian proprietors by individuals, and the title was confirmed by the Virginia Assembly. Later, under the land laws, large tracts were purchased from Indian owners by the colony itself, and title to individual portions was granted by the governor, while the surviving Indians were allowed to live on residual "allotments" (reservations).[7] Jefferson's account has been basically confirmed by later historians. In 1655 these procedures were regularized by the Virginia Assembly in an act which prohibited future private sales of lands by any Indian to any white individual. Thus, Virginia gradually came to accept the legal thesis that the native occupants possessed the right of soil and that their lands could be legally alienated only by a cession to representatives of the colony, particularly the governor, who (before the Revolution) held his authority from the Crown. It was this understanding, well-established by the time of his birth, that Jefferson was expressing in the *Notes.*[8]

By the early eighteenth century, when the "upper country"—consisting of the lands of the Piedmont, where Jefferson lived, and the Shenandoah valley—was becoming of interest to white settlers, the original inhabitants, the Siouan-speaking Monacans, were no longer living there, having dispersed among other native communities to the south. No record of the purchase of any of the Piedmont lands from the Siouans themselves seems to exist. Lewis Evans, whose *Analysis of a General Map of the Middle British Colonies in America* (1754) is cited as an authority by Jefferson in the *Notes,* expressed the opinion that some of the lands of the Monacans were seized by Virginia through force. Other Monacan lands, he believed, were acquired by the Iroquois through conquest.[9]

The Iroquois themselves claimed to have conquered several tribes in Maryland and Virginia, including the "Toderichroonies," their term for all the Siouan-speaking tribes of the southeast, and raids by the Iroquois on Virginia's dependent tribes continued into the eighteenth century. The general disorder produced by these incursions led Governor Spotswood in 1721 to propose a treaty with the Iroquois Confederacy, which at that time consisted of the Mohawks, Oneidas, Onondagas, Cayugas, and Senecas. They lived in villages in what is now New York State, extending roughly from the Hudson River west to Lake Erie. (A sixth tribe, the Tuscaroras, joined the confederacy in 1722, making up the last of the Six Nations.) This Treaty of Albany in 1722 settled Iroquois disputes with the Indians of Virginia and established a boundary between the lands claimed by the Iroquois within the chartered limits of the colony and the lands owned by the colony itself, its citizens, or grantees of the Crown.

The Iroquois referred to Governor Spotswood, and to other governors of Virginia, as Assaraquoa, "The Great Sword," probably because of the ceremonial swords they wore (the term may also have been the origin of the designation "Long Knives" for Virginians). At Albany in 1722, Governor Spotswood represented himself as the spokesman for all the surviving Indians of Virginia, including the Powhatans, Nottoways, Meherrins, and the various Siouan groups. A boundary was fixed between these tribes and the Six Nations, who agreed not to allow their warriors to travel east of what was identified in the treaty as the "high ridge."[10] Virginia's interpretation of this agreement was that it cleared all Indian title to lands within its charter limits south of the Potomac and east of the main range of the Allegheny Mountains, thus freeing for settlement not only the Piedmont but also the great Valley of Virginia, through which ran the waters of the Shenandoah River.

The Albany Treaty was one of the "purchases made in the most unexceptionable form" that Jefferson alluded to in the *Notes.* This was also one of the purchases most important to Jefferson personally, because Monticello and other properties he owned were located on the lands allegedly conveyed to Virginia by the Iroquois. Within two decades after the Albany treaty, plantations were being established in substantial numbers in the Piedmont and the Shenandoah valley, between the Blue Ridge and the Alleghenies. Peter Jefferson was one of those who availed himself of the opportunity created by the Albany treaty, in 1735 patenting a thousand acres in the Piedmont along the Rivanna River, one of the tributaries of the James. Here in Albemarle County he built Shadwell, the house where in 1743 Thomas Jefferson was born; nearby, Thomas would build Monticello and the city of Charlottesville would rise. After a six-year period living at Tuckahoe, an estate farther down the James that his father was managing for his deceased friend Peter Randolph, Thomas Jefferson at the age of nine returned to Shadwell and spent the rest of his youth there until his departure for William and Mary College in Williamsburg at the age of seventeen.

Settlement of Albemarle County and the Piedmont proceeded without complaint or interference from the Indians. But the Valley of Virginia was a different matter. The Iroquois understanding of the agreement signed at Albany in 1722 was that the Blue Ridge to the east, not the Allegheny mountains to the west, was the boundary meant by the phrase "high ridge," and that therefore settlers in the Shenandoah valley were trespassers on Indian land. Although there were no Iroquois or other Indian settlements in the valley, Iroquois war parties frequently traveled the Warriors' Road through the valley to attack their traditional enemies, the Catawbas and the Cherokees in the Carolinas, and the settlers from time to time interfered with them.

An Iroquois speaker explained the seriousness of the problem to Virginia's representative: "We are engaged in a War with the Catawbas which will last till the End of the World for they molest us and speak contemptuously of us which our warriors will not bear and they will soon go to War against them again . . . Some years ago we made a new Road on the outside of your Inhabitants tho' they had seated themselves down upon our land. Now your People seated themselves down again upon the new Road and shut it up and there is no more room for a new Road because of the Terrible Mountains full of stones and no Game there so that the Road cannot be removed."[11]

The issue was still unresolved in 1742, when Virginia militiamen killed a number of Iroquois warriors passing through the valley. This incident precipitated the very important 1744 treaty signed at the county courthouse in Lancaster, Pennsylvania, then a sixteen-year-old frontier village. After some legalistic skirmishing, in which the Indian side proved themselves, in the opinion of white observers, better organized and more cogent in argument than the elegantly dressed, supercilious gentlemen of Virginia and Maryland, Virginia's and Maryland's representatives acceded to the Iroquois demands, agreeing to keep open the Warriors' Road and to pay a quantity of goods and 200 pounds in gold. In return, the Six Nations agreed not to join forces with the French, and signed "a Deed recognizing the King's right to all the lands that are, or shall be, by his Majesty's Appointment in the Colony of Virginia."[12] Subsequently Virginia publicly advertised the precise route of the Warriors' Road, the procedures to be followed in securing passports from magistrates, and the requirement that local settlers provide Indians of the Six Nations and their tributaries with food during their passage to and from the Catawba country.

To the Six Nations this "deed" meant, for practical purposes, a cession of the Valley of Virginia and the (to them) relatively worthless Appalachian Mountains. They had no intention of releasing their claims, or the claims of their dependents and allies, to lands further west, between the Appalachians and the Mississippi River. The Iroquois held on to these claims for another forty years, and even their relinquishment at Fort Stanwix in 1784 did not extinguish the claims of the tribes actually resident in the region. Jefferson would spend the years of his presidency (1801–1809) attempting to buy these same lands once again, this time from their actual occupants.

Virginia, however, took the Iroquois cession literally. According to Virginia's understanding of the 1744 treaty, the Six Nations sold Virginia its rights not just to the Valley of Virginia but to all of the land west of the "high ridge" (however that is defined) *that lay within the colony's charter.* The Virginians had explained to the Iroquois that their charter from the Great King gave them sovereignty over a vast tract extending to the South Sea. Thus, in their view, the Treaty of Lancaster quieted the claim of the Six Nations to a large part of greater Virginia, including the region along the Ohio and Great Lakes that had been conquered by the Iroquois and their ancestors, and also the territory immediately south of the Ohio, where few Indians lived anyway. The Six Nations' deed was, in Virginian eyes, a license to speculate and settle new lands west of the Alleghenies.

In the forefront of these ventures was none other than Thomas Lee, Virginia commissioner at the Lancaster treaty, member of the Governor's Council, and former manager of the Fairfax Estate, a 5,000,000-acre tract comprising the Northern Neck of Virginia, which included lands between the Potomac and the Rappahanock rivers and part of the Shenandoah valley. (The Fairfax Estate had been granted to an ancestor of the present owner, Baron Thomas Fairfax, who on his return to Virginia would become the only English peer resident in America.) Although at first the aristocratic Lee and his homespun Pennsylvania interpreter, Conrad Weiser, did not get along, Lee learned to respect Weiser as an authority on Iroquois affairs. It was probably Lee who arranged for the publication in Williamsburg of the minutes of the Lancaster treaty. In a preface to this pamphlet, for the benefit of Virginians unacquainted with the northern Indian nations, the anonymous editor included a description of "the Power, Strength, and Confederacy of the Six Nations of Indians, their present Tributaries, Allies, and form of Government." The information was supplied by Conrad Weiser. But Lee went further, and in August after the treaty he wrote to Weiser asking for a full account of the religion and government of the Six Nations, in addition to information about the number of fighting men in each nation and more about their tributaries and allies. Weiser replied at length in a general letter that he sent not just to Lee but to others; it was eventually published (in part) by Benjamin Franklin.[13]

Lee became acting governor of Virginia but died unexpectedly in 1750. We do not know whether Jefferson ever saw the Weiser–Lee correspondence or the version of Weiser's letter published by Franklin, which anticipated his own ethnological interests. But in *Notes on the State of Virginia,* Jefferson included among his list of documents important for understanding the history of Virginia the "1744 June. Treaty with the Indians of the 6 nations at Lancaster." His copy was probably the Williamsburg pamphlet.[14]

Another effect of the Lancaster treaty was the movement of most of the remaining Monacans north to join their kinfolk in Pennsylvania under the protection of their former enemies, the Iroquois. Some of the Piedmont Siouans, a generation earlier, had settled first at Shamokin (Logan's birthplace) and then moved farther north along the Susquehanna. By 1754, according to Weiser, there were less than ten families of these Susquehanna Siouans left "and as good for nothing people as any among the Indians . . . the Six Nations minds them no more than the English do the Nigers."[15] But of course there were others left in southern Virginia and North Carolina, and the migration north from Virginia was a straggling one that continued for many years.

A little band of mourners visited a burial mound near Charlottesville around 1750 by Jefferson's reckoning. This was most likely a family of Tutelos visiting the grave of their ancestors one last time before leaving Virginia forever. Jefferson would later excavate the mound in an early exercise in archaeological research.

The Loyal Company of Virginia

The Treaty of Lancaster of 1744 seemed to open the door to the unrestricted settlement of Virginia's lands west of the Blue Ridge mountains. In April 1745 the Governor's Council granted permission to several dozen

George Washington. Engraving by Read after a portrait by John Trumbull, 1775. Courtesy of the Huntington Library, San Marino, California.

persons to take up and survey various tracts, amounting in all to about 300,000 acres in what is now western Virginia and West Virginia. These individualistic ventures were not, however, located in the more remote regions on the waters of the Ohio and Mississippi Rivers, west of the "Great Mountains" (the Alleghenies) where it had been Thomas Lee's dream to establish English settlements. Believing that these more distant settlements required more capital and more extensive preparation, in 1747 Lee and a number of associates, including George Fairfax, Lawrence Fairfax, Augustine Washington, and Thomas Cresap (father of Michael Cresap) organized the Ohio Company of Virginia for the purpose of taking up "a large tract of 500,000 acres of land on the branches of Allegheny and settling a Trade with the several nations of Indians." They expected to settle this land "with strangers, and to build a fort." George Washington, a surveyor of the Fairfax Estate, later joined the company. Because the company proposed a major settlement in the Ohio country itself, which had never been attempted before, the council and Governor Gooch declined to sign off on the company's request and wrote to the Board of Trade in London for instructions. The king approved a grant of 200,000 acres in March 1749, and the good news reached Virginia by June.[16]

News of the approval of the Ohio Company's petition spurred a number of other petitions for grants of land on the waters of the Mississippi River. On July 12, 1749, five such petitions were granted by the Governor's Council, totaling 1,450,000 acres. Of these, the largest, amounting to 800,000 acres, and the only one in which the Jefferson family had an interest, was that of the Loyal Company of Virginia. Adjacent to the Loyal Company's tract in southwestern Virginia was a tract taken up by the Greenbrier Company.[17] Jefferson later bought lands originally surveyed by the agents of both companies and would exert himself politically in their favor.

The Ohio Company was dominated by the Fairfax and Washington interests. The Loyal Company, by contrast, was primarily an Albemarle County group. Its leader was Dr. Thomas Walker, an eminent Fredericksburg physician and real estate speculator, who in 1741 had acquired the 11,000 acre estate named Castle Hill in Albemarle County by virtue of marriage to the widow of the former owner. Five of the forty charter members of the company were Meriwethers; four others were Lewises. One Peachy Gilmer was probably related to Dr. George Gilmer of Williamsburg, Walker's Edinburgh-trained physician-mentor. Another charter member was the Reverend James Maury, soon to become young Thomas Jefferson's schoolmaster and later remembered in Jefferson's autobiography as "a correct classical scholar." Maury was an Anglican minister whose glebe was a 400-acre farm donated to the church by Nicholas Meriwether, also a member of the Loyal Company. James Maury was later to gain fame—or infamy, depending on one's point of view—as one of the Anglican ministers who brought suit against the Virginia legislature for back pay in "The Parsons' Cause." Patrick Henry gained notoriety in defending against this suit so successfully that Maury and the others were awarded only one penny in arrears—a signal victory for those, like Jefferson, who opposed religious establishment.

All in all, the charter members of the Loyal Company were either friends and relations of Thomas Walker or fellow landowners in Albemarle County—including Peter Jefferson and his best friend, Colonel Joshua Fry.[18] Fry was a former professor of mathematics at William and Mary College (which had the privilege of licensing public surveyors) and had in 1746 been appointed as one of the Crown's commissioners in completing the survey of the Fairfax estate. He now served as the chief executive of Abemarle County, being commander (lieutenant) of the militia, presiding judge of the county court, chief surveyor, and the county's representative in the House of Burgesses. Lieutenant Colonel Peter Jefferson was also a magistrate and an assistant county surveyor. Fry's estate, the large Viewmont plantation, was located about fifteen miles south of Jefferson's Shadwell.[19]

One of the first needs of the Loyal Company was to extend the survey of the line between Virginia and North Carolina, which in 1728 had been run by William Byrd and others only as far west as the foothills of the Blue Ridge. By the terms of the Loyal Company's charter, its land was to run from the North Carolina line north and west. In 1749 Fry and Jefferson were appointed to survey the line farther westward into the heart of the Appalachians. Thomas Walker the next year penetrated the mountains beyond, exploring what is now eastern Kentucky but failing to cross into the bluegrass prairie country. Later Walker would continue the survey, moving the line as far west as the Tennessee River. In 1751 Fry and Jefferson published their famous map of Virginia on the basis of their own surveys and the prior surveys and maps of others.[20]

After the end of the French and Indian War the Loyal Company made surveys in the valleys of the Holston and the New (Great Kanawha) rivers and their tributaries, among the mountains of southern West Virginia; but before the Revolution the Loyal Company apparently never attempted to make settlements or sell land west of the Appalachians. With Walker as its chief agent, it seems to have contented itself with surveying and selling about a thousand lots, amounting to some 200,000 acres. The French and Indian War and the War of Independence hampered business, however, and many titles were not completed until after the Revolution. Later on, the Loyal and Greenbrier companies were allotted millions of acres in Kentucky. The affairs of the Loyal Company were still not resolved by the time of Walker's death in 1794, and the last suit was not settled until 1872.

In addition to buying and selling land, the members of the Loyal Company had another, overarching goal: discovering the Northwest Passage, the fabled water route to the Pacific Ocean. About 1752, according to a letter of James Maury written in January 1756, Colonel Fry seems to have conceived a grand scheme of exploration in search of the mountain pass where, supposedly close together, sprang forth the waters that flowed respectively east into the Mississippi River and west to the Pacific Ocean.

Fry apparently had studied Daniel Coxe's geographical speculations in *Corolanus* (1741), of which he owned a copy, about the feasibility of the passage to India via the rivers running through interior parts of America. According to Maury, the plan was far advanced when it was aborted by the death of Colonel Fry in 1754 and the onset of the French and Indian War.[21]

The capable "friend and neighbor" Maury referred to who had explored the region "to the westward" and was taking charge of Fry's enterprise was no doubt Thomas Walker. It is not likely that Peter Jefferson was ignorant of his friends' ambitions to discover the "passage through the garden"; indeed, he was very likely to have been part of it. And his son, young Thomas, was probably aware of the project too, learning of it from his

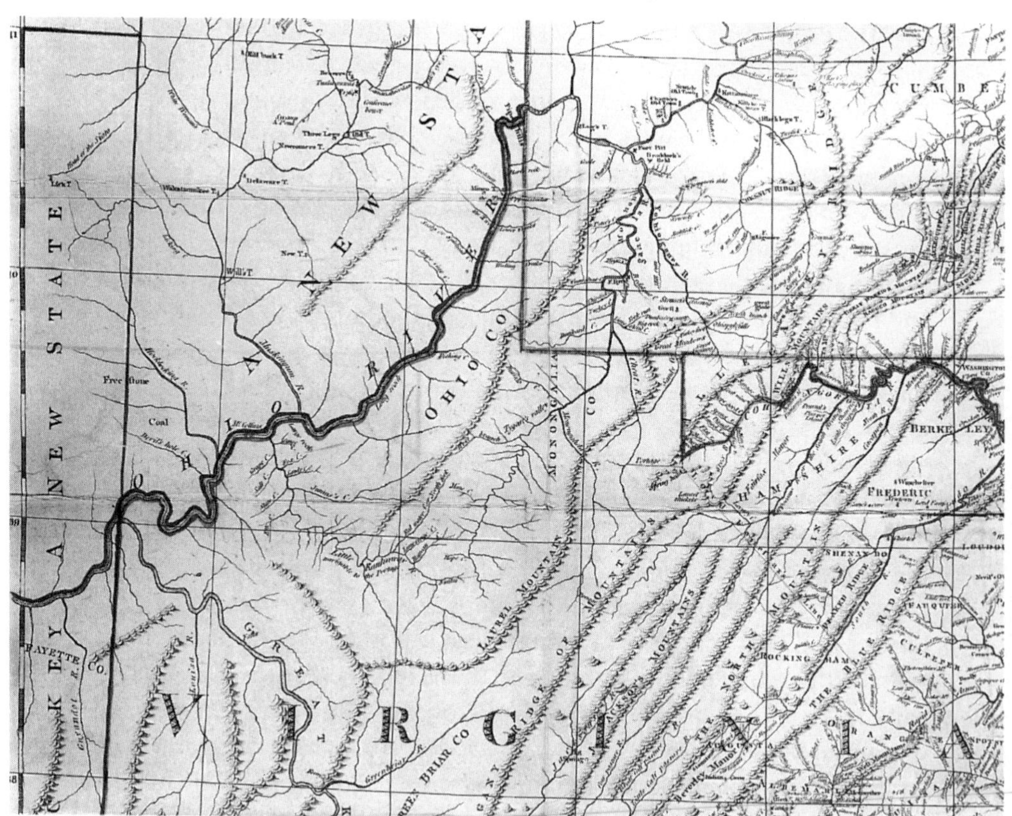

Detail of Jefferson's map from *Notes on the State of Virginia*, 1786–1787. Courtesy of the American Philosophical Society.

father and perhaps others, including Maury, to whom he was sent to school upon his father's death in 1757. The planned exploration would finally take place fifty years later, under President Jefferson's aegis, as the Lewis and Clark expedition.

When Peter Jefferson died, attended in his last illness by Dr. Walker, Thomas Jefferson and his brothers and sisters inherited their father's share in the Loyal Land Company. Of the five men appointed as executors and guardians in his father's will, three were members of the company: Walker, John Harvie (an attorney), and Thomas Turpin (a surveyor and Peter Jefferson's brother-in-law). Members of the Loyal Land Company and their relatives were among Thomas Jefferson's mentors and associates throughout his life.

While the Loyal Company was rather modestly confining its activities to lands east of the Allegheny Mountains, the Ohio Company was pursuing a much more aggressive policy. Its plan was to establish a major fort, trading post, and settlement of 150 families between the Allegheny Mountains and the Ohio River. The company's first act, in 1749, was to build a storehouse on the Potomac at the mouth of Wills Creek, the head of canoe navigation, and to hire an experienced frontiersman, Christopher Gist, to explore the region to the north. In 1752 the company engaged the services of Thomas Cresap to construct a road north from Wills Creek at the head of navigation on the Potomac to Redstone Creek, which flows into the Monongahela; a storehouse was constructed at the confluence of Redstone Creek and the Monongahela by a Pennsylvania trader, William Trent. In January 1754, Trent was commissioned a captain of militia by Governor Dinwiddie and authorized to raise a company of one hundred men to build a fort at the forks of the Monongahela and Allegheny rivers (the site of present-day Pittsburgh), about thirty miles north of Redstone. Colonel Joshua Fry was placed in command of the Virginia troops stationed there, and George Washington was made his second in command. Trent took his body of men—never more than fifty—to the forks in the dead of winter and began to build the fort. But in April a French army of a thousand men, proceeding south along the Allegheny River, overwhelmed the thirty-three Virginians, who surrendered the post. The French proceeded to construct Fort Duquesne on the site.

Meanwhile, Governor Dinwiddie had received instructions from England to use force if necessary to drive the French out of the Ohio country. He dispatched Colonel Fry's regiment to counter the French move, but

Fry died during the march, allegedly as a result of a fall from his horse. Washington, taking over from Fry, unwisely led his small force north from Wills Creek to do battle with the French. After a minor victory over an advance party, he was forced to retreat to the Great Meadows on Redstone Creek, where he hastily constructed Fort Necessity. Surrounded, outnumbered, and outgunned, Washington surrendered.

Thus began the Seven Years War between Great Britain and France, better known in America as the French and Indian War because of the alliance of western Indian tribes with the French. Hostilities lasted until 1760, when the French were defeated by the British. And thus also, for practical purposes, ended the attempt of the Ohio Company to create the first English settlement west of the Appalachians. Legal maneuverings, of course, went on for years and were quickly translated into political intrigues, with which, eventually, Thomas Jefferson became involved.[22]

The Proclamation of 1763

At the conclusion of the French and Indian war, the Treaty of Paris in 1763 allowed Great Britain to assume sovereignty over French possessions in North America east of the Mississippi River. This inaugurated an era of confusion in British politics over Indian policy, the fur trade, and the demands of frontier settlers. Factional disputes in Parliament and in the royal establishment made the process of obtaining lands uncertain, but the main tendency was toward increasing regulation by the British of the colonies' relations with the tribes of the Mississippi valley.[23]

Pontiac's Rebellion—an uprising of Native Americans against the British between 1763 and 1766—prompted the Crown to respond to long-standing complaints about "great frauds and abuses [that] have been committed in the purchasing lands of the Indians." In response to the disaffection of many Ohio tribes and even some Iroquois, the Crown issued its Proclamation of 1763, which reserved, "for the use of the said Indians," all the land west of the sources of the rivers that flowed into the Atlantic Ocean. The Proclamation Line ran from Lake Ontario south to the Gulf of Mexico, for most of the distance along the crest of the Appalachians. The colonial governments were prohibited from warranting surveys or issuing patents for any lands west of the line. No private citizens were permitted to make purchases or to settle beyond the line, and settlers already there were to be removed. East of the line, all lands still in Indian possession were to be acquired only by special license from the Crown by the governor or proprietor of the colony at a public treaty.[24]

No one was happy about the Proclamation of 1763. The Ohio Indians resented the continuing presence of British forts on their land and objected to the newly centralized management of the Indian trade. Moreover, they protested the new settlements of Scotch-Irish from Virginia and Maryland that were being made on the old Ohio Company's claim at Redstone Creek and the Monongahela River, in defiance of the Proclamation. These rough frontiersmen were determined to drive out by force and intimidation the small groups of Delawares still remaining in the region. In one celebrated incident in the spring of 1767, the leader of these outlaw squatters and Indian traders, none other than the "infamous" Captain Michael Cresap of Maryland, allegedly murdered a prominent Delaware war captain, which outraged the Iroquois, who considered the Delawares to be under their protection. The whites, in their turn, resented royal interference in both the private and public purchasing of Indian lands, in the regulation of the whiskey trade, and even in protecting the Indians from murderous frontiersmen.

The pressure on the British government to secure a new cession west of the Proclamation Line was intense. The recently formed Illinois Company, led by Sir William Johnson (the newly appointed superintendent of Indian affairs for the northern colonies), Benjamin Franklin and his son William (since 1763 the royal governor of New Jersey), and a group of Pennsylvania merchants in the Indian trade, wanted a grant of 63,000,000 acres between the Illinois River and the Mississippi to be set up as a new colony. Franklin, in London, lobbied enthusiastically for the scheme, but it fell through. The group then reorganized itself as the Indiana Company of "suffering traders," who were seeking to recoup their losses in the recent wars by a generous grant of land. Still other groups, including one led by the prominent Indian agent George Croghan, himself a "suffering trader," pressed hard for a new cession.

Through a loophole in the Proclamation that allowed for "special leave and license" by the Crown to make purchases of Indian land west of the line, Virginia in 1768 was granted the right to quiet the claims of the Six Nations and the Cherokees to lands south of the Ohio. A treaty with the Six Nations was accordingly negotiated at Fort Stanwix in New York under the direction of Sir William Johnson, the Crown's superintendent of Indian affairs for the northern colonies. Virginia was represented by Dr.

Thomas Walker, the agent of the Loyal Company. The Six Nations were the only Indians consulted. The Board of Trade had ordered that the western boundary of the Iroquois cession should be set at a line drawn due south from the mouth of the Great Kanawha River (in present West Virginia) to the North Carolina border. But Walker persuaded Johnson to accede to his and the Six Nations' request that the boundary be set at the mouth of the Tennessee River, in far western Kentucky, and run up the Tennessee as far as its fork at the Holston River. If taken literally, this would include land in North Carolina, South Carolina, Georgia, and Alabama, for the Tennessee makes a deep swing to the south before flowing north to the Ohio. These boundaries, even if understood to apply only to Kentucky, not only took in all of the hunting grounds of the Shawnees south of the Ohio but also the overlapping claim of the Cherokees, whose lands the Board of Trade understood to extend east to the Great Kanawha—several hundred miles east of the Tennessee!

The Board of Trade was aware that the Cherokees also laid claim to lands in Kentucky. In order to quiet the Cherokee claim, a second commissioner from Virginia, Andrew Lewis from Staunton in the Shenandoah valley, who had originally expected to join Walker at Fort Stanwix, met instead with John Stuart, the Indian superintendent for the southern colonies; and the Cherokees at separate treaties in 1768 and 1770 released their lands east of the Kentucky River.[25]

Jefferson's Investments in Western Lands

Jefferson was aware of the 1768 Treaty of Fort Stanwix, by which, in conjunction with the Cherokee cessions, Virginia had (in her own opinion) perfected her title, subject to royal dispensation, to a vast extent of land west of the Appalachians. He included that treaty, together with the deed from the Iroquois to some of the suffering traders, as the last of the important state papers of Virginia to be itemized in the *Notes*. The Crown initially allowed settlement only as far down the Ohio as the Little Kanawha. But even this limited extension opened a substantial territory to investment by well-placed eastern speculators, such as George Washington, Benjamin Franklin, George Croghan, Patrick Henry, Thomas Walker, Andrew Lewis—and Thomas Jefferson.

In January 1769 Jefferson joined Thomas Walker and a number of associates, including Patrick Henry, an enthusiastic speculator, and his own legal mentor, George Wythe, in petitioning the Governor's Council for a grant of 45,000 acres at the confluence of the Little Kanawha and the Ohio Rivers, in the neighborhood of present-day Parkersburg, West Virginia. Jefferson noted in his memorandum book, where he kept record of at least a part of his real estate transactions, that his share was 5,000 acres.[26] The significance of this location goes beyond the prospect of selling lots to farmers. In the *Notes,* Jefferson observed that a branch of the Little Kanawha "interlocks with the western of Monongahela, [and] may one day admit a shorter passage from the latter into the Ohio." Speaking of the western fork of the Monongahela, he declared it to be "navigable in the winter 10 or 15 miles toward the northern of the Little Kanawha, and will admit a good wagon road to it."[27] His map in the *Notes* shows an "8-mile" portage between the two streams. In 1754 the Ohio Company had already built a road from its storehouse at Wills Creek, on the Potomac, to Redstone Creek, a western branch of the Monongahela. What Walker and Jefferson saw at the mouth of the Little Kanawha was no less than one possible terminus of Virginia's passageway to the western waters via the Potomac, the road to Redstone, the Monongahela, and the upper waters of the Little Kanawha.

Again, in the spring of 1769, Jefferson joined with Patrick Henry and twelve others in petitioning the Governor's Council for a grant of 50,000 acres on the Ohio River below the mouth of the New (Great Kanawha) River.[28] Lands along the Ohio between the Little Kanawha and the Great Kanawha presumably were included in the 200,000 acres surveyed in 1770 by George Washington on behalf of himself and the regiment that had served under him in the French and Indian War; perhaps for this reason, the petition of Henry, Jefferson, and company does not seem to have been approved.[29]

In late 1771 Jefferson learned that before the French and Indian War a number of parcels of western land had been surveyed by Andrew Lewis to which title was never completed. These included seven parcels of land, amounting to between 20,000 and 25,000 acres, west of the Fairfax property line which Jefferson and his associates now wanted to acquire.[30] Some of the properties were vacant, some were settled by persons claiming to have purchased them of Lewis, some were occupied by squatters. These lands were all in what is now West Virginia on the Greenbrier River and its branches, one of the tributaries of the Great Kanawha. Jefferson planned to "get grants" and listed as "Names to use" John Walker, Thomas

Nelson Jr., George Wythe, several Lewises, two Carters, two Randolphs, and members of families affiliated with the Jeffersons, including Dabney Carr and Francis Eppes, among others. The fate of this adventure in unpatented real estate is unfortunately not recorded in the memorandum books.[31]

In January 1773 Jefferson, with Thomas Walker acting as his agent, apparently sold the Jefferson family's share in the Loyal Company grant and in another grant on Walker's Creek, a tributary of the Great Kanawha. Jefferson noted carefully that he took three-eighths of the proceeds of both sales. Perhaps he was acting as trustee on behalf of two of his father's heirs, of whom there were eight living at the time of their father's death in 1757. By 1773 at least one, perhaps two, of the original heirs had died, and he may have been holding their eighth shares in trust for other descendants of Peter Jefferson.[32]

Again on November 29, 1773, Jefferson noted in his memorandum book that "I am this day taken in by Augustine Claiborne as a partner with himself, Matthew Talbot and William Owen in an order of council for 40,000 as. of land in Augusta County on Little river [probably the Little River shown on Jefferson's map in the *Notes* flowing into the Great Kanawha in extreme southwestern Virginia] dated Nov. 5, 1750. Note there are three others named in the order, but they were only nominal and he supposes Talbot or Owen to be dead, so that I shall come in for 10,000 as. at least."[33]

And again, in February 1777, we find Jefferson agreeing to join J. Harvie and Christopher Clarke in taking up 5,000 acres of land apiece "on Kentucky."[34] This venture was mentioned by Jefferson in a letter to James Madison in 1784, in which he stated that in 1776 or 1777 he had joined Harvie and some others in an application for western lands but that the scheme was dropped. In the same letter he also mentioned joining in 1782 "some gentlemen in a project to obtain some lands in the Western parts of North Carolina" but that he withdrew that same year. "Lands in Western North Carolina" would almost certainly be in Cherokee territory, or former Cherokee territory.[35]

If we add up the acreages of western land which Jefferson made at least initial attempts to acquire from 1769 to 1777, we find that they total a substantial amount: about 35,000 acres, assuming that he expected the equivalent in value of at least 5,000 acres in those transactions where his share is not specified in acres. All of this land lay west of the Appalachians on waters flowing into the Ohio River, and the applications for grants were all based on the assumption that Virginia had acquired them by cessions from the Six Nations, the latest occurring at Fort Stanwix in 1768, and from the Cherokees in 1768 and 1770. But in comparison with Patrick Henry, George Washington, and Benjamin Franklin, Jefferson was a cautious speculator. Most if not all of the Loyal Company's actual surveys lay in the southern end of the Valley of Virginia, and "Lewis's rich lands" were along the Greenbrier River in Greenbrier and Pocahontas counties in the eastern parts of West Virginia. The lands on the Great Kanawha River were also in West Virginia, an area of mountains and narrow valleys later to be exploited as coal country. The 45,000 acres below the mouth of the Little Kanawha that he and others petitioned the Governor's Council for in 1769 was within territory ceded by the Iroquois in 1768, and the 5,000 acres "on Kentucky" mentioned in February 1777 was probably within the limits of the Cherokee cessions and occurred at a time when Kentucky was rapidly filling up with speculators and settlers.

Western land company investments and sales were for the most part noted by Jefferson in his memorandum books. Apparently he thought of them separately from the category of "Lands and slaves bought [and] sold," including plantations and town lots, and from the shares inherited by him and his siblings, which were listed in his "Personal stock" accounts. Land company shares were, strictly speaking, not real estate holdings; they were comparable to shares in a mutual fund or a mutual insurance company. The investor was assessed his portion of company expenses, in this case legal and surveying costs, received his part of the profits (if any), and could sell all or part of his share, but he never received exclusive personal title to any particular parcel of land unless he purchased it from the company.

The accounts of "Lands and slaves bought and sold," by contrast, included transactions from 1764 to 1778 in lands to which Jefferson personally held title and which were not part of his inherited plantations at Monticello, Shadwell, Poplar Forest, and elsewhere. All but one of the tracts mentioned in the personal stock accounts lay east of the Blue Ridge, on the waters of the James River and its tributaries, southwest of Monticello in Bedford and Amherst counties and southeast in Cumberland County, plus 157 acres at the Natural Bridge in Botetourt County and a "lot in Richmond town" bought of Colonel Byrd. The lands in the settled parts of Virginia were bought and sold at prices ranging from £1 to £2 per acre. The total value of lands sold was not inconsiderable, amounting to some £7,456 in the years from 1764 to 1778, exceeding by far the value of lands purchased (about £1,658).[36]

The amounts recorded in the memorandum books for expenses in connection with the land company speculations are small, a few hundred pounds at most. How much, if anything, he ever profited from the earnings of these land companies, or from the sale of shares, is not revealed in these accounts. But the fact that his interest was genuine gleams through the terse language of the notations: "5000 acres for my part" on the Ohio (1769), "Pd. Patrick Henry toward the grant we are petitioning for [on the Ohio]" (1769), "Gave Patrick Henry these names of trustees to insert with my own," "I shall come in [with Claiborne, Talbot and Owen], for 10,000 as. at least [as Claiborne] supposes Talbot or Owen to be dead" (1773), "Agreed to join J. Harvie & Christopher Clarke in taking up 5000 as. ld. apiece on Kentucky & pd. J. Harvie 48/towards expence of entries &c." (1777).

The two land company ventures in which Jefferson invested in 1769 do not appear to have resulted in actual sales of land to settlers or in profits to the participants. The petitions to the Governor's Council may never have been acted upon because of the legal limbo in which the governor found himself as a result of the Proclamation of 1763; and in 1773 the governors of all the colonies were prohibited from making further grants of land. The two other ventures in prerevolutionary times, in 1771 and 1772, involved taking up lands already granted to others in the 1750s but to which title had not been perfected. There is no record of success or profit from these speculations either.

Land Company Schemes

In the period from 1763 to the Revolution, speculative land companies and would-be settlers were faced with several choices of strategy for dealing with a British ministry that seemed more interested in maintaining peace with the Indians than in serving the expansionist plans of the colonies. One approach was to attempt to work directly with the Virginia government, assuming that the legal procedures for patenting land already purchased from the Indians continued in effect. This seems to have been the approach taken by the Loyal Company, the Greenbrier Company, and the smaller companies in which Jefferson had an interest. The claims of most of these companies lay on or north of the Great Kanawha, thus complying with the terms of the 1768 Treaty of Fort Stanwix and the ministry's declaration of 1769 approving settlement only as far down the Ohio as the Great Kanawha.

But there were other approaches as well being tried by less scrupulous groups. One of these was the creative scheme of some settlers from the Holston River area in southwestern Virginia, who around 1769 crossed into North Carolina and Tennessee and established a settlement on the Watauga River, a tributary of the Holston that flows south from the southwest corner of Virginia. They made no purchase from the Cherokee claimants to the region but instead arranged an eight-year "lease," thus seemingly avoiding a direct violation of the 1763 prohibition of private purchases (but of course violating the Proclamation's prohibition of settlements west of the mountains). The Watauga settlement expanded onto the banks of the Holston and other streams in what is now Tennessee, and in 1772 these settlements united in the Watauga Association. They were an independent-minded militant community, prepared to defend themselves against all comers, British or Indian, and eventually after the Revolution formed the nucleus of the short-lived State of Franklin (1784–1788). As U.S. President, Jefferson would take measures to ensure that their encroachments on Cherokee land would be legitimized by appropriate land cessions.[37]

Another tactic, technically legal but requiring extensive skullduggery, was to ignore Virginia's claim to lands west of the Appalachians and to approach the British ministry directly. This was the strategy of the association that was variously known as the Walpole Company, the Grand Ohio Company, and the Vandalia Company. The consortium was composed of wealthy and influential Pennsylvanians with interests in the Indian trade and of wealthy and influential Englishmen with friends in high places. The American principals were Benjamin Franklin and Samuel Wharton. Franklin at the time lived in London as postmaster-general and agent for the colonies in lobbying against the repressive policies of the British government. Wharton, once the major Philadelphia importer of goods for the Indian trade, his firm now in receivership, was in London to plead the case for a royal grant to the Indiana Company of suffering traders. Other American associates included Franklin's son William, Sir William Johnson, George Croghan, and William Trent.

The British associates were a whole galaxy of stars. In London, their most active ally was Thomas Walpole, a prominent banker and member of Parliament. Others included Thomas Pownall, Franklin's friend and author of the famous map and topographical description of the middle British colonies in North America; Camden, the lord chancellor; Hertford, the lord chamberlain; George Grenville, recently prime minister and enforcer of the Stamp Act; Thomas Bradshaw, current prime minister; Lord North, to be appointed prime minister in 1770; Sir George Colebrook, director of the East India Company; other members of the Privy Council and Parliament; and various other men of distinction and money. The company soon took in the suffering traders and the remnants of the old Ohio Company and in a few months renamed itself the Grand Ohio Company.

The company's first petition to the Board of Trade was for 2,400,000 acres of the land ceded by the Iroquois at Fort Stanwix. To their surprise, the chairman of the board suggested that they ask for a much larger grant, on the order of 20,000,000 acres, sufficient for a new colony—to be carved out of Virginia—bounded on the south by a line running from the mouth of the Scioto River (north of the Ohio about 150 miles downstream from the Great Kanawha) to the Cumberland Gap and thence up to the head of the Greenbrier River. It was to become a proprietary colony, governed by the company itself. The Grand Ohio Company accordingly submitted a revised proposal along these lines. The bounds thus delineated of course embraced the tracts for which Jefferson and others had been applying to the Governor's Council, as well as "Lewis's rich lands" and other tracts claimed and surveyed by the Loyal Company and its companion Greenbrier Company.

The plan thereafter ran an unsteady course through the royal bureaucracy. In 1770 the Lords of the Treasury approved it; in April 1772 the Board of Trade recommended against it; in July 1772, influenced by Walpole's impassioned defense, the Committee of Council recommended that the king approve the petition; and in August the king ordered the plan to be carried into execution. By May 1773 the Board of Trade had prepared a procedure for separating the Grand Ohio Company's lands "from the colony of Virginia" and establishing on them "a distinct colony, under the name of Vandalia" (the name having been chosen to honor Queen Charlotte, "as her majesty is descended from the Vandals").

But the plan was further delayed by the opposition of the attorney general and solicitor general, who believed that Franklin, the colonial agitator, did not deserve any consideration from the king. Franklin offered to make a public resignation from the company (while secretly continuing as a member). The matter dragged on until the spring of 1775, when the Committee of Council suspended further action on the project until the Revolution was crushed. But the final demise of the scheme was delayed until 1781, when Franklin and Wharton presented a memorial to Congress, which had inherited the Crown's title to lands purchased from the Indians and preemption rights to lands unpurchased. But Congress chose not to sell off its public lands in tracts greater than 2,000,000 acres. Thus ended at last the Grand Ohio Company's attempt to detach Kentucky from Virginia.[38]

A more serious rival for Kentucky lands was the Transylvania Company. Its prime mover was Judge Richard Henderson, a backwoods lawyer from North Carolina who had succumbed to Kentucky fever as early as 1764, when he was about twenty-nine years old. Henderson was a flamboyant character, given to high living and grandiose schemes for western colonization. He employed Daniel Boone and others to scout out Kentucky lands, and in August 1774 Henderson and several other North Carolinians organized the Louisa Company with the purpose of renting or purchasing land on the Ohio from the Indian tribes "now in possession thereof." Six months later the company was reorganized under the name Transylvania Company.[39]

The company proceeded in sublime indifference to the Proclamation of 1763, the claims of the Crown and Virginia to sovereignty over Kentucky lands, and the potentially competing claims of other land companies. Assuming that the Cherokees remained the owners of the lands, Henderson visited the Cherokees and proposed to purchase their lands west of the Great Kanawha. He ignored the king's representatives in Indian affairs, the governors of Virginia and North Carolina, and the southern Indian superintendent, John Stuart, who according to edict should have managed such a matter.

In this he may have been guided by the specious "Camden-York opinion," which already had been used by the Wataugans to rationalize their proceedings with the Cherokees and by the Walpole Company to add backbone to their petition. The Camden-York opinion had been formulated to give license to the East India Company to acquire land from pagan princes in India, without first obtaining grants from the British Crown, and lawyers in America quoted it (leaving out the restrictive references to south Asian moguls) to justify private purchases from the Native Americans. In March 1775, at the Treaty of Sycamore Shoals on the Watauga River, the Henderson Company signed a treaty with certain chiefs of the Cherokees. The Indians, of whom about a thousand were present, allegedly received £2,000 in lawful money, perhaps as much as £8,000 worth of trade goods, and after the treaty was signed, rum "to a great amount." The Transylvania Company received what it considered to be a valid deed to an enormous tract of country: all that land, south of the Ohio, between the Kentucky and Cumberland Rivers, embracing the western two-thirds of Kentucky and much of central Tennessee and amounting to tens of millions of acres.

Even before the treaty was consummated, the company had advertised, promising 500 acres to each of fifty soldiers who would protect the settlers and 500 acres to each settler (plus 250 acres more for every titleable person in his party), and liberal grants of land to those who would set up iron works, saw mills, salt works, and grist mills, bring in flocks of sheep, and so on. All settlers were advised that they could purchase only from the company and would pay quit-rents to the company (not to Virginia or the Crown) and would be governed by the company. The enterprise would be *de facto* a new colony. A vague hope was expressed, in a memorial sent to the Continental Congress in 1775, that the Crown would accept the new arrangement.

Virginia officials were, understandably, upset by news of these proceedings. The governor of Virginia issued a proclamation denouncing "one Richard Henderson, and other disorderly Persons," declaring the "pretended purchase, made from Indians," to be invalid and ordering the officers of the law to evict any settlers claiming lands from Henderson, by force if necessary. He wrote to the ministry in London, seeking support. Nevertheless, the Transylvania Company went ahead with its plans. Daniel Boone and others established settlements in 1775 and 1776 under the company's aegis.

But at the same time, other settlers entered Kentucky, seeking title under a suddenly congenial Virginia government policy of surveying and selling lots in the territory east of the Kentucky River, and the adherents of the Loyal and Greenbrier companies actively opposed Henderson. The unraveling of the Transylvania Company's claims finally came about as a result of a revolt by actual settlers in Kentucky. Disgruntled by the high-handed conduct of the self-assumed proprietors and doubting the legality under Virginia law of the Sycamore Shoals purchase, a convention was held in Harrodsburg, under the leadership of George Rogers Clark, to set up an alternative, interim government independent of the Henderson associates. In July 1776 this group sent a deputation including Clark and John Jones, a nephew of one of Jefferson's legal associates, to Williamsburg to negotiate with the government of Virginia about legitimizing their settlement under the government of Virginia. Henderson and his colleagues also repaired to Williamsburg to plead their case. In October the Virginia Assembly took up the matter of Kentucky.

In part, the issue had been decided already, for on June 29, with the promulgation of a Virginia Constitution, Jefferson's proviso had been adopted declaring "that no purchase of lands should be made of the Indian natives but in behalf of the public by authority of the General Assembly."[40] The practical issue now became one of organizing a county government which could provide an adequate militia for the defense of the inhabitants. Thomas Jefferson became the sponsor of a bill to divide the vast Fincastle County into two counties, one of which would be the home of the Transylvanians. A bitter backroom debate ensued, and out of these negotiations emerged a committee, of which Jefferson was the chairman, to reconsider the bill. This committee proposed, and on November 25 the assembly passed, an amended act which divided Fincastle into not two but three counties. And the Virginia Assembly would now have six representatives from its western marches instead of just two—six sturdy settlers and Indian fighters of the kind Jefferson was coming to see as the backbone of the country.

There were other land issues to be settled, however. What was to be done about the claims of the land companies, now that Virginia's declaration of sovereignty had invalidated both private purchases from the Indians and royal land grants? In 1778 the assembly disposed of these matters. Henderson, who had at least brought in settlers, was awarded 200,000 acres on the Green River in western Kentucky, under the administration of the county of Kentucky. The old Loyal Company and the even older Greenbrier Company were recognized as having surveyed and sold lands to settlers in southwestern Virginia according to proper procedures, and the titles so produced were recognized.

The other land company claimants, including the old Ohio Company, Vandalia (Walpole), and Indiana (suffering traders) companies, received nothing. The settlers in Kentucky who found themselves without legal title, now that most of the land companies' claims had been denied, were allowed to preempt up to 400 acres of land and to pay Virginia a nominal price for it later. And a bill to establish a Land Office was drafted by Jefferson to fill the void and clear the chaos that resulted when the Crown's administration ceased to exist in 1776.[41] Jefferson's bill, however, did not limit the amount of land any one individual might acquire from the state, thus leaving the way open for favored land companies to develop large tracts. He undoubtedly saw a role for land companies in the creation of the infrastructure of roads, ferries, river landings, mill and town sites, and warehouses and stores needed by settlers in a new country, and he did not condemn all such investment as mere speculation, even though his ultimate objective was a commonwealth of small farmers.[42]

The Madison Letter

In the years from 1776 until he assumed the governorship of Virginia in 1779, Jefferson's land-related policies and activities in the Virginia Assembly were at odds with the interests of powerful people in Virginia and elsewhere in the young nation. Furthermore, he was vulnerable to the charge—whether fair or not—that he had a personal financial interest in policies that favored certain land companies and not others, or that he had rushed to profit from the demise of Henderson's claims in Virginia and North Carolina by investing, in February 1777, with John Harvie and Christopher Clarke in 5,000 acres "on Kentucky." And as governor, his apparent neglect of defenses for Tidewater Virginia in favor of Clark's campaign in the Ohio valley might be construed as serving primarily the interests of speculators in western lands.

Rumors circulated in later years that Jefferson expressed an interest in becoming a partner in the Transylvania Company. A grandson of one of the founding members of the company told Lyman C. Draper in 1846, "It is a tradition that Patrick Henry and Thomas Jefferson desired to become partners in the company; but Col. Henderson preferred not to have them admitted . . . lest they should supplant the Colonel in the guiding spirit of the company. Had they been admitted, the validity of the purchase might never have been questioned."[43] But there does not appear to be supporting evidence for this "tradition." Nothing appears in Jefferson's memorandum books or correspondence to suggest that he had an actual financial interest in the Henderson Company. Indeed, he reputedly told one of Henderson's representatives that he hoped to see a "free government" established west of Virginia, presumably a new state governed by its own inhabitants, not by a proprietary company.[44] As for other schemes of private purchase from the Indians in which he might have participated, there is no evidence that he availed himself of these opportunities either.

Many of Jefferson's friends and associates were participants in land companies that planned to profit from private purchases from the Indians illegally made in defiance of the Proclamation of 1763. Included were Thomas Walker, Thomas Walker Jr., Matthew Maury, Patrick Henry, George Washington, Benjamin Franklin, New Jersey Governor William Franklin, two other royal governors (Dunmore of Virginia and Johnson of Maryland), and many other members of the state legislatures and the Continental Congress. The combination of these schemes with revolutionary and counter-revolutionary politics produced a tangle of intrigue and conflicts of interest that must have been deeply confusing to players and spectators alike.

Jefferson's concern about the damaging effect of rumors about his "western land jobbing" came to the surface in 1784, when he began to fear that they might impede his ability to perform public duties. Writing to George Washington from the seat of Congress in Annapolis on March 15, 1784, he foresaw a rivalry between the Hudson and the Potomac rivers for "the commerce of all the country Westward of L. Erie, on the waters of the lakes, of the Ohio & upper parts of the Mississippi." In order for Virginia to engross the better part of this trade, a passage via the creeks and portages from the falls of the Potomac to the upper waters of the Monongahela River or its tributary, the Youghiogany, would have to be opened. To finance this major public works project, he had lately "pressed this subject" on his friends in the Virginia Assembly, proposing to have a special tax laid to raise £5,000 to £10,000 a year. And in order to supervise the great work, he suggested to Washington (now retired as commander-in-chief) that he turn his "great hand" to direct the business. He concluded by assuring Washington that "my zeal in this business is public & pure," and he urged the General to "view me as not owning, nor ever having a prospect of owning, one inch of land on any water either of the Patowmac or Ohio."[45] Washington agreed to head the Potomac project.

Two months later, in May 1784, Congress appointed Jefferson to serve as minister, along with John Adams and Benjamin Franklin, to negotiate treaties of friendship and commerce in Paris and other European capitals.

Jefferson's Denial of an Interest in Western Lands

You mention that my name is used by some speculators in Western land jobbing, as if they were acting for me as well as themselves. About the year 1776 or 1777 I consented to join Mr. Harvey and some others in an application for lands there: which scheme however I believe he dropped in the threshold, for I never after heard one syllable on the subject. In 1782. I joined some gentlemen in a project to obtain some lands in the Western parts of North Carolina. But in the winter of 1782, 1783, while I was in expectation of going to Europe and that the title to Western lands might possibly come under the discussion of the ministers, I withdrew myself from this company. I am further assured that the members never prosecuted their views. These were the only occasions in which I ever took a single step for the acquisition of Western lands, and in these I retracted at the threshold. I can with truth therefore declare to you, and wish you to repeat it on every proper occasion, that no person on earth is authorized to place my name in any adventure for lands on the Western waters, that I am not engaged in any one speculation for that purpose at present, and never was engaged in any, but the two before mentioned. I am one of eight children to whom my father left his share in the loyal company; whose interests however I never espoused, and they have long since received their quietus. Excepting these, I never was nor am now interested in one foot of land on earth, off the waters of James river.

This appointment stirred new misgivings about his land deals. In 1782 he had entered into the land venture in western North Carolina. But learning in early 1783 that he might be dispatched to Europe, he promptly withdrew from this enterprise. Later, from Paris, on November 11, 1783, he wrote to his friend James Madison an extraordinary letter (see above) denying any prior interests in western lands except the 1777 investment toward the 5,000 acres "on Kentucky" and the brief North Carolina involvement in 1782.[46]

That Jefferson felt it necessary to assure his friends that he was not guilty of conflicts of interest resulting from transactions in western real estate is somewhat surprising. George Washington and Patrick Henry were notorious speculators and so was his fellow minister, Benjamin Franklin. There is no reason to suspect that his proposal to Washington about the Potomac–Ohio project was intended to increase the value of secret real estate holdings along the route or that he would steer European investment to his own properties in North Carolina. The other, earlier ventures from 1769 to 1773 seem to have come to naught, and in any case they were relatively small, conservative investments, not likely to make anyone rich. There is no indication in the memorandum books or his accounts that he realized a profit from his series of abortive speculations in western land; very likely he lost money by them.

Presumably Jefferson was prompted to avoid even the appearance of evil. The categorical denial that he "ever took a single step for the acquisition of western lands," apart from the North Carolina and Harvie ventures, was a flat-out lie which probably was intended in part to facilitate the conduct of his mission to France, unencumbered by suspicions that he had used or was using public office to promote his own private financial schemes.

Jefferson was also very sensitive to criticism of his conduct as governor during the Revolutionary War. The assembly had considered investigating him for neglecting the defense of the eastern part of the commonwealth in favor of supporting George Rogers Clark's campaign against the British and Indians in the lands beyond the Appalachians. Jefferson had thus turned Virginia's part in the revolutionary struggle into mostly an Indian war. It could be said by political enemies that he had committed a large share of the state's resources to the protection of Virginia's settlements in West Virginia and Kentucky, where Jefferson and his friends had financial interests that would be advanced after the war by immigrants eager to purchase lands.

So let us turn now to consider Jefferson as Indian fighter.

CHAPTER TWO

The Indian Wars

JUST AS Thomas Jefferson lived in a world of speculation in Indian land, so he lived also in a world in which Indians themselves were a constant presence. The bitter wars with the Powhatans, although a hundred years in the past, lingered in folk memory as well as in historical tracts, and young Jefferson, as a scion of Virginia gentry who were intimately involved in western lands and Indian affairs, must have been made aware of border warfare from an early age. He probably grew up with the traditional view of Native Americans as the enemy.

The French and Indian War, precipitated by the Ohio Company's attempt in 1754 to make settlements west of the Alleghenies and by Washington's sally against the French in the company's defense, had brought down upon Virginia's northern frontier a savage assault by the Indians of the Ohio country. Attacks began in 1755 and continued through 1758, and in 1763 raiders returned, inspired to join Pontiac's Rebellion against the English. To protect the plantations on the northern edge of settlement, Colonel George Washington, in command of the Virginia militia, directed the building of a chain of forts in northern Virginia along the Roanoke River and the north and south branches of the Potomac to protect Fairfax Estate in the Northern Neck, the Valley of Virginia, and the valley of the Greenbrier. In spite of these defensive measures, dozens of settlers' families were massacred, forts were attacked and burned, and pitched battles were fought between Virginia militia detachments and parties of Indians led by French officers. Losses were considerable.

The settlers at the south end of the Valley of Virginia, and in the valleys of the Holston and the New rivers across the mountains, at first fared better. But relations with the Cherokees in North Carolina and present Tennessee soon soured, and between 1758 and 1760 a separate Cherokee War was waged. Peace between the Virginians and the Cherokees was not made until November 1760, and an uneasy truce prevailed thereafter for fifteen years, despite repeated encroachments on Cherokee lands by white hunters and settlers and occasional murders of Cherokees by Virginians and Carolinians.[1]

The French and Indian War was being fought while Jefferson was in his teens, but he certainly would have been sharply aware of many of the events. His father's friend, Colonel Fry, had died on the way to confront the French in 1754, and after Peter Jefferson's own death in 1757, Thomas had gone to school at the house of the Reverend James Maury, a proponent of a strong military defense against the marauding Indians. In his correspondence with kinfolk in England and probably in conversation with his pupils, Maury spoke of terrible Indian depredations by the Cherokees and Shawnees—the laying waste of settlements in the Valley of Virginia, all the way from the Potomac to the Holston River. He spoke of havoc and desolation in the southwest, the theft of 2,000 head of cattle and horses from English settlers, which the Indians drove to the French stronghold at Fort Duquesne, and the potential abandonment of all settlements west of the Blue Ridge. Such fears can hardly have failed to impress the young scholar with the terrors of Indian warfare.[2]

In 1760 Jefferson went to Williamsburg to study at the College of William and Mary and remained there for two years, during which he became friends with his professor of mathematics, William Small, his legal mentor, George Wythe, and the royal governor, Francis Fauquier. The four had "frequent dinners" together and Jefferson, an intelligent, talented, and personable young man, played violin at concerts in the palace. He recalled his association with these sophisticated and well- informed gentlemen as the occasion of hearing "more good sense, more rational and philosophical conversations than in all my life besides."[3] No doubt the talk also included some discussion of the events of the day, including the ongoing war with the Cherokees, for the governor commanded Virginia's troops in that struggle and directed Virginia's participation in the peace settlement.

Toward the end of his college days in Williamsburg Jefferson was exposed to another side of the Indian character. Following the peace settlement, several Cherokee leaders, including the chief Outacite from the Overhills part of the tribe, were invited to visit England. En route, their party spent several days at Williamsburg, accompanied by a number of other Cherokees; and the night before they embarked, Outacite delivered a speech of farewell to his followers. Jefferson remembered the occasion nostalgically some fifty years later, in a letter to John Adams: "Before the Revolution, the Indians were in the habit of coming often and in great numbers to the seat of government, where I was very much with them. I knew much the great Outacite, the warrior and orator of the Cherokees; he was always the guest of my father on his journeys to and from Williamsburg. I was in his camp when he made his great farewell oration to his people the evening before his departure for England. The moon was in full splendor, and to her he seemed to address himself in his prayers for his own safety on the voyage, and that of his people during his absence; his sounding voice, distinct articulation, animated actions, and the solemn silence of his people at their several fires, filled me with awe and venera-

Outacite (left) and two other Cherokee leaders in London, 1762. Engraving, artist unknown. Courtesy of the British Museum.

tion, although I did not understand a word he uttered."[4] This charming anecdote leaves unclear the actual frequency of Outacite's visits to Shadwell during Jefferson's youth.

After the French and Indian War ended in 1760, the next of Virginia's frontier wars prior to the Revolution was the conflict with the Shawnees, formerly resident in Kentucky, who still claimed the right to hunt there and to prevent encroachment by Virginia's hunters, explorers, land speculators, surveyors, and settlers. As we have seen, in the spring of 1774 the murder of Logan's family occurred along the Ohio River, precipitating Lord Dunmore's War. Governor Dunmore ordered Colonel Andrew Lewis, an experienced Indian fighter from the French and Indian War, to lead one army of Virginians against the Shawnees, while he himself commanded another, setting forth from Fort Pitt. Colonel Lewis's command reached the Ohio River first, at the mouth of the Great Kanawha, with the intention of crossing it to destroy the Shawnee towns, but the Shawnees crossed the Ohio and attacked first at Point Pleasant. In a pitched battle, the Virginians prevailed and the Indians retreated across the river, but it was a bloody encounter: of Lewis's army of about 800 men, 81 were killed, including Lewis's brother, and 140 wounded; about 200 Shawnees were killed, out of a force equal in size to the Virginians'.[5]

At the subsequent peace treaty, the Shawnees accepted the terms dictated by Lord Dunmore. They yielded their hunting rights south of the Ohio in return for a white promise not to hunt north of the Ohio, agreed to return prisoners and stolen property and to stop harassing boats on the river, and allowed the whites to set the conditions of future trade. By this treaty, it seemed, the security of the lands claimed by Virginia speculators and land companies was now obtained, and settlers flocked to Kentucky. Indeed, charges were made immediately that the whole war was contrived and provoked for this very purpose. According to Thomas Wharton (a land speculator himself), Patrick Henry explicitly charged that Lord Dunmore, wishing to settle his family in America, "was really pursuing this war in order to obtain by purchase or treaty from the Natives a tract of Territory." Henry thought Dunmore had designs on the north side of the Ohio; the historian Thomas Abernethy, however, is of the opinion that Dunmore's "chief concern [was] the settlement of central Kentucky."[6]

In the period between Lord Dunmore's War and the Revolution, when he first served as lieutenant (commanding officer) of the Albemarle

County militia, Jefferson penned a series of bellicose remarks about Native Americans and their British instigators which certainly reflected and appealed to a conventional Virginian image of Indians as cruel and ruthless enemies. But by 1775 he had specific—if mistaken—reasons for charging the British with instigating Indian attacks. In order to understand Jefferson's life-long ambivalence toward Native Americans, one must ask what information he was privy to throughout the formative revolutionary period, both when he was a militia officer and later, from 1779 to 1781, when he served as governor of Virginia.

The War with the Cherokees

Around the time that the battles of Lexington and Concord on April 19, 1775, signaled the outbreak of armed conflict between the colonists and Britain, rumors began to circulate in the south about the supposed activities of the aging superintendent of Indian Affairs for the southern colonies, John Stuart, in inciting an attack by the Indians. On August 4, 1775, Purdie's *Virginia Gazette* published an extract of an anonymous letter supposedly written from Charleston, South Carolina, on June 29, making the charge explicit: "We lately learned by intercepted letters, and otherwise, that there have been endeavours to set the Indians upon us. Mr. Stewart, the superintendent of Indian affairs, is accused of being the person who has forwarded this wicked design, and he is fled for safety."[7] Stuart, despite his infirmities, had indeed fled from Charleston in May and soon after proceeded to Savannah, Georgia, and thence to Pensacola, Florida. But in fact, in line with prevailing British policy, Stuart was urging the southern Indians *not* to attack the frontiers but to remain neutral in the conflict.

In September 1775, however, Stuart received from General Gage, commander-in-chief of British forces in North America, a letter advising him that the rebels had already "open'd the Door" to Indian warfare by bringing down the "Savages" against the British in Boston. Stuart was ordered to urge the southern Indians to "take arms against his Majesty's Enemies, and to distress them all in their power."[8] Gage's authority to persuade the Indians to take up the hatchet had been given by the ministry in England (just as John Dickinson had charged in his 1775 draft of the "Declaration [of] the Causes and Necessity of their Taking Up Arms," which Jefferson helped write).[9] But Stuart nevertheless refused to interpret his orders as implying that the Indians should be encouraged to launch "an indiscriminate attack upon the Provinces." Rather, he thought they should be encouraged to serve as auxiliaries to Loyalist troops in a "concerted Plan," presumably against revolutionary military units.

Stuart continued to drag his feet through the winter of 1775–1776. In the spring he dispatched his brother Henry to visit the Overhills Cherokees, many of whom, independent of British urging, were threatening to go to war against the Wataugan settlements in what is now northeastern Tennessee. The Cherokees complained that the original "lease" of their lands, and later the Henderson purchase itself in March 1775 at the Treaty of Sycamore Shoals, had been fraudulent. Stuart, with the help of the resident British trader Alexander Cameron, persuaded the Cherokees to send letters in May warning the Wataugans to vacate the disputed lands within twenty days.

The Wataugan response was duplicitous. On the one hand, a reply to Stuart and Cameron expressed friendship for the Indians and loyalty to the king (but no promise to give up their settlements). But a forged letter, purportedly from Henry Stuart, was sent to the revolutionary conventions in North Carolina and Virginia and to the Continental Congress and was published in Purdie's *Virginia Gazette* on June 7, 1776. This letter described a British plan to send an army north from Florida, mobilizing Creek and Cherokee warriors along the way, to attack and destroy all rebel settlements on the Carolina and Virginia frontiers.[10]

This forged letter may very likely have been in Jefferson's mind in July 1776 when he wrote in his draft of the Declaration of Independence that the king "has endeavored to bring on the inhabitants of our frontiers the merciless Indian savages, whose known rule of warfare is an undistinguished destruction of all ages, sexes, and conditions of existence."[11] The same charge, in the same language, had a month before been included in the preamble to his draft of a constitution for Virginia.[12] But the ultimate source of the paragraph was more likely the anonymous letter from South Carolina of 1775, which mentioned in the same breath fears of a slave rebellion and an Indian onslaught. This charge was given even wider currency by Thomas Paine's *Common Sense* (published February 14, 1776), which referred to "that barbarous and hellish power, which hath stirred up the Indians and the Negroes against us."[13] Thus Jefferson's allusion in the

"An Indian Warrior Entering His Wigwam with a Scalp." Engraving by Barlow, 1789. An image of the "merciless savages" (and perhaps rebellious black slaves) killing and scalping helpless settlers while British soldiers look on. Courtesy of the Library of Congress.

Declaration reflected widespread belief in the south and even in Pennsylvania that the British were scheming to turn loose the Indians upon the back settlements and to rouse the slaves in revolt.

By the summer of 1776 the situation in Cherokee country was rapidly deteriorating. At the beginning of July word reached the Overhills that southern Cherokee warriors had attacked South Carolina frontier settlements. Dragging Canoe, the leader of the anti-Wataugan faction among the Overhills, now launched his own war parties against the Wataugans. The Wataugans fled their farms, some of them congregating in a fort on the Watauga River, others fleeing into Virginia. Dragging Canoe planned first to take the Wataugan fort but was ambushed by Wataugan bush fighters before he reached it. The Cherokees lost thirteen men, and Dragging Canoe was severely wounded.

In retaliation, the Cherokees abandoned their military-style formation, broke up into small parties, and attacked isolated settlements, burning cabins and killing eighteen whites. These guerrilla raids continued through the summer of 1776. Jefferson was so incensed by the Cherokee raids that in August he was writing: "Nothing will reduce these wretches so soon as pushing the war into the heart of their country. But I would not stop there. I would never cease pursuing them while one of them remained on this side the Mississippi. So unprovoked an attack & so treacherous a one should never be forgiven while one of them remains near enough to do us injury."[14]

In retaliation, militia armies from Georgia, the Carolinas, and Virginia launched a massive assault on the Cherokees, destroying virtually all their undefended towns. The Overhills towns, where Old Tassel and other peaceable chiefs lived—those who had signed the treaty with Henderson at Sycamore Shoals the year before—were destroyed along with the rest, for Dragging Canoe and his warriors also made their headquarters there. Many Cherokees did not return for a time to their burnt-out villages and ruined cornfields and potato plantings, seeking shelter instead with the British in Florida or with the western Creeks. Dragging Canoe and his followers removed to Chickamauga Creek, near present-day Chattanooga, Tennessee, and came to be referred to as the "secessionists."[15]

Jefferson in later years recalled with relish the victory of the Virginians in their attack on the Overhills settlements. In his biography of Meriwether Lewis, written in 1813, in speaking of his protégé's descent from an illustrious family, Jefferson saluted the paternal uncle, Nicholas Lewis, in language reminiscent of his words of nearly four decades earlier: "Nicholas Lewis, the second of his father's brothers, commanded a regiment of militia in the successful expedition of 1776, against the Cherokee Indians, who, seduced by the agents of the British government to take up the hatchet against us, had committed great havoc on our southern frontier, by murdering and scalping helpless women and children according to their cruel and cowardly principles of warfare. The chastisement they then received closed the history of their wars, prepared them for receiving the elements of civilization, which, zealously cultivated by the present government of the United States, have rendered them an industrious, peaceable and happy people."[16] Perhaps Jefferson never learned that Stuart had done his best to hold back Dragging Canoe and his warriors, who were as enraged at the British as at the Americans. But the expedition of 1776 did not close the history of the Cherokee wars. Jefferson should have recalled his own ordering forth of Virginia's troops in an assault on the still defiant Cherokees in 1780 and 1781, when he was governor of Virginia.

The Overhills chiefs, now rid of Dragging Canoe, were glad enough to make peace, negotiating a treaty with the Carolinians and Georgians in May and with the Virginians in July 1777. Peace came at a price, of course—over 5,000,000 acres of land—and many Cherokees, resenting the cession, joined Dragging Canoe at Chickamauga. Violations of these treaties occurred on both sides, the Wataugans quickly overstepping the agreed-upon boundaries and the Chickamaugans scalping and burning with increased fury. Meanwhile, the peaceable chiefs in the Overhills were without supplies because the Americans were financially unable to give them relief and the British pack-trains were being intercepted by the Chickamaugans.

Old Tassel sent a plaintive protest to the governor of North Carolina: "Brother . . . We are a poor distressed people, that is in great trouble . . . your people from Nolichucky [the Wataugans] are daily pushing us out of our lands. We have no place to hunt on. Your people have built houses within one days walk of our towns. We don't want to quarrel with our elder brother; we therefore hope our elder brother will not take our lands from us, that the Great Man above gave us. He made you and he made me, we are all his children . . . We are the first people that ever lived on this land; it is ours."[17] No response, apparently, was forthcoming, and the bloody frontier war continued.

In April 1779 Governor Patrick Henry dispatched a force of three hundred Virginians, joined with an equal number of North Carolinians, to attack the Chickamaugans. They met no resistance, the warriors being absent on their own mission against white frontier settlements, and they were able to burn eleven Indian towns and carry away peltries, ammunition, and 20,000 bushels of corn. The Chickamaugans, undaunted, simply moved their towns westward and renewed their attacks on the Wataugans and other settlers. And they were now joined by Cherokees who had fled to shelter among the British in Florida. There was even an imminent threat that the Indians to the north and to the south, seduced by British agents and led and supplied by British officers, would combine in a pincers movement to cut off Kentucky.[18]

When Jefferson became governor of Virginia later that year, he was well aware of the division among the Cherokees and regarded the Overhills towns, led by friendly chiefs like Old Tassel, as deserving of Virginia's protection. The state, indeed, had gone to some expense to supply them with necessities, in order to forestall their turning to the British in desperation. Outrage and horror at Indian atrocities could be vented violently on British instigators and their Indian allies, but the politic parallel response was to buy the friendship of as many potential enemies as possible. As one of Jefferson's more sympathetic biographers, Merrill Peterson, succinctly put it: "Divide and rule, aid the friendly in peace, exterminate the incorrigibles—this was Jefferson's Indian policy."[19]

In June 1780 Jefferson decided to act against the Chickamaugans. He ordered 250 militia from Washington and Montgomery counties in southwest Virginia to join with troops from the Carolinas in an attack on the Chickamaugan towns. He intended to "strike a decisive and memorable blow against those hostile towns, taking great care that no injury be done to the friendly part of the nation . . . I have no reason to suppose that the Carolinians would propose to confound together the friendly and hostile parts of the Cherokee nations: it is my duty however to guard against possibilities, and to direct that our people do by no means cooperate against the friendly towns. They have our faith pledged for their protection and tho we cannot oppose force on their behalf in such an event, it is our desire that every thing short of that be exerted in their favour."[20]

The expedition, despite its officers' professions of success, fell far short of expectations. It was December before the little army got under way. The Wataugan contingent refused to go beyond the Hiwassee River, which meant that the force stopped fifty miles short of the new Chickamaugan towns on the Tennessee River. Instead, alleging that the friendlies were really hostile, they destroyed virtually all of towns in the Overhills district, despite desperate appeals from the friendly chiefs. The three officers, Arthur Campbell and Joseph Martin for Virginia and John Sevier for the Wataugans, reported proudly to Jefferson that they had laid waste the eleven principal towns: "No place in the Overhill Country remained unvisited." They had killed twenty-nine men and taken seventeen prisoners, "mostly women and children." Old Tassel, however, escaped injury. About a thousand houses were burned, 50,000 bushels of corn and other provisions were destroyed, and the "Archives of the nation," consisting of a variety of copies of treaties, commissions, and letters, were seized. Nancy Ward, the pro-American female ceremonial chief who had earlier warned the Wataugans of Dragging Canoe's pending attack and who had brought overtures for peace, was carried off with her family.[21]

In March 1781 Jefferson appointed commissioners from Virginia to join with those from North Carolina to conclude a peace treaty with the friendly Cherokees. He planned in the negotiations to remove "any just complaint . . . as to their Boundary."[22] But before the treaty could be held, the authority was transferred from the governors to the American general in the region, Nathaniel Greene. By the time Jefferson left office as governor on June 1, 1781, Cherokees were again marauding in Powell's valley and the Shawnees were striking at settlements on the Holston River.[23] Peace between the Cherokees and the United States was not officially declared until the Treaty of Hopewell in 1785.

Trouble North of the Ohio

Farther north, Indian affairs during the early days of the Revolution appeared to be going more smoothly, despite Continental suspicions that British commanders in Canada were urging the Six Nations and their tributaries in the Ohio valley to attack the frontiers from New England to Kentucky. Such fears prompted efforts to bring the natives over to the American side. In March 1775 Stockbridge Indians in Massachusetts offered to serve as Minutemen, an offer gratefully accepted by the provincial Congress, and Ethan Allen invited native participation in his campaign.[24] But Virginia took the lead in the attempt to assure the neutrality, if not the alliance, of the Native Americans north of the Ohio.

In June 1775 Virginia appointed commissioners to negotiate a treaty with the Ohio Indians: Thomas Walker, Andrew Lewis, John Walker, James Wood, and Adam Stephen. The Walkers and Andrew Lewis, of course, were well known to Jefferson. James Wood carried the invitation to the tribes and reported that the Wyandots and the Shawnees were greatly distressed by the Americans' conduct, particularly the Shawnees, who still resented the encroachments onto their hunting grounds on the Kentucky River. Delegates from Virginia and the Continental Congress attended; the Indian tribes present were the Shawnees, the Delawares, and the Six Nations. On his arrival at Fort Pitt in September, Walker wrote to Jefferson notifying him of their arrival and of the disaffection of the Wyandots, who, he suggested, had "acceded to the terms proposed to them by [General] Carlton and [Indian superintendent] Johnson."[25] We may assume that Walker (and others) kept Jefferson closely informed on Indian affairs during the next year.

The principal accomplishment of the treaty was an endorsement of the Fort Stanwix land cessions of 1768 and an agreement that the Ohio River would forever be the boundary between red and white. The Shawnees thus were again officially precluded from hunting in Kentucky, and Virginians were prohibited from trespassing north of the river. The attending tribal representatives from the Delawares, the Shawnees, and the Six Nations promised to remain neutral in the family squabble among the whites. Reassured by the good news of Indian neutrality in the Ohio valley, the Continental Congress turned its attention to more easterly British threats and to the bold but ill-fated invasion of Canada by Benedict Arnold. Virginia was left to defend Kentucky and her other western borderlands by herself, with garrisons along the Ohio at Pittsburgh, at Wheeling (along the Ohio near the site of Logan's massacre), at the mouth of the Great Kanawha, and three fortified settlements in Kentucky at Boonesborough, Harrodsburg, and St. Asaph's.[26]

These measures proved to be tragically ineffective. Despite the treaty, by October 1776 raids from Indians north of the Ohio had forced the settlers who had flooded into Kentucky to abandon all but the three major fortified settlements. The Shawnees and the Mingoes in particular were still enraged by their losses during Lord Dunmore's War and sought revenge. Rumors flew that the commanding British officer at Detroit, Henry Hamilton, had urged the Indians to bring him fresh American scalps and that a vast confederacy was forming among the Ohio Indians with the intention of striking the frontiers and even taking Pittsburgh. In

February 1777 a little army of Ohio Indians descended on Virginia's remaining frontier forts and settlements, laying siege to Wheeling on the Ohio and Boonesborough in Kentucky. Fearful of offending peaceful factions, however, Virginia Governor Henry held back from sending a punitive expedition into the country north of the Ohio.

Efforts to ensure the neutrality of a majority of the Ohio tribesmen were compromised by a continuing series of assaults and murders of peaceable Indians by frontiersmen who were unable or unwilling to discriminate between friendlies and hostiles. These incidents culminated in November 1777 with the barbarous murder of the pro-American Shawnee chief Cornstalk, while he was detained as a hostage during a mission of peace. Thus ended all hope of a reconciliation with the Shawnees and the rest of the Ohio tribes. Governor Henry had the murderers brought to trial, but they were acquitted because no one would testify against them.

The Indian attacks on the Virginia frontier intensified. In the spring of 1778 a force of four hundred men attacked the forts and settlements on the Great Kanawha and the Greenbrier, where settlements had been made under patents from the Loyal Company of Virginia and where Jefferson had planned his own investments; they were driven off with difficulty.[27]

George Rogers Clark's Ohio Campaign

Virginia's main response to these incursions was the famous Ohio campaign of George Rogers Clark.[28] The situation in Kentucky had become desperate; the population had been reduced to about one hundred armed men, confined to the three fortified settlements at Boonesborough, Harrodsburg, and St. Asaph's. In December 1777 Clark broached a military plan to Governor Patrick Henry that would, if successful, deliver Kentucky from devastation at the hands of the Indians. The plan was to capture the British forts in Indian country, along the Illinois and Wabash rivers, and ultimately at Detroit, thereby depriving the marauding tribes of access to British trade goods and military assistance and forcing them to end their attacks on Kentucky. A fort would also be constructed along the Mississippi below the mouth of the Ohio.

Henry approved the plan, and it was endorsed by the Virginia Assembly and the Governor's Council. Henry consulted with Jefferson, George Wythe, and George Mason, and they also approved the plan. In order to provide further incentives for Clark and his volunteers from Kentucky,

George Rogers Clark. Oil on canvas by John Wesley Jarvis, c. 1820–1834. Courtesy of The Filson Club Historical Society, Louisville, Kentucky.

these three even wrote privately to Clark, assuring him that the assembly would reward him and his associates with land grants in conquered territory.[29] Apparently persons interested in the Illinois and Wabash land companies, including Patrick Henry and Continental General Hand at Pittsburgh, who supplied Clark's expedition with boats to descend the Ohio, gave additional support to the proposal.

At first Clark's campaign worked brilliantly. In July 1778 his little band of 175 volunteers occupied the undefended village of Kaskaskia, the old French settlement and trading emporium on an island in the Mississippi between St. Louis and the mouth of the Ohio, and recruited its menfolk into a militia. That persuaded the French inhabitants of the nearby towns to take the oath of allegiance to the United States. French emissaries were sent to Vincennes, some distance up the Wabash, urging the inhabitants to join the Americans; they happily complied and occupied the fort. Thus, without having to fight a single battle, Clark was able to claim that he had driven the British out of the southern part of the Ohio country and secured the allegiance of its French-speaking inhabitants.

The next task was to neutralize the hostile Indians. Although many Virginians imagined that all the tribes of the north of the Ohio were on the British side and that as many as 8,500 screaming warriors were about to descend upon them, in actuality only a few tribes had entered the war against the United States. The Illinois tribes, including the Kaskaskias and Peorias, were pro-American and some of them were actually aiding the American forces. Farther north, the Sac and Fox, the Winnebagos, the Menominees, and the Miamis were essentially neutral. It was mainly the portion of the Ottawas, Potawatomis, and Chippewas in the neighborhood of the British stronghold at Detroit, the Wyandots on the Sandusky, the Delawares on the Muskingum, and especially the Shawnees from the southern parts of what is now Ohio who were on the warpath.

Clark tried to use his apparent military success, and an offer to temporarily provide trade goods from New Orleans to replace British goods from the north, to convince the Ohio tribes to come to the American side. In August 1778 representatives of the more westerly nations met with Clark at Cahokia and renounced any affiliation with the British. A similar conference at Vincennes brought the Indians on the Wabash to announce that they too would abandon the British.

A temporary setback occurred in September 1778 when Lieutenant Governor Hamilton at Detroit, leading a force of about 500 whites and Indians, forced the surrender of the small American garrison at Vincennes and reoccupied the fort. Hamilton even boldly proposed to mobilize the southern tribes in the spring for a simultaneous invasion of the frontiers from both south and north, in a pincerlike assault. But Clark and a band of 270 hardy French and Americans made their historic winter march across the "drowned lands" of central Illinois to surprise Hamilton and his garrison at Vincennes in late February. Hamilton was forced to surrender the British fort after a short siege, and he himself was taken back to Kentucky and eventually put into the hands of Governor Thomas Jefferson.

In December 1779 Clark and Jefferson met in Richmond to plan his grand assault on Detroit, the center of British influence in the territory west of the Appalachians. Jefferson was already intending to cede to Congress Virginia's claims to western lands north of the Ohio; this expedition would secure to the United States uncontested control of the Ohio watershed and the southern shores of the Great Lakes. Washington grudgingly approved the scheme and Congress agreed to supply the powder, but the bulk of the 2,000 troops would be Virginia militiamen from the western counties.

The expedition had to be aborted, however: many of the soldiers mutinied and refused to march, the Continental commander at Fort Pitt was uncooperative, and by August 1781, when Clark abandoned the effort,

Jefferson had been replaced as governor. The only military legacy of the occasion was a foray by a detachment of undisciplined militia from the Monongahela and Redstone region. Part of this group, with the aid of friendly Delaware warriors, surprised and destroyed the Delaware town of Coshocton and a returning Delaware war party.[30]

The fort on the Mississippi built by Clark in April 1780 (Fort Jefferson) was besieged by the Chickasaws and abandoned in June 1781.[31] An Indian treaty at Pittsburgh in September 1779 with the recalcitrant Wyandots and Delawares had brought professions of friendship, but the mood of the Delawares was soured by the experience of a delegation that had recently visited Philadelphia, appealing for help in converting to the white man's way of life. Congress made an equivocal response to these overtures, promising after the war "to encourage and promote your Civilization by inducing Ministers, Schoolmasters, Tradesmen and Husbandmen to reside among you." And on their journeys both to and from the capital the little band of peacemakers were repeatedly threatened with murder by frontiersmen and were forced to take circuitous detours to avoid the danger.

No accommodation with the Shawnees or the Mingoes was ever made by Clark, who hated the Shawnees in particular. Indeed, his prisoner, Henry Hamilton, reported a conversation in which Clark said "that he expected shortly to see the whole race of Indians extirpated, that for his part he would never spare man, woman or child of them on whom he could lay his hands." Jefferson apparently shared much of Clark's animus, proposing "the total suppression of their savage insolence and cruelties" and even suggesting the extermination of the Shawnees.[32]

In short, the recapture of Vincennes had been the high point of Clark's campaign in the northwest. After that, the American cause in that quarter suffered continuing reverses. Clark's difficulties in building on his initial success were the result, essentially, of two factors: his, and Virginia's, inability to establish an adequate trade network, in large part because Virginia Continental currency was valueless and could not be used to purchase goods; and the continuing attacks of whites on Indians, which were as barbarous and nondiscriminating as those perpetrated on whites by the "merciless savages" they sought to destroy. As historian Richard White has phrased it, "Murder gradually became the dominant American Indian policy."[33]

As a result of American failure to provide trade goods or to establish

Joseph Thayendaneken, Mohawk chief, also known as Joseph Brant. From a drawing prepared to accompany James Boswell's article on Brant in *London Magazine,* July 1776. Courtesy of the Library of Congress.

law and order on the frontier, British influence over the Indians and the French in the region regained strength. And as it did, Indian attacks on the Kentucky frontier resumed in full fury. In 1780 a joint British–French expedition against Kentucky destroyed two settlements and forced the abandonment of two others. In 1781 the Mohawk war captain Joseph Brant, fresh from a campaign of terrorism in the Mohawk valley in New York, led a band that ambushed and defeated a large body of Clark's troops near the Ohio River. Then in 1782 the Shawnees decimated the best of Kentucky's Indian fighters at the battle of Blue Licks.[34] By December 1782, when the British command ordered its Indian allies to cease attacking the Americans, the British had been able to organize the Ohio tribes into a quasi-confederacy that would, in a few years, be able to fight American armies to a standstill in the northwest.

Jefferson's Persecution of Henry Hamilton

Clark's principal trophy from the recapture of Vincennes was the hapless British commander Henry Hamilton. He had seen his French militiamen desert to the Americans, his Indian allies mostly melt away, and Indian prisoners bloodily executed in the streets of Vincennes by tomahawks in the hands of Clark himself and his fellow banditti (or so Hamilton alleged). Clark at first wanted "to put . . . to death or other ways treat . . . as I thought proper" all the British garrison, in revenge for "the cries of the Widows and fatherless on the Frontiers."[35] After allowing the British to surrender instead, he dispatched the "hair-buyer" Hamilton to Kentucky and thence to Virginia, where he arrived in handcuffs in the middle of June 1779, just after Jefferson's election by the assembly to the governorship. Dealing with Hamilton was one of the first, and ultimately one of the more annoying, episodes of his administration.

Hamilton was put in jail and prosecuted as a war criminal, along with another officer captured at Vincennes and the justice of the peace from Detroit.[36] The Council, with Governor Jefferson presiding, decided that Hamilton had incited the Indians to practice their "accustomed cruelties" on American citizens without respect to age, sex, or condition—just as Jefferson had charged in the Declaration of Independence. More generally, British officers in America were charged with disregarding the rules of civilized warfare, including the mistreatment of American prisoners (in contrast with the supposedly humane and gentlemanly conduct of the Americans toward their prisoners). Hamilton and his associates were sentenced to be placed in irons and incarcerated in the dungeon of the local jail, prohibited from conversing with anyone except their jailer, and denied the use of writing materials. Jefferson heartily approved and executed the sentence, and notified Congress of the action, which he said conformed to the popular sense of justice. Congress applauded the measures taken by Virginia, and General Washington replied to Jefferson's notification with approval.

Doubts were cast on the propriety of these proceedings, however, by British General William Phillips, second in command to General John Burgoyne. Phillips, whose British and Hessian troops were captured at Saratoga, marched seven hundred miles to Virginia and was quartered in Albemarle County near Jefferson. The senior British officers immediately rented local estates, and some became friends and frequent visitors for dinners, musical entertainment, and philosophical conversation with the Jeffersons; officer-prisoners were gentlemen, after all, who deserved to be treated with courtesy. Phillips pointed out that Hamilton had formally surrendered in writing to Clark and deserved to be treated as a prisoner of war, that is, humanely, according to the conventions of civilized warfare, which forbade the kind of trial and punishment being meted out to Hamilton and his associates.

Phillips no doubt touched a nerve in Jefferson, who had a few months before written to then-Governor Patrick Henry in favor of mitigating the hardships of prisoners: "The practice, therefore, of modern nations, of treating captive enemies with politeness and generosity, is not only delightful in contemplation, but really interesting to all the world, friends, foes, and neutrals."[37] And there was the question of the British retaliating by treating American prisoners with even greater rigor. By *lex talionis,* what would be the fate of George Rogers Clark, the butcher of Vincennes, if the same standard were applied to him and other prisoners from Virginia in the event of capture by the British?

Jefferson wrote a hot but legalistic reply to General Phillips's letter of protest, adducing as evidence of Hamilton's guilt a proclamation he had allegedly issued authorizing "general massacres of men, women, and children." He asserted that Hamilton had hired the Indians and that "the known rule of warfare with the Indian Savages was an indiscriminate butchery of men, women and children." He claimed to have evidence of "his particular cruelties to our Citizens, prisoners with him" at Detroit, and he argued that because the articles of capitulation did not explicitly state that the prisoners from Vincennes were prisoners on convention, rather than prisoners at discretion, the rigors of his confinement were not legally excluded.[38]

But Jefferson also was politic enough to seek the advice of George Washington. And Washington, concerned about British retaliation on American prisoners, now qualified his approval, suggesting that Hamilton was indeed a prisoner on convention and should not be kept in irons. Congress declined to intervene, leaving the matter to Virginia. Jefferson and the council decided to take Washington's advice, removing the irons and offering to release the prisoners from confinement as soon as they signed a parole, which required them to promise to neither do nor say anything offensive to the United States. When the prisoners refused to accept restrictions on their speech, Jefferson became equally obdurate, and Hamilton and his two companions remained in jail for another year. Washington then intervened once more, suggesting that they be exchanged, and Virginia finally agreed to release Hamilton to the authorities in New York, where he signed his parole and shortly was returned to England.

The intensity of Jefferson's hatred of Hamilton for, as he saw it, setting the merciless savages upon innocent settlers was perhaps not atypical of even enlightened gentlemen of Virginia. He had the initial support of the Council and the Congress. But the precipitate manner in which he rushed to judgment deserves a little examination. How valid was his information about Hamilton's conduct? And what were his sources of information about Indian atrocities and about Hamilton himself?

Jefferson entered the arena of governorship with a preformed conviction—expressed in the Declaration—that the British ministry, the civil and military authorities in Canada, and the Indian superintendencies both north and south were plotting to unleash savage warriors upon the frontiers. But the charge, contained in his letter to Phillips, that the British sent joint parties of whites and Indians, and sometimes Indians alone, "not against our forts, or armies in the field, but the farming settlements on our frontiers," was certainly not entirely true.[39] Indian forces had a long history of confronting European troops on the field of battle. A British and Iroquois army under Colonel Barry St. Leger had inflicted a signal and well-known defeat on an American army under General Herkimer in August 1777 and laid unsuccessful siege to Fort Stanwix; only after lifting that siege did Iroquois raiders devastate the settlements in the Mohawk valley. The Cherokees had initially attacked the Wataugan forts in 1775. A year before, in Lord Dunmore's War, the battle of Point Pleasant was initiated by an Indian attack on an American army. And over a decade before that, Pontiac's warriors had attacked British forts and laid siege to the garrison at Detroit. During the French and Indian War, the Ohio Indians had destroyed an army of whites, including British regulars commanded by General Braddock, before Fort Duquesne, and Indians both north and south had made frontal assaults on, and laid siege to, major fortifications along all the frontiers. But it is true that the rules of warfare among "polished nations" prohibited the slaughter of noncombatants, men as well as women and children, and the torture and execution of prisoners. The Americans subscribed to these rules, even if they were not always followed by frontiersmen.

One of Jefferson's principal advisors on these matters was of course George Rogers Clark himself. Clark was an Indian hater from way back, but in practice he could distinguish friend from foe and sought to gain Indian tribes to the American side by diplomatic and commercial means. During the period of his governorship Jefferson was a loyal supporter of Clark, urging him on to construct Fort Jefferson on the Mississippi (which was important for securing the trade route from New Orleans) and to defend the Kentucky settlements by chasing the British out of the lower Ohio country and going on to attempt to take Detroit. Jefferson probably learned from Clark that "in every house, where they murdered or carried away the family, [the Indians] left one of [Hamilton's] proclamations."[40]

The source of the characterization of Hamilton as the "hair-buyer" and of Jefferson's charge of atrocities committed under Hamilton's orders on American prisoners at Detroit was probably John Dodge. Dodge was a pro-American trader among the Wyandots at Sandusky. In June 1776 he was arrested, jailed, and kept in irons by the British at Detroit as a suspected American spy. He was released in 1777 but again arrested in January 1778 and shipped off to Quebec in a prison ship. He escaped, got to Boston in the fall of 1778, and then went on to meet George Washington and members of the Continental Congress. He then proceeded to Williamsburg, where he appeared as the only witness against Hamilton and the other prisoners, vowing that "they will be hanged without redemption."[41]

In 1779 Bradford in Philadelphia published his *Narrative of the Capture and Treatment of John Dodge,* a lurid account of his experiences among enemy Indians and the British at Detroit. During the fall of 1775, he claimed, a war party from the vicinity of the lakes came by his place and told him that the governor at Detroit had warned the Indians not to attend the Pittsburgh treaty because the Americans would murder them all, and had gone on to say that if the Indians joined the British "he would give them twenty dollars a scalp" and that they were "not to spare man, woman, or child." Such stories had reached the ears of the Indian commissioners (who included Jefferson's neighbor Thomas Walker) as early as August 1777 through the American agent at Pittsburgh George Morgan. And in 1780 Dodge published an even more sensational account detailing the sufferings of a Virginia lad held captive by Hamilton for eventual burning at the stake by the cruel savages. The poor fellow, Dodge said, had died of fear before he could be tortured and killed.[42]

These stories of atrocities instigated by Governor Hamilton would seem, in historical hindsight, to have been gross distortions. At Detroit and elsewhere the British traditionally supplied Indians with weapons for hunting and defense, equipment that could be used for purposes of war. And Hamilton did recruit Indians to serve under the command of British officers (an uncertain relationship at best) in joint expeditions against American strongholds (including the one he led to Vincennes). Indians supplied by British merchants and ostensibly led by British officers did carry out a campaign of terror against frontier settlements in New York, Pennsylvania, Kentucky, the Carolinas, and Georgia.

But some Americans who met him spoke well of Hamilton. Daniel Boone, after his capture by Indians, said that the governor at Detroit treated him "with great humanity."[43] And historians such as Randolph Downes and Merrill Peterson regard the verdict of the council against Hamilton as based "on little more than frontier opinion and rumor and the treacherous testimony of John Dodge."[44] Jefferson, who of course met Dodge on the occasion of his testimony against Hamilton, at first accepted him at face value and in later years published his population estimates for a number of Indian tribes along with those of more reputable authorities in *Notes on the State of Virginia.*[45] But even Jefferson and Clark came to question Dodge's veracity. After his return to Ohio "to conduct a commerce with the Indians on behalf of this state [Virginia]," Dodge was accused of "gross misapplication or mismanagement." Jefferson instructed Clark, if it proved necessary, to "remove him from his office."[46]

The Good Indians

Jefferson's preoccupation with fighting the Indians and the British in the western counties of Virginia attracted criticism of his conduct as governor. Virginia was ill-prepared for General Benedict Arnold's invasion in the winter of 1780–1781. General Greene, commander in the south, commented acidly, "History affords no instance of a nation being so engaged in conquest abroad as Virginia is at a time when all her powers were necessary to secure herself from ruin at home."[47] Jefferson was stung by these reproaches even though the assembly eventually refused to conduct a proposed inquiry, which might have led to official censure, and instead voted to thank him for his "Ability, Rectitude, and Integrity as chief Magistrate."[48]

In almost the last act of his governorship, while Virginia's refugee assembly and council were reassembling at Charlottesville in late May 1781,

"Indian of the Nation of Kaskaskia." Engraving by Gen. Victor Collot, a French spy who traveled in the Ohio and Mississippi valleys in 1796 and observed the growing American influence in the Middle West. Courtesy of the Beinecke Library, Yale University.

Jefferson was visited by a delegation of Kaskaskia Indians headed by a mixed-blood chief named Jean Baptiste du Coigne, who brought with him his wife and son. They had come from the Illinois country and were pro-American. Du Coigne himself had served as Clark's emissary to the Wabash Indians and had come to the rescue of an American garrison besieged by hostile Indians. He had no doubt learned of the great governor of Virginia from Clark, and his infant son bore the name Jefferson.

The Kaskaskia chief was formally presented to Jefferson, with whom he smoked "the pipe of peace." Ordinarily Jefferson did not smoke, but he thought it "a good old custom handed down by your ancestors, and as such I respect and join in it with reverence. I hope we shall long continue to smoke in friendship together." The two men exchanged gifts, Jefferson presenting the chief with a silver medal and a commission (not otherwise described) and du Coigne giving Jefferson several buffalo skins bearing carefully painted figures, which were duly hung on the walls of the main entrance hall at Monticello and perhaps formed the nucleus of his celebrated collection of Indian artifacts.

As part of the state visit, du Coigne delivered a "friendly discourse" before Jefferson and some members of the assembly. It was a statement of friendship and alliance on behalf not only of the Kaskaskias but of other tribes in the Illinois country. Jefferson in reply offered an explanation of the war with England ("They at length began to say we were their slaves") and an optimistic assessment of its course ("They have now waged that war six years, and have not yet won more land from us than will serve to bury the warriors they have lost"). He went on to urge the Indians not to take up the hatchet against the British unless the British attacked them first; in that case, they had the right to take revenge, and "General Clark will . . . show you the way to their towns." He apologized for the interruption in the flow of trade goods and promised an ample supply as soon as the war was over (and "the English cannot hold out long").

But the most interesting part of Jefferson's little speech was its conclusion: "You ask us to send schoolmasters to educate your son and the sons of your people. We desire above all things, brother, to instruct you in whatever we know ourselves. We wish to learn you all our arts and to make you wise and wealthy. As soon as there is peace we shall be able to send you the best of school-masters; but while the war is raging, I am afraid it will not be practicable. It shall be done, however, before your son is of an age to receive instruction."

It is not clear how soon the "best of school-masters" reached Kaskaskia to teach young Jefferson du Coigne, but apparently the lad was still living in 1796, when Jefferson gave his French friend and fellow anticlerical philosopher Constantin Volney, then traveling in America, a letter of introduction to the Kaskaskia chief, in which he offered to take care of "my name sake Jefferson." What is most significant in his reply to du Coigne is its adumbration of what later became known as the civilization policy: the plan of the federal government to send teachers, missionaries, and capital goods into the villages of friendly Indian tribes to teach them white methods of agriculture and domestic husbandry.

As is clear from his growing awareness of the importance of distinguishing between friendly and hostile tribes and his sympathetic response to du Coigne, Jefferson's experience as war governor was mellowing his perception of the Native Americans as enemies. No longer were they merely "merciless savages" from whom, at great price in blood and treasure, America's lands had been wrested by force. They were now, as he put it to du Coigne, some sort of brothers: "We, like you, are Americans, born in the same land, and having the same interests." This stance of paternalistic solicitude that Jefferson increasingly displayed as the Revolutionary War was coming to an end was accompanied by the development of a scholarly interest in Indian language, culture, and history that continued for the rest of his life and influenced the course of ethnological research in America. It is to that subject that we now turn.[49]

CHAPTER THREE

Notes on the Vanishing Aborigines

AFTER Jefferson left the Virginia governor's office in 1781, his letters to George Rogers Clark shifted from matters of war—which continued unabated in both the east and the west—to matters of science. In December 1781 he asked Clark to send to Monticello "some teeth of the great animal whose remains are found on the Ohio" and commented that in his retirement he was eager to pursue studies in natural history. In Clark's reply, in addition to remarks about animal bones, he alluded to "the powerful nations that inhabited those regions," perhaps a reference to the vanished builders of the impressive ceremonial mounds that dotted the Ohio valley.[1]

Jefferson's curiosity about the mammoths of the Ohio valley had been piqued by a visit of some Delaware Indians to Williamsburg about the time he was becoming governor. After matters of business had been discussed, the Indians were asked some questions about their country, and particularly what they knew of the large bones found at Great Salt Lick on the Ohio. Years later, Jefferson described the response with relish: "Their chief speaker immediately put himself into an attitude of oratory, and with a pomp suited to what he conceived the elevation of his subject, informed him that it was a tradition handed down from their fathers, That in antient times a herd of these tremendous animals came to the Big-bone licks, and began an universal destruction of the bear, deer, elks, buffaloes, and other animals, which had been created for the use of the Indians: that the Great Man above, looking down and seeing this, was so enraged that he seized his lightning, descended on the earth, seated himself on a neighbouring mountain, on a rock, of which his seat and the print of his feet are still to be seen, and hurled his bolts among them till the whole were slaughtered, except the big bull, who presenting his forehead to the shafts, shook them off as they fell; but missing one at length, it wounded him in the side; whereon, springing round, he bounded over the Ohio, over the Wabash, the Illinois, and finally over the great lakes, where he is living at this day."[2] Jefferson, who believed that nature would never permit any link to fall from the Great Chain of Being, took this as confirmation of the mammoth's continued existence to the north and west of the Great Lakes.

Jefferson's interest in natural history was further stirred by the queries of François Marbois, the secretary of the French legation in Philadelphia, whose questionnaire on the new states with whom France was now aligned had come into Governor Jefferson's hands in mid-1780. By late fall Jefferson was busy at Monticello gathering information to answer the queries. Although work on the project was delayed by General John Burgoyne's invasion of Virginia and the evacuation of the capital to Charlottesville, as well as by his own retirement in June 1781 and by the death of his wife in September, he was able to put a completed manuscript of *Notes on the State of Virginia* in the hands of Marbois by the end of December. In the following several years before its first publication in Paris in 1785, Jefferson sent the manuscript to a number of friends and acquaintances for their comments and corrections.

Information on Native Americans was contained in two sections of the *Notes,* one entitled "Productions, Mineral, Vegetable and Animal" and the other "The Aborigines." The first Indian essay was an elegiacal mixture of salutation and farewell, crystallized in the story of Logan, which, as we have seen, served in later years to rationalize Jefferson's and future generations' drive westward to fulfill America's destiny. The other was largely a statistical review of the decline of the native population. But even in this essay, omissions, errors, and distortions, however unintended or unavoidable most of them may have been, also had the practical function of further sanctioning the cause of white settlement in the New World.

Jefferson's Elegy for the Indians

In the first section of the *Notes,* Jefferson's praise of the racial characteristics of Native Americans was couched as a rebuttal to the popular French naturalist the Comte de Buffon. Buffon's *Histoire naturelle* argued that the peculiar environment of the New World had stunted the development of its native flora and fauna (including the aborigines) and retarded even the European colonists who settled there. Jefferson staunchly defended the productivity of his native land, trotting forth facts and figures on the large quadrupeds of America, including the mammoth whose bones were found in Ohio, and which, he claimed on the basis of Indian fables like the Delaware legend, still lived in the north and west of the continent.

He then proceeded to refute Buffon's assertion that "the savage of the new world" was defective in sexual ardor and potency ("the most precious spark of the fire of nature") and therefore was timid and cowardly, stupid, incapable of love or loyalty, lacking any sort of communion, commonwealth, or "state of society." To the contrary, declared Jefferson, "the Indian of North America" was as ardent as the white man, free, brave, preferring death to surrender, moral and responsible without compulsion by government, loving to his children, caring and loyal to family and friends, and equal to whites in vivacity and activity of mind. The women, to be sure, were forced to submit to unjust drudgery and, owing to their circumstance, produced fewer children. But that was the result of culture, not nature. "It is civilization alone which replaces women in the enjoyment of their natural equality."

He went on to consider in particular the equality of Indian intelligence with that of whites and argued that when all the facts were in hand, "we shall probably find that they are formed in mind as well as in body, on the same model with the 'Homo sapiens Europaeus.'" As proof of this natural equality of mind, he cited the Indians' bravery and skill in warfare, of which "we have multiplied proofs, because we have been the subjects on which they were exercised," and their "eminence in oratory." The example of Indian oratory which he brought forward was, of course, Logan's Lament.

Jefferson turned next to a comparison of Indians "in their present state with the Europeans North of the Alps, when the Roman arms and arts first crossed those mountains." He pointed out that it took sixteen centuries before the Anglo-Saxons produced an Isaac Newton. The implication was clear: given time and exposure to European civilization, the Native Americans too could rise to the same level of culture as the whites, as Enlightenment theories of progress would predict.[3] Writing to General Chastellux a few years later (in 1785), he declared that he had "seen some thousands [of Indians] myself, and conversed much with them, and have found in them a masculine, sound understanding . . . I believe the Indian to be in body and mind equal to the white man."[4]

The question thus arose whether the Native Americans, when "civilized," might be admitted to membership in the new republic. Jefferson does not seem to have advanced that idea at this period, but twenty years later he was to embrace it, confidentially. In a letter to Benjamin Hawkins in February 1803, he expressed the opinion that citizenship and amalgamation with whites was inevitable: "In truth, the ultimate point of rest and happiness for them is to let our settlements and theirs meet and blend together, to intermix, and become one people. Incorporating themselves with us as citizens of the United States, this is what the natural course of things will, of course, bring on, and it will be better to promote than to retard it . . . We have already had an application from a settlement of Indians to become citizens of the United States."[5] The means of promoting this idea was the conversion of the Indians to the white man's way of agriculture, domestic manufactures, and education—a policy to be pursued by Congress and President Jefferson in the ensuing years.

This vision of a Native American citizenry blending happily into white society depended upon Jefferson's belief in the inherent racial equality of Indians with whites and their innate capacity for climbing the ladder of cultural evolution. To the other ethnic minority within the bosom of the United States, the blacks of African descent, most of them slaves, Jefferson was less generous. In the section of the *Notes* devoted to his proposed revision of the laws of Virginia, he described blacks as physically ugly, offensive in body odor, and oversexed but underloving. "They are more ardent after their female, but love seems with them to be more an eager desire, than a tender delicate mixture of sentiment and sensation. Their griefs are transient." But what truly disqualified blacks from membership in white society, according to Jefferson, was their inferiority in mental faculties. They were, he felt, "in reason much inferior, as I think one could scarcely be found capable of tracing and comprehending the investigations of Euclid." In art and oratory, they stood far below the Indians, and although gifted in music, were incapable of writing a decent poem (Phyllis Wheatley's productions, he felt, were "below the dignity of criticism").[6]

That said, he nevertheless deplored the immorality of the institution of slavery, although he defended what he regarded as the humane practices of Virginia slaveowners like himself and compared them favorably with those of ancient Rome, even though the Romans' slaves were mostly white. And he proposed, unsuccessfully, a bill for the emancipation of all slaves born after a certain date, thus anticipating a gradual abolition of slavery as current slaves eventually died. But these free blacks ought not be allowed to remain within the state (as emancipated slaves were not by current law).

The deep-rooted prejudices among whites, and the memory of past injuries among blacks, "will divide us into parties, and produce convulsions which will probably never end but in the extermination of the one or the other race."

The only solution was to educate the free black children in tillage and artisanship and then, when the females reached eighteen and the males twenty-one years, "they should be colonized to such place as the circumstances of the time should render most proper," where they could have their own country—perhaps the West Indies or even Africa. To replace them, white immigrants should be invited to come to Virginia, lured by "proper inducements." Failing such a solution, he foresaw in the perpetuation of the slave system the inevitable corruption of white masters, the degeneration of the yeomanry into sloth and depravity, until God himself intervened and permitted the "extirpation" of the slave masters. In an oft-quoted passage from the *Notes,* Jefferson wrote: "Indeed I tremble for my country when I reflect that God is just: that his justice cannot sleep for ever: that considering numbers, nature, and natural means only, a revolution of the wheel of fortune, an exchange of situations, is among possible events: that it may become probable by supernatural interference."[7]

This was Jefferson in apocalyptic mode. But there was something of the same tone underlying his hope for eventual amalgamation with the Indians. In the section on "The Aborigines" he drew attention to the virtual extinction of the native population of Virginia, and he lamented that "we have suffered so many Indian tribes already to extinguish" without saving even records of their languages.[8] And there is discernible in his story of Logan's Lament a kind of mordant fascination with the image of the Indians as a conquered and dying race. For Jefferson did believe that those Native Americans who refused to sell their hunting grounds, now depleted of game, and adopt "civilization," or who even took up arms against the United States, were destined for extinction.

The Tidewater Indians of Virginia

"The Aborigines" provided a largely statistical review of the decline of the Indian population in Virginia. In 1743, when Jefferson was born, the Indians east of the Appalachian Mountains were already becoming a distant memory. The Algonkian-speaking chiefdoms of the Powhatan Confederacy, whose prosperous agricultural villages had spread throughout the

Tidewater countryside at the beginning of the previous century, were now reduced to a remnant, a few bands of survivors of war and plague living on tiny allotments of land. The Siouan-speaking villagers of the Piedmont had also been greatly reduced in numbers, and most of their survivors had moved away to live as refugees among the Iroquois to the north and the Catawbas to the south. A few Susquehannocks from the Susquehanna valley, who had fled into the colony toward the end of the seventeenth century to join local Iroquoians (the Nottoways and Meherrins), clustered on small reservations in the south near the Carolina border.

"Very little can now be discovered of the subsequent history of these tribes severally," Jefferson wrote. He counted as living descendants of the Powhatans only three or four men of the Mattapony tribe ("and they have more Negro than Indian blood in them"), living on fifty acres of land on the Mattapony River, and ten or twelve Pamunkeys, on three hundred acres of "very fertile land" on Pamunkey River. (Both reservations still exist, about thirty miles northwest of Williamsburg.) Of the Nottoways, "not a male is left. A few women constitute the remains of that tribe."[9]

Actually, a good deal was known in Jefferson's time about the Powhatans, thanks to the writings of Captain John Smith and other early seventeenth-century chroniclers of Virginia. In addition, the watercolors of John White preserve vivid images of the appearance, the material culture, and the rituals of the nearby and culturally similar Carolina Algonkians. Jefferson was familiar with Smith's account, but he did not have access to White's watercolors. He did not discuss ethnographic information about the Powhatans or other Virginia Indians.[10]

The tribes living along the shores of the Chesapeake Bay, and particularly those of the Powhatan Confederacy (which was actually a quasi-empire held together by force and hierarchy), were estimated by Jefferson to have numbered on the order of 2,400 warriors or 8,000 souls at the time of the arrival of the first colonists at Jamestown in 1607.[11] At first, relations between colonists and local tribes were by and large peaceable, both sides being eager for trade. But after Powhatan's death, his nephew Opechancanough, resentful of the tobacco planters' insatiable hunger for Indian land, in 1622 launched a surprise attack on the colonists that resulted in the death in one day of about 350 settlers and the devastation of all the settlements except those around Jamestown. A war of extermination was declared against the Indians that continued for fourteen years.

A second war in 1644, again led by Opechancanough, started with the

"The Manner of Their Fishing." Watercolor by John White, c. 1585, showing a Carolina Algonkian weir with a fish trap and a dugout canoe with fire. Courtesy of the British Museum.

A panoramic view of the Carolina Algonkian town of Secoton.
Watercolor by John White, c. 1585.
Courtesy of the British Museum.

death of 500 whites in the first day, but this conflict lasted only a couple of years. Opechancanough was captured and shot, and the confederacy disintegrated. The separate tribes made their own treaties of peace, abandoning much of their land in the process and accepting reservations, which were further reduced in size thereafter by piecemeal purchases. Despite these concessions, peace eluded the Powhatans: they were harassed by raiding Iroquois from the north and massacred in 1675 during Bacon's Rebellion by Virginians, who accused them of depredations actually committed by invading Susquehannocks.

These wars, the introduction of alcohol, and repeated epidemics of measles, smallpox, and other European diseases drastically reduced the Tidewater Indian population. A census taken in 1669 showed a total of 525 warriors or (using Jefferson's ratio of 10:3) 1,750 souls, a loss of 78 percent in the sixty-two years since the founding of Jamestown.[12] By 1705, when Robert Beverley published his *History and Present State of Virginia,* his total for the Powhatans plus other survivors was less than 500 warriors, and he concluded that "The *Indians of Virginia* are almost wasted."[13]

The Middle Plantation treaties of 1677 had confirmed to the survivors their small reservations, for which each community paid a tribute of three arrows for the land and twenty beaver skins for protection each year. The protection was from neighboring Indians, of whom they were "much in fear." Beverley observed that they "live poorly" and were a "harmless people." In 1727, when William Byrd of Westover published his *Natural History of Virginia* in Switzerland (which he wrote in German in the hope of attracting good European farmers to the colony), he declared that there were "very few wild or native Indians in Virginia." He still allowed them as many as 500 men able to bear arms but declared them to be "excessively gentle and easy-going."[14]

Jefferson's estimate that in the 1780s the last of the Powhatans amounted to not more than four Mattapony men and twelve Pamunkey men, with only the eldest preserving "the last vestiges on earth, as far as we know, of the Powhatan language," would seem to have been wildly inaccurate.[15] James Mooney, an authority on Native American demography and especially on the Indians of the southeast, asserted in 1928 that the Powhatan remnants in Jefferson's time "must have numbered not far from 1,000," and he counted at the time of his writing at least 700.[16] More than a thousand persons claiming descent from Powhatan ancestors—Pamunkey, Mattapony, and Chickahominy—still inhabit small state reservations and other rural communities in eastern Virginia.[17]

It is difficult to understand Jefferson's underestimation of the number of surviving Tidewater Algonkians. The sources that he cited were out of date, the latest being Beverley's 1705 book, but he must have been familiar with the region where the Indian communities were located, east of Richmond or north of Williamsburg. When Jefferson was in college and later when he was a practicing lawyer, member of the House of Burgesses, and finally governor, the Algonkians were still paying their annual tribute to the governor at Williamsburg and later Richmond. Perhaps Jefferson's error can be ascribed to the existence of small, uncounted remnant groups living in out-of-the-way niches who later joined the reservation communities. Whatever the case may have been, it should be kept in mind that Jefferson was writing a usable history, intended to promote confidence among Europeans who might wish to invest or emigrate to a safe and secure Virginia, one whose Indian population no longer posed a threat to white settlement.[18]

The Indians of the Virginia Piedmont

In Captain Smith's time, the stretch of country between the fall line and the Blue Ridge Mountains—and perhaps also the Valley of Virginia west of the Blue Ridge—from Maryland south to the Carolina border was occupied by tribes of Siouan Indians who spoke a language radically different from that of the Tidewater Algonkians. Smith reported that they were organized in two large, allied confederacies, the northern being called the Mannahoac and the southern the Monacan; modern usage embraces both under the rubric Monacan. Like the Powhatans, the Siouan tribes of the Piedmont depended upon a combination of female horticulture and male hunting for subsistence but would seem to have been less hierarchial in social organization than the Powhatans. They may also have traded their own Blue Ridge copper with the Powhatans during lulls in the fighting, and may have served as middlemen, conveying copper, iron trade goods, and wampum from the north down to the Chesapeake region.

Smith and his colonists visited outlying territories of the Piedmont tribes on a couple of occasions, with some armed conflict, but he depended largely on information given him by the Powhatans and by Mosoc, a bearded captive Monacan, and by an informant who described village locations. Later, travelers' journals and official accounts recorded the changing locations of the Monacans, who by 1700 were coming to be known by other terms applied to various component groups, such as the Saponis, Tutelos, and Ocaneechis.[19]

Very little cultural information is revealed in either Smith's or later accounts, except for the narrative of William Byrd, who served on the commission that surveyed the dividing line between Virginia and North Carolina in 1728. The surveying party hired a Saponi Indian named Bearskin to accompany it as a hunter. Bearskin spoke enough English to provide some account of the traditional religious beliefs and rituals of his people, and Byrd included the substance of these interviews in his journal. Bearskin came from the Indian town at Fort Christanna in southern Virginia. Two Indian towns had been established there in 1714 as a collection point for the several tribes of the Piedmont who had a generation earlier fled into North Carolina. In 1728 remnants of at least four Monacan subgroups, named by Byrd the Ocaneechis, the Saponis, the Tuteloes, and the Steukenhocks, were living there, all "speaking the same language, and using the same Customs."[20]

In later years (in 1816 and 1817), Jefferson was called upon to evaluate the authorship and authenticity of Byrd's still unpublished "Secret History of the Dividing Line," and in that correspondence he revealed no prior acquaintance with it.[21] But Jefferson can hardly have been totally unaware of Byrd's work, for in 1751 his father and Joshua Fry had run a continuation of Byrd's line westward into the mountains and had published their famous map of Virginia based in part on his surveys.

In addition to Byrd's narrative, Jefferson might also have been aware of John Lederer's book, published in 1672, describing his travels in Virginia and the Carolinas during which he visited several Saponi villages.[22] Apart from Smith's accounts, however, Jefferson's only cited source for the numbers and locations of the Piedmont tribes actually living in Virginia is the 1669 official census of Virginia Indians, which lists fifty Tutelo warriors living with other tribes in southeastern Virginia and thirty Monacan warriors living in a town at the fork of the James River, above the falls.[23]

If there was little information available to Jefferson about the culture of the Piedmont Indians, there was even less about their language. Captain Smith recognized that they spoke a different tongue from the Powhatans but was able to communicate, on the brief occasions of contact, through Powhatan interpreters. Neither Smith nor anyone else seems to have collected any Siouan vocabularies to permit linguistic comparison, although the place names and translations provided Byrd by Bearskin might have served that purpose (but Byrd's history was not published until 1844). Jefferson gained the impression that the Powhatans, the Manahoacs, and the Monacans spoke languages of "three different stocks, so radically different that interpreters were necessary where they transacted business" and that the several tribes that constituted each of the three confederacies in turn spoke various dialects perhaps mutually intelligible.[24]

Jefferson himself, in his later vocabulary-collecting days, never obtained a word list from any of the Siouan remnants, and his pleas for salvage of the native languages before they became extinct came too late for local antiquarians. Not until nearly a hundred years later was Tutelo at last recognized as a Siouan language related to the languages of the Siouan-speaking tribes of the west. In 1870 the linguist and ethnologist Horatio Hale visited the Cayuga settlement on the Six Nations Reserve at Grand River in Ontario and there met Nikonha, the last pure-blooded Tutelo, allegedly 106 years old. From him Hale obtained a vocabulary of nearly one hundred words that clearly identified his language as Siouan. Nikonha died the next year, but Hale was able to obtain more words and phrases from a couple of "children of Tutelo mothers by Iroquois fathers." This additional information enabled him to construct a preliminary analysis of the grammar. In 1883 Hale published his linguistic results in the *Proceedings of the American Philosophical Society,* along with a historical sketch of the Tutelos and their companions and a speculative theory that the Siouan tribes of the west in fact had emigrated from an eastern homeland. Today there are apparently no surviving fluent speakers of the Tutelo language.[25]

It is sad to contemplate that Siouan languages spoken by thousands of Native Virginians were apparently never learned by any white man, that not even a vocabulary was recorded until over 250 years after white people encountered them, when the language itself was on the edge of extinction. It may have been the Siouan tribes of the Piedmont that Jefferson was thinking of when he wrote in the *Notes,* "It is to be lamented, then, very much to be lamented, that we have suffered so many of the Indian tribes already to extinguish, without our having previously collected and deposited in the records of literature, the general rudiments at least of the languages they spoke."[26]

Jefferson's only mention in the *Notes* of Piedmont Indians in his own neighborhood was a notice of mortality. There was a barrow, or burial mound, containing the bones of about a thousand persons, located on low ground near the Rivanna River, about two miles above its main fork at

Charlottesville and not far from the site of the former Monacan Indian town of Monasickapanough. By the time that Peter Jefferson and other settlers arrived in the 1730s and 40s, no Indians had resided in the immediate area for many years, and on the mound itself grew trees as much as twelve inches in diameter.

Probably in the late 40s or early 50s, according to Thomas Jefferson, a group of Indians visited the mound. They "went through the woods directly to it, without any instructions or inquiry, and having staid about it some time, with expressions which were construed to be those of sorrow, they returned to the high road [probably the road from Richmond to Staunton in the Shenandoah Valley], from which they had detoured about half a dozen miles to pay this visit, and pursued their journey."[27]

Some time before writing his *Notes,* Jefferson had a trench dug across the middle of the mound, so as to reveal the series of successive strata deposited during the gradual buildup of the mortuary. He was able to conclude that it contained the remains of men, women, and children, the disarticulated skeletons bundled together as if they were periodically being given a secondary burial after the flesh had been removed.[28]

Research by modern ethnohistorians fills out and mostly confirms Jefferson's brief account of the Piedmont Siouans' demise and departure from Virginia. Before the 1670s they lived beyond the frontier settlements, their lands unoccupied by whites, alternately feuding and trading with the Powhatans to the east and with the Massawomecks to the west. Iroquois warriors from the north attacked the Monacans, who took refuge still farther to the south, first moving onto the islands in the Roanoke River, near the North Carolina border, at the Ocaneechi trading center. By 1700 these refugees, now known as Tutelos and Saponis, had moved southward to take shelter with the Tuscaroras in North Carolina and probably with the Catawbas in South Carolina. But the Tuscaroras themselves were dislodged by the whites in a major war in 1711, and many began moving northward into Pennsylvania in 1712.

A few Tuscaroras, and associated Tutelo and Conoy fugitives from earlier Iroquois assaults in Virginia and Maryland, remained behind, most of them after 1714 on the Roanoke River near Fort Christanna. Eventually the Tutelo and Saponi remnants in Pennsylvania joined the Iroquois in New York and after the Revolution moved onto the Six Nations Reserve in Ontario, where a few descendants remain to this day. People claiming to be Monacans also live in Amherst County, Virginia, in the midst of the

Blue Ridge mountains, on the upper reaches of the James River, and are active in recovering their ancient history.[29]

The Mysterious Massawomecks

The ancient Indian tribes of Tidewater and Piedmont Virginia were of little concern to eighteenth-century Virginians. Of far more importance, as young Jefferson grew up, were the Indians to the westward. Beyond the Blue Ridge, beyond the newly settled Valley of Virginia, beyond the Appalachian Mountains lay imperial Virginia's vaster domain, ranging from the North Carolina boundary northward across the Ohio valley and westward in a great swath to the Pacific Ocean (at least as Virginians interpreted their 1609 charter). The land between the Appalachians and the Mississippi, called the Ohio country for the Ohio River which bisected it, was occupied in Jefferson's time by diverse tribes who had moved into the vacancy created by the Iroquois wars in the seventeenth century. These tribes included, among others, the Sac and Fox, the Illinois, the Miamis, and the "Three Fires"—the Ottawas, Potawatomies, and Chippewas—and even more recently, in the eastern part of the region, tribal remnants from Pennsylvania, New Jersey, and Canada, especially the Delawares, the Shawnees, and the Wyandots, accompanied by some Iroquois, locally called Mingoes.

South of the Ohio River, the demographic pattern was different. What are now the states of West Virginia and Kentucky (but were then the western counties of the colony of Virginia) in the seventeenth and eighteenth century seem to have been home to few resident Indians, although in previous centuries mound-building cultures had flourished there and north of the river as well. Occasionally hunting parties from the Cherokees and Catawbas to the south, and no doubt also hunters from the north, penetrated the region, and for a time there were a few Shawnee villages, but mostly it was traversed by war parties of Iroquois coming down to strike their enemies, particularly the Cherokees and Catawbas. Kentucky came to have the reputation of a "dark and bloody ground."

Success in the wars of the seventeenth century encouraged the Iroquois to claim, in their perennial negotiations with the British, conquest of the whole Ohio country, from the Great Lakes south at least to the Virginia–North Carolina boundary. This assumed conquest, in their eyes, reduced the status of any actual Indian residents of the region to mere tributaries, tenants at will, whose lands could be sold by the Iroquois to Europeans whenever they chose. Colonial governors and land speculators were only too glad to take the Iroquois claim at face value, on such occasions as the Lancaster treaty of 1744. Unfortunately for Virginia, and later for the United States, the resident tribes did not accept the Iroquois interpretation of their land tenure.

None of this information appears in the text of Jefferson's *Notes on the State of Virginia.* He contented himself with one brief paragraph: "Westward of all these tribes [i.e. the Indians of the Tidewater and Piedmont], beyond the mountains, and extending to the Great Lakes, were the *Massawomecks,* a most powerful confederacy, who harassed unremittingly the *Powhatans* and *Manahoacs.* These were probably the ancestors of the tribes known at present by the name of the *Six Nations.*"[30] This is an extraordinary statement, both for the positive misinformation it contains and for the failure to mention facts with which Jefferson should have been familiar.

Jefferson's identification of the Massawomecks with the Six Nations Iroquois is mistaken. "Massawomeck" is the word originally used by the Powhatans of Captain Smith's time to denote their enemies to the north and west and probably did not refer to the Iroquois at all. Furthermore, in the seventeenth century, and indeed even in the eighteenth, the five tribes that made up the original Iroquois Confederacy never lived west of the Appalachian Mountains. The Mohawks, Oneidas, Onondagas, Cayugas, and Senecas lived in villages in what is now New York State, extending roughly from the Hudson River west to Lake Erie. The sixth tribe, the Tuscaroras—also speakers of an Iroquoian language—emigrated from North Carolina to Pennsylvania and New York after 1712. Many took refuge among the Five Nations and eventually were accepted as the Sixth Nation of the Iroquois Confederacy. About the middle of the eighteenth century, some Iroquois people (including Logan) did make their residence in what is now eastern Ohio and became known as Mingoes.

A second piece of misleading information (if not misinformation) concerns the number of Indians in the various tribes west of the Appalachians. The section of *Notes on the State of Virginia* on "The Aborigines" concludes with a census and gazetteer of the Indian tribes of the United States. This census, arranged in tabular form, reproduces the numbers contained in several reports by well-known authorities: Colonel Bouquet, Thomas Hutchins, and George Croghan. Some figures were provided informally by John Dodge, who was Jefferson's star witness against Governor Hamilton "the Hair Buyer"; Jefferson later came to consider them unreliable. The entries in the original lists, however, were not figures for the total population but were rather warrior counts, in keeping with the traditional practice of estimating only the number of fighting men that a tribe could mobilize. Conventionally, the figure for the total population was obtained by multiplying the warrior count by a factor of four or five (although elsewhere Jefferson used a factor of three).

But Jefferson's list does not mention that he is presenting only the warrior count; he introduces the list as a statement of "the nations and numbers of the Aborigines which still exist in a respectable and independent form." Thus, for instance, he cites John Dodge's estimate of the Six Nations population in 1779 as 1,600 souls; the total actually was on the order of 10,000. Furthermore, Jefferson's omission of the Virginia Indians implied that they were extinct. Actually, as we have seen, several hundred still lived on small reservations and enclaves. The omission of the information that the numbers were only warrior counts was most likely a slip of the pen; but however it came about, it had the practical effect of minimizing whites' apprehension of Indian interference with their settlements.[31]

Why did Jefferson assert that the Iroquois Confederacy (the Six Nations) or their ancestors were the sole occupants of the country west of the Appalachian Mountains in the seventeenth century? The answer would appear to be simple economic interest. In 1722, 1744, and 1768 the colony of Virginia, and land companies and speculators associated with it, bought a large part of that land from the Iroquois and were prepared to acquire the rest from the same "owner." Although in 1781 Virginia was preparing to cede to Congress her claims to land north of the Ohio, in the *Notes* Jefferson was silently validating Virginia's exclusive claim to Kentucky by asserting that the Six Nations had once held title and that such other populations as could be found there were of minor importance. Jefferson's identification of the Massawomecks as the aboriginal proprietors of all that part of the Old Dominion lying immediately to the west of the Appalachians, and as being the ancestors of the Six Nations themselves, thus appears to be a peculiar and arbitrary construction.

In another confused passage, he suggested that the Monacans, "better known latterly by the name of *Tuscaroras,*" were probably connected with the Massawomecks and with the Eries, "a nation formerly inhabiting on the Ohio," who spoke a language akin to Tuscarora.[32] These errors of identification likewise lent support to Virginia's legal claim to have purchased the Piedmont, the Shenandoah valley, and the territories west of the Appalachians from the Six Nations at Albany in 1722, at Lancaster in 1744, and at Fort Stanwix in 1768.

Scholarly opinion about the actual identity of the Massawomecks has been divided. Some, like Jefferson, have concluded that they were indeed the Five Nations (that is, the Six Nations minus the Tuscaroras). Jefferson's own authority for his assertion that the Massawomecks were the Five Nations, or their ancestors, would seem to have been the Reverend William Stith, a native of Virginia and president of William and Mary College. Stith's *History of the First Discovery and Settlement of Virginia* was published in Williamsburg in 1747, and Jefferson listed it right after Captain Smith's work in his bibliographical essay in the *Notes.* There he described Stith as "a man of classical learning," though he criticized his work as being choked with "details often too minute to be tolerable."[33] But Jefferson did follow Stith's characterization of the Massawomecks as "a great and powerful Nation of *Indians,* inhabiting upon some of the Lakes of *Canada,* and the original perhaps of those, at present known by the Name of the *Senecas* or *Six Nations.*"[34]

The most recent, and authoritative, opinion on the identity of the Massawomecks is that of James Pendergast, who concluded that the Massawomecks were an Iroquoian-speaking tribe, or group of tribes, who early in the seventeenth century occupied a region between Lake Erie and Lake Ontario, west of the Five Nations, where they were known to the French as Antouhonorons. They began to raid and trade into the Chesapeake Bay region sometime prior to 1627 and eventually migrated south to a location along the headwaters of the Potomac, Monongahela, and Youghiogheny rivers, where they continued their commerce with the Virginia Indians well into the middle of the seventeenth century. Their fate thereafter is not known.[35]

Jefferson's Style of Ethnology

Jefferson's approach to Native American ethnology—the study of customs, beliefs, and institutions—tended to be historical. The section on "The Aborigines" of Virginia is entirely historical, apart from the table listing tribes and their present locations and numbers. So few Native Americans still remained in the part of the state east of the mountains that his account of them amounted to little more than a recital of the names of the extinct tribes and confederacies.

Next followed the account of his excavation of the Indian burial mound along the Rivanna River, near Monticello. His methodology was exemplary and well suited to the theoretical question that prompted him, namely, the popular opinion that such mounds were the mass graves of victims of a furious battle, buried on the spot. After initial surface collecting of a disorderly mixture of bony fragments, Jefferson ordered a perpendicular trench to be dug across the barrow, which revealed the stratigraphy of the site and permitted rational inference about the history of the mound and the method of interment (the deposit of collections of bones at successive intervals, each deposit being covered by a layer of earth). As noted earlier, archaeologists have given Jefferson high marks for his sophisticated excavating technique.[36] Jefferson did not continue his archeological researches into burial mounds, however, even when retirement would have given him the opportunity.

The only place in the *Notes* where Jefferson describes Indian customary behavior is in the essay "Productions Mineral, Vegetable, and Animal." It betrays little interest in the details of native social institutions, which, of course, he was committed to replacing with "civilized" ones, and it ignored not only the monumental earthworks of the Ohio and Mississippi valleys but also the high cultures of the Incas and Aztecs. The commentary contra Buffon emphasizes the estimable moral qualities and intellectual abilities of the Indians, not what later scholars would refer to as their culture. He appraises their character in a style perhaps reminiscent of dinner-table conversation among a family evaluating the worthiness of their neighbors. He makes no mention of the rules of kinship, those systems of consanguinity and affinity that were the backbone of Native American social structure and that would fascinate scholars of the next generation, beyond recognizing affection for children and "other connections." He praises the "care" and "indulgence" with which children are treated, and the heartbreak felt when they died.

Jefferson does not deal with the division of labor by gender, whereby the women were responsible for producing the crops of corn, squash, and beans that were the major staples of the native diet. He correctly notes that all forms of compulsion are prohibited in Indian society (a cardinal virtue, in his eyes), but he ignores major features of the political organization, such as the role of women in nominating the traditional chiefs who represented clans and lineages or the recent ascendancy of nonhereditary "chiefs" who achieved eminence as brave warriors and orators eloquent in council, or the structure of ethnic confederacies like that of the Iroquois. In the *Notes* he has nothing to say about religious beliefs and rituals, which of course he would be apt to dismiss as superstitious nonsense in any case.[37]

Jefferson was modest in his claim to be an authority on Native Americans. "Of the Indians of South America I know nothing," he admitted, and he labeled the available published accounts of them as mere "fables." He gave some credit to more general works on human nature and to what he himself had "seen of man, white, red, and black." Of the Indian of North America, "I can speak . . . somewhat from my own knowledge, but more from the information of others better acquainted with him, and on whose truth and judgment I can rely."[38]

Jefferson's most trusted advisor on Indian ethnology was Charles Thomson, to whom Jefferson sent (by the hand of Marbois) a copy of the *Notes* in 1781. In response, Thomson wrote an extended commentary on Indian affairs, which Jefferson published in the *Appendix* to the *Notes* in 1800. Jefferson probably first became acquainted with Thomson when this upright scholarly gentleman was elected to the American Philosophical Society in 1785, and he later knew him as the perennial secretary of the Continental Congress. The two corresponded regularly on a variety of scientific subjects, and when Thomson—a devoted Presbyterian and a classicist—produced his own translation of the Old Testament from the Greek, about the time that Jefferson was completing his "Philosophy of Jesus," they exchanged views on the true Christian morality.[39]

Thomson had a wide reputation as an absolutely honest man. He had traveled in Indian country, visiting the Delaware settlement at Wyoming along the Susquehanna in company with the Moravian missionary Christian Frederick Post, and had served as secretary to Teedyuscung, the Delaware Indian spokesman at treaties at Easton, Pennsylvania, in 1757 and 1758. His notes were so carefully taken that they became the official minutes. In 1759 Thomson published a notorious book, *Enquiry into the Causes of the Alienation of the Delaware and Shawanese Indians from the British Interest,* charging that mistreatment of the Delawares by the Crown and the colonists had caused them to take the French side in the French and Indian War and to lay waste the frontiers of Pennsylvania.

Thomson became known, in the words of an admiring biographer, as "the leading authority on all questions relating to the Indians."[40] His "commentaries" on the Indian material in the *Notes* are partly a corroboration of Jefferson's refutation of Buffon, point by point, with allusions to moral similarities between the Indians and the ancient Hebrews and Romans. He too made sweeping generalizations: "All the nations of Indians in North America lived in the hunter state, and depended for subsistence on hunting, fishing, and the spontaneous fruits of the earth, and a kind of grain which was planted and gathered by the women, and is now known by the name of Indian corn. Long potatoes, pumkins of various kinds, and squashes were also found in use among them. They had no flocks, herds, or tamed animals of any kind." This is accurate enough except for the omission of reference to beans, an important part of the diet, and of course it does not describe contemporary Indians who had been more or less acculturated.

He goes on to describe the Indians' "patriarchal" style of government in some detail, their mode of burial, and the history of several wars. Thomson is perhaps weakest in identifying the various tribes outside the territories of the Iroquois, whom he also calls Mingoes (a term generally used to refer to transplanted Iroquois in the Ohio valley), mismatching the Monacans with the Tuscaroras and the Saponis with the Unami branch of the Delawares, and mislocating the Tutelos as aboriginal residents of the Delmarva peninsula (that is, the eastern shore of the Chesapeake).[41]

Still, Thomson was one of the best choices Jefferson could have made as critical reader of the Indian portions of his manuscript. Most of the other colonial authorities on the Indians were unavailable, and the earlier Indian agents and superintendents, who were generally very well-informed, were either dead or relocated in Canada or Florida. Jefferson did write to Thomas Walker but seems to have gotten no useful response from him. He also consulted George Rogers Clark, whose later elaboration on the Cresap affair Jefferson mostly ignored and concealed, and Thomas Hutchins, for population estimates. At that time he seems not to have known well enough the Moravian and other missionaries who might have given helpful comments, although he did consult later with John Heckewelder on the Cresap affair and published his lengthy discussion in the *Appendix*.

From Savagism to the Corps of Discovery

The picture of the Indians presented in *Notes on the State of Virginia* was painted with a broad brush—a panorama of universal attributes of character and temperament supposedly shared by all Native Americans. It articulated a general view which Roy Harvey Pearce has characterized as an "American theory of savagism"—that "the savage [is] one whom circumstances, for good and for bad, have held in an early state of society." Pearce, indeed, suggested that the idea of savagism was "first outlined" by Jefferson.[42] This schematic view of the Indians was derived in part from the Scottish philosophers' teaching that a moral sense of right and wrong is part of human nature, in part from a belief in the importance of environment in shaping the manners and moral refinement of different societies, and in part from the Enlightenment belief in universal stages of progress toward modern civilized society. Thus the Indians could be regarded as inherently the equals of whites and yet as culturally inferior, childlike, in their savage state.[43]

The theory of a scale of progress or Great Chain of Being was fully current in the literature of the Enlightenment by the time Jefferson was writing in the 1780s.[44] Montesquieu, one of Jefferson's most closely read authors, had in 1748 in *De l'esprit des lois* sketched out the familiar three-tiered schema of human progress from savagery to barbarism to civilization. And William Robertson's *History of America,* which appeared in 1777 and which Jefferson regarded as essential reading for any aspiring law student (despite his rejection of Robertson's repetition of Buffon's thesis), presented the conventional typology of savage, barbarian, and civilized man.

This Enlightenment belief in universal progress was explicitly invoked by Secretary of War Henry Knox in his proposal to President Washington in 1789 to commence a program of civilizing the Indians.[45] Jefferson, of course, supported the Indian civilization policy throughout his life. But he also shared with Knox the belief that "favorable circumstances" were needed for a people to make progress. Unfavorable circumstances might include an unfriendly environment or, in the case of the blacks, a racially based incapacity to rise above a certain rung on the ladder of perfection.

Later in life, with more information, he became explicit in his delineation of the positions of the Native Americans on the ladder of cultural progress. Writing to a friend in 1824, he observed: "Let a philosophic observer commence a journey from the savages of the Rocky Mountains, eastwardly towards our sea-coast. These he would observe in the earliest stage of association living under no law but that of nature, subsisting and covering themselves with the flesh and skins of wild beasts. He would next find those on our frontiers in the pastoral state, raising domestic animals to supply the defects of hunting. Then succeed our own semi-barbarous citizens, the pioneers of the advance of civilization, and so in his progress he would meet the gradual shades of improving man until he would reach his, as yet, most improved state in our seaport towns. This, in fact, is equivalent to a survey, in time, of the progress of man from the infancy of creation to the present day."[46]

Despite these generalizations, Jefferson was aware of the need for specific studies of individual tribes, each of which had its own unique language, customs, and history. He may have had this in mind when he called for a "natural history" approach to ethnology. "To our reproach it must be said, that though for a century and a half we have had under our eyes the races of black and of red men, they have never yet been viewed by us as subjects of natural history."[47] His proposal in the *Notes* for reform of the Brafferton Institution at William and Mary envisaged resident missionaries who would move from tribe to tribe spreading the Gospel and collecting information on the cultures, languages, and histories of Native American tribes.[48] Evidently Jefferson was less interested in teaching Indian boys Latin and Greek, or even in converting them to Christianity, than in obtaining information that would contribute to his own study of the origin of tribes and of the Indian "race."

Jefferson's 1793 instructions, on behalf of the American Philosophical Society, to the French botanist André Michaux for his exploring expedition up the Missouri to the Pacific Ocean explicitly requested him to record "the names, numbers, & dwellings of the inhabitants, and such particularities as you can learn of their history, connection with each other, languages, manners, state of society & of the arts & commerce among them."[49] The plans of the American Philosophical Society's 1797 Committee on History included inquiry "into the Customs, Manners, Languages and Character of the Indian Nations, ancient and modern."[50]

Jefferson's instructions in June 1803 to Meriwether Lewis in preparation for the great trip to the Pacific Ocean called for many ethnographic details on the Indian tribes he would meet along the way (see opposite).[51] Lewis and Clark received additional questions from Benjamin Rush and Caspar

Jefferson's Instructions to Lewis and Clark Regarding Indians

The commerce which may be carried on with the people inhabiting the line you will pursue, renders a knowledge of those people important. You will therefore endeavor to make yourself acquainted, as far as a diligent pursuit of your journey shall admit, with the names of the nations & their numbers; the extent & limits of their possessions; their relations with other tribes of nations; their language, traditions, monuments; their ordinary occupations in agriculture, fishing, hunting, war, arts, & the implements for these; their food, clothing, & domestic accommodations; the diseases prevalent among them, & the remedies they use; moral & physical circumstances which distinguish them from the tribes we know; peculiarities in their laws, customs & dispositions; and articles of commerce they may need to furnish, & to what extent. And considering the interest which every nation has in extending & strengthening the authority of reason & justice among the people around them, it will be useful to acquire what knowledge you can of the state of morality, religion, & information among them; as it may better enable those who may endeavor to civilize & instruct them, to adapt their measures to the existing notions & practices of those on whom they are to operate.

Wistar, the eminent Philadelphia physicians and members of the Philosophical Society to whom Jefferson had advised them to turn for guidance. Rush in particular was something of an ethnologist himself, having in 1774 published his *Enquiry into the Natural History of Medicine among the Indians in North America.* He had delivered a short list of questions to Alexander McGillivray on the occasion of the Creek chief's visit to New York, and another to Timothy Pickering on the eve of his visit to the Senecas in 1791. Rush sent his list of some twenty questions to Lewis in May 1803, covering "Physical History & medicine," "Morals," and "Religion."[52]

Clark collated Rush's list, another list from Wistar, possibly some from Benjamin Smith Barton, and Jefferson's suggestions, along with, no doubt, some thoughts of his own, into a master set of notes and queries in 1804. (Later in the century, "Notes and Queries" would become the technical

William Clark (left) and Meriwether Lewis (right). Oil on paper, c. 1810, and oil on wood, c. 1807, by Charles Willson Peale. Courtesy of Independence National Historic Park Collection.

"Captains Lewis & Clark Holding a Council with the Indians." From Patrick Gass, *Journal of Voyages and Travels of Corps of Discovery under the Command of Capt. Lewis and Capt. Clarke,* 1810. Courtesy of the Beinecke Library, Yale University.

term for this kind of check-list ethnography.) Clark's list of nearly one hundred topics amounted to an outline of cultural materials, divided into ten categories: "1st. Physical History and Medicine. 2nd. Relative to Morals. 3rd. Relative to Religion. 4th. Traditions or National History. 5th. Agriculture and Domestic economy. 6th. Fishing & Hunting. 7th. War. 8th. Amusements. 9th. Clothing Dress & Ornaments. [10th.] Customs & Manners Generally."[53]

These categories cover much of what a twentieth-century ethnographer

"Bird's Eye View of the Mandan River, 1800 Miles above St. Louis." Oil on canvas by George Catlin, 1837–1839. The earth lodges were forty to sixty feet in diameter and could house twenty to forty people. In the central plaza, shown here, the barrel shaped edifice, called "the big canoe," contained the tribe's sacred medicines. National Museum of American Art, Washington, DC / Art Resource, NY.

would include under the concept of "culture." What are most conspicuously missing are entries for kinship and political organization. In their journals and reports, Lewis and Clark did record much cultural information, the value of which has been emphasized by twentieth-century ethnohistorians, but unfortunately none of it became available in print until a two-volume history of the expedition by Nicholas Biddle, based on the explorers' journals, was published in 1814. The full text of the Lewis and Clark journals did not see print until a century and more later, beginning with the Philosophical Society's manuscript edited by Reuben Gold Thwaites in 1901 and culminating in the recent edition of Gary Moulton.[54]

But a partial account of the fruits of their inquiries was transmitted to the President and the secretary of war from the Mandan village on the upper Missouri in the spring of 1805, and the President communicated it in turn to the Congress. Eventually it was published in the *American State Papers, Vol. 1, Indian Affairs.* This "statistical view of the Indian nations inhabiting the territory of Louisiana, and the countries adjacent to its Northern and Western boundaries," contained information tabulated according to nineteen categories (see opposite).[55] Thus, concerning the Mandans, about whom Lewis and Clark were well informed, having spent the winter of 1804–1805 at the Mandan village, they recorded a rather bland account (see page 102).[56]

Lewis reported that the Mandans had "no idea of an exclusive right to any portion of country," an assertion of dubious validity. With respect to some of the tribes farther down the Missouri, he made a point of ascertaining the possibility of inducing them to make room for Indian tribes from the eastern side of the Mississippi, a possibility the more probable the less territory the local tribes claimed. Thus, of the Grand Osage he wrote that two villages might be prevailed on "to relocate and thus leave a sufficient scope of country for the Shawnees, Delawares, Miamies, and Kickapoos." The Otoes likewise would not "object to the introduction of any well-disposed Indians."[57]

The most richly textured observations in Lewis and Clark's journals were made of those tribes (such as the Mandans and the Clatsops on the Pacific coast) among whom the explorers spent several months' time instead of just passing through their territory as quickly as possible. Thus, among the Mandans, Clark's journal records much detail about a ceremony in which young warriors required their wives to have sexual intercourse with respected older men, or with interesting visitors—members of

Lewis and Clark's Nineteen Categories

A. The names of the Indian nations, as usually spelt and pronounced in the English language.
B. Primitive Indian names of nations and tribes, English orthography, the syllables pronouncing the sounds by which the Indians themselves express the name of their respective nation.
C. Nicknames, or those which have generally obtained among the Canadian traders.
D. The language they speak; if primitive, marked with a *, otherwise, derived from, and approximating to, the______.
E. Number of villages.
F. Number of tents, or lodges, of the roving bands.
G. Number of warriors.
H. The probable number of souls.
I. The rivers on which they rove, or on which their villages are situated.
J. The names of the nations, or companies, with whom they maintain their principal commerce or traffic.
K. The place at which their traffic is usually carried on.
L. The amount of merchandise necessary for their annual consumption, estimated at the St. Louis prices, in dollars.
M. The estimated amount, in dollars, of their annual returns, at the St. Louis prices.
N. The species of peltries, furs, and other articles, which they annually supply or furnish.
O. The species of peltries, furs, and other articles, which the natural production of their country would enable them to furnish, provided proper encouragement was given them.
P. The places at which it would be mutually advantageous to form the principal establishments, in order to supply the several Indian nations with merchandise.
Q. The names of the Indian nations with whom they are at war.
R. The names of the Indian nations with whom they maintain a friendly alliance, or with whom they are united by intercourse or marriage.
S. Miscellaneous remarks.

Lewis and Clark's Account of the Mandans

A. Mandans.
B. Maw-dan—Ma-too-tonka, 1st village; Rop-tar-ha, 2d village.
C. Mandans.
D. Some words resembling the Osage.
E. Two.
F.
G. 350.
H. 1,250.
I. On both sides of the Missouri, 1,612 miles from its mouth.
J. The Hudson bay and Northwest companies, from their establishment on the Assinniboin.
K. At their villages.
L. 2,000.
M. 6,000.
N. Principally the skins of the large and small wolves, and the small fox, and beaver, also, corn and beans.
O. The same as the Ricaras . . . except the grisly bear; they could furnish, in addition, the skins of a large species of white hare, a very delicate fur.
P. At or near the mouth of the Yellow Stone river.
Q. With no nation, except a defensive war with the Siouxs.
R. With all nations who do not wage war against them.
S. These are the most friendly, well disposed Indians, inhabiting the Missouri; they are brave, humane, and hospitable. About 25 years since, they lived in six villages, about 40 miles below their present villages, on both sides of the Missouri. Repeated visitations of the small-pox, aided by frequent attacks of the Siouxs, has reduced them to their present number. They claim no particular tract of country; they live in fortified villages, hunt immediately in their neighborhood, and cultivate corn, beans, squashes, and tobacco, which form articles of traffic with their neighbors, the Assiniboins; they also barter horses with the Assiniboins, for arms, ammunition, axes, kettles, and other articles of European manufacture, which these last obtain from the British establishments on the Assinniboin river. The articles which they thus obtain from the Assiniboins, and the British traders who visit them, they again exchange for horses and leather tents, with the Crow Indians, Cheyennes, Wetepahatoes, Kiawans, Kanenavish, Staitan, and Cataka, who visit them occasionally, for the purpose of traffic; their trade may be much increased; their country is similar to that of the Ricaras; population increasing.

Jefferson "Peace and Friendship" medal of 1801, given to various Indian chiefs by Lewis and Clark. Courtesy of the American Numismatic Society.

"The Interior of the Hut of a Mandan Chief." Engraving with aquatint, hand-colored, after a watercolor by Karl Bodmer, c. 1834. Courtesy of the Joslyn Art Museum, Omaha, Nebraska; Gift of Enron Art Foundation.

the Corps of Discovery, for example. (In Biddle's published summary of the expedition's history, this event is discreetly described in Latin.) Among the Clatsops, customs relating to trade with Europeans, who had been well-established there long before Lewis and Clark arrived, were subjects of prime interest. But the explorers had not been asked nor trained to serve as professional ethnologists. While their observations have been invaluable to latter-day ethnohistorians, they did not advance the art of comprehensive ethnographic description.

Jefferson's Cabinet of Curios

As early as the 1780s Jefferson began his cabinet of curios and mementos in the entrance hall and library at Monticello, starting with the two painted buffalo hides from the Kaskaskia chief in 1780, one painted with a battle scene, the other with a native map of the lower Missouri River basin. In the *Notes,* as part of his defense of Native American genius, he remarked, "The Indians will often carve figures on their pipes not destitute of design and merit. They will crayon out an animal, a plant, or a country, so as to prove the existence of a germ in their minds which only wants cultivation."[58] He had little opportunity to expand his collection in the 1780s; relations with most of the Indian nations were not peaceable until after the war, and then he was off to Paris. But in the 1790s the collection at Monticello probably expanded somewhat, and it was thereafter greatly augmented with numerous items collected by Lewis and Clark and other Indian agents and philosophical gentlemen on the frontiers.

Jefferson's Indian Hall generally impressed visitors to the house; one guest described it as "the most varied complete collection that has ever been made," containing "offensive and defensive arms, clothes, ornaments, and utensils of the different savage tribes of North America." It was an extremely heterogeneous cabinet, full of all sorts of things hung on the walls in great profusion: portraits of great men, including Christopher Columbus, Sir Walter Raleigh, Bacon, Newton, and Locke; paintings of classical subjects; mounted heads and horns of wild animals; minerals and crystals; fossil shells and bones, including the jaws of a mastodon; and, as Silvio Bedini puts it, "with aboriginal art and artifacts layered over the whole": buffalo robes, peace pipes, clothing, war clubs, bows and arrows, shields (some of them hanging from horns and antlers), and wampum. The Indian materials evidently were classified as natural curiosities,

"Portrait of a Young Chief of the Sack Nation of Indians." Watercolor by David Bourdon. According to family tradition, this was part of Jefferson's collection at Monticello, most likely given to him in 1805 by a delegation of Native Americans from the "Missouri and Mississippi." Courtesy of Monticello/Thomas Jefferson Memorial Foundation, Inc.

memorabilia, curious productions of the New World's antique human inhabitants, shown along with extinct animals like the mastodon and *Megalonyx Jeffersoni* (the giant sloth).

No complete list of Jefferson's collection exists; apparently he left no catalogue of his own, and after his death the collection was dispersed, passing through various hands, some of it finding a resting place at the Peabody Museum of Archaeology and Anthropology at Harvard University. Lewis and Clark sent three shipments of artifacts to Jefferson in Washington. The first, accompanying a delegation of Osage Indians, arrived in July 1804 and probably included mostly Osage items; their fate is unrecorded, except for some pieces now at the Peabody. The second, and largest, came from Fort Mandan in August 1805 and consisted of Mandan artifacts. It was divided, as Lewis requested, between Monticello and the

Peale Museum in Philadelphia (located at Philosophical Hall). Jefferson kept a Mandan bow and a quiver of arrows, a cooking pot, four buffalo robes and other items of dress, and a buffalo hide painted with a representation of a famous battle. A third shipment containing items from the northwest coast, including Clatsop hats, was sent from St. Louis on the return of the expedition in the fall of 1806.

How carefully Jefferson recorded the provenance of his artifacts—by tribe, by collector, by date, by location, and so on—is not clear. The surviving artifacts at the Peabody are generally "attributed" to tribal groups or culture areas on the basis of stylistic features and information by correspondents and observers. The miscellany of items in the Peabody collection includes (putatively) a Mandan eagle-bone whistle and buffalo robe, a Sac and Fox tobacco pouch, a flute from the northern Plains Indians, an Osage warrior's insignia, a Crow cradle, and an Ojibwa knife sheath.[59]

Collecting Indian curios was an avocation of Jefferson's friends and associates as well. In February 1797 a resident of the western country, George Turner, a member of the American Philosophical Society's 1797 Committee on History, donated to the society a remarkable collection of nearly twenty items from a number of tribes: boys' leggings, a "Calumet of Peace," and a "Conjurors' Mask," from the Missouri; arrows made by the Sacs and by the Miamis, a sea-otter skin blanket acquired by the celebrated British explorer Alexander Mackenzie on the northwest coast in 1794, a wooden statue of a beaver from the Kaskaskias, a pair of garters "tipped with tin and Porcupine quills" from the Wabash and another pair from the Creeks; and various items with tribal provenance unspecified or of archaeological origin.[60] Where these items were deposited is not clear; probably they were displayed in Peale's Museum on the premises. Some of Peale's collection and other artifacts belonging to the society eventually came to rest in the University of Pennsylvania's Museum of Anthropology and Archeology.

The allusion to Mackenzie is interesting because it suggests a possible contact of Jefferson with the first European to cross the continent and reach the Pacific Ocean—an object contemplated in the society's Michaux expedition in 1793. Mackenzie, who visited Philadelphia in 1798, probably gave Turner the blanket at that time. But there is no record of a visit by Mackenzie to the society, or of a meeting with Jefferson, and his book describing the adventurous journey did not appear until late in 1801.[61]

In any case, the information to be gained about the particular cultures of specific Native American communities from explorers' accounts and poorly documented collections of artifacts was far too thin and skimpy to lead to anything approaching the standards of ethnological research that came into vogue in America in the second half of the nineteenth century. The hallmark of the later disciplines of anthropology and sociology was precisely the requirement that data be collected by the sort of "philosophic observer" that Jefferson once alluded to, men (and women) who resided among the subjects of study, spoke the language, and were there for the primary purpose of research.

CHAPTER FOUR

Native Americans through European Eyes

JEFFERSON'S VIEW of America as expressed in *Notes on the State of Virginia* faced some formidable competition when it was first published in 1785 in Paris. *Letters from an American Farmer* by J. Hector St. John de Crevecoeur—a Frenchman by birth—had been published (in English) in London four years earlier and had became an instant success.[1] Despite its quasi-fictional mode of presentation, Crevecoeur's book provided far more detailed and complete data on many aspects of American life than did Jefferson's *Notes,* and for years in Europe it remained the standard work on America. In the United States, it earned Crevecoeur membership in the American Philosophical Society.

With the advantages of an excellent Jesuit education and military experience as a French officer during the French and Indian War, Crevecoeur had emigrated from Canada to the English colony of New York. He traveled extensively as a surveyor before settling down in 1769 as a gentleman farmer in Orange County. During the Revolution, however, he was accused by the Americans of being a Tory and by the British, who imprisoned him, of being a Rebel. He escaped to England, wrote his book, and went home to France. In 1783, now a famous author, he returned to the United States as French Consul in New York, only to find his estate at Pine Hill despoiled, his wife dead, and his children in the care of a kind stranger from Boston. Jefferson knew Crevecoeur in the 1780s first through his book on America and later as a correspondent on a favorite subject, horticulture. While Jefferson was serving as minister in France, he became acquainted with Crevecoeur's young sons and took an interest in their education.[2]

Crevecoeur's book inspired a cult of devotees to his images of an American Arcadia. The *Letters* describe in glowing terms the fishing settlements of New England and the prosperous farming communities of long-settled parts of New York and Pennsylvania. But when he cast his eye southward,

Crevecoeur's portrait of America revealed a dark side, not only in his grim vignette of a condemned black slave, blinded and attacked by birds, dying slowly in an iron cage suspended from a tree, but also in his account of the sorry state of the trans-Appalachian settlers who had planted their homesteads in places too far from the markets where they had expected to sell their products (see page 197). A careful resident observer who spoke the language of his subjects, he vividly described the poverty, terror, and demoralization on the frontier as Indian war came closer and closer.

The Jesuit Tradition of Ethnography

The true pioneers in ethnography as carried out by resident observers were the French Jesuits. They were, to be sure, in the Americas to save the souls of the heathen, but they were heirs to a thousand years of Roman Catholic experience with the problems of converting pagans. They knew, for instance, that what Roman and Christian law considered to be impediments to marriage were not prohibited among the "savage" peoples they encountered in Europe north of the Alps. Degrees of cousinhood that were unacceptably close in Rome were permitted among the heathen. Polygamy was customary in some tribes. Should the church demand the dissolution of happy and respectable existing unions because of technical differences in marriage laws? It was necessary to understand local custom in order not to destroy the fabric of old societies or (perhaps still worse) alienate the natives from their would-be saviors.

If these European situations required close study, how much more so in the New World, where truly exotic customs were to be encountered. Among the Iroquois in New France, for instance, the basis of formal social structure was kinship, organized by rules unfamiliar to Europeans. Every tribe was divided into several clans, membership in which was inherited from the mother; each of these matrilineal clans belonged to one of two sides, whose representatives played reciprocal roles on ceremonial occasions; "chiefs" were chosen to sit in council by lineages in each of the clans. Members of the same clan, no matter how remotely related, were forbidden to marry, but in some systems first cousins of different clans (cross cousins) might do so. A man's mother's brother's daughter might be the perfect choice for a wife.

The terms for kinfolk did not have the same meaning in Native American languages as they did in French or English. Thus the term "father"

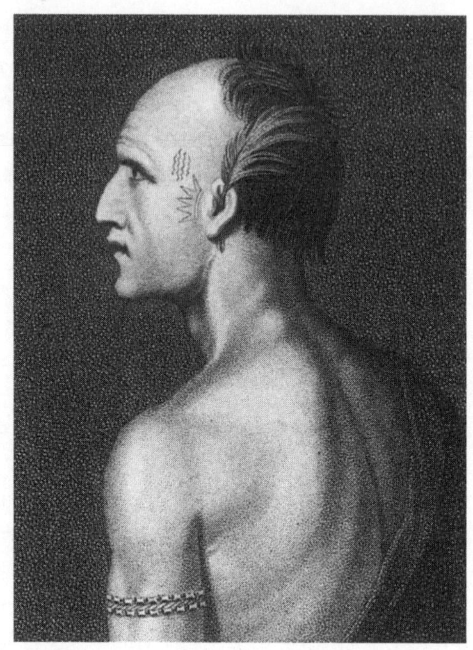

"Koohassen, Warrior of the Oneida Nation." Aquatint by the Parisian artist Bonfils, for Crevecoeur's *Voyage dans la Haute Pensylvanie et dans L'etat de New-York, par un Membre Adoptif de la Nation Oneida,* 1801. Courtesy of the Beinecke Library, Yale University

(meaning male biological parent or spouse of mother) might have only a partial equivalent in an Indian language, the native term including not only father in the European sense but also a variety of other male relatives. Jefferson had become aware of this semantic problem by 1825, remarking to a correspondent that "the Cherokee [language] has no name for 'Father' in the abstract, but only as combined with some one."[3] That "someone" was the father's brother, and also an indefinitely large number of others, all the male members of the father's matrilineal clan. But Jefferson's writings generally do not betray any familiarity with the ubiquitous system of clans, the widespread practice of matrilineal descent, and so on. And his anticlerical bias, generated by his bitter opposition to the Anglican establishment in colonial Virginia, coupled with his firm adherence to what he understood to be the pure teachings of Jesus, made it impossible for him to perceive Native American religion as anything but superstitious nonsense, and religious prophets who opposed his policies as anything but impostors.

Not so the Jesuits. They were heirs to an old tradition of scholarship and education and worked hard to describe accurately what they saw and heard among the heathen, whether they approved of it or not. They spent years in residence, learned the language of their hosts, prepared dictionaries and grammars for the instruction of novices at Jesuit academies in France, and wrote up their observations in formal accounts that were published for the instruction of those who would follow. These *Jesuit Relations,* first published in the mid-seventeenth century and republished with English translation by Reuben Gold Thwaites in seventy-three volumes from 1896 to 1901, have proved to be a gold mine of information to twentieth-century ethnohistorians. Jefferson probably did not have access to any of these Jesuit manuscripts or publications, though he did read a Jesuit missionary's ethnographic summary, Father Joseph-François Lafitau's *Moeurs des sauvages Ameriqains, comparées aux moeurs des premiers temps,* published in Paris in 1724.[4] Making use of the reports of Catholic missionaries in both North and South America, and relying on his own experience as a missionary for years among the Mohawks in Canada, Lafitau devoted chapters to religion, political government, marriage and education, occupations of men in the villages, occupations of the women, warfare, embassies and trade, and much more. Whether Jefferson had read the work by the time he wrote the *Notes* is not known, though he purchased a copy in France in 1789. But in any case, Jefferson's own preoccupation with historical questions, and particularly with the origin of the Indians, seems to have interfered with his appreciation of Lafitau's writings.

This bias is nowhere more clearly expressed than in his correspondence with John Adams in 1812. Adams had asked whether there was "any book that pretends to give any account of the traditions of the Indians," and Jefferson had replied that "the early travellers among them . . . chiefly French" had given some account of their "traditions . . . customs and characters." He went on to recommend two books, which, however, he set about at once to criticize severely. He first took to task Father Lafitau, whose work he dismissed out of hand.

Jefferson wrote: "Unluckily Lafitau had in his head a preconceived theory on the mythology, manners, institutions and government of the ancient nations of Europe, Asia and Africa, and seems to have entered on those of America only to fit them into the same frame, and to draw from them a confirmation of his general theory. He keeps up a perpetual parallel, in all those articles, between the Indians of America and the ancients of the other quarters of the globe. He selects, therefore, all the facts and adopts all the falsehoods which favor this theory, and very gravely retails such absurdities as zeal for a theory could alone swallow. He was a man of much classical and scriptural reading, and has rendered his book not unentertaining. He resided five years among the northern Indians, as a Missionary, but collects his matter much more from the writings of others than from his own observation."[5]

Actually, although Lafitau did compare Native American institutions to those of the Greeks and other early European civilizations (and believed that Indians had migrated from Europe eons ago), his descriptive information is by no means all "falsehood" and "absurdities." In writing about Iroquois political organization, which he regarded as prototypical for Native Americans generally, after admittedly tedious comparisons with ancient Greek institutions, Lafitau provides a remarkably accurate description of the system of chiefs and chiefs' councils. He recognized that chiefs represented matrilineal clans and indicated both the scope and limitations of their influence; he considered the role of the leading women as a council of advisors to the chiefs; he gave a finely detailed account of the requickening ceremony by which blood-feuds were aborted; and he gave a succinct and accurate analysis of the classificatory kinship system which anticipated the classic work of Lewis Henry Morgan on the Iroquois by 125 years.[6] None of the eyewitness observations Lafitau reported were seriously contaminated by his own ideas about the similarity of Indian institutions to those of the ancient Greeks and Romans.[7]

Jefferson was similarly dismissive of another substantial authority, the English trader among the southern Indians, John Adair, author of *The History of the American Indians, Particularly Those Nations Adjoining the Mississippi, East and West Florida, Georgia, South and North Carolina, and Virginia* (published in London in 1775): "Adair too had his kink. He believed all the Indians of America to be descended from the Jews; the same laws, usages, rites, ceremonies, the same sacrifices, priests, prophets, fasts and festivals, almost the same religion, and that they all spoke Hebrew. For, although he writes particularly of the Southern Indians only, the Catawbas, Creeks, Cherokees, Chickasaws and Choctaws, with whom alone he was personally acquainted, yet he generalizes whatever he found among them, and brings himself to believe that the hundred languages of America, differing fundamentally every one from every other, as much as Greek from Gothic, yet have all the common prototype. He was a trader, a man of learning, a self-taught Hebraist, a strong religionist, and of as sound a mind as Don Quixote in whatever did not touch his religious chivalry. His book contains a great deal of real instruction on its subject, only requiring the reader, to be constantly on his guard against the wonderful obliquities of his theory."[8]

Jefferson was particularly incensed by Adair's references to a priesthood among the southeastern Indians, and he gave Adams his own summary of the religious institutions of the Indians (see next page). While he was certainly correct in distinguishing between the secular men and women who officiated at certain ceremonies and the shamans who performed magic for individual clients, he was wrong in denying the existence of priests, in the sense of public religious servants of the community.[9]

Constantin Volney

Jefferson did not like it when any writer disparaged any aspect of American life, and he hoped—vainly, as it turned out—that a young French scholar whose acquaintance he had made in Paris would correct some of the bad impressions left by his countrymen and other Europeans. That scholar was Constantin François Chasseboeuf Volney, one of the intellectual idealists who frequented the salons of Baron Holbach and Madame Helvetius and who saw, as did Jefferson, in the early Revolution the dawn of a new era of freedom. The brilliant son of a lawyer, Volney received a fine education, went on to study medicine, and then decided to commit himself to "l'étude des peuples," that is to say, the comparative study of different national, ethnic, and religious groups.

This was a nascent discipline, a mix of what now might be called cultural anthropology or ethnology, comparative sociology, political science, and human geography. Volney inherited some money and decided spend it by undertaking a long journey, á la Herodotus (about whose travels he had published a book), for the sole purpose of giving to the world "a new fund of information."

He took ship to Cairo, the first step on his private expedition to the Middle East. Once there, "he felt the necessity of speaking the language of the country that he wished to know," and so he entered a Coptic monastery where he learned Arabic. Then he set forth on foot, with a pack on his back and a gun on his shoulder, on a three-year tour of the cities, towns, and Bedouin encampments of Egypt and Syria (including all of present day Syria, Lebanon, Israel, and Palestine). When he returned to Paris, he published *Voyage en Syrie et en Egypt, pendant les annés 1783, 1784 et 1785,*

Jefferson on Native American Religions

You ask further, if the Indians have any order of priesthood among them, like the Druids, Bards or Minstrels of the Celtic Nations? Adair alone, determined to see what he wished to see in every object, metamorphoses their Conjurers into an order of priests, and describes their sorceries as if they were the great religious ceremonies of the nation. Lafitau called them by their proper names, Jongleurs, Devins, Sortileges; De Bry pradesitiatores; Adair himself sometimes Magi, Archimagi, cunning men, Seers, rain makers; and the modern Indian interpreters call them conjurers and witches. They are persons pretending to have communications with the devil and other evil spirits, to foretell future events, bring down rain, find stolen goods, raise the dead, destroy some and heal others by enchantment, lay spells, etc. . . . In the solemn ceremonies of the Indians, the persons who direct or officiate are their chiefs, elders and warriors, in civil ceremonies or in those of war; it is the head of the cabin in their private or particular feasts or ceremonies; and sometimes the matrons, as in their corn feasts . . . The present state of the several Indian tribes, without any public order of priests, is proof sufficient that they never had such an order. Their steady habits permit no innovations, not even those which the progress of science offers to increase the comforts, enlarge the understanding, and improve the morality of mankind. Indeed, so little idea have they of a regular order of priests, that they mistake ours for their conjurers, and call them by that name.

which instantly earned him wide acclaim for opening the eyes of Europeans to a little-known Islamic civilization, then dominated by the Turks. Much of the work dealt with the geographical divisions and civil administration of the region, but it also contained chapters on religion, agriculture, artisans, merchants, arts and sciences, and traits of character. For example, he disputed Montesquieu's assertion that people in warm climates are always indolent and given to despotic regimes, arguing that "the habits of the character of the Orientals are varied according to the form of their governments & the spirit of their religion." The book became the indispensable guide to Napoleon's army in its invasion of Egypt ten years later.[10]

Jefferson left France in 1789, but his association with Volney continued. Volney had gone to Corsica, where he developed an experimental estate to provide an example of modern, improved agriculture among "a people firmly attached to ancient customs." This was just the kind of experiment that interested Jefferson, both on his own account at Monticello and as a device for civilizing the Indians, and subsequent correspondence during the next couple of decades included much exchange of agricultural information. But it was Volney's American tour that is most relevant to Jefferson's view of the frontier Indians. Volney seems to have intended an ethnographic survey of America comparable to his earlier travels in Egypt and Syria, including both the Native Americans and whites of various ancestries, particularly French.

In preparation for the trip, Volney visited Jefferson at Monticello, spending about three weeks there in June 1796. In his private journal he recorded a curious vignette describing Jefferson among his slaves. The field hands he observed to be haggard and fearful, cringing at the master's shaking of the whip he carried, suddenly galvanized by the threat into strenuous labor, only to return to indolence after Jefferson passed by.[11] This is not the image of the benevolent Virginia slaveowner that Jefferson cultivated. But the scene does not seem to have lessened Volney's and Jefferson's mutual admiration. Jefferson provided Volney with copies of his printed word list for collecting Indian vocabularies and wrote several letters of introduction for Volney, including one to his old friend the Kaskaskia chief John Baptiste du Coigne, effusively expressing friendship and the wish that the Kaskaskias not be "disturbed in their lands."[12] (Seven years later, Jefferson would scheme to persuade du Coigne to sell the tribe's territory (see page 213).

It is not clear whether Volney ever met with du Coigne or delivered Jefferson's letter to him. His original plan had been to go to St. Louis and thence down the Mississippi to Kaskaskia, but he seems to have reached only Vincennes on the Wabash. There, toward the end of the summer he observed the Indians returning from the hunt, many of them drunken and violent, and he decided to abandon his plan to live among the natives and learn their language (see page 213). Their independence of authority, which to Jefferson was admirable, horrified Volney.

He wrote: "I at first entertained the design of going to live a few months among them, to study them as I had done the Bedoween Arabs; but when I had seen these specimens of their domestic manners; and many of the inhabitants of the place, who acted as tavern keepers to them, and were accustomed to go and trade among them, assured me, that the laws of hospitality did not exist among them as among the Arabs; that they had neither government nor subordination; that the greatest war-chief could not strike or punish a warrior even in the field, and that in the village he was not obeyed by a single child except his own; that in these villages they dwelt singly, in mistrust, jealousy, secret ambushes, and implacable vengeances, in a word, that their society was a state of anarchy, of a ferocious and brutal nature, where want constitutes right, and strength laws, and besides, as they made no provision, a stranger ran the hazard of being starved without any resource; I felt the necessity of relinquishing my design. My greatest regret was the being unable to acquire any notions of their language, and obtain a vocabulary."[13]

Volney was also disillusioned by the meager (and boring) way of life of the frontier settlers among whom he traveled. All thought of planting himself in this wilderness for very long vanished, and he was overcome with longing for Philadelphia and Monticello. He returned as fast as possible, north across Illinois and Indiana by way of a military road cut only two years before and took ship for Philadelphia, where he arrived in November.

Jefferson, in the meantime, was anticipating a report from "a philosophical observer . . . on the aboriginals of America." But Jefferson would have to wait. Although Volney wished to talk with him about these things, dined with him in Philadelphia, and visited Monticello again before leaving America in 1798 (in haste, after being accused under the Alien and Sedition Acts of being a French secret agent), their subsequent correspondence suggests that Jefferson's curiosity was not assuaged. Volney was elected to membership in the American Philosophical Society in January 1797, no doubt on Jefferson's recommendation, and the two corresponded for at least a decade thereafter.[14]

Volney's *View of the Climate and Soil of the United States of America* was published in Paris in 1804, and an English translation appeared in London in the same year. Jefferson first received his copy from the author in August, promptly deposited it in the Library of Congress, and did not consult it until winter, after returning from his "autumnal visit to Monticello." He wrote to Volney expressing his "great satisfaction" with the work in February 1805.

Jefferson's comments, though polite, were evasive. He declined to take up one of Volney's main points, that the geology of a country must be studied in order to understand its civilization, confessing that he did not know "the face of the country" beyond Staunton, Virginia, the farthest west he had traveled, and stating that he had never bothered much with "geological inquiries, from a belief that the skin deep scratches which we can make or find on the surface of the earth, do not repay our time with as certain and useful deductions as our pursuits in some other branches." Most of Jefferson's letter takes issue with Volney's observations on climate and on yellow fever. At some length, Jefferson compared the gray skies of Europe to the azure blue of America and corrected Volney's views on the yellow fever. But he said not a word about Volney's observations on white settlers or anarchical Indians, nor did he respond to Volney's doubts about the existence of a practical route to the Pacific up the Missouri River and across the Rocky Mountains.[15]

Jefferson also ignored Volney's series of interviews with the Miami leader Little Turtle, which from the standpoint of ethnographic method is the most interesting part of Volney's book. While at Vincennes, Volney had been advised that William Wells, the white captive of the Miamis who had learned "several dialects" (particularly Miami) and was now serving as interpreter for General Anthony Wayne, was the best person to contact in the Indian country. He did not have an opportunity to consult with Wells during the trip, but by good fortune Wells arrived in Philadelphia a year later as the guide and interpreter for Little Turtle. Little Turtle was already known to Americans as a famous war chief who had delivered a catastrophic defeat to the American army in the northwest. Now he had come to Philadelphia to solicit Congress and the Society of Friends for technical assistance, because he believed that the Indians in the Ohio country must adopt the white mode of agriculture.[16]

At the time Volney learned of his presence, Little Turtle had been inoculated for small pox and was receiving medical treatment for gout and rheumatism. Volney obtained an introduction to Wells and "the savage chief," explained that he wanted to study Native American languages and customs, and gained their consent to be interviewed. Volney made "nine or ten" visits to their quarters in January and February 1798. The method of

Little Turtle, Miami war chief. Lithograph by C. B. J. Févret de Saint Mémin after a portrait by Gilbert Stuart, 1797. Courtesy of the Smithsonian Institution.

inquiry was to obtain a Miami vocabulary, which Volney duly published as an appendix to his book. The list of English nouns to which Miami equivalents were provided (in both English and French orthography) substantially overlaps Jefferson's printed list, but Jefferson's includes kinship terms which are lacking in Volney's. Volney, on the other hand, attempts to provide Miami equivalents of the conjugations of several English verbs (to eat, to drink, to beat), and Volney was acutely aware of the problem of rendering native sounds in European alphabets.

But the linguistic inquiry also provided an entry into other subjects. As Volney put it. "In the course of conversation many curious remarks occurred, which I preserved with the more care, because the facts, coming without preparation, were the less to be suspected of alteration, and the habit of seeing me, added to my being a frenchman, diminished in the Little Tortoise that spirit of suspicion and distrust, which sway the savages in all their discourse. Every day after my visit I wrote down what appeared to me most interesting; and these observations, united with those I collected during my travels from the most judicious witnesses, form the materials of what I have reduced to order."

Part of Volney's information came directly from Wells, in English (in which Volney evidently was fluent), part from Little Turtle, via Wells as interpreter. The conversations were not guided by a formal schedule but flowed freely among subjects of mutual interest and curiosity: clothing, skin color and physiognomy, racial origins, child-rearing, values, aids and impediments to acculturation, the blood feud, relative rates of population growth. In fact, Volney was so much impressed by the Miami chief, "a person superior in understanding to most of the savages," that he went on to compare him favorably to the *philosophes* of Europe.[17]

Whatever the worth of his specific accounts of the Wabash Indians' drunkenness or of Little Turtle's eloquence, Volney's main contribution to the development of ethnology lay in method. His remarkable innovation was that his field work was conducted as a purely scholarly enterprise; it was not an incidental by-product of a diplomatic, commercial, or military expedition, or even of a tour undertaken for pleasure and adventure. Volney was a resident professional observer who learned the language of the people he intended to study and recorded data systematically, very much in the style of a twentieth-century ethnographer. When circumstances prevented residential field work, he turned to another standard research technique, identifying a capable interpreter and a prime informant and interviewing them on linguistic and other subjects in extended sessions, paying due attention to the establishment of good rapport. To be sure, his categories of inquiry were unsophisticated by later standards, but, like Jefferson's, they were appropriate to his time.

It is difficult to judge whether Volney's example influenced Jefferson. Jefferson, of course, was contemptuous of the observations of casual travelers, which he dismissed as "mere fable." He admired the tradition of comparative sociology exemplified by Montesquieu, whose analyses of European polities Jefferson read carefully, and by Alexander Humboldt, whose treatise on the geography and governments of the countries of New Spain, based on extensive travels through Central and South America and the Caribbean between 1799 and 1804, he praised as a "great work" full of "treasures of . . . learning."[18] He himself habitually compared Greek, Roman, what he imagined to be old Anglo-Saxon, British, and American institutions, and contrasted "priest-ridden" monarchical societies with secular democratic ones, for guidance in framing policy for America. Insofar as Volney's work belonged to that tradition of the comparative study of civilizations, like his *Travels in Syria* and *Les ruines,*

Jefferson admired it. But very fine-grained studies of contemporary Indian institutions did not especially interest him. As a scholar, Jefferson was personally uninterested in those Indians who were living in a "middle ground" of mixed white and native institutions. In principle he favored stationing resident "philosophical observers" in Indian communities, but in practice as an administrator he was content to leave the ethnographic documenting of Indian history, manners, and customs to the grosser observations of military men, like Lewis and Clark, and missionaries, like the Brafferton professors. His own scholarly interests were primarily in Indian origins.

Jefferson was also acquainted with another student of the Indians, John Heckewelder, whose researches in the field demonstrated the merit of Jefferson's call for resident philosophical observers. Heckewelder (one of the authorities to whom Jefferson turned to verify his account of the Logan massacre) was the same age as Jefferson, an English-born son of Moravian refugees from Germany. In 1754 he had come with his parents to the Moravian settlement at Bethlehem in Pennsylvania, where he was trained in the European manner as a multilingual missionary. Heckewelder was elected to the American Philosophical Society in 1797, in recognition of his knowledge of Indian languages and traditions, and after his retirement from the mission field he had become the protégé and collaborator of Peter Stephen DuPonceau, a friend of Jefferson's and the society's resident expert in the fledgling science of linguistics (see Chapter 10). His *History, Manners, and Customs of the Indian Nations Who Once Inhabited Pennsylvania and the Neighboring States* was first published in 1819 by the society.[19]

French Enlightenment Ethnography

The growing French tradition of sending off professional observers like Volney found its most focused expression in an organization founded in late 1799 to promote "anthropology": the comparative study of man. *Société des Observateurs de L'homme,* ancestor to the more famous *Société d'Anthropologie de Paris,* embraced physical anthropology, cultural anthropology (the customs and usages of peoples), and linguistics, aiming for a comparative dictionary of all known languages. This grand design to study "men and manners" around the world, which Rousseau had suggested as early as 1755 in his *Dissertation on the Origin and Foundation of the Inequality of*

Man, attracted as early members a sparkling array of French scientists, including the biologists Cuvier and Lamarck, the psychiatrist Pinel, the explorer Bougainville, the linguist Destutt de Tracy, and of course Volney. Its motto was *connais-toi toi-même,* perhaps an echo of Alexander Pope's famous couplet in *An Essay on Man:*

> Know then thyself; presume not God to scan,
> The proper study of mankind is man.

The society was encouraged in its work by the *Institut National,* the premier institution of Napoleon's scientific establishment, of which Volney was a member, and it was able to mount one scientific expedition, to Australia. Although the expedition itself was a disaster, it was guided by a remarkably sophisticated memoir on research methodology, prepared by Citizen Degerando, an associate member of the *Classe des sciences morales et politiques* of the institute. Degerando was contemptuous of the incomplete and biased accounts of societies visited by travelers who stayed only briefly, for other purposes, and never learned the language. He demanded prolonged residence, fluency in the alien language, and systematic observation according to a predetermined set of standard categories that would permit comparison and eventual generalization. The society fell afoul of the imperial transformation of Napoleon's administration and passed out of existence in 1804, along with the institute's *Classe des sciences morales et politiques,* to which Volney had been appointed. Its spirit, however, lived on in America, perhaps in attenuated form, but eventually to flourish in the linguistic and ethnological programs of the American Philosophical Society and its friends.[20]

Part of the French interest in the comparative study of man was carried forward in America by the wives of French diplomats and soldiers. Among these were two ladies of Paris who accompanied their husbands to the United States in the first decade of the nineteenth century, Mme Victor DuPont and the Baroness Hyde de Neuville. Victor DuPont was the elder of the sons of Pierre Samuel DuPont de Nemours, the friend and correspondent of Jefferson. His brother Eleuthere Irene would found the famous gunpowder works along the Brandywine, where Victor would eventually also establish himself as proprietor of a woolen mill. Victor was a perennial visitor to the United States on various diplomatic missions in the 1780s and 90s, and in 1802 he and his wife arrived in the United States to stay. After failing in business in New York, he acquired land in the new Holland Company purchase in western New York and in 1806 moved with his wife and children to the frontier community of Angelica, where a number of other French emigrés had gathered. He built a farmhouse, established a tannery, opened a country store, and soon was commissioned a major in the militia and appointed clerk of Allegheny County. The family remained only three years, however, removing to join brother Eleuthere on the Brandywine in 1809.[21]

The little town of Angelica was situated on the upper waters of the Genesee River, not far from Caneadea, one of the small Seneca reservations that were left along the banks of the Genesee after the Treaty of Big Tree in 1797. Victor's wife, Gabrielle, took a lively interest in her new surroundings in America, an interest she shared with her friend, the Baroness Hyde de Neuville, who paid a long visit to Angelica in 1808. The Baroness was a watercolorist and made drawings of the first log cabin at Angelica and of one of the early settlers. But she is chiefly famous for her paintings of several of New York state's Indians in 1807 and 1808, remarkable both for their early date and for the care with which she delineated costume and pose.[22]

Gabrielle DuPont's contribution to the ethnography of the Iroquois is less well known. Some time after her arrival in Angelica, she wrote a quasi-fictional account of the ongoing process of "civilization" among the nearby Senecas and of the patterns of interaction between them and the white settlers. The novel is an account of an Indian reformer, Tippewa, who, as a result of divine inspiration, is passionately convinced of his people's need to acquire not only the technology but also some of the spirit of European civilization, but without abandoning the best values of their own culture. He makes friends with a philosophical white storekeeper, Cheriwanee, with whom he has endless conversations on these subjects, presumably in French. Eventually he sends his son and a young girl of the tribe to France for their education, and on their return years later the son takes over as chief of the tribe, over which Tippewa has gained "entire supremacy," and marries the girl in a proper Catholic ceremony.

Interspersed among philosophical conversations (a literary device acceptable at the time for developing not only social issues but character) and the sometimes forced twists and turns of the plot are sketches and vignettes that display the spirit of the French ethnographer at his or her best. Mme DuPont was no Jane Austen, but she was probably an equally keen observer of the local scene. Her account of her visit to Caneadea (which she misnames Oneida) is a vivid description of a Seneca village in the midst of social change: a field of stumps, horses grazing among fruit trees, warriors and women, deer, bear, panther, and buffalo skins, scenes of indolence—but most notably no mention of liquor (see page 125). Mme DuPont was not an unqualified admirer of the "uncivilized" Indians but she felt compassion for them, surrounded as they were by whites who would soon "altogether banish the poor loitering savages in spite of the humane measures adopted by the government to protect their waning independence." She joined in sympathy with Tippewa, who wanted Cheriwanee to go with a deputation of Indians to Washington to protest the seizure of land in violation of a treaty by "the *Man King* [perhaps a play on the name of one of Jefferson's successors as President, James Monroe] who by sad chance to us governs here in these distant parts instead of our own people."

What Mme DuPont was describing actually was Seneca society in the midst of a revitalization movement led by a religious prophet, Handsome

First cottage at Angelica, New York. Watercolor and pencil by Baroness Hyde de Neuville, 1808. © Collection of The New-York Historical Society.

"Mary, Squah of the Oneida Tribe." Watercolor and pencil by Baroness Hyde de Neuville, 1807. © Courtesy of The New-York Historical Society.

Gabrielle DuPont's Springtime Visit to a Seneca Reservation

[After crossing a meadow where Indian horses are grazing,] presently will the traveller perceive those poor Children of Nature, some pretty much as She created them, others miserably and oddly accountred. Some few on horse-back in the guise of Warriors tho forgetting or rather despising the restraint of nether garments, otherwise pompously clad in our best clothes and most indifferent gold laces, Feathers short rare and of brightest hues ornamenting their Caps, and worn always as badges of skill and cunning in their many exploits. As to the Women or *Squaws* their aspect saddens the observer at the first glance, and still more so on a closer inspection. They present much less of the semblance of beings freely enjoying the gifts which Nature opens to them than they are the image of servitude and brutality. There is a silly & undetermined expression in their countenances which is anything but propessing [sic] and which is peculiar to them. They are remarkable for their long and lanky hair, and large feet turned inwards, their faces rather square than oval, bespattered with paints of different hues, their cheeks, ears and noses laden with tawdry ornaments, their waists and arms generally secluded by a blanket not always clean, but in whichever light they are seen it is always under an unpleasant aspect. These poor Indians have cause occasionally to be surprised at the impinging boldness of the Pale faced Neighbours as they term the White Settlers. This interference is irksome to them tho' rendered less so from habit. Seldom do they express Curiosity or Surprise, they neither raise nor turn aside their heads at one's approach, following quietly their occupation nor evincing by word or gesture having noticed the interruptions. It were as well however not to try their patience too much, nor allow one's visit to be of long duration lest it might excite their suspicion, also to endeavour to be to them what they are to us when visiting the *Settlement,* to follow one's path and not seek to initiate one's self too much in their concerns. They have no Police to protect their rights and [illegible] their peace, but still do they wish to be and indeed *are* masters in the narrow homes left them by the encroaching Whites.

Madame Victor C. (Gabrielle) DuPont. Oil on canvas by Louis Leopold Boilly, c. 1796–1802. Courtesy of the Hagley Museum and Library.

Lake. The absence of any mention of drunken Indians was not a prudish avoidance on her part; Handsome Lake's temperance drive had made teetotallers of most of the Senecas by this time. The mingling of the two communities in an effort to save a child dragged into the forest by a wolf, and in the country store whose appearance and functions are described in living detail, are valid reflections of the efforts at racial accommodation of the prophet and of the Quakers on the Allegheny Reservation a few score miles away to the west of Angelica. All in all, despite some lapses (including a tendency to use Algonkian terms like "manitoo" and "kitchi manitoo"), her novel is an extraordinary achievement in recognizing the power of religious enthusiasm in bringing about major cultural change.[23]

But this insight was denied to Jefferson, as was Volney's and Gabrielle DuPont's interest in describing the rich texture of daily life. Unlike Jefferson, she knew that she was only an ethnographer, referring to herself as a "traveller coming to study their ways" (both the reservation Indian and the white communities). The work apparently was never published, but it has been preserved, along with other autobiographical narratives, among the Victor DuPont Papers at the Hagley Museum and Library. There is no reason to suppose that Jefferson ever saw it; but Gabrielle was well aware of his Indian policies and disapproved of some of them. She certainly moved in the social circle of Jefferson's friends and acquaintances, and it is not impossible that he heard of her efforts to study the Indians. Her husband, Victor, had been naturalized as an American citizen in 1800, and in 1804 he had corresponded with Jefferson. In 1815 he accompanied his father, Jefferson's philosophical friend DuPont de Nemours, on a visit to Monticello. Victor's brother Eleuthere was also a correspondent of Jefferson's and in addition an active member of the American Philosophical Society.

But even if Jefferson was exposed to her ideas, he would view the contemporary cultural mixtures on the Indian reserves and the ongoing processes of culture change as evanescent phenomena, temporary phases in the transformation to civilized society, not authentically Indian and thus of no scholarly interest.

The Indians Jefferson Knew

So far as we know, Jefferson never attempted to visit any of the communities of trans-Appalachian Indians with whom so much of his public policy dealt. But he did meet with numerous Indian delegations in his various official capacities as governor of Virginia, secretary of state, and President. The roster of names is impressive: du Coigne, McGillivray, Handsome Lake, Little Turtle, Shahaka, and many others. That he enjoyed personal association with these Indian visitors is certain: he maintained helpful contact with du Coigne over the years; was solicitous of Shahaka's safe turn to the Mandan village (see Chapter 8); saw to inoculations for small pox; went out of his way to provide for the comfort of Little Turtle.

His intimacy with some of these visitors on at least one occasion provoked resentment in the European diplomatic corps. Jefferson customarily held receptions for visitors to the United States on New Year's day, and January 1, 1806, was no exception; Jefferson, dressed in a black suit ("his gala dress on these occasions"), welcomed his guests as usual. But this time those invited included the Indian delegation sent forward by Lewis and Clark—a number of Osages and some representatives from five other tribes, more than twenty men in all. The secretary to the British legation, Augustus Foster, complained in his journal that Jefferson spent so much time apart with his Indian guests that the British minister, Anthony Merry, who was chronically offended by Jefferson's casual manner, took it

Chief of the Little Osages. Crayon on paper by C. B. J. Févret de Saint Mémin, c. 1807. © Collection of The New-York Historical Society.

as an insult to the Crown's representative and departed in a huff after five minutes. Foster reported that Jefferson was "as much attached to them from Philanthropy and because they were savages as if they were his own children, while he paid them infinitely more attention than he ever vouchsafed to show to a Foreign Minister."[24]

It was Jefferson's habit to experiment with his Indian visitors, trying to elicit some expression of "astonishment or surprise" at the novelties he showed them, but he was never able to succeed until wine-coolers filled with ice appeared on the table. It was a hot July day, and the Osage delegation did react to the presence of cracked ice with wonder and awe.[25]

This group created a major sensation in the capital. They were exotically accoutred, some naked from the waist up, heads shaven, faces painted red, ears green, black stripes from crown to chin, feathers and quills tied to long hair in back. Another delegation including the Mandan chief Shahaka and his family and a number of Osages arrived about a year later. Portraits were painted of a number of them by St. Mémin (see page 365);

they were the subject of detailed accounts in the *National Intelligencer.* But ethnographic research was not Jefferson's purpose in bringing the Indians to Washington. They were here to be impressed by the power and benevolence of the United States and to be recruited as agents of tribal accommodation. There would have been little time in either his own or their schedules for the patient collection of vocabularies and the conducting of interviews about native traditions.[26]

More and more, Jefferson's concern focused on the search for the historical origins of the doomed Indian race. John Adams, with whom he corresponded on this subject, himself was not interested in Indians in a scholarly way, and he saw no point in research into their ancient past and ultimate point of origin. He put his opinion forcefully to Jefferson: "The various ingenuity which has been displayed in inventions of hypothesis, to account for the original population of America, and the immensity of learning profusely expended to support them, have appeared to me for a longer time than I can precisely recollect what the physicians call the *Literas nihil Sanantes.* Whether serpents' teeth were sown here and sprang up men; whether men and women dropped from the clouds upon this Atlantic Island; whether the Almighty created them here, or whether they emigrated from Europe, are questions of no moment to the present or future happiness of man. Neither agriculture, commerce, manufactures, fisheries, science, literature, taste, religion, morals, nor any other good will be promoted, or any evil averted, by any discoveries that can be made in answer to these questions."[27] Both Adams and Jefferson professed sympathy for the Indians; but only Jefferson strove for some measure of understanding.

CHAPTER FIVE

In Search of Ancient Americans

THOMAS JEFFERSON was red-headed and ruddy-complexioned like the Welsh Tudors who once occupied the British throne and sent forth the first colonists of Virginia. But Jefferson was also heir to another ancestral tradition, one which claimed that at least some of the aboriginal inhabitants of America were Welshmen like himself. According to legend, in 1170 Prince Madoc of Wales and his company sailed westward in ten ships and never returned; it was said that the adventurers reached America and left descendants among the Indians. The story of Prince Madoc gained new currency in Queen Elizabeth's time because it rationalized the Tudor claim that the British presence in the Americas was far antecedent to the explorations of Columbus, Cortez, and Pizarro. Hakluyt's *Voyages* (1582–1600) popularized the Madoc legend, and supposed sightings of blond, blue-eyed Indians who spoke Welsh periodically reinforced it.

Jefferson himself had heard reports that far up the Missouri River a blond, blue-eyed, Welsh-speaking tribe—the Mandans—still existed and were the architects of great fortifications requiring skills exceeding those of neighboring peoples. Jonathan Carver, in his *Travels* (1778), among others, had claimed that the builders of the great mounds and earthworks of the Mississippi watershed were American descendants of the Welsh prince and his twelfth-century explorers. Jefferson read some of the works of these eighteenth-century purveyors of the Madoc theory and seems to have been sufficiently intrigued to ask Lewis and Clark to inquire about blond, blue-eyed, Welsh-speaking Indians as they explored the Missouri River. The Corps of Discovery did in fact encounter Mandans answering this physical description, and Jefferson went to particular pains to entertain the Mandan chief Shahaka when a Mandan delegation visited Washington in 1806.

Jefferson habitually sought precedents for his moral, legal, and political views in paragons of antiquity—in Jesus, in the democratic freemen, authors, and orators of ancient Greece and republican Rome, and in the sturdy yeomen of Anglo-Saxon England. Perhaps, as Jefferson was severing his roots in Britain and the Old World, he found congenial the thought that he and his fellow colonists had collateral roots in a Native American antiquity.

The Mound-Builders

The vast domain of pre-Revolutionary Greater Virginia, stretching by charter from sea to sea, was strewn with the relics of by-gone Native American civilizations—the remains of pyramids, mounds, ceremonial enclosures, and stone-walled roads, the oldest of which date back 5,000 years. Such structures were found west of the Appalachians in the Ohio valley, in the southern provinces, and across the Mississippi along the lower reaches of the Missouri. These monumental earthworks ("build-

Grave Creek mound in present-day West Virginia. Engraving, 1848.
Courtesy of the British Museum.

ings," as a recent authority, Roger Kennedy, has insisted they be called) were large and quite distinct from the small burial mounds or "barrows" of the kind excavated by Jefferson along the banks of the Rivanna River. Some of them were pyramids hundreds of yards across at the base and a hundred feet high. Others were enormous walled enclosures, whose construction required architectural and engineering techniques for laying out nearly perfect squares, circles, and octagons. Although these buildings were commonly called "forts" by early observers—and fanciful images of Armageddon-like battles were concocted to account for their construction—they were actually ceremonial centers. Some in the south were still being used for ritual assemblies well into the colonial period.[1]

The ceremonial mounds had been observed by French and English traders and military men since early in the eighteenth century at least. The massive Grave Creek Mound, a few miles south of present Wheeling, West Virginia, and others were seen by George Washington on surveying trips as early as 1772. The Moravian missionary David Zeisberger recorded in his diary of 1772 the discovery of huge earthworks on the upper Muskingum River, in present Ohio. The Reverend David Jones published an account of mounds along the Scioto River near present Circleville, Ohio, in the *Royal American Magazine* in 1775 and had mentioned these mounds in his earlier book, *A Journal of Two Visits Made to Some Nations of Indians in . . . 1772 and 1773*.

His account in the *Journal* (printed in 1774) lamented a lost civilization: "North of this town [Chillicaathee, a Shawnee settlement on Paint Creek] are to be seen the remains of an old fortification, the area of which may be fifteen acres. It lies near four square, and appears to have had gates at each corner, and in the middle likewise. From the west middle gate, went a circular entrenchment including about ten acres, which seems designed to defend on all quarters. This circle included a spring. Mr. Irwine [an Indian trader] told that another exactly in this form is to be seen on the river Siota, the banks of which remain so high as to intercept sight of men on horseback. 'Tis evident to all travelers that this country has been inhabited formerly by a martial race of mankind enjoying the use of iron, for such entrenchments, as appear in various places, could not have been made otherwise: but of this part of antiquity, we shall remain ignorant."[2] Communication about these ruins by word of mouth and written correspondence was no doubt extensive as well.

Yet Jefferson does not mention these "forts" in his *Notes on the State of*

Virginia. In a preface to his report on the archeological dig near Charlottesville, he remarked: "I know of no such thing existing as an Indian monument: for I would not honor with that name arrow points, stone hatchets, stone pipes, and half-shapen images. Of labor on the large scale, I think there is no remain as respectable as would be a common ditch for the draining of lands: unless indeed it be the Barrows, of which many are to be found all over this country. These are of different sizes, some of them constructed of earth, and some of loose stone. That they were repositories of the dead, has been obvious to all."[3]

Even giving due credit to Jefferson's customary and prudent scientific skepticism, his failure even to mention the massive earthworks reported by early travelers is difficult to understand. Granted, he might have missed Jones's book and report in the *Royal American Magazine;* he could have dismissed Carver as an unreliable source, which he was; and of course the Moravian missionaries' diaries were not yet published. But Jefferson knew George Washington, George Rogers Clark, and many other western travelers very well and is likely to have conversed with them about western lands because of their mutual interest in land speculation and military expeditions. At a minimum, there were two concentrations of mound-builder architecture that Jefferson should have known about by the time he was writing the *Notes:* the numerous mounds along the Great Kanawha River, and the Old Fort at Redstone.

In the case of Great Kanawha mounds, Jefferson, as we have seen, had purchased shares in real estate ventures there and on the Little Kanawha. He believed that a portage or canal between the river's headwaters and those of the James or Roanoke rivers might become a commercial route to the Ohio country.[4] Patrick Henry and the other speculators associated with him in these ventures would not have committed monies to the project without having received some reports or surveys of the region. And such reports could hardly have missed the structures Jefferson's friend Bishop James Madison (president of William and Mary College and cousin of the statesman bearing the same name) later described in a paper published by the American Philosophical Society in 1803: "Upon the Kanhawa, to the extent of 80 or an 100 miles, and also upon many of the rivers which empty their waters into it, there is scarcely a square mile in which you will not meet with several [mounds]. Indeed they are as thick, and as irregularly dispersed, as you have seen the habitations of farmers, or planters, in a rich and well settled country." Madison emphasized the monumental scale of these supposed "fortifications," which he correctly declared to be no fortifications at all but mortuary and ceremonial centers. On the "low grounds" of the Great Kanawha he found one that he compared to the pyramids of Egypt: a truncated cone, 140 yards in circumference at its base, 40 feet in height, with a flat platform on top about 12 feet in diameter. He estimated it to be forty times the size of Jefferson's Rivanna barrow.[5]

As impressive as the relics in the Great Kanawha valley were, they were dwarfed by the remains of the so-called Old Fort at Redstone, a monument of particular interest to Virginians of Jefferson's time. This was originally a massive pre-Columbian earthwork whose moat and wall enclosed a large interior court. The Old Fort was located on the south bank of the Monongahela River, near Redstone Creek (the present site of Brownsville, Pennsylvania)—the first convenient landing and embarkation point on the Ohio drainage for travelers who crossed the Alleghenies from Fort Cumberland on Wills Creek, at the head of navigation on the Potomac. Redstone quickly became a strategic center for Virginia's trade into the Ohio valley.

Virginia claimed sovereignty over the area, which lay within the charter limits of the Ohio Company of Virginia. In 1753 the Old Fort was described on a company map as follows: "There has been an Indian Fort there some years ago. The Ditch is now to be seen. Here the Indians always fled upon an Alarm as it was reckoned the strongest Fort they had, several thousands have lost their lives in the Attack of it, but it never was yet taken."[6] Another contemporary source, Colonel Henry Bouquet, described the structure in 1759 as "the Remains of an Indian Retrenchment of a circular form," perched on a hill overlooking the river. Across the river rose a "conical pointed hill, the highest eminence in view," perhaps suggestive of the great conical mound left by the architects of Grave Creek Mound on the Ohio, some forty miles to the west.

As late as 1791 the Old Fort at Redstone was still intact enough to be used as the first meeting place for the organizers of the Whiskey Rebellion. But by 1810 the Indian structure and the later colonial fort built in 1759 had been virtually obliterated by the thriving town of Brownsville, although small mounds were left and the remains of the ancient ramparts and Indian bones were still being uncovered by settlers when they dug cellars for their new homes.[7]

As a youth, in the course of learning about the events of the French and

Indian War, Jefferson must have become aware of Redstone as the base of the Ohio Company's operations in the Ohio valley and of the road from Wills Creek to Redstone. Redstone was the intended destination of the regiment under the command of his father's neighbor and partner, Colonel Joshua Fry, in 1754 (an expedition directed by George Washington after Fry's death at Fort Cumberland); and Braddock's Road to and from the site of Washington's defeat near Fort Duquesne took him along the valley of the Redstone.

In 1766, after the French and Indian War ended, the Redstone valley and specifically the site of the Old Fort was occupied by a group of settlers acting in defiance of the Ohio Company's charter. This community, mostly composed of Virginians and Marylanders, had been formed by Thomas Cresap, the original surveyor of the path from Wills Creek to Redstone, who had obtained an improper private land grant from the Six Nations. The presence of this illegal settlement was galling to both Virginia and Pennsylvania authorities, for it lay in an area of disputed sovereignty between the two provinces (Pennsylvania's western boundary had been specified as to its longitude but never actually surveyed). The boundary dispute with Pennsylvania occupied Jefferson's attention as a delegate to the Continental Congress in 1776, and one of his last actions as governor of Virginia was to agree to a postponement of the astronomical observations necessary to the final survey.[8]

A leading figure among these outlaws was Thomas Cresap's son Michael Cresap, who, it was claimed, murdered a Delaware Indian chief at Redstone in 1767. This and other murders by the Redstone squatters for a time threatened to abort the forthcoming treaty at Fort Stanwix, by which the Six Nations ceded their land east of the Ohio River.[9] Michael Cresap obtained title to the Old Fort at Redstone from Virginia some time before 1774, the year in which John Logan's kin were murdered, precipitating Lord Dunmore's War.

All of this was known to Jefferson. Given the history and strategic importance of Redstone, it seems highly improbable that Jefferson would never have heard of the Old Fort there (let alone other monumental architecture in the Ohio valley) before putting pen to paper in 1781 for the *Notes.* Why, then, his omission of any mention of the road from Wills Creek to Redstone and his outright denial of the existence of any Indian monument larger than a drainage ditch?

Probably part of the explanation is that he was merely expressing conventional doctrine: the Indians were "savages" and therefore incapable of monumental architecture, and accounts of great fortifications were mere Indian fables and tales told by travelers who exaggerated the size of small burial mounds like the one excavated by Jefferson himself. Part of the answer may also be that at the time Jefferson favored improving waterways as commercial routes to the west, rather than roads like the one from Fort Cumberland to Redstone Old Fort. But an even more practical explanation presents itself if one takes into account the prime purpose of the *Notes,* which was to attract European investment. Mention of massive Indian fortifications and the slaughter of thousands of combatants would not accord well with the picture drawn in the *Notes* of the Indians as either vanished, vanishing, or peaceable and capable of being civilized.

As the number of reports confirming the existence of the great monuments increased, Jefferson's denial of the mound-builders' culture could not be maintained. In the late 1780s, the Society of the Cincinnati and John Cleves Symmes's newly chartered Ohio Company began their settlements along the north shore of the Ohio River in the neighborhood of Cincinnati and Marietta. On the Muskingum at Marietta, General Samuel Parsons made a map of the extensive earthworks found there and sent a copy and description to Ezra Stiles, President of Yale College, who in turn forwarded Parsons's letter to Jefferson in Paris. Parsons claimed that bricks had been found.

Jefferson's response to Stiles in September 1786 was still skeptical. He observed: "When we reflect how long we have inhabited those parts of America which lie between the Alleghany & the ocean, that no monument has ever been found in them which indicated the use of iron among its aboriginal inhabitants, that they were as far advanced in arts, at least, as the inhabitants on the other side of the Alleghany, a good deal of infidelity may be excused as to the new discoveries which suppose regular fortifications of brickwork to have been in use among the Indians on the waters of the Ohio. Entrenchments of earth they might indeed make: but brick is more difficult. The art of making it may have preceded the use of iron, but it would suppose a greater degree of industry than men in the hunter state usually possess. I should like to know whether general Parsons himself saw actual bricks among the remains of fortification."[10]

But a year later he had come to accept the reality of the mounds, pyramids, and other large structures of the Ohio valley. His consultant on Indian matters for the *Notes,* Charles Thomson, had written to him on the subject and had enclosed a letter from Symmes, who speculated, as had William Robertson, that the earthworks had been created by the highly civilized Aztecs and then abandoned under attack by the savage hordes around them. Jefferson, in a letter to Thomson of September 20, 1787, conceded the existence of "the antiquities found in the western country." But with proper scientific caution he urged that more exact research be undertaken (see next page).[11]

Also in 1787 a monograph, *Observations on Some Parts of Natural History,* was published by Benjamin Smith Barton, a young American medical student at Edinburgh. It described the mounds and in particular exuberantly extolled the seventy-foot-high Grave Creek Mound as a "stupendous eminence . . . One of the most august monuments of remote antiquity."[12] Barton could not believe that Indians could raise such noble piles of earth, and so he attributed the structures to Danish invaders, notable builders of barrows in Europe, who later, in his theory, would found the Toltec civilization of Mexico. Jefferson, whose own book was being brought out in London in the same year, may very well have seen this early treatise of Barton's, and the two men would later become associated in linguistic research and the affairs of the American Philosophical Society.

About this same time Jefferson was expressing interest in the theory of Dr. Andrew Turnbull, a Scottish physician of Charleston, South Carolina, that the Creek Indians were descended from Carthaginians whose ships strayed from Hannibal's fleet and wound up in America. "I see nothing impossible in his conjecture. I am glad he means to appeal to the similarity of language."[13] But he does not mention the speculation that there were mounds of Carthaginian origin and would probably have rejected the idea, as he did other theories of trans-Atlantic origins for the mound-builders, such as those of his fellow authority on the west, John Filson; but he could accept speculations of affiliation based on "affinities of sound."[14]

After he returned from France in 1789, Jefferson began to receive even more convincing evidence of the high culture that once had spread over the central part of the continent. In 1790 Harry Innes, his agent in Kentucky, sent him a description of an Indian "fort" near Lexington, along with a ten-inch statuette of a kneeling woman giving birth. Jefferson was delighted, calling it "the best piece of workmanship I ever saw from their hands." About the same time, the newly appointed governor of the Northwest Territory, Arthur St. Clair, began sending Jefferson Indian artifacts from his capital at Cincinnati. Two other kneeling figures, from Tennessee,

Jefferson on Theories about the Mound-Builders

I wish that the persons who go thither would make very exact descriptions of what they see of that kind, without forming any theories. The moment a person forms a theory, his imagination sees, in every object, only the traits which favor that theory. But it is too early to form theories on those antiquities. We must wait with patience till more facts are collected. I wish your Philosophical Society would collect exact descriptions of the several monuments as yet known, and insert them naked in their Transactions, and continue their attention to those hereafter to be discovered. Patience and observation may enable us in time, to solve the problem, whether those who formed the scattering monuments in the western country, were colonies sent off from Mexico, or the founders of Mexico itself? Whether they were the descendants or the progenitors of the Asian Redmen? The Mexican tradition, mentioned by Dr. Robertson, is an evidence, but a feeble one in favor of the one opinion. The number of languages radically different, is a strong evidence in favor of a contrary one.

were added to Jefferson's Indian collection at Monticello in 1799.[15] And a spate of publications and personal correspondence throughout the 90s, and indeed for the rest of his life, kept Jefferson informed of the grandeur and number of the Indian architectural constructions.

In 1793, for instance, the American Philosophical Society in its *Transactions* published an account by Major Jonathan Heart of the works at a number of sites in Ohio, including those at Grave Creek, Marietta, and Chillicothe; he had already described the Marietta mounds in the *Columbian Magazine* in 1787. Heart's contribution was posthumous, for he had been killed in battle by the Indians in 1791. Jefferson was also familiar with the renowned botanist William Bartram's *Travels through North and South Carolina,* published in Philadelphia in 1791, which contained accounts of southern mounds, and cited the work in private annotations to his copy of the Stockdale edition. He talked and corresponded on the subject of mounds with Winthrop Sargent, fellow member of the American Philosophical Society, secretary of the Northwest Territory, and later governor of the Mississippi Territory.[16]

Clearly Jefferson was convinced of the existence of monumental architecture west of the Appalachians by the time he became president of the American Philosophical Society in 1797. In that same year he became a member of the society's newly formed Committee on History, which issued an appeal for information on a variety of subjects, including the Indian mounds. The committee wished "to obtain accurate plans, drawings, and description of whatever is interesting . . . and especially of ancient fortifications, Tumuli, and other Indian works of art, ascertaining the materials composing them, their contents, the purposes for which they were probably designed, &c."[17] And six years later, in his instructions to Meriwether Lewis on the eve of the Corps of Discovery's departure up the Missouri, Jefferson included among the kinds of information about the Indian nations he desired the category "their . . . monuments." In the fall of 1803, Jefferson was impressed by surveyor William Lytle's maps of "ancient fortifications" in the neighborhood of Cincinnati and requested more information about "Those works of Antiquity."[18]

These Jeffersonian queries about monuments, forts, and tumuli refer to them as being Indian in origin, not the relics of wandering Aztecs, Vikings, or long-lost Jewish tribes. Jefferson was impatient with exotic speculations and tended to minimize the size and significance of the structures. In this he had support from his friend Constantin Volney, who had personally viewed with admiration the stone monuments of Egypt and the Near East and who deprecated the Indian earthworks in his *View of the Climate and Soil of the United States of America.* The works along the Ohio gave "no indication of skill in the military or in any other art," he claimed.[19] Bishop James Madison agreed with Jefferson and Volney, arguing in an 1804 paper in the Philosophical Society's *Transactions* that the earthworks had been constructed by people with no higher technology than that of the Indians of recent times.[20]

It was not until he had retired from the office of President, however, that Jefferson became fully aware of the quantity, size, and grandeur of the monumental architecture of the mound-builders. A western traveler, Henry Brackenridge, in July 1813 sent Jefferson some reprints of his newspaper accounts of the hundreds of ancient structures at Cahokia, across from St. Louis, and other sites along the Mississippi and Missouri rivers.

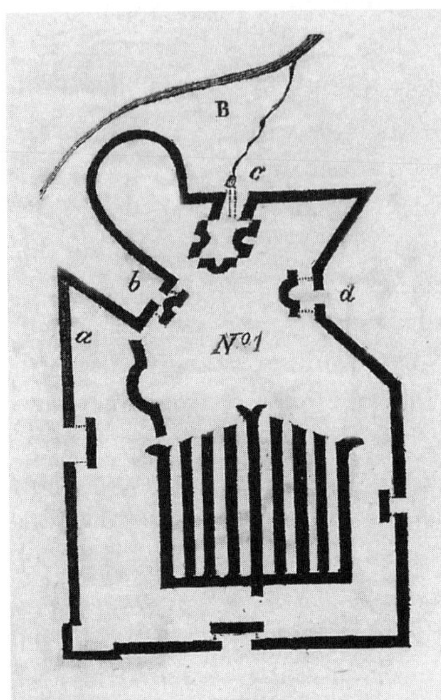

East Fork works, drawn by surveyor William Lytle, c. 1803, and published by Hugh Williamson, *Observations on the Climate in Different Parts of America*, New York, 1811.
Courtesy of Houghton Library.

Jefferson was deeply impressed by these descriptions of the ancient "fortifications" that Brackenridge had found in the west, and he confessed that he "never before had an idea they were so numerous."[21] In 1820 Caleb Atwater, a postmaster at Circleville, Ohio, described the remarkable geometrical precision with which the circle and square earthworks in the vicinity had been laid out, based on measurements more exact than the local white inhabitants would have been capable of making.[22]

It was Albert Gallatin, however, Jefferson's former secretary of the U.S. treasury, who continued Jefferson's cautious approach to the study of the mounds. Although archaeology was not his main interest, he did include under "General Observations" in his *Synopsis* several pages of discussion of "those ancient tumuli, fortifications, and other remnants, both east and west of the Mississippi." He noted that their origin was unknown to the Indians presently occupying the area. He dismissed the possibility that these earthworks had been created by European immigrants. "There is nothing in their construction, or in the remnants which they contain, indicative of a much more advanced state of civilization than that of the

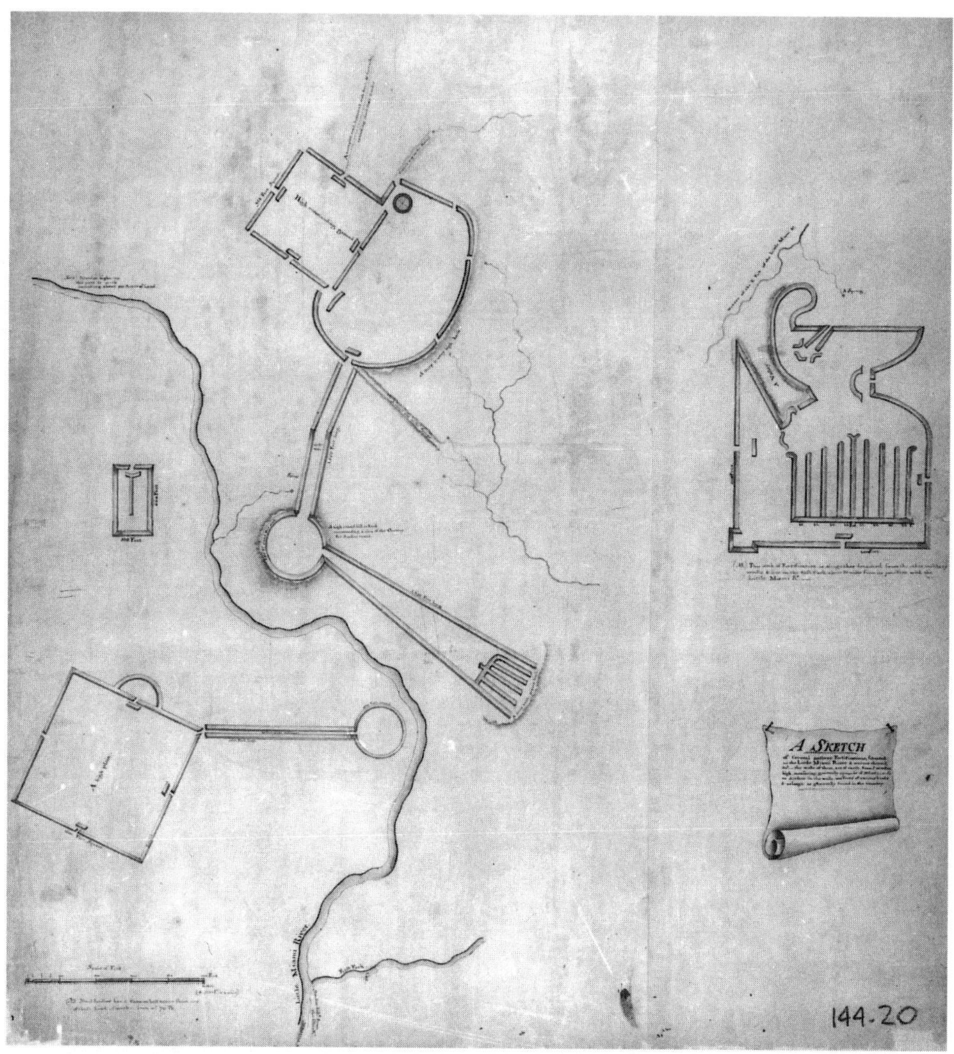

East Fork and Milford works, drawn by surveyor Isaac Roberdeau of the Corps of Engineers, 1823. The scroll identifies it as "A Sketch of several ancient fortifications situated on the Little Miami River & waters thereof, etc. The walls of them are of earth from 5 to 10 feet high, measuring generally upwards of 30 feet across." National Archives, Military Archives Division; print courtesy of Hugh McCulloch, Ohio State University.

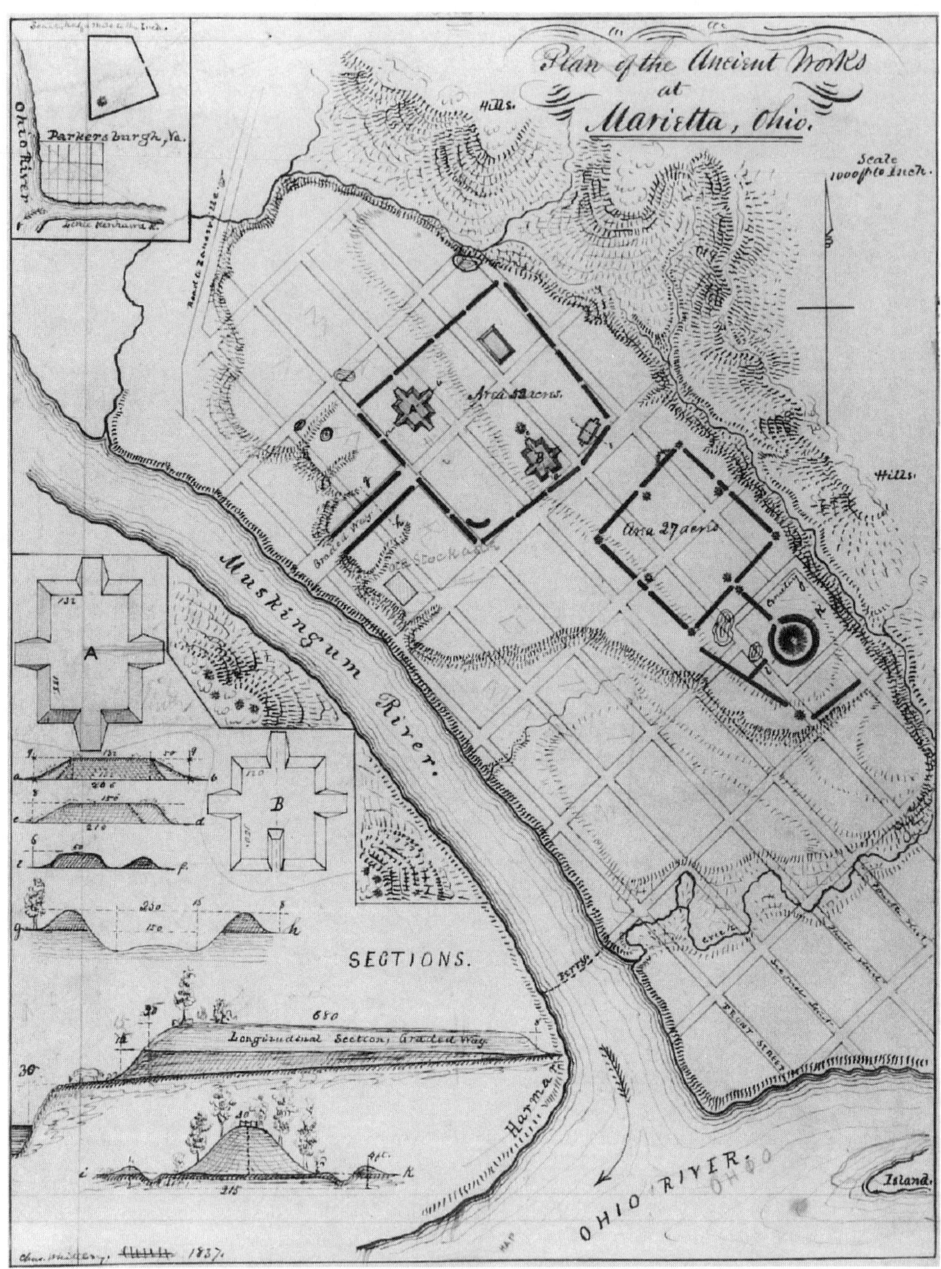

Earthworks on the Muskingum River. Ink and graphite on paper, 1837, from Charles Whittlesey, *Plan of the Ancient Works at Marietta, Ohio.* Courtesy of the Library of Congress.

present inhabitants. But it may be inferred from their number and size, that they were the work of a more populous nation than any now existing; and if the inference is correct, it would necessarily imply a state of society, in which greater progress had been made in agriculture." He doubted whether the structures had ever been intended as forts; native forts were sturdy wooden palisades, not pyramids and circular mounds. Probably they, like the Mexican pyramids, "were connected with the worship of the nation." And of course, like Jefferson, he wanted "full and precise descriptions."[23]

This fuller and more precise study was accomplished in the next decade by two Ohio residents, Ephraim George Squier and Edwin H. Davis. Impressed by the concentration of earthworks near their homes in Chillicothe, Squier and Davis began in 1845 to explore, map, and draw the structures in their vicinity. In 1846 they approached the American Antiquarian Society and the American Ethnological Society (of which Gallatin was president) for funds to carry forward the investigation. Although these organizations declined to subsidize the field research, they, along with Silliman's *Journal of Arts and Science,* offered to publish the findings.

The ponderous tome, heavy with maps and engravings, that Squier and Davis supplied to the Ethnological Society promised to cost more for publication than that slender organization could afford, even with Gallatin's support. But the new Smithsonian Institution, headed by the physicist Joseph Henry, was looking for just such a scientific contribution to demonstrate its commitment to serious, methodologically sound science, clean of fruitless speculation. The resulting publication in 1848 of Squier and Davis's *Ancient Monuments of the Mississippi Valley,* the first of the Smithsonian's Contributions to Knowledge series, was a landmark in the history of American archaeology, comparable to Gallatin's own triumphant *Synopsis.*

As Gallatin (and Jefferson) had asked, Squier and Davis eschewed speculation and stuck to precise description and illustration. Echoing Gallatin's opinion, they pointed out similarities to Central American monumental ceremonial architecture, inferred a large agricultural population, probably the ancestors of the civilized Mexicans, with "fixed and well-defined . . . customs, laws, and religion," more sophisticated in technology and culture than present-day Indians. Gallatin, who had recommended to Henry that the Smithsonian publish the monograph, was pleased by the book.[24]

The Vocabulary Project

Jefferson's obsession with the origins of Native Americans is most clearly revealed in his approach to the study of Indian languages. His interest in this subject evidently commenced early in his career, and by the 1780s he had formulated a program of research into the origin of "the aboriginal inhabitants of America" by means of the systematic collection of vocabularies and grammars. He outlined the plan in the *Notes* (see opposite).[25]

Although Jefferson's speculation about the large number of linguistic stocks or families ("radical ones") in the Americas as compared to Asia has proved to be exaggerated, the principle of measuring the antiquity of the divergence of two languages from a common ancestral tongue by the number of cognates in a standard lexicon or word list of terms referring to universal concepts contains the germ of the idea behind the twentieth-century development of lexico-statistics. Jefferson, like other philologists of his time, might have employed the concept of a tree, the branches successively differentiating as they became more distant from the trunk. But the lack of a standard orthography in these early years made comparison of word lists a chancy exercise and rendered impossible the tracing of systematic sound changes. The genealogical tree as a model for the "filiation" of languages does not appear to have been introduced until the second or third decade of the nineteenth century.[26]

Jefferson's initial hypothesis was that the ancestors of the Indian "race" probably originated in Asia or Europe and eventually, at some time in the remote past, emigrated into North America, either across the Bering Strait or across the North Atlantic via Iceland and Greenland.[27] But he gradually came to favor a reverse hypothesis: that the point of origin was in the Americas and that emigration had gone the other direction, across the Bering Strait into Asia, where people of similar color and physique resided. His reasoning was that the greater multiplicity of languages in the Americas was evidence of a longer period of differentiation from a common ancestral tongue. By 1786, in a letter to Yale President Ezra Stiles, who, like Jefferson, was a polymath interested in languages, he developed the American-origin hypothesis more firmly: "I suppose the settlement of our continent is of the most remote antiquity. The similitude between its' inhabitants & those of Eastern parts of Asia renders it probable that ours are descended from them or they from ours. The latter is my opinion, founded on this single fact. Among the red inhabitants of Asia there are

Jefferson's Plan to Study Indian Antiquity through Languages

A knowledge of their several languages would be the most certain evidence of their derivation which could be produced. In fact, it is the best proof of the affinity of nations which ever can be referred to . . . It is to be lamented then, very much to be lamented, that we have suffered so many of the Indian tribes already to extinguish, without our having previously collected and deposited in the records of literature, the general rudiments at least of the languages they spoke. Were vocabularies formed of all the languages spoken in North and South America, preserving their appelations of the most common objects in nature, of those which must be present to every nation barbarous or civilised, with the inflections of their nouns and verbs, their principles of regimen and concord, and these deposited in all the public libraries, it would furnish opportunities to those skilled in the languages of the old world to compare them with these, now, or at a future time, and hence to construct the best evidence of the derivation of this part of the human race . . .

But imperfect as is our knowledge of the tongues spoken in America, it suffices to discover the following remarkable fact. Arranging them under the radical ones to which they may be palpably traced, and doing the same by those of the red men of Asia, there will be found probably twenty in American for one in Asia, of those radical languages, so called because, if they were ever the same, they have lost all resemblance to one another. A separation into dialects may be the work of a few ages only, but for two dialects to recede from one another till they have lost all vestiges of their common origin, must require an immense course of time; perhaps not less than many people give to the age of the earth. A greater number of those radical changes of language having taken place among the red men of America, proves them of greater antiquity than those of Asia.

but a few languages radically different, but among our Indians the number of languages is infinite which are so radically different as to exhibit at present no appearance of their having been derived from a common source. The time necessary for the generation of so many languages must be immense."[28]

A decade later, writing to Dr. John Sibley, the Indian agent for Lower Louisiana, to whom he was sending copies of his word list and a request to collect vocabularies, he characterized the question of American origin as "still undecided."[29] Apparently he maintained to the day of his death his belief that linguistic comparison was "the only index by which we can trace their Filiation." But it was a daunting task, and his own efforts to identify families of related languages were frustrating, as he confessed in 1825: "I am persuaded that among the tribes on our two continents a great number of languages, radically different, will be found. It will be curious to consider how so many, so radically different, have been preserved by such small tribes in coterminous settlements of moderate extent. I had once collected about thirty vocabularies formed of the same English words, expressive of such simple objects only as must be present and familiar to every one under these circumstances. They were unfortunately lost. But I remember that on a trial to arrange them into families or dialects, I found in one instance that about half a dozen might be so classed, in another perhaps three or four. But I am sure that a third, at least, if not more, were perfectly insulated from each other."[30]

Jefferson's plan to develop the comparative study of Indian languages, based on standardized vocabulary lists, was a pioneering effort when he began it in the early 1780s. His proposal in the *Notes* was likely drafted before Peter Pallas published, in 1781, his compilation of two hundred vocabularies of Asian languages, the *Linguarum totius orbis comparativam;* it long preceded Benjamin Smith Barton's publication of comparative vocabularies of Indian languages in 1799 and Adelung and Vater's famous *Mithridates,* a vast compilation of vocabularies from around the world published in six volumes from 1806 to 1817, including North and South America (these volumes appeared in 1815 and 1816, based in part on Barton and Barton's sources). Albert Gallatin's 1836 *Synopsis of the Indian Tribes of North America,* based on an unpublished essay of 1823, expanded on the earlier collections of vocabularies, some of them obtained from tribes in the Louisiana Purchase, and was inspired in part by Gallatin's association with Jefferson as his secretary of the treasury and long-time friend and confidant.

While in France from 1784 to 1789, Jefferson was prevented from pursuing his linguistic researches in America. He may have known of Empress Catherine's support of the study of exotic languages in the Russian empire but apparently did not become aware of Pallas's book until 1806, when he read a review of the work by Volney. The second edition contained a number of American Indian vocabularies, procured for Pallas by the empress herself, who had applied to Lafayette, who turned to Washington to obtain them. The empress also had given Pallas a 285-item word list; Jefferson, basing his impression on Volney's review, thought there were only 130 (the number reported in volume I), and found that only 73 were shared with his own 250-word list. He wrote to the American minister in St. Petersburg at once, requesting that he send him a copy of Pallas's work, and in due course Jefferson received both the first and second editions, the latter containing the additional Native American and African vocabularies.

Jefferson had high hopes that a comparison based on these 73 shared words of his own American Indian sample and Pallas's Asian one would "enable us, by a comparison of language, to make the enquiry so long desired, as to the probability of a common origin between the people of Colour of the two continents." In 1806, indeed, Jefferson thought that he had "made such progress [in his vocabulary project], that within a year or two more I think to give to the public what I shall then have acquired."[31]

Jefferson's own collecting began soon after his return to the United States, when, in company with James Madison, he visited the Unquachog Indians at Poosepatuck on Long Island. It was an unplanned excursion and Jefferson was not prepared. Of the twenty survivors of the tribe, only three "old women" remained who could speak the language. Two of these, and a young woman who "knew something of the language" and perhaps served as interpreter, got together with Jefferson, Madison, and their host, General William Floyd. Jefferson prepared an impromptu list of about 200 English words, written literally on the back of an envelope, and secured the Unquachog equivalents.[32]

This experience seems to have inspired Jefferson to make his own 250-item word list, which he had printed for use in gathering American Indian vocabularies. In December of the next year, while he was in official residence in Philadelphia, he (or James Madison on his behalf) made an excursion to the Delaware reservation at Brotherton and collected another vocabulary, this time on the printed form. The recorder was careful to explain the relation of his orthography to Delaware phonetics: "The orthography used in the Indian words has no mute or superfluous letter. The sounds of the letters are according to the French. The c, the g, the w & the x are rejected, for the hard [>] the h, for the c soft the s, for the ch the tsh, for the g and k, & for the w the v is used. The a has two sounds, the a open & the a broad. The common method of accenting is omited, & the emphatical syllable formed by an additional letter."[33]

So far as is known, these are the only vocabularies personally recorded by Jefferson (if indeed he visited Brotherton himself); they were mutually unintelligible Algonkian dialects. For the remainder of his collection, he relied on a network of Indian agents, travelers, missionaries, and resident gentlemen who had close and frequent contact with various Indian communities, in the hope, as he put it to William Dunbar, of making "as extensive a collection as possible of the Indian tongues."[34]

As early as 1786 he was writing to Benjamin Hawkins enclosing "queries on the subject of the Indians." At the same time he sent copies to a number of other correspondents. Hawkins replied promptly, but by August he had heard nothing from the rest. He was not discouraged and declared, "I shall proceed, however, in my endeavors, particularly with respect to their language, and shall take care so to dispose of what I collect thereon, as that it shall not be lost." A year later he wrote again to Hawkins from Paris, thanking him for the vocabularies and assuring him that collecting lexicons was "an object I mean to pursue, as I am persuaded that the only method of investigating the filiation of the Indian nations is by that of their languages."[35]

Hawkins had been a member, along with Jefferson, of the committee of the Continental Congress overseeing Indian affairs, and in 1785 he served as one of the commissioners to negotiate treaties of peace and settle boundary questions with the southern tribes. Acting as chairman, Hawkins was successful in persuading Old Tassel and other Cherokee chiefs to sign the first Treaty of Hopewell in November 1785. He was also involved in peace and boundary negotiations with the Choctaws, Chickasaws, and Creeks.

After Hawkins's appointment as Creek agent and superintendent of Indian affairs south of the Ohio, Jefferson continued to rely on him to collect vocabularies, now according to the printed form. Hawkins prepared his vocabularies with special care, seeking "the purest source" and identifying the informants and interpreters.[36] His Cherokee, Creek, Choctaw, and Chickasaw vocabularies, transmitted to Monticello in 1800, were eventually donated by Jefferson to the American Philosophical Society.[37]

Vocabularies supplied by others in response to personal appeals and sent directly to Monticello were also preserved and eventually collated and edited by Peter Stephen DuPonceau at the American Philosophical Society. Martin Duralde sent Jefferson Chitimacha and Atacapa vocabularies from Louisiana in 1802; these were said to be dialects of Natchez. Duralde had received a copy of Jefferson's list from William Dunbar of Natchez, the premier naturalist of the old southwest and long-time correspondent of Jefferson, who helped elect him to membership in the American Philosophical Society.[38] Along with the dialects, Duralde sent a sketch of Chitimacha religious beliefs. Judge David Campbell in 1800 provided another Cherokee vocabulary, and General Dan Smith of Tennessee, whom Campbell had inspired, independently secured a Chickasaw vocabulary about the same time. Miami was obtained from William Wells and Little Turtle in Philadelphia in 1798 and again by William Thornton in Philadelphia in 1802. A Mr. Murray of Maryland secured a fragmentary lexicon from a small remnant Nanticoke community (consisting of four or five "wigwams" and a board house with one glass window) in 1792. A Nottoway vocabulary was secured as late as 1820 by John Wood, a professor of mathematics at William and Mary.

By about 1802 or 1803, by means of this network of personal correspondents, Jefferson had accumulated twenty-two vocabularies that met his standards. As he put it in 1805: "Very early in life . . . I formed a vocabulary of such objects as, being present everywhere, would probably have a name in every language; and my course of life having given me opportunities of obtaining vocabularies of many Indian tribes, I have done so on my original plan, which, though far from being perfect, has the valuable advantage of identity, of thus bringing the languages to the same points of comparison."[39] The twenty-two vocabularies were not all based on his printed word list, however, some being actually entered on his broadside, some on handwritten copies of it, some on spur-of-the-moment lists of English words. Some were incomplete; and the orthographies were various, some being in French, some in English. But Jefferson was well-enough satisfied to put together a systematic comparative vocabulary of the twenty-two languages from the sources mentioned above and others not identified, entered on a copy of his standard word list. This presumably was thought of as a preliminary exercise, his long-term goal being to make "as extensive a collection as possible of the Indian tongues" and discover the secret of the peopling of the Americas.

Jefferson's "Manuscript Comparative Vocabulary of Several Indian Languages" is evidently a careful collation of the lexical materials available to him before the arrival of the Lewis and Clark items. It comprises some thirty sheets of paper, written on both sides in Jefferson's small, meticulous, clear hand. The tribal names are listed on the left, from top to bottom, twenty-two in all, in addition to "English" and "French" at the top of the column. Across the top of each page are three English words, and below each of them is a column listing the equivalent in French and in the several Indian languages. The list of languages includes representatives of both northern and southern Iroquois, Algonkian, Muskogean, and (again) Chitimacha and Atacapa.

The list of English names for various objects and relationships deemed by Jefferson to be universal concepts is quite long; at least 140 are legible, and there were several dozen others, lost when the tops of several pages were destroyed. His total list amounted to 250 English words. They form several groups: numbers (integers, tens, hundreds), body parts below the neck (the body, belly, back, side, wrist, hand, finger, toe, skin, nails, thigh, leg, foot), face and neck (eye, nose, cheek, tongue, ear, neck, chin, lip, mouth, tooth, the hair, the beard, the face), time (a day, a month, a year, spring, autumn, winter, today, tomorrow), familiar opposites (life, death, good, bad, large, small), food stuffs (food, meat, fat, blood, bread, Indian corn), fauna (buffalo, eagle, hawk, pheasant, partridge, crow, blackbird, crane, turkey buzzard, raven, owl, turkey, swan, fly, mocking bird, snake), natural phenomena (air, land, sky, fire, earth, darkness, day, night, moon, star, light), weather (fog, rain, snow, cold, smoke; cloud, hail, ice, frost, dew), and gender (a man, a woman, a boy, a girl), and kinship (brother, sister, husband, wife, father, mother, daughter).

Obviously not all of the items are found everywhere even in the present United States, let alone throughout the world; and the English kinship terms do not have precise equivalents in the Indian languages represented. For example, the Iroquois terms for what the English language refers to as "brother" and "sister" also refer to parallel cousins. But for practical purposes, applied to tribes east of the Mississippi and south of the Great Lakes, the list would do well enough.[40]

The purchase of Louisiana provided an opportunity for the expansion of the vocabulary project, for knowledge of the Indian languages and the filiation of the tribes would now be of importance not only to scholarship but also to governance and commerce. The leader of the Red River Expedition of 1806, Thomas Freeman, was told to collect information about the Indians' "languages, traditions, monuments,"an instruction virtually identical to the one Jefferson had given to Lewis and Clark. Zebulon Pike's expeditions in 1805–1807 up the Mississippi and west to Colorado, New Mexico, and Texas apparently bore no such obligation, the orders having come from Wilkinson to conduct secret military excursions, unknown at the outset even to Jefferson. No vocabularies seem to have been obtained from the Freeman southwestern expedition, although Dr. John Sibley of Natchitoches, an advisor to the Freeman expedition and Jefferson's original choice to lead it, later secured vocabularies of Adayes and Caddo for Adelung and Vater's *Mithridates*.[41] But by far the most significant collection of vocabularies of the western Indians was made by Lewis and Clark. In 1804 Jefferson received Iowa and Sioux vocabularies forwarded by Captain Amos Stoddard, interim governor of the new territory. The Corps of Discovery accumulated other vocabularies during the remainder of the trip, perhaps ten or twelve, and Lewis brought them to Washington on his triumphal return in 1806.[42]

The tragic fate, in 1809, of Lewis's contribution, as well as part of Jefferson's own compilation, is described by Jefferson in a letter to Benjamin Smith Barton of that year (see next page). From this letter it would appear that the vocabularies sent by Stoddard, plus the nine sent by Lewis in a shipment of Indian artifacts from St. Louis in the fall of 1806, plus any given to Jefferson when Lewis returned to Washington, were destroyed, along with some of Jefferson's own. A few, unmentioned in the letter to Barton, remained at Monticello.[43]

The American Philosophical Society

In addition to his network of Indian agents, naturalists, and explorers, Jefferson had access to another resource for the advancement of the vocabulary project: the American Philosophical Society itself. In its first

Jefferson's Loss of His Papers in the James River

I received last night your favor of the 14th and would with all possible pleasure have communicated to you any part or the whole of the Indian vocabularies which I had collected, but an irreparable misfortune has deprived me of them. I have now been thirty years availing myself of every possible opportunity of procuring Indian vocabularies to the same set of words: my opportunities were probably better than will ever occur again to any person having the same desire.

I had collected about 50, and had digested most of them in collateral columns and meant to have printed them the last year of my stay in Washington. But not having yet digested Capt. Lewis's collection, nor having leisure then to do it, I put it off till I should return home. The whole, as well digest as originals were packed in a trunk of stationary & sent round by water with about 30 other packages of my effects from Washington, and while ascending James river, this package, on account of it's weight & presumed precious contents, was singled out & stolen.

The thief being disappointed on opening it, threw into the river all it's contents of which he thought he could make no use. Among these were the whole of the vocabularies. Some leaves floated ashore & were found in the mud; but these were very few, & so defaced by the mud & water that no general use can ever be made of them . . . Perhaps I may make another attempt to collect, altho' I am too old to expect to make much progress in it.

half-century, the society, "held in Philadelphia for the Promotion of Useful Knowledge," largely reflected the interests of those members who were primarily concerned with mathematics and the natural sciences. But the membership included lawyers, judges, and men of letters, a growing number of whom sought an intellectually wider role for the society.

When Jefferson was elected president in 1797, the society's quarters in Philosophical Hall (constructed in 1789 in the State House yard, immediately adjacent to Independence Hall) housed a variety of persons and institutions. The society itself occupied a large room on the second floor, where meetings were held and a collection of scientific instruments (such as telescopes and precise balances and rules) and a library (which included treatises on technical subjects, maps, manuscripts, and its own publications) were located. The rest of the building was leased to "desirable tenants," such as the celebrated painter Charles Willson Peale, who lived there with his large family and his famous museum. Peale's portraits and his specimens of the natural history of America, ranging from mastodon skeletons to mounted birds and animals to American Indian costumes and other relics, were on display for the public's edification. After Peale removed his establishment in 1811, another distinguished artist, Thomas

Philosophical Hall, erected 1786–1789.
Home of the American Philosophical Society.
Courtesy of the American Philosophical Society.

"The Artist in His Museum." Oil on canvas by Charles Willson Peale, 1822.
Courtesy of the Pennsylvania Academy of the Fine Arts, Philadelphia;
Gift of Mrs. Sarah Harrison (The Joseph Harrison, Jr. Collection).

Sully, moved in with his own family and gallery. A third long-term resident of the Hall was John Vaughan, a businessman who rented space in the cellar to store his stock of imported wines and liquors. Vaughan became treasurer and librarian of the society and lived in the Hall from 1803 until his death in 1841.[44]

On his election as president of this august institution, Jefferson declared that the American Philosophical Society "comprehends whatever the American World has of distinction in Philosophy and Science in general." The operative phrase was "in general," for Jefferson, although well trained in mathematics and the use of scientific instruments and an

"The Exhumation of the Mastodon."
Oil on canvas by Charles Willson Peale, 1806–1808.
Courtesy of the Maryland Historical Society, Baltimore.

admirer of the accomplishments of Franklin in electricity and Rittenhouse in astronomy, wanted an expanded definition of the society's sphere. He acted quickly to establish the Committee on History, with himself as a leading member, to investigate "the antiquity, changes, and present state" of the United States. The other members of the committee were General James Wilkinson, then commander-in-chief of the U.S. Army and an amateur naturalist and ethnologist; Judge George Turner, federal magistrate at Kaskaskia (and one of only three persons ever expelled from the society, in his case for embezzling funds); Charles Willson Peale; Dr. Caspar Wistar, the eminent physician and professor of medicine at the University of Pennsylvania; Dr. Adam Seybert, secretary of the society; and Franklin's nephew Jonathan Williams, chairman, a military engineer whom Jefferson later appointed as the first superintendent of the military academy at West Point. Jefferson's colleagues on the committee were all active in intellectual pursuits, contributing papers to the society's *Transactions* or sending to Jefferson or the society such items as Indian relics and fossil bones.

The committee desired to collect information under four heads:

1. To procure one or more entire skeletons of the Mammoth, so called, and of such other unknown animals as either have been, or hereafter may be discovered in America.
2. To obtain accurate plans, drawings and descriptions of whatever is interesting (where the originals cannot be had) and especially of ancient Fortifications, Tumuli, and other Indian works of art: ascertaining the materials composing them, their contents, the purposes for which they were probably designed, &c.
3. To invite researchers into the Natural History of the Earth, the changes it has undergone as to Mountains, Lakes, Rivers, Prairies, &c.
4. To enquire into the Customs, Manners, Languages and Character of the Indian nations, ancient and modern, and their migrations.

The committee announced its plans for research in an advertisement in the society's *Transactions* and appealed to "every lover of science . . . who have taste and opportunity for such researches" to communicate with the committee. The program of the committee reads remarkably like an expansion of the prospectus of studies outlined by Jefferson in *Notes on the State of Virginia* a few years earlier: fossils, geology and geography, Indian archaeological sites, and Indian languages, customs, and history. If sufficient materials could be assembled, it could have led to an up-to-date *Notes on the United States of America.* But such a document was not to be.[45]

Although there were some communications to the members of the committee, a few of which were duly published in the *Transactions,* the response to the appeal seems to have been tepid. By 1801 Jefferson himself was fully occupied with the business of the presidency. And the other member of the society who perhaps most nearly shared Jefferson's interests in paleontology and American Indian studies, the eminent Philadelphia physician and naturalist Benjamin Smith Barton, was not a member of the committee. But Barton did donate to the society, through the hand of the committee chairman Jonathan Williams, a copy of his just-published book, *New View on the Origin of the Tribes and Nations of America* (1797).

Barton's absence from the 1797 committee is difficult to explain. A notable member of Philadelphia's scientific community and professor of natural history, botany, and *materia medica* at the University of Pennsylvania, he was in the process of preparing for publication a major work on the medicinal plants of the United States. It was to be a follow-up to Dr. Benjamin Rush's 1774 *Enquiry into the Natural History of Medicine among the Indians of North America and a Comparative View of Their Diseases and Remedies with Those of Civilized Nations.* Barton was a nephew of the famous astronomer David Rittenhouse and son of an Episcopalian rector whose pastimes were botany and mineralogy. His interest in natural history had been developed in childhood at Lancaster and York, Pennsylvania, where his hobby was collecting specimens of the flora and fauna of the nearby woods and fields. He had received a medical education at Edinburgh, and in addition to all this, he had prepared and published a British edition of Samuel Stanhope Smith's *Essay* on race.

But there was a somewhat devious side to Barton's personal conduct. He had left Edinburgh abruptly, without receiving a degree, leaving behind a trail of unpaid debts and accusations that he embezzled a large sum of money entrusted to him as one of the presidents of the Royal Medical Society of Edinburgh. After a brief sojourn on the continent, he returned to Philadelphia in the fall of 1789. Despite the lack of a degree, he was able to enter practice as a physician and was promptly elected to membership in the American Philosophical Society and a professorship at the University of Pennsylvania, where he eventually succeeded Benjamin Rush as professor of medicine. In the meantime, however, embarrassed by his lack of a medical degree, in 1796 he solicited one from a German acquaintance, Professor C. D. Ebeling of Hamburg. Ebeling was able to arrange for the granting of an honorary degree of Doctor of Medicine from Christian-Albrechts University at Kiel. He had hoped, however, to receive this honor from the more prestigious medical school at Göttingen, and he actually told some relatives and acquaintances that he had received his degree there in 1789, after leaving Edinburgh.[46]

Although Barton does not seem to have been personally close to Jefferson, he knew of his interest in American Indian antiquities and languages from reading the *Notes.* In 1796 he sent to the Reverend Doctor Joseph Priestley a communication concerning the identity and origin of the mound-builders. Barton, noting as had others that the mound-builders were carriers of a more advanced civilization than the natives recently encountered in these parts, a civilization reminiscent of the high cultures of Mexico and Peru, speculated that the mounds had been built by outliers of the Toltecs, the predecessors of the Aztecs, and that the Toltecs in turn were descendants of Danes from northern Europe. He had voiced his Danish hypothesis as early as 1787, while still a medical student at Edinburgh, in a paper published in a British journal.

He declared his intention to produce, in two or three years, a great work: "It is now about ten years since I first turned my attention to the subject of the American monuments, and since I began to collect materials for a work which is intended to involve the physical and moral history of the aboriginal Americans. In this work, the favourite object of my earlier and my present days, I hope I shall be able to demonstrate the physical antiquity of America; the remoteness of its population; the countries from which it was peopled; and the fewness of its radical languages. I trust, I shall also be able to vindicate, from the aspersions of certain popular and eloquent writers, the intellectual character of the Americans. And although I shall not be able to show that highly civilized nations had ever possessed the countries of America, previously to the discovery of Columbus, yet it will be easy to demonstrate, that these countries were formerly possessed by nations much farther advanced in civilization, than the greater number of the nations north of the empire of Mexico; by nations who must have been extremely numerous."[47]

Although Barton's intentions would seem to press in the directions sketched by Jefferson in the *Notes* (published in London a year before

Barton arrived in Edinburgh), his only mention of Jefferson was to disagree with him. He asserted that "the radical languages in North-America are but few," an opinion the opposite of that "entertained by an enlightened American philosopher" (identified in a footnote as "Mr. Jefferson"). Barton, was, in fact, correct in seeking to combine apparently distinct languages in common families; linguists today are still debating the number of North American Indian language stocks, the more radical scholars proposing less than a dozen, the more conservative on the order of sixty. Barton, of course, had a very small sample of languages to work with, in the form of imperfectly recorded vocabularies. But the available sources on Algonkian were relatively rich, and he and others were able to recognize that there were many "dialects" of that stock (which he termed "Lennape").[48]

The next year, when *New View* appeared, Barton went out of his way to assure Jefferson (now vice-president of the United States as well as president of the American Philosophical Society) of his high esteem. He dedicated the work "To Thomas Jefferson, L.L.D." (that is, to a fellow recipient of an honorary degree) and added a flattering salute: "These pages are, with peculiar propriety, addressed to you. I know not that any person has paid so much attention to the subject which they involve; I know of no one who places a higher value upon the question which I have ventured to discuss. Although, in the progress of my inquiry, I have differed from you, in one or two essential points, I cannot suppose that on that account the investigation of the question will be less agreeable to you. I am confident, from my personal acquaintance with you, that you are anxious for the discovery of truth, and ardent to embrace it, in whatever form it may present itself. It is the jewel which all good and wise men are in pursuit of. It is the punctum saliens of science."[49]

The theoretical content of the work pretty much repeated his original thesis: that all races of man can fall from high to low, can degenerate; that also, like other races, the Indians are capable of progress, and just as today's civilized nations were once rude and barbarous, so too can the Indians ascend from savagery to civilization; therefore, current programs to civilize and Christianize the Native Americans have every prospect of success. The evidentiary part of Barton's work, however, was not material culture but language, specifically, comparative vocabularies. Barton used a 54-item English word list, beginning with "God" and ending with "I (Ego)." The sample was drawn from publications mostly concerning the Indians of North America east of the Mississippi, with a few from Spanish writers in South America and three or four Asian languages from Pallas.

Perhaps, in the context of this flurry of Bartonian enterprises, Jefferson sensed that the society was harboring in Barton not a collaborator but a competitor; it is easy to imagine that the circular letter of 1797 was an effort on Jefferson's part to recapture for himself the initiative lost to Barton. For Barton in fact had produced a significant contribution. He was the first to recognize that Cherokee was one of the Iroquoian family of languages, and his suggestion that the Indians of the northern and southern hemispheres had the same origin is no longer disputed. Finally, he was perhaps the first to detect specific affinities between Asian and American Indian languages.

Whether Jefferson saw Barton as a rival in 1797 may never be known, but he was most gracious to Barton in later years. In 1809, when Barton wrote Jefferson asking for copies of Meriwether Lewis's vocabularies for use in preparing a revised edition of the *New View,* Jefferson sent the poignant letter quoted above, describing the maritime disaster of 1809 that aborted Jefferson's personal program to investigate the languages and antiquity of the American Indians. But after Jefferson's departure from the presidency and return to philosophical pursuits, a new and more productive program of linguistic research would soon commence at the American Philosophical Society, under Jefferson's benevolent eye.

CHAPTER SIX

Civilizing the Uncivilized Frontier

BEFORE LEAVING for France in 1784 to serve as United States minister, Jefferson briefly returned to Congress and there took the lead in developing a public land policy for the new nation. Jefferson's policy, which was eventually enacted in the land ordinances of 1784, 1785, and the Northwest Ordinance of 1787, included a formal recognition that the lands beyond the Appalachian mountains were to be secured by peaceful purchase from their native inhabitants, exclusively by the United States or its agents.

On his return from France in 1789, Jefferson served in two Federalist administrations—under George Washington as secretary of state and under John Adams as vice-president—where he was necessarily involved in the contentious and bloody world of Indian affairs. His earlier philosophical speculations about the vanishing Indians, crystallized in the story of Logan, were now put to the test, as he helped formulate practical policies that would implement his views on how to obtain, humanely if possible, the lands that the Native Americans were bound to lose in one way or another.

The Northwest Ordinance

In 1779, as governor of Virginia, Jefferson had established a new Land Office to replace the one vacated by the Crown's agents in 1776. It faced a daunting task: not only to satisfy the needs of petitioners in the long-settled portions of the state east of the Appalachians but also to refresh a depleted treasury by selling western lands to speculators and would-be settlers, who were pressing on into West Virginia and Kentucky despite wartime conditions. But Jefferson, along with other responsible statesmen, did not believe that Virginia's claim to the territory north of the Ohio River was worth pursuing in the face of so many intractable problems: a seemingly endless war with western tribes, the difficulty of governing a fractious frontier population, and the constant pressure of speculative land companies to detach parts of Virginia's domain and form new colonies or states. He came to believe that territory beyond the Appalachians, especially that portion north of the Ohio, should be administered by the Congress until such time as new states might be formed out of lands acquired from their Indian occupants.

In January 1781 Jefferson transmitted to Congress an act of cession by Virginia of her lands north of the Ohio—a move which persuaded Maryland, the last holdout, to ratify the Articles of Confederation. Congress objected to certain conditions laid down by Virginia, including her rejection of the claims of certain land companies, but Virginia refused to modify her terms of cession, and a stalemate ensued. The politics of this situation revolved around the pretensions of several land companies that had made private purchases of Indian lands prior to the Revolution, in defiance of British policy. They now came back to claim from Congress the land titles disallowed by the Crown.

The Illinois-Wabash Company presented a memorial; an earlier memorial, drafted by Benjamin Franklin and Samuel Wharton on behalf of the Vandalia Company, was submitted anew; and memorials were submitted in support of the claims of George Croghan and of the Indiana Company. Eventually, if grudgingly, the states supporting the land companies' claims yielded ground, and in March 1784 Congress accepted in principle Virginia's insistence that the ceded lands in the Northwest Territory (all of the United States north of the Ohio River and west of Pennsylvania, consisting of the present states of Ohio, Indiana, Illinois, Michigan, Wisconsin, and part of Minnesota) be considered a national domain, with Congress alone possessing the right to make treaties, buy land, wage war, and manage Indian affairs.[1]

In March 1784, immediately after Congress's acceptance of the Virginia cession, as chairman of a congressional committee "appointed to prepare a plan for the temporary Government of the Western territory," Jefferson submitted a report that provided for public, not private, purchase of land from the Indians: "Resolved that the territory ceded or to be ceded by Individual States to the United States whensoever the same shall have been purchased of the Indian Inhabitants and offered for sale by the U.S. shall be formed into distinct states."[2] This view of a peaceful, orderly process of acquiring Indian land by government purchase was eventually embodied in the land ordinance of 1785, providing for the survey and sale of "the territory ceded by the individual States to the United States, which has been purchased of the Indian inhabitants."[3] And of course it was repeated and amplified in the more famous Northwest Ordinance of 1787, which required that "The utmost good faith shall always be observed towards the Indians, their lands and property shall never be taken from them without their consent, and in their property, rights and liberty, they shall never be invaded or disturbed, unless in just and lawful wars authorized by Congress; but laws founded in justice and humanity shall from time to time be made, for preventing wrongs being done to them, and for preserving peace and friendship with them."[4] Jefferson's plan envisioned the eventual formation of nine new states. Although Jefferson was in Paris by the time the two ordinances were passed by Congress, they were indeed his legacy and the legacy of most of the other gentlemen of the Enlightenment who led the new nation.

But not all Americans shared Jefferson's sentiments. While he watched from a distance in Paris, some American leaders put forth the view that those Indian tribes that had sided with the British during the Revolution had forfeited their right of soil, and as a conquered people might justly be driven off the land or exterminated by war if they resisted white occupation. Under this conquest theory, from 1784 to 1789 the United States conducted a series of treaties, some of them fraudulent, with Indians both north and south of the Ohio, by which they "gave peace" to the conquered tribes in return for a cession of land, with trivial compensation. The treaty signed at Fort Harmar (at Marietta, Ohio) in January 1789 was the culmination of these negotiations. It was intended to quiet Indian objections to the coercive "peace" treaties signed by unqualified representatives of several tribal groups from 1784 to 1787 and to substitute a general purchase from all the tribes of the Ohio valley. The Treaty of Fort Harmar, however, was similarly defective: none of the tribes in the ceded area sent representatives, and the few from the northern tribes who straggled in were not leading men. The treaty purported to cede to the United States the southern two-thirds of Ohio and all of Ohio east of the Muskingum River. But it, like its predecessors, was practically worthless as soon as it was signed. Powerful factions within the Indian nations rejected these treaties, mobilized the confederacy of western tribes anew, and commenced a guerrilla war against the whites.[5]

Complicating the efforts of the federal government to stabilize the situation were precipitous moves to plant settlements west of the Appalachians. North of the Ohio, land companies had established forts at Marietta and Cincinnati. South of the Ohio, Georgia—whose charter limits extended from the Atlantic Ocean to the Mississippi River embracing the present states of Georgia, Alabama, and Mississippi—denied that the Indian tribes had any right of soil at all and proceeded to grant extensive tracts along the Mississippi to the so-called Yazoo land companies, in defiance of any claim of Congress. Georgia and her citizens insisted that the Indian resident population, numbering upwards of 100,000 people, were only tenants at will.

The tangle of conflicting interests was all the more difficult to resolve because of the vague wording of the Articles of Confederation, which cautiously gave to Congress the "right and power of . . . regulating the trade and managing all affairs with the Indians, not members of any of the states, provided that the legislative right of any state within its own limits be not infringed or violated." Furthermore, the Articles gave to each state the power to engage in war against any Indian tribe, without consent of Congress, if it "shall have received certain advice of a resolution being formed by some nation of Indians to invade such state, and the danger is so imminent as not to admit of a delay."[6]

Much stronger language, giving Congress exclusive authority to form alliances, make war, and buy land, had been proposed by Benjamin Franklin (whose own financial interests were involved) and John Dickinson (another Pennsylvanian anxious to curtail the western expansion of Virginia in the Ohio valley). The weaker compromise language was described by James Madison as "obscure" and "contradictory," "absolutely incomprehensible." Madison suggested firmer language at the Constitutional Convention, complaining that under the ambiguous guidelines laid down in the Articles, several states had "entered into treaties and wars" with Indian tribes.[7]

But the Constitution as adopted in 1787 was even more vague on Indian relations than the Articles, mentioning Indians only as an afterthought in the section giving Congress the power "to regulate commerce with foreign nations and among the several states, and with the Indian tribes." Implicitly, in the enumeration of the executive powers of the President, the Indian tribes were included in the power "to make Treaties, provided two thirds of the Senators present concur." Important negotiations and agreements with Indian tribes, whether peace, alliance, trade, or sales of land were the object, had been traditionally conducted under the authority of the sovereign. This practice was continued by the President with respect to Indian tribes, with the full formality of ratification by the Senate, until late in the nineteenth century.[8]

Although Jefferson in Paris was not much concerned with Indian matters—except for correspondence about Indian languages and antiquities, buying books, and seeing his own *Notes on the State of Virginia* through the press—he was kept informed, at least to a degree, about governmental activities. After the treaties of Hopewell with the Cherokees in 1785 and the Choctaws in 1786, his former congressional colleague, now treaty commissioner, Benjamin Hawkins, wrote him an account of the sad implications of the constitutional stalemate over federal versus states' rights in the management of relations with the Indians.

Hawkins was pessimistic about the fate of the Native Americans: "You will see by the Treaties which I enclose how attentive I have been to the right of these people; and I can assure you there is nothing I have more at heart than the preservation of them. It is a melancholy reflection that the rulers of America in rendering an account to Heaven of the aborigines thereof, will have lost everything but the name. The interposition of Congress without the cooperation of the Southern States is ineffectual, and Georgia and North Carolina have refused by protesting against their authority. The former will not allow that the Indians can be viewed in any other light than as members thereby, and the latter allows a right of regulatory trade only without the fixing of any boundary between the Indians & Citizens, as they claim all the land Westward according to their bill of rights and that the Indians are only tenants at will."[9]

Jefferson in reply deplored the want of American concern for justice to the Indian tribes: "The attention which you pay to their rights also does you great honor, as the want of that is a principal source of dishonor to the American character, the two principles on which our Conduct towards the Indians should be founded, are justice and fear. After the injuries we have done them they cannot love us, which leaves us no alternative but that of fear to keep them from attacking us, but justice is what we should never lose sight of & in time it may recover their esteem."[10]

Knox's Civilization Policy

Alarmed by the deterioration of Indian relations in both the northwest and the south, Secretary of War Henry Knox decided that the conquest theory was a poor basis for constructing an Indian policy that would

Henry Knox, Secretary of War and author of the United States' civilization policy toward Native Americans. Oil on canvas by Charles Willson Peale, c. 1783. Courtesy of Independence National Historical Park Collection.

advance the true interests of the United States. It would be wiser to turn to the more pacific language of Thomas Jefferson as expressed in the Northwest Ordinance of 1787. Accordingly, in July 1789 he wrote a letter to President Washington outlining the alternative policies of war or peace and the measures needed to be successful at each of them. War against the Creeks, who would if attacked doubtless consolidate a "general confederacy" of southern Indians allied to Spain, would be a daunting prospect, requiring an army of at least 5,000 men (in addition to whatever was needed north of the Ohio) at a cost of $1,500,000 annually. To enforce a peaceful settlement of boundary disputes with the Creeks and Cherokees would also require a military force, but a much smaller one, of at least 500 troops, stationed in a string of posts on the Indian side of the boundaries.

The need for such a force, Knox admitted candidly, was in large part owing to the ungovernable nature of the frontier whites: "The angry passions of the frontier Indians and whites, are too easily inflamed by reciprocal injuries, and are too violent to be controlled by the feeble authority of the civil power . . . There can be neither justice or observance of treaties, where every man claims to be the sole judge in his own cause,

Henry Knox's Policy of Purchasing Indian Land

It would reflect honor on the new Government, and be attended with happy effects, were a declarative law to be passed, that the Indian tribes possess the right of the soil of all lands within their limits, respectively, and that they are not to be divested thereof, but in consequence of fair and bonafide purchases, made under the authority, or with the express approbation, of the United States. As the great source of all Indian wars are disputes about their boundaries, and as the United States are, from the nature of the government, liable to be involved in every war that shall happen on this or any other account, it is highly proper that their authority and consent should be considered as essentially necessary to all measures for the consequences of which they are responsible.

No individual State could, with propriety, complain of invasion of its territorial rights. The independent nations and tribes of Indians ought to be considered as foreign nations, not as the subjects of any particular State. Each individual State, indeed, will retain the right of pre-emption of all lands within its limits, which will not be abridged; but the general sovereignty must possess the right of making all treaties, on the execution or violation of which depend peace or war . . .

Although the disposition of the people of the States, to emigrate into the Indian country, cannot be effectually prevented, it may be restrained and regulated.

It may be restrained, by postponing new purchases of Indian territory, and by prohibiting the citizens from intruding on the Indian lands. It may be regulated, by forming colonies, under the direction of Government, and by posting a body of troops to execute their orders.

and the avenger of his own supposed wrongs . . . In such a case, the sword of the republic only, is adequate to guard a due administration of justice, and the preservation of the peace . . . All offences committed by individuals, contrary to the treaties, should be tried by a court martial, agreeably to a law to be made for that purpose . . . The disgraceful violation of the

Henry Knox's Civilization Policy

As population shall increase, and approach the Indian boundaries, game will be diminished, and new purchases may be made for small considerations. This has been, and probably will be, the inevitable consequence of cultivations. It is, however, painful to consider, that all the Indian tribes, once existing in those States now the best cultivated and most populous, have become extinct. If the same causes continue, the same effects will happen; and, in a short period, the idea of an Indian on this side the Mississippi will only be found in the pages of the historical.

How different would be the sensation of a philosophic mind to reflect, that, instead of exterminating a part of the human race by our modes of population, we had persevered, through all difficulties, and at last had imparted our knowledge of cultivation and the arts to the aboriginals of the country, by which the source of future life and happiness had been preserved and extended. But it has been conceived to be impracticable to civilize the Indians of North America. This opinion is probably more convenient than just. That the civilization of the Indians would be an operation of complicated difficulty; that it would require the highest knowledge of the human character, and a steady perseverance in a wise system for a series of years, cannot be doubted. But to deny that, under a course of favorable circumstances, it could not be accomplished, is to suppose the human character under the influence of such stubborn habits as to be incapable of melioration or change—a supposition entirely contradicted by the progress of society, from the barbarous ages to its present degree of perfection . . .

Missionaries, of excellent moral character, should be appointed to reside in their nation, who should be well supplied with all the implements of husbandry, and the necessary stock for a farm. These men should be made the instruments to work on the Indians; presents should commonly pass through their hands, or by their recommendations. They should, in no degree, be concerned in trade, or the purchase of lands, to rouse the jealousy of the Indians. They should be their friends and fathers. Such a plan, although it might not fully effect the civilization of the Indians, would most probably be attended with the salutary effect of attaching them to the interest of the United States.

treaty of Hopewell, with the Cherokees, requires the serious consideration of Congress. If so direct and manifest contempt of the authority of the United States be suffered with impunity, it will be in vain to attempt to extend the arm of Government to the frontiers. The Indian tribes can have no faith in such imbecile promises, and the lawless whites will ridicule a government which shall, on paper only, make Indian treaties, and regulate Indian boundaries."[11] Knox went on to sketch a new philosophy of Indian relations, a set of "proper principles . . . for the government of Indian affairs," that included a formal recognition of the Indian right of soil (see page 167) and a program of "civilization" of the Indians (see opposite). His view represented the guidelines under which Jefferson as President would later conduct his own Indian policy.[12]

The administration proceeded promptly to carry out Knox's new policy. In September 1789 American commissioners met with the great Creek leader Alexander McGillivray, a literate man whose Scottish father had married the daughter of a French officer and a Creek woman. McGillivray had been educated in Charleston and on his return to the Creek country became head chief of that nation and acknowledged leader of the Seminoles of Florida. He was said to be able to mobilize 10,000 warriors. His business partner was William Panton, the Scottish leader who from his headquarters at Pensacola in Spanish Florida supplied the Creeks and other southern tribes and who brought McGillivray and his Creeks and Seminoles into alliance with Spain. A bitter war with the Georgia and North Carolina settlers in the Cumberland valley was being carried on despite early treaties, which McGillivray repudiated, ceding the disputed lands. But the terms now being offered by the Americans, like the terms put forward at Fort Harmar a few months before, included a confirmation of the earlier cessions, albeit with compensation. McGillivray angrily rejected the offer and stalked away without farewell.[13]

In the eyes of some, such an insult required war to vindicate the national honor. But Washington rejected this suggestion and instead chose to follow Knox's policy of conciliation. He sent a personal emissary to invite McGillivray to visit him at the capital to discuss the terms of peace. McGillivray accepted, made a triumphal tour, lodged with Knox, visited the Spanish ambassador along with Knox and Jefferson (who by this time was back in the country serving as secretary of state), and with the accompanying Creek chiefs on August 7, 1790, signed a treaty of peace and friendship with the United States. The treaty established boundaries acceptable to the Creeks, promised that white encroachment could be punished by the Creeks "as they please," and promised the Creeks material assistance—domestic animals, implements of husbandry, and white interpreters to teach their use—in the process of attaining "a greater degree of civilization."[14]

Not made public were six articles intended to open the Creek trade to the United States, to educate four Creek youths in the north at any one time, and to bribe the loyalty of McGillivray and the other chiefs. McGillivray was made Indian agent of the United States with the rank of brigadier-general and a salary of $1,200 per year. McGillivray then took the oath of allegiance to the United States. Not to be outdone, the Spanish quickly appointed him their superintendent-general of the Creek nation at a salary of $3,500 per year. In addition to his two salaries, he received $100,000 in compensation for estates confiscated by Georgia during the Revolution, and he shared with Panton in the profits of the £40,000 worth of trade goods imported annually. At the time of his death in 1793 he owned several plantations, sixty Negro slaves, and a large stable of horses.

Simultaneously with the Creek treaty, on July 22, 1790, Knox and Washington were able to persuade Congress to pass the first Trade and Intercourse Act, which set the pattern for federal regulation of Indian relations for the next century. It provided for the licensing of traders, prohibited any purchases of Indian land by any private persons or any state except at a public treaty "held under the authority of the United States," and provided for the trial and punishment in state or territorial courts (not by military court-martial, as Knox had suggested) of any white person who trespassed on Indian land or committed other crimes against Indians.[15]

The War for the Northwest Territory

Jefferson had rather reluctantly assumed his duties as secretary of state in New York in March of 1790, just in time for McGillivray's visit. Washington's cabinet at that time consisted of only four positions: secretary of state, secretary of war, secretary of the treasury, and attorney general. The treasury secretary was Alexander Hamilton, with whom Jefferson would shortly become embroiled in a feud over fiscal policy and general philosophy of government. The attorney general was Edmund Randolph, an old friend and political protégé from Virginia, whom Jefferson counted on to balance the federalist leanings of Hamilton and Knox but who eventually earned Jefferson's disgust as "the most indecisive [person] I ever had to do business with" for not always siding with his patron in cabinet disputes.[16]

But it was the portly Major General Henry Knox, Washington's brilliant artillerist during the Revolution, who, as secretary of war, directly managed Indian affairs under the general guidance of his revered mentor, the President. To his credit, Knox was responsible for drafting the memorandum to Washington outlining the peace-and-civilization policy in 1789 which led to the passage of the Trade and Intercourse Act of 1790. But he had also been responsible for the unfortunate Indian treaties of 1784 to 1789 and for the military defense of the disputed frontiers. Although Knox was inclined to maximize the power of the federal government, and was far less of a francophile than Jefferson, he was an amiable man of Enlightenment principles, whose Indian policy did not offend Jefferson. Like Knox, Jefferson also favored combining the promotion of peace and civilization for the friendly tribes with a readiness to war upon the merciless enemy savages.[17]

The importance of Indian affairs to the young republic was prominently displayed within weeks of Jefferson's arrival in New York, when McGillivray swept in with his Creek entourage to negotiate the August 7, 1790, treaty of peace and friendship. But the aspect of Indian relations that most attracted Jefferson's attention, although he was powerless to intervene, was the war in the Northwest Territory, which was going badly.

During the previous spring, Arthur St. Clair, governor of the Northwest Territory, had sent a peace emissary to the hostile Western Confederacy, which consisted of Wyandots, Delawares, Shawnees, Ottawas, Chippewas, Miamis, Kickapoos, Weas, Kaskaskias, Potawatomies, and others. But the hostiles reiterated their refusal to accept the boundaries specified in the Fort Harmar treaty of January 1789 and demanded that the Americans recognize the confederacy as the sovereign power with whom they would henceforth have to negotiate. They also asked for a promise to open trade at the levels they enjoyed with the British and a guarantee that the raids from Kentucky would cease. This response convinced St. Clair that no accommodation was possible with the "renegade" Indians, and he at once began preparations for a large expedition, amounting to 320 regular army troops and 1,133 militia, under the command of Colonel Josiah Harmar (who had founded the fort at Marietta that bore his name).

In October of 1790 Harmar's little army burned several unoccupied Miami towns, but after that suffered two disastrous defeats. The Indians ambushed part of the force on October 19, killing 20 regulars and 40 militiamen. And again on October 22, while the survivors were retreating, a detachment of regulars and militia who had been sent back to the Miami villages came under surprise attack; 183 men were killed and many wounded. Congress now appropriated $300,000 for a new expedition; and as before, a peace emissary was dispatched to persuade the recalcitrant tribesmen to accept the Fort Harmar boundary and, simultaneously, to invite the Iroquois to join the Americans in a war against the western confederates. The American proposals were spurned by the now-contemptuous western Indians and also by the Iroquois, who were indignant at being asked to attack their former allies. St. Clair commenced his preparations for a major campaign.[18]

News of this impending campaign did not entirely please Jefferson. To Senator Charles Carroll of Maryland, signer of the Declaration and erstwhile colleague in the Continental Congress, he wrote in April complaining of the expense of the interminable Indian wars and their tendency to require the raising of troops and an elevation of the national debt as "some" (that is, the hated Hamiltonians) favored anyway. "Our news from the westward is disagreeable. Constant murders committing by the Indians, and their combination threatens to be more and more expensive. I hope we shall give them a thorough drubbing this summer, and then change our tomahawk into a golden chain of friendship. The most economical as well as most humane conduct towards them is to bribe them into peace, and to retain them in peace by eternal bribes. The expedition this year would have served for presents on the most liberal scale for one hundred years; nor shall we otherwise ever get rid of any army, or of our debt. The least rag of Indian depredation will be an excuse to raise troops for those who love to have troops, and for those who think that a public debt is a good thing."[19] Yet in July Jefferson mentioned in a letter to John Adams "that we expect hourly to hear the true event of Genl. Scott's expedition. Reports have favorable hopes of it."[20]

Scott's expedition was indeed successful: 700 mounted Kentucky militia destroyed several Wea towns on the upper Wabash, killed 32 warriors, and returned with a number of prisoners. But Scott's foray was only a preliminary, as was a less successful raid in August led by Lt. Colonel James Wilkinson of Kentucky, lately a schemer to detach the southeastern United States as a separate republic allied with Spain. (He would eventually become involved with Jefferson in the administration of the Territory of Louisiana and in the prosecution of Aaron Burr for a similar, treasonous secession plot). In October General St. Clair himself led an army of 2,000 men, including hundreds of regular soldiers, with substantial artillery, up the Miami River. St. Clair's army blundered into an ambush and was virtually destroyed by an Indian army of approximately 1,200 warriors led by the Miami war chief Little Turtle. The Americans lost 630 men killed and 270 wounded, and the panic-stricken survivors—mostly Kentucky militia—abandoned their artillery and wounded and in two short days fled back to the safety of the forts from which they had set forth a month before.

St. Clair's defeat was catastrophic for western expansion. The progress of settlement in the lands supposedly purchased at Fort Harmar in 1789 and their organization under the Northwest Ordinance of 1787 ground to a halt. Frontier settlements north of the Ohio were abandoned as the inhabitants fled to the forts at Marietta, Cincinnati, and even back to Pittsburgh, Wheeling, and Louisville. The Indians exulted. At a grand council in the fall of 1792 the revitalized Western Confederacy rejected American offers to negotiate a peace and demanded nothing less than American relinquishment of all claims north and west of the Ohio and even compensation to the Shawnees for the lands they had been forced to surrender at the end of Lord Dunmore's War, almost two decades earlier.

Despite the insulting (in American eyes) arrogance of the confederacy, the peace policy adumbrated by Knox and advocated by Washington and Jefferson remained in place. In July 1793 the United States' response to the Indian demands was carried to Detroit by three American commissioners—Timothy Pickering and Benjamin Lincoln of Massachusetts and Beverly Randolph of Virginia. Pickering, then postmaster general, would in 1795 succeed Knox as secretary of war and would serve as secretary of state during Jefferson's vice-presidency. The distinguished commissioners were instructed to make major concessions, including the return of all the lands ceded at Fort Harmar except the tracts in southern Ohio that had already been granted to the Ohio Company and the land company known as Symmes Associates. The forts at Marietta and Cincinnati would be evacuated, and the United States would admit that the King of England had not had the right to give Indian land to the Americans at the end of the Revolutionary war, as the United States had claimed under the conquest theory, since he had never purchased it himself.

But the confederate representatives rejected the United States' offer.

They insisted on complete American withdrawal from Ohio and suggested that the $50,000 compensation offered the Indians be used instead to compensate the poor settlers who would have to remove. Thus the negotiations failed and the war ground on until, in the summer of 1794, an even larger American army under General Anthony Wayne defeated the Indians at Fallen Timbers in northern Ohio. A year later, at the Treaty of Greenville, the broken Indian confederacy, assembled in discord and defeat, signed away all of southern and eastern Ohio, substantially confirming the Fort Harmar boundaries. It was the end of effective Indian resistance north of the Ohio River to the advance of white settlement into the territory between the Appalachians and the Mississippi.[21]

Mr. Secretary

Jefferson could only watch from the sidelines while Knox, as secretary of war, managed Indian affairs, both diplomatic and military. But dealing with British interference in the Indian wars was another matter. All members of the administration assumed that the resistance of the Native Americans in Ohio was being encouraged by the British, whose army still occupied a string of forts in American territory south of the Great Lakes and whose traders still supplied the Indians with guns and ammunition. Before they would give up these posts, the British insisted that the Americans settle the financial claims of English commercial creditors and mistreated Loyalists. Negotiations about these sensitive issues in foreign affairs lay within the purview of the secretary of state, and because British garrisons on American soil were implicated in the continuing war with the Indians, Jefferson was thus indirectly involved in Indian affairs.

George Hammond, the first British ambassador to the United States, arrived in Philadelphia in late October 1791, a few days before St. Clair's defeat by Little Turtle. Jefferson had met Hammond at Versailles, and in these first discussions Hammond, who was young, arrogant, and aggressive, made it clear that there would be no negotiations regarding the normalization of relations until the failure to carry out the terms of the 1783 treaty of peace were addressed. According to the British, the Americans had not settled their unpaid debts to British merchants or compensated Loyalists for confiscated property. On the American side of the ledger, the British had not relinquished posts in the Northwest Territory nor compensated the Americans for about 3,000 stolen slaves.

Hammond's tactic was to stall. In December Jefferson asked for a statement of the British position in writing, but Hammond did not deliver it until March 1792. Jefferson responded in May with his own lengthy memorandum of some 250 manuscript pages, a tour de force legalistically citing chapter and verse of British misconduct and American virtue.[22] The memorandum pointed out that the failure to evacuate posts on the frontier seriously hurt American interests "by depriving us of our fur trade" and "by intercepting our friendly and neighborly intercourse with the Indian nations, and consequently keeping us in constant, expensive, and barbarous war with them."[23]

Hammond was stunned. The two men met at dinner to discuss, in particular, the matter of the posts. Shortly after delivering his own memorandum, Hammond had received a secret communication from Lord Grenville, who, encouraged by the Indian success in defeating St. Clair, now proposed that in exchange for abandoning the posts, an Indian barrier state be created in the Northwest, effectively ending American plans for settlement. But after receiving Jefferson's memorandum, this proposal seemed so far-fetched that Hammond did not even mention it to Jefferson.

The two men did discuss their two countries' policies toward the Indians, however. Hammond told Jefferson that the British—and therefore the Indians—believed that it was the American intention "to exterminate the Indians and take the lands." Jefferson assured him that, to the contrary, "our system was to protect them, even against our own citizens: that we wish to get lines established with all of them, and have no views even of purchasing any more lands of them for a long time." The United States did not claim a right of soil, by conquest or declaration of sovereignty. "We consider it as established by the usage of different nations into a kind of jus gentium for America, that a white nation settling down and declaring that such and such are their limits, makes an invasion of those limits by an other white nation an act of war, but gives no right of soil against the native possessors."[24]

While Jefferson was pursuing his inconclusive and ultimately fruitless negotiations with Hammond, Hammond was consulting behind his back with Jefferson's rival in the cabinet, Alexander Hamilton. Hammond liked Hamilton better than Jefferson and indiscreetly said so to a friend of Jefferson's. "The Secretary of the Treasury is more a man of the world than Jefferson and I like his manners better, and can speak more freely to him.

Jefferson is in the Virginia interest and that of the French. And it is his fault that we are at a distance. He prefers writing to conversing and thus it is that we are apart."[25] And a few days after the dinner conversation, Hammond wrote to his government in London that he had learned from Hamilton that Jefferson's memorandum did not reflect the views of the American administration, that the President had not read it, that the Cabinet had not approved it, that all opposed its intemperate violence and peculiar asperity—false charges all, for the President had read and approved it, as had Randolph, Hamilton, and Jefferson's friend and adviser James Madison.

Hammond's underhanded meddling in America's Indian affairs even included a secret meeting with the Mohawk emissary Joseph Brant, whose arrival in Philadelphia in June 1792 Jefferson noted with approbation. Brant was there to confer with Knox and to carry American proposals regarding peace, boundaries, and civilization to the Western Confederacy. In his meeting with Hammond, Brant revealed the nature of the American offer (he believed it would be rejected by the majority but might prove attractive to the Wyandots, Delawares, and Shawnees) and advised him that British agent McKee had already, in 1791, urged the Indians to demand the creation of a barrier state.[26]

As it turned out, Brant was unable to make the trip to meet with the Western Confederacy and sent his son Isaac instead. But Isaac's misrepresentation of the proposals carried by his father made him appear to the Indian advocates of peace as an "Emissary of the Devil." Rumors flew that the Americans were selling poisoned liquor, that the Indians were all to be driven across the Mississippi, and that the offer to teach the Indians to raise cattle and tend their fields like white men was merely a ruse to turn Indian men into women (who were the native horticulturists) or "beasts" like oxen and packhorses, to raise corn for the white men. At the end, the tribesmen left the fall meeting with guns and ammunition, supplied by McKee, to continue the war to victory.[27]

The Americans could gain only marginal satisfaction from a peace treaty with friendly Weas, Kaskaskias, and Potawatomies at Vincennes (a treaty rejected by the Senate) and from a perilous visit of friendly chiefs, under threats of murder by Kentuckians, to Philadelphia, where Jefferson's old acquaintance, du Coigne, served as speaker and delivered an address to Washington. Jefferson, as a member of the cabinet, very likely met du Coigne again on this occasion.[28]

Jefferson was never able to secure a response from Hammond. The posts were, however, finally turned over pursuant to a treaty completed in England in 1795 by John Jay, a strong Federalist and an ally of Hamilton, after Wayne's success at Fallen Timbers. The Jay Treaty was a galling affront to Jefferson, because it sacrificed American interests in maritime commerce to a Britain now desperately at war with America's ally, France; British creditors were even to be compensated while American slave holders were not.[29]

Another Jeffersonian frustration involving Indian affairs lay to the south. Jefferson hoped to establish an American right to navigate the Mississippi through Spanish Louisiana. But the Spanish felt no obligation to concede such a right. They themselves were on the offensive, organizing the four southern tribes in confederation to defend Spain's claims west of the Appalachians from intrusion by Georgians and Carolinians. Marauding parties of Indians harassed Americans from Florida to the Tennessee River. In Jefferson's opinion, only war could resolve the impasse to the south, as it had in the north. But in the south no war came.[30]

Jefferson resigned his office as secretary of state at the close of 1793, disgruntled with his own failure to achieve diplomatic success with either Britain or Spain and dismayed by the seeming drift of government under the Federalists toward an almost monarchical centralization of power. But he never relinquished his legal opinion that the aboriginal Indian occupants of the continent possessed the right of soil, including both their settlements and hunting grounds, and that formerly the British Crown and now the government of the United States had only a preemptive right to purchase, exclusive of other white sovereignties.

The Whiskey Rebellion and States' Rights

Federal control over the purchase and settlement of Indian land, and over Indian trade, was eroded not just by the Indian resistance and British complicity but by many frontier Americans themselves, who refused to recognize federal or even state authority in outlying areas. From pre-Revolutionary times on, ambitious and greedy individuals had sought to "purchase" tracts of land from local Indians without the participation or knowledge of either tribal councils or colonial, state, or federal authorities, and to evade trade regulations by bringing liquor into Indian country, cheating Indians in bargaining over furs and hides, and offering shoddy goods. Disputes with Indians over hunting rights, trade transactions, and interference with Indian women were often settled by knife or gun. And no matter what the circumstances, white culprits could never be convicted by white juries.

No wonder, then, that responsible men in government regarded the undisciplined, Indian-hating frontiersmen as the principal obstacle to peaceful purchase and settlement of the west. Knox and Washington believed that only military force could restrain whites on the frontiers and keep them from encroaching on Indian lands, trading without licenses, and committing unprovoked acts of violence. Jefferson in principle agreed with them. But shortly after becoming Washington's secretary of state, Jefferson was confronted with political issues that called forth from him a different reaction—a vehemently populist, pro-settler, states' rights philosophy of republicanism, in response to what he saw as the centralizing, pro-urban monarchical drive of the Federalists. This philosophical position made unthinkable the maintenance of a permanent military apparatus sufficient to suppress white trespasses on the Indian frontiers. In the decentralized political world that he was endeavoring to create, his social ideals with respect to the rights of Indians and a humane civilization policy could never be realized.

Jefferson's responses to two political crises, neither one directly involving Indians, illustrate the dilemma and foreshadow the ambivalence of Jefferson's Indian policy during his administration. The first event was the Whiskey Rebellion of 1793–94. This was a protest, centered mainly among Scotch-Irish settlers in western Pennsylvania, particularly in the Monongahela–Redstone district, against an excise tax on whiskey that had been levied by Congress at Hamilton's urging.[31] Whiskey was a commodity of vital importance to these frontier settlers, for whom it was virtually the only product that could be readily preserved, transported a great distance, and converted into cash. In addition to resolutions and memorials decrying the whiskey tax, the settlers' resistance took the form of tax evasion and physical harassment of revenue collectors.

At first this challenge to the government's authority to levy and collect taxes offended Jefferson as much as it did Washington and Hamilton. But as the resistance grew more organized and intense, the Federalists began to accuse the so-called democratic societies on the frontiers of fomenting not only a pro-French, anti-government policy in foreign affairs but also of provoking the Whiskey Rebellion itself. Eventually President Washington ordered a 12,000-man militia, accompanied by the hated Hamilton himself, into the disaffected region; ringleaders were captured, tried, and convicted (and eventually pardoned by Washington). Jefferson was outraged by these high-handed proceedings. He considered the rebels not to have done "anything more than riotous . . . The excise law is an infernal one."[32] He foresaw the potential for a perhaps justifiable separation from the union by western agriculturists, who now shared an intense detestation of the government as a result of the unilateral declaration of war by one political faction against another.

The second event that stimulated Jefferson's growing populism and raised his anti-Federalist ire was passage of the Alien and Sedition Laws of 1798, which provided for the expulsion or incarceration of alien residents of, or visitors to, the United States if they were deemed dangerous to the country, and made assembly to oppose any act of the government, or publication of writings hostile to the government, punishable by fine or imprisonment. Jefferson's friend Volney was forced to leave the country precipitously as an enemy alien; several anti-Federalist editors were jailed. The acts were clearly intended to suppress the political activities of the Jeffersonian Republicans. As the constitutional crisis between the Federalists and the Republicans dragged on, intensified by the prospect of war with revolutionary France, the Alien and Sedition Laws came to represent to Jefferson an evil plot of pro-British monarchists, like John Adams, to destroy the Republican opposition. Jefferson saw a dire threat to state and local governments by the increasing seizure of powers by a central government, a seizure not sanctioned by the Constitution.

In response, in 1798 he secretly composed the "Kentucky Resolutions," a body of anti-Federalist opinions on the Alien and Sedition Laws which included the claim that the states had the right to nullify laws and acts of the general government that it considered to violate the Constitution by assuming undelegated powers. Those resolutions, and a comparable set drafted by James Madison for Virginia, raised the specter of a dissolution of the Union. Although the resolutions as actually passed by the Kentucky and Virginia legislatures did not contain the word "nullification" and were generally milder in tone than the original drafts, they constituted another signal to the "General Government" to keep its hands out of local affairs.[33]

None of these Jeffersonian declarations of local sovereignty over local issues and the right of dissent—even armed dissent—directly addressed the Indian boundary question. Jefferson did not openly advocate that federal authorities condone outrages committed on friendly Indians. But in the interest of the Republican principle of minimizing the interference of the general government in the political and economic activities of its citizens, he was not about to support Henry Knox's old recommendation that a standing army be deployed on the frontiers to protect the Indians or that white offenders be tried by military court martial.

The "Civilized" Indians

Jefferson was not personally familiar with the situation in Indian country, even though he sought to improve conditions by introducing "civilization." He never saw with his own eyes any Indian community, civilized or not, except for the town on Long Island that he and Madison visited in June 1791 and (possibly) the tiny reservation at Brotherton, in central New Jersey, where he or a friend collected a vocabulary in 1792.

The one-day excursion to the village of Poosepatuck was an impromptu affair. The two future presidents had stopped at the home of General William Floyd on their way back from their northern tour, and Floyd escorted them on a side trip to the nearby Indian village where Jefferson recorded a vocabulary.[34] The inhabitants spoke an Algonkian language and were descendants of the Unquachog nation, who once shared eastern Long Island with the Montauks, Shinnecocks, and other native peoples, the whole combined native population of the island amounting to no more than 5,000 souls. The Unquachog reservation had been granted to his Indian neighbors in 1700 by Colonel William Smith, who owned a manor of about 17,000 acres in the area of present-day Mastic and Moriches, on Great South Bay. The original grant by Smith was 175 acres; by the time of Jefferson's visit, it had been whittled down to less than 50 acres, and the population had dwindled, as a result of disease and wars with the Indians of the mainland, to a few dozen families. Jefferson counted only about "20 souls" but he probably underestimated, as was his wont; a century later, the number had risen to "about twenty families . . . to some extent intermarried with negroes."

The aboriginal economy had depended on horticulture, fishing, and clamming and oystering, and, for a cash crop, the manufacture of wampum from the shells of clams, locally termed *quahog*. With the decline of the wampum industry toward the end of the seventeenth century, however, the Unquachogs and other Long Island peoples turned to other lines of work to obtain the cash or credit needed to buy trade goods. Wage work for local white whalers and fishermen became the chosen male occupation. Christian missionaries were preaching to the people at Poosepatuck from the middle of the eighteenth century; English surnames were adopted; and a new institution of "kings" and "queens" was developed to provide spokespersons for dealing with the whites.[35]

What Jefferson was presented with at Poosepatuck in 1791, therefore, was a "civilized" Indian community, perpetuated by only a remnant of the former population, living by subsistence agriculture, fishing and gathering, and working for wages on local whaling and fishing boats owned by whites, with whom they shared the catch. How much he actually perceived of this hybrid culture is not revealed in his record of the visit. He probably thought the community was moribund. But actually, like dozens of other remnant groups along the eastern seaboard, it was very much alive, and the reservation and its multiracial population survive to this day as a tribal enclave in largely white suburbia.

The other community of "civilized" Indians that Jefferson may have visited in the 1790s was the Delaware reservation named Brotherton in central New Jersey, about forty miles east of Philadelphia. In December 1792 a vocabulary in the Delaware language, entered on Jefferson's printed form, was collected at "Edgepuluck West New Jersey." As in the case of the Poosepatuck, the population was recorded: "Their numbers about forty years ago were abut 280, are now about 30." The style of notetaking is similar to the Unquachog vocabulary, but the handwriting is not Jefferson's; possibly this is a later transcription, perhaps by DuPonceau, who recorded at the bottom of the form the words "Mr. Thos. Jefferson," or it may have been recorded by James Madison, who like Jefferson was in Philadelphia attending Congress in 1792.[36] Either man could have encountered English-speaking Delawares from Brotherton in Philadelphia, where members of the tribe peddled their brooms and baskets for cash.

The Brotherton Indians had been an established and well-known community in New Jersey from about 1758, when the village was established as the gathering place for all 280 of the Delaware Indians still residing in the state, until 1802, when most of the remaining 100 or so members, including 63 adults and their children, sold the tract and moved to New Stockbridge in New York State. The site was acquired by white farmers and entrepreneurs but is still known today as Indian Mills for the saw and grist mills the Indians left behind.

What Jefferson saw, if he visited Brotherton, was a planned community that had been established by the government of New Jersey as partial recompense for the relinquishment by the Delawares (including the Munsees) of all their claims to land in both northern and southern New Jersey. A tract of 3,000 acres was purchased from a prosperous landowner that encompassed several houses, a saw mill, outbuildings and fences, orchards and cleared land. The governor announced that "we are going to build a Town for them . . . and a grist Mill." Lots were laid out for private ownership, and ten houses were erected.

The village occupied a small oasis on the edge of the pine barrens, in which the Indians were granted the further right to hunt, trap, cut timber, and gather basket materials, and they were allowed free passage down the river to the sea for fishing. The saw mill and grist mill, it was expected, would not only serve their own needs but would "raise a little money for other purposes"—an essential consideration for an economy that could no longer expect to count on the fur trade for the purchase of essential dry goods, fabrics, and hardware. For a time the village prospered and the Indians built a meeting house and school, a blacksmith shop, and a store. The spiritual needs of the community were served by the Reverend David Brainerd, the missionary, and by his brother, the Reverend John Brainerd, after David Brainerd's death. An Indian convert, Stephen Calvin, served as the schoolmaster for Indian children.[37]

Through Brainerd and Calvin, the College of New Jersey at Princeton, then a Presbyterian institution, maintained a close interest in the welfare of the Brotherton Indians. Brainerd obtained admission to Princeton for Bartholomew Calvin, a son of Stephen's, and Bartholomew and other Indian students at the college obtained the personal interest of Samuel Stanhope Smith, Jefferson's old opponent on the issue of racial differences and from 1785 a fellow member of the American Philosophical Society. Smith was a strict disciplinarian as a theologian, teacher, and academic administrator (he was president of Princeton from 1795 to 1812, when he resigned in protest against "student insubordination"). But on philosophical issues, and particularly as regards racial differences, he might be described as a liberal, asserting a theory of rapid physical evolution as a result of the influence of climate and "the state of society" and promoting the teaching of the natural sciences and the humanities in traditional bastions of religious and classical studies.

Smith's *Essay on the Causes of the Variety of Complexion and Figure in the*

Human Species, first published in Philadelphia in 1787, introduced "a young Indian" as an example of the incomplete progress of the Indian physique toward white standards resulting from being "too far advanced in savage habits." His mouth was still too large, his lips too thick, his cheekbones too high, his complexion too dark; but the eyes were less vacant, the expression "less lugubrious," than those of his brethren back on the reservation. And he was capable of blushing![38] This young Indian was probably George White Eyes, son of the Delaware chief White Eyes, who had been murdered by white men on the Ohio in 1778. He was brought to Princeton in 1779 at the age of eight and was now about fifteen years of age, busily studying Latin and Greek. Although he won a prize at grammar school commencement, he quit college at eighteen and returned to his home in Ohio.

Two other Ohio Delaware youths came with George White Eyes to study at Princeton. They were John and Thomas Killbuck, sons of the friendly Delaware chief Killbuck, who brought them to Philadelphia in 1779 with the Delaware delegation's eastern tour. It was this Killbuck whom Michael Cresap had threatened to kill in 1774. John and Thomas were less successful at Princeton than George White Eyes. Thomas took to drink, and John made a servant girl pregnant; both departed for Ohio in 1785.[39]

By the time George White Eyes and the Killbucks had arrived at Princeton, Bartholomew Calvin (born about 1757) had probably completed his course of studies. After leaving Princeton, Calvin went on to a long and productive career as teacher and community representative in dealings with white officialdom. The Calvins were no doubt a success story in the eyes of enlightened educators, who believed that the Indians were as capable of progress as anybody and that it was worthwhile to make the effort to help them on the path of civilization. But the fate of the Brotherton community was disappointing. Although they were far away from "the Wild Indians" to the north and west, they were not insulated from other noxious influences. Whites persisted in selling them liquor, and drunkenness was a problem that John Brainerd was unsuccessful in stopping. Whites trespassed on Indian land to cut timber, refused to pay debts, and suspected that young Brotherton males were slipping away to join the hostiles.

In 1762 a disastrous fire completely destroyed the saw mill, eliminating the source of cash needed to pay debts incurred for food, clothing, and nails for construction. An appeal to the legislature for financial aid was denied, and the saw mill was not rebuilt; a petition for permission to lease part of their land to white farmers was also denied. By the mid-1770s the population at Brotherton had dwindled to about sixty, and these few were described by a Quaker visitor as "poor Indians . . . in very low circumstances as to food and raiment."[40]

In 1795 the reservation was visited by a German traveler, the physician and naturalist J. F. H. Autenreith, who described a pleasant-looking village with "nice winding paths like an English park" leading to the log houses, set among well-tilled fenced fields and orchards, "entirely European-American in manner." Some of these fields may by then have been leased to whites for cultivation and timbering, however. He visited with "their leader" and his family, found them to be Asiatic in physiognomy but "dressed like white Americans"; everyone spoke English, and the leader was able to read and write. All the men were at least nominal Christians and denied virtually any knowledge of the old religious beliefs and rituals. Only about nine families were reported to remain.

In 1796 all the farm land was leased to three white men, who were to pay rent in cash or necessaries for the benefit of the remaining Indians. In 1802 the band sold the tract and removed to the refugee Algonkian settlement at New Stockbridge on the Oneida Reservation in New York State and again moved to Wisconsin a couple of decades later. In 1832, in a final act of separation from New Jersey, Bartholomew Calvin, now seventy-six years old, persuaded the legislature to purchase the residual hunting and fishing rights of the Delaware Indians, which had not been sold along with the Brotherton tract, for the sum of $2,000. In 1839–1840, during the great removal, the Wisconsin community of intermingled Delawares and Mahicans trekked west across the Mississippi, some to Kansas and some to Oklahoma, where their descendants remain.[41]

Another community of "civilized" Delawares of which Jefferson probably was aware during the 1790s but never visited was the Moravian village of Goshen on the Tuscarawas River, a tributary of the Muskingum in eastern Ohio. The Moravians had secured from Congress in 1788 a grant of 12,000 acres in the Northwest Territory for the establishment of a mission to the Delaware Indians, among whom they had worked to build small "civilized" Christian settlements ever since 1740, when they founded their own utopian community at Bethlehem in Pennsylvania. After the war ended, Congress renewed the grant in the ceded area south of the Greenville line, and in spring 1797 three tracts were surveyed of 4,000 acres each. One of these was Goshen, near the site of an earlier Moravian mission. In the fall of 1798 the veteran missionary David Zeisberger and a little band of thirty-one Indian converts from the Thames River mission in Ontario disembarked from their canoes and commenced building the town.[42]

Goshen was from the first a carefully planned enterprise, intended to carry out both the civilization policy of the federal government and the evangelical purposes of the Society of the United Brethren for the Propagating of the Gospel among the Heathen. Across the river the Moravians built a new white settlement, Gnadenhütten, near the site of the former mission village where the converts had been massacred not quite twenty years before. Here a community of friendly white Moravians led by John Heckewelder would trade eastern dry goods and hardware for surplus furs, meat, and baskets produced by the Goshen Indians; and Goshen would be a training ground for new missionaries and native helpers, who then would go on to establish mission stations among the wild Indians to the west, particularly the heathen and apostate Delawares on the White River in Indiana. The nearest white settlements that could serve as a source for further goods and services, such as blacksmithing and gun repair, were located on the Ohio River in what is now West Virginia.

The Indian population at Goshen remained in the range of forty to seventy converts during its first six years, but the Moravian settlement, attracting farmers and artisans from Pennsylvania, grew rapidly, amounting to about two hundred residents within the same period. Life at Goshen was a successful combination of Indian economy and Moravian discipline. The master of the village was David Zeisberger, who promulgated a list of nineteen specific regulations (see next page).[43] But this theological dictatorship was in other ways tolerant of native custom, and a viable hybrid culture combining elements of the by-now traditional fur trade economy and state-of-the art European farm practice developed.

The spring and winter hunts were extensive undertakings and were compared by the Indians to the annual harvests of the white people. Hundreds of deer were taken each winter, and nearly two hundred bear were killed in the spring of 1800 alone. The men dragged their prey back to the camp, where the women and children scraped and prepared the skins and dried the meat. In the early spring the people moved out to the sugar-making camps. Private property was encouraged, each male convert building his own house, fencing, planting (in small hillocks, for at first the

David Zeisberger's Regulations of Indian Life at Goshen

1. All converts must worship one God, but the one and only true God, who made us and all creatures, and came into this world in order to save sinners; to him alone we pray.
2. We will rest from work on the Lord's day, and attend public service.
3. We will honor father and mother, and when they grow old and needy we will do for them what we can.
4. All residents must have prior approval from both the Native Helpers and the missionaries before they can live in the village.
5. All residents must refuse to have any association with thieves, murderers, whore mongers, and drunkards.
6. All dancing, sacrifices, heathen festivals, and games are prohibited.
7. Witchcraft will not be permitted during hunting.
8. All villagers must renounce and abhor tricks, lies, and deceits of Satan.
9. There must be prompt obedience to the missionaries and the Native Helpers who are appointed to preserve order in the village.
10. We will not be idle, nor scold, nor beat one another, nor tell lies.
11. Whoever injuries the property of his neighbors shall make restitution.
12. A man shall have but one wife, he shall love and provide for her; and a woman should have but one husband, be obedient to him, care for his children, and cleanly in all things.
13. All villagers must renounce the use of rum, and traders are prohibited from bringing liquor into the village.
14. Prior consent be received from the Native Helpers before contracting any debt or selling any goods from traders.
15. Permission must be received from the Native Helpers before going hunting.
16. Young persons shall not marry without the consent of their parents, and the missionaries.
17. All members of the village must willingly assist in community projects, such as building fences, repairing public buildings, etc.
18. Hospitality must be shown to all strangers. All residents must contribute corn from their private stores whenever needed, or sugar for lovefeast.
19. No villagers will go to war or buy anything from warriors taken in war. [This statute was adopted during the revolutionary war.]

fields were not plowed), and tending his own crop of corn and vegetables and feeding his own family. This was in contrast to aboriginal practice, in which women worked the fields communally and men did not assume the role of *pater familias.* The peach and apple orchards, however, were a cooperative project; the surplus of fruit was sold to nearby white settlers and the cash proceeds devoted to village enterprises.

The houses and church were solidly constructed of logs; the Indian converts themselves notched the timbers with hatchets, smoothed the surfaces with broad-axe and plane, and split clapboards and shingles. Using hand tools, expert Indian carpenters constructed canoes that sold for twenty-five dollars; and men and women manufactured large quantities of baskets, brooms, and chairs, which were taken by the wagonload to sell in Pittsburgh, the Monongahela valley, and at Wheeling on the Ohio.

In the village school, adults and children were instructed in both Delaware and English, and many became literate enough to engage in written correspondence with friends and relatives in other Delaware villages. The schedule of classes was adapted to the annual cycle of hunting and sugar-making. Church services were held twice a day, also in the school. In the morning, Scriptures were read and sermons delivered; in the evening, worship was combined with discussion of more secular issues, such as the assignment of communal duties and the resolution of disputes, and the meeting concluded with the singing of hymns, often led by the accomplished married couples' choir. The Moravians had always been famous for their musical love feasts, and the tradition was continued at Goshen.

But this frontier idyll was not to last. Farther to the west, the Shawnee Prophet Tenskwatawa was urging the Indians of the northwest to shun the white man's ways and return to the customs of their ancestors. In 1805 a young man, Henry, the son of a leading Goshen convert, committed suicide. To Zeisberger, this act was an unpardonable sin, and he refused to permit a Christian burial. The family was enraged and left the mission, fifteen in all. About the same time, and apparently out of disillusionment with the stone-hearted Zeisberger, drunkenness became a major problem in the village, the liquor being supplied surreptitiously by merchants from New Philadelphia, a non-Moravian white settlement only a few miles away.

Zeisberger died in 1808. His assistant for a time was able to rebuild the mission, and it survived the suspicions of white neighbors during the War of 1812. But alcohol remained a problem, the population dwindled, and the last of the Goshen community left the valley of the Muskingum in 1821, joining the White River Delawares in the trek west of the Mississippi.[44]

Several other civilization projects among the Indian nations north of the Ohio were sponsored by religious bodies with the blessing and minor financial encouragement of the federal government. The Quaker meeting in Philadelphia in 1798 launched a very successful program among the Iroquois in New York State. Episcopal missionaries had long worked among the Mohawks, and the Calvinist, Samuel Kirkland, had become a permanent resident at Oneida. And the Moravians had followed their Algonkian converts from one European-organized settlement after another as the frontier moved west throughout the eighteenth century. Logan the Great Mingo had been a product of Moravian influence at Shamokin and had in fact known Heckewelder and Zeisberger both in Pennsylvania and later along the Muskingum in the years before Lord Dunmore's War. Jefferson can hardly have been ignorant of this thrust of civilizing missionary benevolence among the Iroquois of New York and the Algonkians of the Northwest Territory; he had recommended a similar program for the Brafferton Institution at William and Mary.

South of the Ohio, the course taken by the Federalist civilization program was somewhat different. Despite two centuries of war and disease, large native populations still hunted and resided on extensive tracts of land that they had claimed for many generations; they were not refugees on reservation communities surrounded by whites. And they had not yet been much missionized. The agents of "civilization" in the south had traditionally been the resident traders, mostly representatives of the British-owned Panton, Leslie, and Company, now based in Florida. In the 1790s each town among the Creeks, Cherokees, Choctaws, and Chickasaws had its own resident trader, who usually lived with a native wife, raised a family of children by her, and in some cases built up a virtually baronial lifestyle that served as a model for emulation by the chiefly elite among the Indians.

Among the Creeks of Hillabee Town in present-day Alabama, a Scottish trader, Robert Grierson, had acquired 40 black slaves, 300 cattle, 30 horses, and land for raising cotton, which was cleaned at Grierson's own cotton gin. Following his example, leading Hillabee Indians were also farming and raising cattle; one (perhaps a so-called half-breed son of Grierson's) owned 130 head of cattle and 10 horses. The Hillabee community was destroyed by Andrew Jackson's army in 1813. Also among the Upper Creeks, an English trader named Richard Bailey had lived for forty years with his Indian family; his estate boasted beehives, cotton (which his wife and daughters spun, wove, and fashioned into clothes), 7 black slaves, 200 head of cattle, 150 hogs, and 120 horses. The "half-breed" Charles Weatherford, brother-in-law of the Creek leader Alexander McGillivray, bred race horses and built a race track near his house. There were dozens of resident traders all told among the Creeks, maintaining Indian families and keeping a general store in each village, and there were dozens of Creek men who had assumed the southern plantation lifestyle, with slaves and cotton and fine horses. Missionaries were largely absent.[45]

The first federal agent among the southern Indians responsible for, among other things, promoting "civilization" was Colonel Benjamin Hawkins. Hawkins, like Jefferson, was a scion of the frontier aristocracy. His family came from Virginia to North Carolina before he was born; he grew up on his father's tobacco plantation, attended Princeton University, and was employed by North Carolina as commercial agent, procuring supplies for the military during the Revolutionary War. Tradition has it that he also for a time served General Washington as a French-speaking liaison officer. Between 1781 and 1795 he had been a member of the Continental Congress and then the Senate, active in committees on Indian affairs, and a friend and confidant of Jefferson's. He served as United States commissioner in the treaty negotiations with the southern Indians that brought peace, of a sort, to the frontiers of the states south of the Ohio. In 1796, on the basis of his experience in Indian relations and his standing as a Federalist, albeit a relatively liberal one, he was appointed principal temporary agent for Indian affairs south of the Ohio River, and he continued in this capacity through Jefferson's and Madison's administrations until his death at his residence in the Creek country in 1816.

Hawkins was eager to protect "his" Indians from the rapacious efforts of Georgia and his own state of North Carolina to deny federal authority, seize Indian land, and subject the natives to the laws of the state. He and Jefferson had corresponded on the subject while Jefferson was in Paris. Jefferson's reply had been a bit equivocal, appealing to the abstract principles of "justice'" and "fear" (whatever these terms might imply).[46]

Hawkins was also committed to the federal civilization program. He, like the traders, invested a great deal of his own time and money in keeping a model slave-operated farm, where he experimented with new methods of husbandry and taught Indian men how to farm, plantation-style, and the women how to spin and weave and keep house. He declined

Benjamin Hawkins, agent to the Creek nation. Artist and date unknown. From Merritt Pound, *Benjamin Hawkins* (University of Georgia Press, 1951). Courtesy of Harvard College Library.

"Chiefs of the Creek Nation, and a Georgian Squatter."
Engraving by W. H. Lizars, after a drawing by Basil Hall, 1827–1828.
Courtesy of the Beinecke Library, Yale University.

the advances of Indian women who offered marriage, and eventually wed his white mistress. No more attached to organized religion than was Jefferson, he did not actively solicit the visitations of northern missionaries; this meant that English schooling, generally a missionary activity, was not carried out. But in the case of white technology, he was an agent of acculturation in the same mode as the old resident traders and the newer federal trading houses established by the Trade and Intercourse Acts. He dutifully distributed hundreds of plows and other farm equipment provided by the Federalist program.

Where he differed sharply from traders and missionaries was with regard to political organization. He sought to impose on the Creeks, and as best he could on the other tribes, his conception of a centralized Indian state with legislative, executive, and administrative branches, strong enough to unite the several autonomous geographical districts, the factions, and the divided authorities of traditional chiefs and the newer warrior leaders. During Jefferson's administration his efforts had some success, but they were blighted after 1805 by the inflammatory, antiwhite, anticivilization rhetoric of the Red Sticks, followers of the Shawnee Prophet Tenskwatawa and of his brother Tecumseh. During the War of 1812 Andrew Jackson's army crushed the Creeks, and after the war anti-American sentiment continued to hamper the federal civilization program in the Creek country.[47]

"Uncivilized" Whites

Each of the communities of "civilized" Indians had complaints about the conduct of some of the white people whose settlements were closing in upon them. The Brothertons in New Jersey and the Goshen Delawares in Ohio were plagued by bootleg whiskey sellers. The Creeks, Hawkins reported, suffered seriously from the depredations of horse thieves and trespassing whites, who grazed their cattle on Indian lands and set fish traps in their streams.[48] Indians, on the other hand, also committed crimes, particularly horse stealing. Retaliatory assaults and murders occurred on both sides, in defiance of federal and state law and Indian custom. Such incidents as these, set against a recent history of frontier warfare, with all of its bloody atrocities, could not but maintain an atmosphere of distrust and apprehension. The readiness to exploit and to kill was exacerbated by the excessive use of alcohol by Indians and frontiersmen alike.

In these turbulent frontier white communities, "Indian fighters" became folk heroes. The legendary Wetzel family is a prime example. From Lancaster County, Pennsylvania, the Wetzels, along with ten other families, moved to the Virginia frontier near Wheeling in the early 1770s, on the eve of Lord Dunmore's War. Two of the five brothers were captured by Indians early in the Revolution but escaped. Martin Wetzel gained a measure of infamy by participating in the slaughter of prisoners during Brodhead's campaign against the Delawares on the Muskingum in 1781 and by murdering an Indian emissary who was on his way to arrange a peace.

Lewis Wetzel earned a reputation for meanness by murdering an old Indian on horseback who had secretly escorted him to safety after he had been captured and sentenced to be burned at the stake. Reproached for this act, he gave as his excuse: "He made me walk, and he was nothing but an Indian." Lewis, indeed, made a career as a serial killer of Indian men (he claimed never to have killed women except by accident); his biographer enumerates at least 52 killings. He was arrested once for a particularly

"Lewis Wetzel Killing Three Indians." Engraving by Wills De Hass, 1851, from *History of the Early Settlement and Indian Wars of Western Virginia.* Courtesy of Harvard College Library.

offensive murder but escaped and was not punished. The Wetzels never did learn to farm; they suffered eventually from multiple wounds which incapacitated them for useful work. Their trade was killing Indians, and they boasted in a petition for financial aid that they had "with their own hands taken and destroyed thirty two or there abouts Indians."[49]

Some of the killings of peaceful Indians living close to white settlements were probably acts of terrorism calculated to drive away native inhabitants of coveted lands. This apparently was the motive in the murder of Bald Eagle, whose body, with a piece of cornbread stuffed in his mouth, was propped up in the stern of a canoe and set afloat down the Monongahela. Terrorism probably also lay behind the slaughter of five Delaware families, including men, women, and children, at Bulltown on the Little Kanawha.[50]

The near universality of this type of racist contempt and murderous hatred of Indians in the white frontier communities posed a problem of social control for both British and American authorities. In 1767 the British commander General Gage reported to his superiors in England that "All the People of the Frontiers, from Pennsylvania to Virginia inclusive, openly avow, that they will never find a Man guilty of Murder, for killing an Indian."[51] Forty years later, Jefferson would find the same situation embarrassing him in his efforts to maintain peaceful relations with the Indians of the Ohio country. When Governor Harrison complained that the Delawares were justly irritated "in consequence of our being unable to bring to justice any one of those miscreants who have murdered their people," and particularly one William Rea, Jefferson authorized the secretary of war to increase the reward for Rea's capture to $1,000. "Both the Indians and our own people," he averred, "want some example of punishment for the murder of an Indian."[52] In effect, though, Jefferson just wanted another scapegoat.

To white folk on the frontier, there were no good Indians, for even the friendly and civilized ones, including women and children, were guilty in their eyes of aiding and comforting the same warriors who had massacred white families in the past and would do so again if given a chance. Ironically, retribution tended to fall most heavily on the friendly, civilized Indians precisely because they were more trusting and more accessible than the warlike Indians to the west.

In his book *History, Manners, and Customs of the Indian Nations* (1819), John Heckewelder reiterated much of what Jefferson had written earlier

John Heckewelder, Moravian missionary. Oil on canvas by Gustav Anton von Seckendorff (alias Patrick Peale), c. 1822–1823. Courtesy of the American Philosophical Society.

about the admirable moral qualities of the aboriginal Indians. But he expatiated on the depraved character of many of the frontier whites. In the concluding chapter, "The Indians and The Whites Compared," he drew attention to the systematic use of encroachment and violence in provoking a war crisis that could only be resolved by another cession of land. His description of the process was detailed (see opposite).[53] And his prime example of the process in action was, in fact, Jefferson's account of the murder of Logan's family and the consequent Lord Dunmore's War in the *Notes* and in the *Appendix* to the *Notes.* Jefferson had in fact consulted with Heckewelder about the murder and printed his testimony in the *Appendix.* "A precedent, however, may be found, on perusing Mr. Jefferson's Appendix to his Notes on Virginia. On all occasions, when the object is to murder Indians, strong liquor is the main article required; for when you have them dead drunk, you may do to them as you please, without running the risk of losing your life. And should you find that the laws of your country may reach you where you are, you have only to escape or conceal yourself for a while, until the storm has blown over! I well recollect the time when thieves and murderers of Indians fled from impending punish-

John Heckewelder's Description of the Perfidy of Whites

"No faith can be placed in what the Indians promise at treaties; for scarcely is a treaty concluded than they are again murdering us." Such is our complaint against these unfortunate people; but they will tell you that it is the white man in whom no faith is to be placed. They will tell you, that there is not a single instance in which the whites have not violated the engagements that they had made at treaties. They say that when they had ceded lands to the white people, and boundary lines had been established—"firmly established!" beyond which no whites were to settle; scarcely was the treaty signed, when white intruders again were settling and hunting on their lands! It is true that when they preferred their complaints to the government, the government gave them many fair promises, and assured them that men would be sent to remove the intruders by force from the usurped lands. The men, indeed, came, but with chain and compass in their hands, taking surveys of the tracts of good land, which the intruders, from their knowledge of the country, had pointed out to them! What was then to be done, when those intruders would not go off from the land, but on the contrary, increased in numbers?? "Oh!" said those people, (and I have myself frequently heard this language in the Western country,) "a new treaty will soon give us all this land; nothing is now wanting but a pretence to pick a quarrel with them!"

ment across the Susquehanna, where they considered themselves safe; on which account this river had the name given to it of '*the rogue river.*' I have heard other rivers called by similar names."[54]

The demoralization of many frontier communities, particularly in the Monongahela region of western Pennsylvania and the mountain valleys of West Virginia, was exacerbated by extreme poverty. Jefferson in the *Notes* wrote a famous panegyric on the life of the farmer, declaring that "those who labor in the earth are the chosen people of God," virtuous and free in comparison with the artisan population of cities, and he recommended that America remain a nation of husbandmen, exchanging the products of the field and forest for the manufactures of Europe.[55] This glib formula presupposed the availability of markets, both domestic and foreign, to the farmer, an assumption fair enough for plantations like Monticello. But markets were not always available, and frontier man was not always virtuous, as Crevecoeur, writing about the same time as Jefferson, observed. In an essay that remained unpublished until 1923 he vividly described some of the more remote white settlements (see opposite).[56]

Crevecoeur's analysis of the economic problem of the frontier community that had no ready access to market was directly applicable to the very frontier regions that were most aggressive in their greed for Indian land: the valleys of the Monongahela and the Ohio south of Pittsburgh, and the Appalachian plateau in southwestern Virginia and West Virginia. The population of the Monongahela region and adjacent Ohio valley ap-

"American Stage Waggon." Engraving by Isaac Weld, Jr., c. 1799.
Courtesy of the Beinecke Library, Yale University.

Crevecoeur's Description of Poverty on the Frontier

I was once at Pa—an, where several families dwelt on the most fruitful soil I have ever seen in my life. The warmest imagination can't conceive anything equal to it. These people raised what they pleased: oats, peas, wheat, corn, with two days' labour in the week. At their doors they had a fair river, on their backs high mountains full of game. Yet with all these advantages, placed as they were on these shores of Eden, they lived as poor as the poorest wretches of Europe who have nothing. Their houses were miserable hovels. Their stalks of grain rotted in their fields. They were almost starved, not for want of victuals but of spirit and activity to cook them. They were almost naked.

This may appear to you a strange problem. This is representing to you two extremes which you cannot reconcile, yet this relation is founded on fact and reason. This people had not nor could they have, situated as they were, any place where they might convey their produce. They could neither transport, sell, nor exchange anything they had, except of cattle, so singularly were they placed. This annihilated all the riches of their grounds; rendered all their labours abortive; rendered them careless, slothful, and inactive. This constituted their poverty, though in the midst of the greatest plenty. They could not build for want of nails. They could not clothe themselves for want of materials, which they might easily have procured with their wheat. They were inferior to the Indians. Had they had a market, the scene would have been greatly changed. Neatness, convenience, decency of appearance would have soon banished that singular poverty under which they groaned. I stayed five days with them and could not rejoice enough to think that my farm was so much more advantageously situated. Happily for this country[,] we have but few spots among the many which have been discovered [from which] the people may [not] convey what they raise to some markets. But, you'll say, what could induce people to settle on such grounds? The extreme fertility of the soil, necessity, and poverty. This it is, sir, which drives people over the hills and far away.

proached 100,000 by the end of the eighteenth century, but the result of this rapid population growth was an economic and social disaster. Although the land was extremely fertile, the cost of transporting rural produce over the mountains to eastern markets like Baltimore and Philadelphia was prohibitive. In theory, grains, flour, and meats could be floated downstream to the new settlements in Ohio and Kentucky, but these places were producing surpluses of their own, and New Orleans was an unreliable market for political reasons. Unable to sell produce for cash, the western farmer was unable to buy. Many turned to making whiskey, which at least had a market in the Indian country and could be bartered locally for goods and services. It was also consumed at home in large quantities. About one family in ten maintained a moonshine still, usually capable of producing less than one hundred gallons a year.

As the poor got poorer, the few well-to-do increased their holdings, and an extreme contrast appeared between wealthy landowners—who owned the mills, served as sheriffs and magistrates, and collected rents—and dirt-poor tenant farmers. Travelers were appalled at the many one-eyed men, victims of eye-gouging in drunken brawls, and the deplorable housing conditions on the frontier. Single-room cabins of the better sort—even those offering accommodations to travelers—contained whole families and their hired hands. In 1789 a Baltimore merchant, after a disastrous money-losing venture to Pittsburgh, complained that on his way back he had to stay in the cabin of one of the more prosperous families at the foot of Laurel Mountain; it was already occupied by an old man, a girl of eighteen, two hired women, three hired men, miscellaneous children, five dogs, and a bear.[57]

This was not the world of noble yeomen that Jefferson imagined. When he became aware of the desperate economic conditions at Redstone and the Monongahela region it is difficult to know. Unlike Washington, he did not personally cross or even enter the Appalachians, but by the time he returned from Paris he had made the acquaintance of Crevecoeur (though he hoped that Volney would correct Crevecoeur's unfavorable portrait of American frontiersmen).

Political discontent in western Pennsylvania certainly came to his attention in the early 1790s, however, when several movements favoring separation of western counties as separate states were coming to a head. Kentucky became a separate state in 1792, carved out of Virginia's Old Dominion, and Jefferson was one of the architects of the plan to create

"An American Log-house." Engraving by General Victor Collot, c. 1804, one of the earliest images of a typical Anglo-American frontier house. Courtesy of the Beinecke Library, Yale University.

"Place of Worship and Burial Ground at Ligonier Town, Pennsylvania." This camp meeting ground, north of Redstone, was typical of the kind used by many frontier ministers for revivals and regular religious services. Lithograph by Adlard Welby, 1821. Courtesy of the Beinecke Library, Yale University.

new states in the Northwest Territory that Virginia had ceded to Congress; his map in the *Notes* bears the notation "new State" over several areas west of Pennsylvania.

But the desperation of the western counties of Pennsylvania must have come most forcefully to his attention as the Whiskey Rebellion precipitated the military occupation of the region by Washington and Hamilton's 12,000-man army. This was out of all proportion to the Whiskey Rebellion itself, whose most rebellious act was the tar-and-feathering of a few well-to-do revenue collectors. Jefferson saw occupation as a singularly inappropriate imposition on an already desperate population to whom whiskey was not only a dietary staple but a principal medium of exchange. His gentlemanly plantation way of life may have made it difficult for him to imagine or admit that many other farmers were poor, ignorant, and violent, but he could certainly empathize with their resentment of a distant and indifferent authority that was imposing a cruel and burdensome tax. He later appointed one of the more restrained whiskey rebels, Albert Gallatin, to be his secretary of the treasury, and he put into action Gallatin's plan to build a national road from Cumberland in Maryland to Redstone Creek and beyond, so that commerce with the east could be improved.[58]

Farther south, the mountain valleys of what is now West Virginia also harbored a breed of independent-minded frontiersmen. These were the Allegheny Highlands, and settlers from the Potomac and the Shenandoah valleys had been penetrating them since the middle of the eighteenth century. By 1754, Andrew Lewis had surveyed more than 50,000 acres in the Greenbrier valley for the Greenbrier Company, and after the French and Indian War, settlement along the valleys of the Great Kanawha, the Greenbrier, and other Highland streams proceeded apace. By 1790, the Highlands were home to perhaps 20,000 settlers, and many more were streaming westward into Kentucky, whose population by 1790 numbered around 90,000.[59]

The security of these settlers on their lands was, however, extremely precarious. Although the land law of 1779 blocked the claims of the old Ohio Company, the Indiana Company, and other speculative combinations, it still required settlers of lands surveyed by the Loyal and Greenbrier Companies to pay up or be evicted. And it did not protect them later from the machinations of speculators who were owed money by the State of Virginia for wartime services or who bought up the warrants of Revolutionary War veterans and applied them in opposition to settlers who thought they already had title to their tracts. Princely eastern merchants thus acquired hundreds of thousands of acres, as did various public officials, including Albert Gallatin, who acquired nearly 200,000 acres. The frenzy of chaotic land speculation made the titles of actual settlers extremely dubious, for the domains claimed by large dealers, holding vaguely located warrants for hundreds of thousands of acres, typically embraced a patchwork of actual farms whose title was already uncertain.

The result of this rapidly evolving pattern of absentee ownership and of uncertain title for actual residents was a paucity of the sorts of public services provided in eastern regions by schools and churches. As in western Pennsylvania, law and order in the Highlands were not well maintained. When in 1771 Jefferson was joining Patrick Henry, George Wythe, and other gentlemen in an application for "lands on the Greenbrier previously surveyed and claimed by Andrew Lewis," he made note of the persons actually living there.

One tract of 10,000 acres, known as "The Sink Hole Lands," included "Burnside's place." "Burnside," Jefferson observed, "is a great notorious villain obnoxious to everybody near him, who would be glad he could be removed. He is supposed to have murdered one Jno. Moorehead. He claims all the lands thereabouts and keeps people off." Burnside was involved in another confusing dispute involving a tract known as Sparr's Ford on Greenbrier: "'Sparr's ford.' On green Bryar, about 800. as. might be had good. 170.as. was surve. by Lewis as before and sold to Sparr a Dutchman @ £3–10. Sparr went off & sold to Tom. Campbell for 200. of which 20 half Joes are paid. But Sam. Wilson to whom Campbell was indebted 150, takes possn. of the lands for his debt. He and Burnside are at continual war, the possn. sometimes in one, sometimes in the other."[60]

Others who might contest the new claims of Jefferson and company included some who had bought from Lewis but whose titles were unclear because Lewis never patented the land, some "who run off," some absentee purchasers whose claims were contested by settlers who occupied the lots "in opposition," some who were killed and whose heirs, if any, could not be found. Clearly Jefferson was aware of the chaos and demoralization of the Highlands region but was prepared to enter into a speculative venture to "get grants" to "Lewis's rich lands" on the Greenbrier. How the legal tangles would be resolved is not clear.

Many of the settlers on Greenbrier and the other Highland streams were, like their brethren on the Monongahela, in straitened circumstances because they were stranded far from the markets where they could have sold their crop for cash. Jefferson's awareness of this problem was displayed in the *Notes* in the chapter on "Rivers." He discussed various means by which transportation through the mountains by water and short portages could be improved: by a nine-mile canal from the Great Kanawha to the Roanoke, by a portage from the Little Kanawha to the Monongahela, by the much-touted portage from the Potomac to the upper waters of the Ohio, by clearing obstruction in the navigable rivers. Prospective canal and portage routes were dotted in on the map inserted in the *Notes.* This would culminate in Gallatin's elaborate system of internal improvements that would link the developing frontiers with markets on the east coast and along the Mississippi and its waters.

From these depressed, insecure frontier regions in the Monongahela valley in western Pennsylvania and the Allegheny Highlands in West Virginia and southwestern Pennsylvania came some of the most aggressive trespassers on Indian territories. The first cohort were adventurous "long hunters" who, like their Native American counterparts, sought skins and peltries for the fur trade. They were competing with Cherokee and Shawnee commercial hunters, exploiting the same region and on occasion engaging in fatal confrontation with the Indians who laid claim to traditional hunting territories in this "dark and bloody ground." The long hunters were followed by actual settlers who intended to clear the lands for farming and to establish permanent towns. These early settlements were organized community efforts, not independent ventures by individual families, with several extended families forming the nucleus of a cluster of farmsteads, in close enough proximity to provide a measure of common defense against Indian attack.[61]

Among the most aggressive and successful were the Wataugans, a group of settlers who had moved from southwestern Virginia into the region of the Holston, Watauga, and Nolachucky rivers in what turned out to be North Carolina.[62] As early as 1772 they had formed a quasi-independent state governed by a constitution known as "The Articles of the Watauga Association." The Wataugans cooperated with Henderson in obtaining his lease from the Cherokees and in the creation of the Transylvania Company, in whose affairs Jefferson had become embroiled in 1776.

Wataugans were prominent in the Indian wars of the 1770s and 80s; and it was a Wataugan who committed the infamous murder of the Cherokee chief Old Tassel, which itself was an act of retaliation for the massacre of the murderer's family. The event has an uncanny similarity to the story of Logan, except that in this case a white man is the injured party.

In 1778, while peace ostensibly prevailed between the Cherokees and the Wataugans, the family of John Kirk was massacred by an Indian named Slim Tom and his cronies; eleven in all died, including women and children. The Kirk family had thought of Slim Tom as a friend. Kirk soon thereafter killed half a dozen Cherokees who had come into the settlement under a flag of truce, including Old Tassel. Then, in order to abort future hostilities, Kirk wrote a letter to John Watts, Old Tassel's successor, explaining his actions (see next page).[63] The story of Old Tassel's murder has so many parallels with Jefferson's story of Logan that it raises the question whether it was a fabrication inspired by the widely publicized speech. The Wataugans were responsible for an earlier hoax—the fake letter of Stuart urging the southern Indians to go to war on the eve of the Revolution. But whether the Kirk letter was genuine or a self-serving fabrication in one sense does not matter: the story reveals a worldview, a frontier ethos, of indiscriminate vengeance for past wrongs that was shared by both Indians and whites.

The Watauga Association remained a cohesive force for years, expanding into satellite settlements, making ad hoc accommodations with the Cherokees as they moved westward into Tennessee, and even forming the core of the short-lived State of Franklin. The militant Wataugans would continue well into Jefferson's presidency to put pressure on the federal government to legitimize their trespasses. And for the next fifty years the "civilized" Cherokees would continue to resist the seizure of their lands, until they were—most of them—removed to Indian Territory west of the Mississippi.

The Federalist Civilization Program

The civilization program during the years of Federalist ascendancy was carried out partly by direct federal donations of ploughs and other instruments of husbandry, partly by the example of plantation-style farming set by the Indian agents and resident traders, partly by missionaries and converts who taught a mixture of Scripture and the three Rs in schools established in Indian communities, and partly by eastern boarding schools and colleges who took in and educated the sons of influential and friendly

John Kirk's Lament

Sir: I have heard of your letter lately sent to Chucky [John Sevier]. You are mistaken in blaming him for the death of your uncle. Listen now to my story. For days and months the Cherokee Indians, big and little, women and children, have been fed and treated kindly by my mother. When all was at peace with the Tennessee towns, Slim Tom with a party of Satigo and other Cherokee Indians, murdered my mother, brothers and sisters in cold blood, when children just before were playful about them as friends; at the instant some of them received the bloody tomahawk they were smiling in their faces. This began the war; and since I have taken ample satisfaction can now make peace except with Slim Tom. Our beloved men, the Congress, tell us to be at peace; I will listen to their advice if no more blood is shed by the Cherokees, and the headmen of your nation take care to prevent such beginnings of bloodshed in all time to come. But if they do not, your people may feel something more to keep up remembrance of John Kirk, jun.

Captain of the Bloody Rangers

chiefs. In addition, for generations many Indian communities had been acquiring major elements of European technology either through purchases made possible by profits of the fur trade or through the "presents" that became an accepted part of forest diplomacy. At a result, many Indian communities were very similar in material goods and economic lifestyle to inland white communities.

In social organization and religion, however, there were major differences. The axis of social organization in Indian communities was kinship, in fact and metaphor. Religious ritual and belief were generally not Christian, although some communities had Catholic or Protestant congregations. And the political organization was noncoercive, without police, courts, and codes of written laws, a feature that some enlightened whites, like Jefferson and Crevecoeur, found most attractive but that Indian agents, like Hawkins, considered to be an obstacle to progress. "Civilizing" the Indians thus meant, to many government officials and evangelists alike, converting them to Christianity and substituting European-style political institutions, not just persuading the men to plow and tend herds and the women to spin and make soap.

But certain harsh economic and social realities on both sides of the racial frontier hindered the program of civilization. One of these was the difficulty, for both white and Indian frontiersmen, of producing the cash crop needed to purchase necessities—hardware, cloth, furniture, foods in season—that made a sedentary, civilized life possible. As game diminished in Indian country and as native hunting grounds were whittled away by war and purchase, Indian hunters increasingly viewed white hunters as trespassers and lethal competitors who had to be driven out by force. White frontiersmen, for their part, were desperate for cash to buy the same necessities as the Indians, and so turned to long hunting and to whiskey production. Both of these courses of action were certain to lead to bloody encounters of white against white, Indian against Indian, and white against Indian.

Neither side was able to deter violence. This had long been a problem for Indian diplomats, whose peace-making efforts were easily subverted by vengeance-seeking warriors; the plaintive excuse was, "We cannot control our young men." On the white side, far from eastern centers of power, it was equally difficult to prevent mayhem and murder by violent men. Efforts to assert federal and state authority in matters of taxation and punishment aroused separatist sentiments in even the most conservative breasts. Why belong to a state that affords no access to market for your goods, that is only interested in you for the tax revenue you represent, that wants to "civilize" the savages rather than drive them off the land, and that abandons you to fight and die alone when the Indians go on the warpath?

Thomas Jefferson, ever the foe of central power (when wielded by others), could not help but be in sympathy with these sentiments of local self-determination and separatism. Furthermore, he seems to have been anxious to avoid condemning the many for the errant acts of a few (a lawyer's proper principle, perhaps). His attitude was: protect the Indians, though not at the expense of white lives, except when one or two outrageously guilty individuals can be blamed. But when he became President, a more important element of Jefferson's Indian policy than his fear of central power, his separatist sympathies, or his civilization program would be his desire to obtain Indian land, at almost any cost.

CHAPTER SEVEN

President Jefferson's Indian Policy

WHEN JEFFERSON assumed the duties of President of the United States in the spring of 1801, Indian affairs at once became a central concern. In his first annual message to Congress he sounded an optimistic chord on this as on other topics: "Among our Indian neighbors also a spirit of peace and friendship generally prevails, and I am happy to inform you that the continued efforts to introduce among them the implements and the practice of husbandry and of the household arts have not been without success; that they are becoming more and more sensible of the superiority of this dependence for clothing and subsistence over the precarious resources of hunting and fishing, and already we are able to announce that instead of that constant diminution of their numbers produced by their wars and their wants, some of them begin to experience an increase of population."[1]

This cheerful picture, which applied primarily to the southern Indians, must be read in the context of another passage in which he looked forward to a rapidly increasing white population and the consequent "settlement of the extensive country remaining vacant within our limits." This was a view he shared with Madison, who believed that the stability of democratic institutions depended on constant expansion of the increasing population into new territory. This "vacant" land was, of course, for the most part owned by the Indians and used by them for hunting and fishing. What Jefferson was foreseeing was the extinction of the "savage" way of life, the assimilation of the surviving Native Americans into the white agricultural economy, and the purchase of useless hunting grounds for white settlement. Peace, land purchases, and the civilization of the friendly tribes (which would proceed *pari passu* with the vanishing of the last few recalcitrant hunters) were the visible principles of Jeffersonian Indian policy.

Less visible, in the happy anticipation of universal peace expressed in Jefferson's first message to Congress, was a fourth principle of Jeffersonian

Indian policy: to prevent the encircling British, Spanish, and French from subverting the all-too-corruptible savages and inciting them to war against the frontiers of the United States.

The Administration of Indian Affairs

When Jefferson took command, a constitutional assignment of powers and an apparatus of law and administration had already been established by the Federalists for the day-to-day management of Indian affairs, and he made few changes in this formal structure. The Constitution made the President responsible for foreign relations, including the negotiation of treaties, and for the armed forces. Washington and Adams had used these powers, insofar as they applied to Indian affairs, to make the secretary of war responsible for guarding the frontiers from Indian attack, primarily by constructing a chain of forts beyond the Indian boundary (as defined by treaties) and garrisoning them with soldiers of the regular army. They, as had the British before them, regarded the Indian tribes as foreign powers, with whom diplomatic relations were to be conducted according to traditional protocol.

To Congress, however, had been given the authority to regulate trade and commerce with the Indian nations. First in 1790, and again in 1793, 1796, and 1799, Trade and Intercourse Acts had been passed that provided for the establishment of government "factories" or trading posts, the "civilization" of the Indian nations, the licensing of private traders, the definition of the boundaries of "Indian country," the prohibition of white intruders, and the cooperative responsibility of Indian superintendents and the military for the enforcement of these laws. Jefferson had earlier opposed the acts as unconstitutional infringements on states' rights; now he was prepared to amplify them. The Trade and Intercourse Act in effect sewed together the pieces of Indian affairs into a single Indian department within the office of the secretary of war, with its own budget, accounts, and correspondence managed in Washington by clerks and accountants and in the field by Indian agents and military commandants.[2]

The President appointed governors in the various territories not incorporated in any state. The territorial governor was *ex officio* the superintendent of Indian affairs for that territory, reporting in that capacity to the secretary of war. In the beginning there were only two organized territories, the Northwest Territory (established in 1787) and the Southwest Territory (established in 1790); but smaller territories, which eventually became states, were soon created, beginning with Mississippi in 1798, Ohio in 1799, Indiana in 1800, and Michigan in 1805. Under the superintendents the secretary of war appointed agents and subagents, interpreters, and factors (storekeepers) to deal directly with Indian people. The superintendents were responsible officially for the administration of the Trade and Intercourse Acts and were authorized to call upon the military to enforce these laws. Agents generally made their headquarters in the neighborhood of army posts, and here too were located the trading posts authorized under the Trade and Intercourse Act. In addition, licensed private traders maintained stores in most Indian villages. Superintendents and agents were also responsible for aiding the work of civilization—dispensing the hardware and dry goods bought for Indian use with the annual congressional appropriation and aiding the small corps of volunteer missionaries and teachers who undertook to convert the heathens to Christianity or to educate them in the three Rs and in the crafts and skills needed by an up-to-date agricultural community.

Jefferson appointed General Henry Dearborn as his secretary of war, and therefore as the primary administrator of Indian affairs. Dearborn was a New Englander, a veteran of many campaigns in the Revolution, including Sullivan's raid on the Iroquois, and had served in Congress, where he may have commended himself to the Republicans by opposing an expansive military establishment. Jefferson thought of him as a plain-living "farmer" and "man of business."[3] The superintendent of Indian affairs of most interest to Jefferson was twenty-seven year old Captain William Henry Harrison, son of Benjamin Harrison of Virginia, who had been a congressional colleague of Jefferson's and his successor as governor. Young Harrison had served as aide-de-camp to General Anthony Wayne during the campaign against the Western Confederacy and had acted for a year as secretary of the Northwest Territory. In May 1800 he was appointed by President Adams to be governor of the newly created Indiana Territory, which embraced the present states of Indiana, Illinois, and Wisconsin and contained most of the Indian land north of the Ohio River of interest to land speculators and of concern to the military. Harrison's father-in-law, Judge John Cleves Symmes, was one of the principal investors in Symmes Associates, one of the land companies whose claims in southern Ohio had made necessary the recent Indian war. Harrison would retain his post as territorial governor throughout Jefferson's administration.[4]

Henry Dearborn. Oil on canvas by Charles Willson Peale, c. 1796–1797. Courtesy of Independence National Historical Park Collection.

Another official in the Indian department who had already earned Jefferson's confidence as an expert on Indian affairs was Colonel Benjamin Hawkins, a former congressional colleague and occasional correspondent on Indian matters (including Indian vocabularies). Hawkins had been intimately connected with Indian affairs since 1785, when he was sent by Congress to arrange treaties with the Creeks. In 1796 he had served as commissioner at the Treaty of Coleraine, necessitated by the Creek's refusal to accede to the Yazoo land companies' fraudulent claims to millions of acres of land granted by the state of Georgia. In the same year Washington appointed him principal temporary agent on Indian Affairs south of the Ohio river. He was reappointed by Jefferson in 1801 and remained the most important agent among the southern Indians until his death in 1816.[5] Dearborn, Harrison, and Hawkins were to be Jefferson's first team in the management of Indian affairs.

There were only a few Indian agencies and factories at the beginning of Jefferson's term. South of the Ohio, Hawkins personally managed the Creek agency. It was located on the Flint River in western Georgia, adjacent to Fort Lawrence. About a day or two's journey to the east was a factory at Fort Wilkinson, on the Oconee River, managed by a subagent under Hawkins's direction. To the north at Tellico Blockhouse, on the Tennessee River in what is now southeastern Tennessee, was the agent to the Cherokee nation, Thomas Lewis (later replaced by Silas Dinsmoor and then Return J. Meigs); a factory was located there as well. In 1802 Samuel Mitchell was appointed agent to the Chickasaws, and Dinsmoor was appointed agent to the Choctaws, in northern and southern Mississippi respectively.

North of the Ohio, within Governor Harrison's superintendency of Indiana Territory, were a number of agents, subagents, factors, and interpreters. Perhaps the most important agency, along with a factory and garrison, was at Fort Wayne, on the Maumee River in what is now northeastern Indiana. Fort Wayne sat astride the old fur-trade portage between the watersheds of the Great Lakes and the Ohio and dominated the heartland of the old Western Confederacy; but it also was not far from the several reservations carved out of the Greenville cession of 1795. From 1795 to 1812, the notable William Wells presided as agent in varying capacities (although in 1801 one William Lyman was made principal agent for the Northwest and Indiana territories). As a child, Wells had been captured and adopted by the Miamis; he had fought as an Indian against Colonel Josiah Harmar, and then for General Wayne. After the wars he returned to the Miamis to live with his Indian wife, daughter of the influential chief Little Turtle, who was, like Wells, a proponent of the Jeffersonian program of civilization for the Indians and knew Jefferson personally. Wells was killed in 1812 during the Indian attack on Chicago; his heart was ripped out and eaten.[6]

Other agents and interpreters circulated among the various tribes, including the Six Nations of New York and the Hurons, Delawares, and Shawnees on reservations in Ohio. But the situation in the Northwest Territory remained politically unstable. British influence was strong, and Indian factionalism was exacerbated by the civilization policy.

Certain ambiguities of status chronically plagued Indian agents. One of these was their uncertain relationship to territorial governors. The governor was technically the superintendent of Indian Affairs, but he was apt to be preoccupied with other official duties and political problems and was not necessarily well-educated on Indian matters and never fluent in the native languages. Furthermore, as administrator of a territory he was responsible to the secretary of state, but as Indian superintendent he answered to the secretary of war. When Jefferson became President, he appointed William C. Claiborne governor of Mississippi Territory; but it was unclear whether Hawkins should report to the governor or the secretary of war.

A further ambiguity of jurisdiction applied to Indians resident on Indian land within states of the Union. The position of the federal government was that federal Indian agents were responsible for their particular tribes and would report to the secretary of war, not to state governors.[7] But the constitutional issues involved in the question of state versus federal versus Indian national sovereignty within the boundaries of states admitted to the Union would flare up again and again, most spectacularly in the 1820s and 30s in Georgia over the issues of state sovereignty and Indian removal.[8]

And still another ambiguity in the situation of the agents was their relation with the military, upon whom they depended for enforcement of the Trade and Intercourse acts. The commanders of the garrisons were under orders to cooperate with and assist the agents, but the agents themselves could not give specific orders. Thus there was room for delay, misunderstanding, and dispute over what was necessary, proper, and feasible. Complaints had to be referred to the secretary of war in Washington or to the territorial governor.

But the agents' principal problem, overriding all these others, was the white frontier community's disregard of the Trade and Intercourse acts and other laws and regulations relating to commerce with the Indians. The trade in whiskey was a salient example. Although at first there was no federal restriction on the liquor trade (a departure from earlier colonial practice), the federal factories were not allowed to furnish liquor. The Northwest Territory early enacted a law prohibiting the sale of intoxicating beverages to the Indians, but the law was ineffective. Hawkins complained repeatedly about the evil done by the liquor trade, and perhaps in response to his pleas Mississippi Territory in 1799 passed a law restricting the traffic.[9] Indian representatives again and again begged federal authorities to limit the liquor trade.

Impressed by the seriousness of the problems caused by unscrupulous traders and drunken Indians, Jefferson in January 1802, in a special message to Congress requesting a renewal of the Trade and Intercourse Act, specifically asked for a prohibition of the liquor trade: "These people [the Indians] are becoming very sensible of the baneful effects produced on their morals, their health, and existence by the abuse of ardent spirits, and some of them earnestly desire a prohibition of that article from being carried among them. The legislature will consider whether the effectuating that desire would not be in the spirit of benevolence and liberality which they have hitherto practiced toward these our neighbors, and which has had so happy an effect toward conciliating their friendship. It has been found, too, in experience that the same abuse gives frequent rise to incidents tending much to commit our peace with the Indians."[10]

The act as passed in March 1802 did contain, in its next to last article, a provision authorizing the President to take measures to restrain the liquor trade.[11] In order to effect compliance with the act and Jefferson's wishes, the secretary of war sent a circular to the Indian agents instructing them to prevent traders from supplying Indians with whiskey, and he wrote to the territorial governors asking them to cancel the licenses of traders who ignored the ban. But the prohibition was ineffective because it could be enforced only in Indian country; whiskey sellers continued to do business with impunity on ceded land just across the border. The evil done by alcohol in some of the Indian communities north of the Ohio was vividly described by Volney in his *View of the Climate and Soul of the United States of America* (see opposite).[12]

Jefferson further responded to the liquor problem by declaring that territorial governments had the legal authority to ban the liquor traffic on ceded lands, and Governor Harrison was able to persuade the legislature of Indiana Territory in 1805 to pass an act, to supplement the "entirely ineffectual" federal measures, outlawing the sale or gift of liquor to an Indian. But the law's enforcement was conditional upon the other territories' passage of comparable legislation; and the other territories did not act. Indiana Territory then imposed a partial restriction, prohibiting the distribution of liquor to the Indians within thirty miles of a treaty site. By 1806 the territories of Louisiana and Orleans enacted a general law. Near the end of his second term, in December 1808, Jefferson begged all the territorial and state governors to propose appropriate legislation. The state of Ohio responded promptly, and a year later at Harrison's urging Indiana Territory finally complied. The territories of Michigan, Illinois, and Mississippi (strengthening earlier laws) followed in 1812, 1813, and 1816. But none of these legal barriers was ever able to stop the widespread abuses of the trade in bootleg whiskey among Indians.[13]

Another source of difficulty in administering the Trade and Intercourse law was encroachment on Indian lands, which was of course prohibited by

Constantin Volney's Description of Drunkenness among Indians

From early in the morning both men and women roam about the streets, for no other purpose but to procure themselves rum: and for this they first dispose of the produce of their chase, then of their toys, next of their clothes, and at last they go begging for it, never ceasing to drink, till they are absolutely senseless. Sometimes this gives occasion to ridiculous scenes; they will lift the cup to drink with both hands like apes, then raise up their heads with bursts of laughter, and gargle themselves with their beloved but fatal liquor, to enjoy the pleasure of tasting it the longer; hand the cup from one to another with noisy invitations; call to one only three steps off as loud as they can bawl; take hold of their wives by the head and pour the rum down their throats with coarse caresses, and all the ridiculous gestures of our alehouse sots. Sometimes distressing scenes ensue, as the loss of all sense and reason, becoming mad or stupid, or falling down dead drunk in the dust or mud, there to sleep till the next day. I could not go out in the morning without finding them by dozens in the streets or paths about the village, literally wallowing in the dirt with the pigs. It was a very fortunate circumstance if a day passed without a quarrel, or a battle with knives or tomahawks, by which ten men on an average lose their lives yearly. On the 9th of August, at four o'clock in the afternoon, a savage stabbed his wife in four places with a knife within twenty steps of me. A fortnight before a similar circumstance took place, and five such the year preceding. For this vengeance is immediately taken, or dissembled until a proper opportunity offers, by the relations, which produces fresh causes for waylaying and assassination.

the act. In some localities, because of the ambiguity of the language of treaties and a failure to carry out actual surveys on the ground (the important Hopewell and Greenville lines, for instance, were not marked out for years), white intrusion on lands claimed by Indians was relatively innocent in intention. But in other places, particularly in the south, the intrusion was a deliberate challenge to the principle of Indian ownership and was massive and persistent. Indian agents again and again called upon federal troops to evict the intruders. Harrison issued a proclamation forbidding hunting and making settlements on Indian lands, and he requested permission of the secretary of war to survey the boundary in Indiana territory. But ugly incidents of trespass, theft, and murder still occurred with little effective prosecution of offenders brought to trial before sympathetic juries. In the south, Hawkins was forced to complain repeatedly to the state and territorial governors of white intrusion, including grazing cattle on Indian lands, rustling Indian horses and cattle, hunting and fishing across the borders, and making illegal settlements.[14]

In Georgia, such problems were most acute with respect to the fork of the Oconee and Ocmulgee rivers. In 1802 under Jefferson's insistence the federal government had assumed the obligation to purchase Indian lands within the state and turn them over to Georgia. The pressure from Georgia to get on with the purchases was intense, and Hawkins was directly ordered by Jefferson to persuade the Creeks to sell the land in the Oconee–Ocmulgee fork: "it is for their interest to cede lands at times to the United States, and for us thus to procure gratifications to our citizens, from time to time, by new acquisitions of land."[15] The lands in question were located in central Georgia, a wedge of territory running north and south, about 140 miles long and 35 miles wide, already overrun by eager intruders. The cession was completed in Washington in 1805 and was, supposed Dearborn, the final purchase needed from the Creeks in his lifetime.

Another "focus of infection" (to use the phrase of historian Francis P. Prucha) was among the Chickasaws north of the Tennessee River in the northern part of what is now Alabama.[16] The invasion began in 1807. In March 1809 agent Meigs and a detachment of troops removed 284 white families, but this was merely a token eviction; the territorial governor estimated that as many as 5,000 families remained, defying the government. Agent Meigs wrote a pessimistic report to the secretary of war: "The great length of this frontier, & the few troops in this quarter, puts it in the power of the people of the character mentioned to impose on the Indians & to put the U States on considerable expence. Should this disposition to make intrusions on Indian lands increase, they will perhaps at last put the few troops here at defiance. These intruders are always well armed, some of them shrewd & of desperate character, have nothing to lose & hold barbarous sentiments towards Indians. They see extensive tracts of

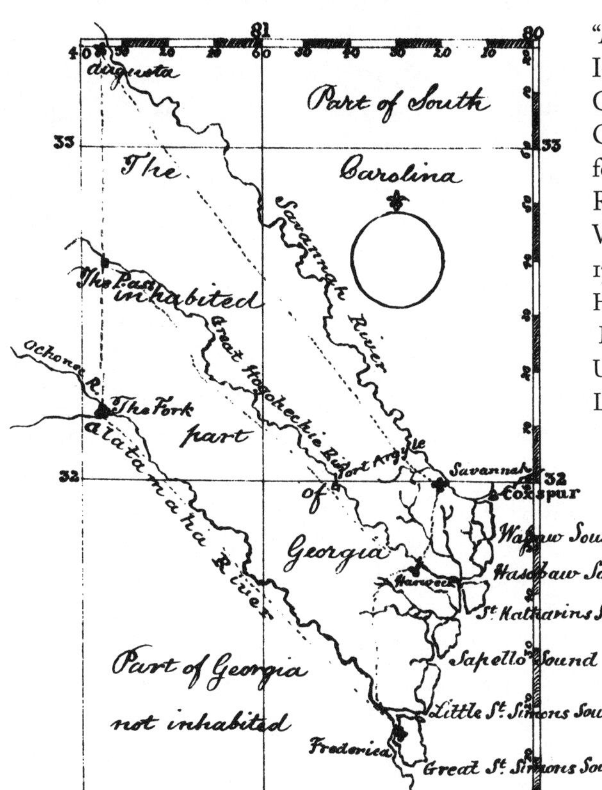

"A Map of the Inhabited Part of Georgia," showing the Oconee-Ocmulgee fork of the Altamaha River. Drawing by William DeBrahm, c. 1756. Courtesy of the Hargrett Rare Book and Manuscript Library/ University of Georgia Libraries.

forest exceedingly disproportioned to the present or expected population of the tribes who hold them. They take hold of these lands, some of them in hopes the land will be purchased, when they will plead a right of preemption, making a merit of their crimes. With these people remonstrance has no effect, nothing but force can prevent their violation of Indian rights."[17]

The settlers in response (no doubt emulating the earlier stand of the Watauga Association) submitted a petition to Congress and to the President (now Jefferson's successor James Madison) pleading to be allowed to remain and denying the right of Chickasaws: "To gratify a heathen nation Who have no better right to this land than we have ourselves; and they have by estemation nearly 100,000 acres of land to each man of their nation and of no more use to government or society than to saunter about upon like so many wolves or bares, whilst they who would be a supporter to government and improve the country must be forsed even to rent poor stoney ridges to make a support or rase their famelies on whilst there is fine fertile countrys lying uncultivated, and we must be debared even from inJoying a small Corner of this land."[18] The War Department never was able to evict the illegal settlers: first the exigencies of the War of 1812, then the Creek War of 1813–1814, preoccupied the Indian agents and the military; finally the Chickasaws gave in and ceded the lands in dispute.

Military and civilian authorities agreed after about 1816 that driving off illegal settlers on Indian lands was impossible. Major General Andrew Jackson, the military commander in Tennessee upon whom Cherokee agent Meigs depended for the force needed to evict illegal settlers, advised the secretary of war that burning cabins and driving off settlers at the point of a gun was ineffectual. The laws could not be enforced. He wrote to the War Department to say that removing illegal squatters was useless; they returned a few days after the soldiers left and "recommenced their plan of robbery."[19]

Compounding the lack of will was the progressive down-sizing of the regular army during Jefferson's administration. The maximum size of the military establishment was set by law in 1802 at 3,289 officers and men. About a third of these were assigned to the corps of artillery defending the Atlantic coast. The remainder, perhaps 2,000 men, were assigned to guard the western frontier, stretching from Forts Ontario and Niagara in the north to Mobile on the Gulf of Mexico. After the Louisiana Purchase of 1803, old French and Spanish forts fell into American hands and others were built, adding to the burden of defending the frontier. In the last year of Jefferson's presidency, when troubles with Spain, the British, and the Indians were threatening, the number of men under arms more than doubled, but not for the purpose of controlling white encroachment on Indian lands.

These frontier forts were generally rectangular enclosures constructed of timber stockades, barracks, supply magazines, and blockhouses at each corner to give a field of fire against attacking Indians or European infantry; artillery bombardment, requiring defensive ramparts of earth and stone, was not anticipated. The garrisons were generally not large—as few as a single company of about one hundred men in peaceable Indian country, more where a threat from Spanish or British forces required a stronger defense. The political disposition of the officer corps changed progressively throughout the period, from about 95 percent pro-Federalist in 1801 to nearly 90 percent pro-Republican in 1809. Republican officers were far less likely to order their men to fire upon rebellious white frontiersmen than their Federalist counterparts had been a decade earlier.[20]

There was, of course, the militia, who theoretically could be called upon, as they had been at the time of Whiskey Rebellion, to put down riotous mobs of law breakers. But the prospect of mobilizing local militia-

Fort Washington, c. 1790, near present-day Cincinnati, Ohio. Engraving.
Courtesy of the Ohio State Historical Society.

men to defend Indians against a horde of intruding white settler families was unthinkable. The settlers *were* the militia, and woe betide any aspiring politician who attempted to set them against their own kind.

In sum, it is evident that the policy of guaranteeing the Indian boundary against intrusion, genuinely intended in the intercourse acts and particularly in Jefferson's bill of 1802, progressively failed during his administration and was by 1816 a nullity. The reason for this failure no doubt lay in part in Jefferson's ethos of decentralization. Chary of infringing upon the rights of "the people," of the states, of territorial governments, the federal establishment had not the political will nor military muscle to exert deadly force against armed and violent frontiersmen and their families. The governors of the states and territories, to whom the agents had to turn for support, were as much the creatures of their local constituents as of the President who appointed them. To make white public officials the guardians of Indian lands was indeed to set the fox to guard the hen house.

Initial Moves toward Obtaining Land

During the first year and a half of his presidency, Jefferson's attention in Indian affairs was directed toward tying up some loose ends left over by his predecessors while formulating a mature policy of his own. Both north and south of the Ohio, the boundaries of Indian-owned territory, although generally described in treaties, were unsurveyed and unmarked, a situation that readily led to trespass and violence. The number of government trading houses needed to be increased. Indian complaints about white encroachment and the failure of the states and territories to punish whites for crimes against Indians had to be addressed in some systematic way, notably by land purchases in sensitive locations. And strategic roads had to be opened across Indian country for the sake of commerce and national defense, particularly a proper road to connect Natchez on the Mississippi with American settlements in Tennessee and Kentucky.

In order to accomplish these tasks in the region south of the Ohio, Jefferson had the secretary of war appoint a commission to negotiate with the four major southern tribes, the Cherokees, Creeks, Chickasaws, and Choctaws. The commissioners were Brigadier General James Wilkinson, the senior general in the United States Army; Benjamin Hawkins, superintendent for the southern Indians; and Andrew Pickens of South Carolina, a former congressman, Revolutionary War hero, and for forty years a leader in campaigns against the Cherokees. They were instructed to obtain from the Cherokees a cession of land and permission to open a road across their remaining territory from Nashville in the direction of Natchez on the Mississippi. After treating with the Cherokees, they were to go on to the Chickasaws and Choctaws, to obtain from them a confirmation of boundaries and permission for the Natchez road to cross their respective territories. Guards and gates would be placed at intervals along the road to prevent Indian horses and cattle from straying.

A codicil was added, at the express direction of the President, modifying the instructions with respect to the Cherokee negotiations; it indicates Jefferson's desire to preserve amicable relations with this powerful Indian tribe: "as by information lately received, it is evident that the Cherokees have testified much dissatisfaction, on hearing that the Government were about to request them to cede more land, it is the wish of the President that you should treat the subject with great tenderness, and that you should not press them on any other subjects than those which relate to roads, and settlers thereon. You will impress upon them the belief, that the United States have no desire to purchase any of their land, unless they are quite willing to sell; that we are not in want of lands, but only wish to be accommodated with such roads as are necessary to keep up a communication with all parts of the United States, without trespassing on the lands of the red people."[21]

In September the commissioners met with the Cherokees and, as Jefferson reported to Congress, "though our overtures to them were moderate, and respectful of their rights, their determination was, to yield no accommodation with respect either to a land cession or the road." Hawkins and his colleagues then went on later in the fall of 1801 to the Chickasaws and the Choctaws, who were more cooperative with respect to the road across their land to Natchez but objected to the building of inns for the entertainment of travelers and insisted on maintaining the ferries themselves. No cession of land was requested, but the Choctaws confirmed to the United States the cession previously made to the Crown in 1765 of a stretch of land east of the Mississippi from Louisiana to the Yazoo River. The next year (1802) they again confirmed to the United States a small tract previously ceded to the Crown in present Mississippi and Alabama just north of the Florida panhandle.[22]

In May and June of 1802, Hawkins and his colleagues visited the Creeks with instructions to secure a cession of land in the fork of the Oconee and

Ocmulgee rivers.[23] This was a somewhat more difficult assignment, for in addition to the usual Indian reluctance to part with ancestral villages and hunting grounds, the Creeks were divided internally by geographical and factional differences. There were the Upper Creeks, the Lower Creeks, and the Seminoles in Florida; and now the adventurer William Bowles, passing himself off as the emperor of the Creeks, was threatening to embroil the southern Indians in a war with Spain to secure for Bowles and his partners Lord Dunmore (now governor of the Bahamas) and the merchant John Miller a monopoly of the lucrative trade of Panton, Leslie, and Company with the southern Indians. This effort divided the Creeks between Bowles and their long-time leader McGillivray, who was an agent of Panton, Leslie. But after prolonged negotiations, Hawkins was able to persuade the Creeks to cede a sliver of land in extreme southeastern Georgia, and another sliver on the eastern side of the Oconee–Ocmulgee fork. Georgia was not happy, however, with the limited nature of this success in quieting Indian claims to her land and accused Hawkins of a lack of zealousness owing to his undue sympathy for the natives. Hawkins was able to take his revenge on the obstreperous Bowles next year, persuading the Upper Creeks to arrest him and turn him over to the Spanish authorities. Bowles died in prison in Morro Castle in Havana in 1805.[24]

Another loose end to be dealt with in this interim period before the formal enunciation of policy in 1803 was increasing the number of factories among the southern Indians. At the beginning of the term, there was one at Tellico among the Cherokees, where J. W. Hooker sold goods at prices the Indians considered exorbitant and lost money nevertheless; and a second among the Creeks at Fort Wilkinson on the Oconee River in Georgia. Jefferson's predecessor, John Adams, had been content to let the factory system languish, but Jefferson saw a use for it in civilizing the Indians, combating foreign influence, and persuading the natives to sell their lands to pay their trading debts. So in 1802 he opened two more in the south, one among the Chickasaws and another among the Choctaws, in direct competition with the well-established British firm of Panton, Leslie, and Company, and two in the north, one at Fort Wayne and one at Detroit, in competition with the British traders from Canada.[25]

Jefferson's Indian Policy

Jefferson was in complete agreement with the popular passion to purchase Indian land. When General Jackson wrote to Jefferson complaining of agent Hawkins's excessive sympathy for the Indians, which might interfere with the zealous pursuit of Indian real estate, Jefferson replied, in February of 1803, with reassuring language: "In keeping agents among the Indians, two objects are principally in view: 1. The preservation of peace; 2. The obtaining lands." He went on to explain that he had complete confidence in Hawkins's dedication to the policies of peace, civilization, and obtaining cessions of land, and he described in some detail the pressure which as President he had brought upon Hawkins to complete the purchase of the Oconee–Ocmulgee fork.[26]

In December of 1802 and the early months of 1803, in several official messages and letters of instruction, Jefferson went on to outline his mature Indian policy. This policy was formulated as much in response to the situation of foreign affairs and domestic politics as to his philosophical views on the origin and future of the Indian race; it was deeply constrained by the fears that dominated him: of external menace (from the British, French, Spanish, and scheming adventurers like Bowles) and of internal assaults on freedom (from the monarchical Federalists); and it was soon to be deeply influenced by the opportunities opened by the Louisiana Purchase.

His first statements of the principles to guide America's relations with the Indians were made before news of the Louisiana Purchase reached him on July 3, 1803. On December 29, 1802, he wrote a private letter to Secretary of War Dearborn outlining in candid terms the purposes and methods of American Indian policy. Indian land should be acquired on the southern and western frontiers, particularly along the Mississippi, so as to provide a well-defended border with France in Louisiana and Spain in Florida. Civilizing the Native Americans would make them willing to sell their increasingly bare hunting grounds for the capital goods needed for white-style agriculture. And the factories, although run honestly and clean of liquor, could induce further cessions by encouraging the natives to run into debts so large that they could be lopped off only by cessions of land. "Our proceedings with the Indians should tend systematically to that object, leaving the extinguishment of title in the interior country to fall in as occasion may arise. The Indians being once closed in between strong settled countries on the Mississippi & Atlantic, will, for want of game, be forced to agriculture, will find that small portions of land well improved, will be worth more to them than extensive forests unemployed, and will be continually parting with portions of them, for money to buy stock, utensils & necessities for their farms & families."[27]

Jefferson followed his private instructions to Dearborn with a special confidential message to Congress on January 28, 1803, on the subject of "trade." The security in which he wished these communications to be kept was needed, he felt, because if the Indians, now almost universally averse to selling any more land, became aware of the real purpose of the factories and the civilization policy, they would reject both. That real purpose, for the present, was the peaceful acquisition of the Mississippi frontier, from the Yazoo north. He recommended therefore the renewal of the Trade and Intercourse Act during the present session of Congress. He also suggested, in the interest of an extension of the fur trade among the numerous tribes west of the Mississippi, an American expedition up the Missouri River to find the northwest passage to the Pacific Ocean, and he requested an appropriation of $2,500 to support a party of ten or twelve soldiers under an "intelligent officer" on their ostensibly literary and scientific traversal of French territory. This proposal was the genesis of the Lewis and Clark expedition.[28]

In February 1803 Jefferson wrote three additional letters, going over the head of his secretary of war to assert clearly to three of Dearborn's subordinates the guidelines of American policy in Indian affairs. In these letters he was just as candid as he had been with Dearborn and with the Congress. One was the letter to Jackson in which he stated the peace-and-lands objective of his policy, his personal confidence in Hawkins, his reliance on progress toward civilization as the means of weaning the native Americans from their hunting grounds, and his intention to secure the lands in the Oconee–Ocmulgee fork.[29] The other two letters, to his principal Indian superintendents Hawkins and Harrison, were more intimate and conveyed somewhat different sentiments, calculated to appeal to different sensibilities. To Hawkins, his old associate, after sharing his smug satisfaction with the expected retirement of Federalist officials to "obscurity and settled disaffection," he went on to state candidly his "private" views on the conduct of Indian affairs. These views were based on a conviction of the inevitable demise of the Indian way of life, the termination of Indian history, and the eventual incorporation of the survivors into the fabric of civilized society as citizens of the United States (see opposite). He added, as a kind of "by-the-way," a beseeching plea to Hawkins to please acquire for the United States, and Georgia, the lands in the Oconee–Ocmulgee fork.[30]

Jefferson wrote privately to Harrison in order to give him a more candid

Jefferson's Policy of Civilization and Assimilation

I consider the business of hunting as already become insufficient to furnish clothing and subsistence to the Indians. The promotion of agriculture, therefore, and household manufacture, are essential in their preservations, and I am disposed to aid and encourage it liberally. This will enable them to live on much smaller portions of land, and, indeed, will render their vast forests useless but for the range of cattle; for which purpose, also, as they become better farmers, they will be found useless, and even disadvantageous. While they are learning to do better on less land, our increasing numbers will be calling for more land, and thus a coincidence of interests will be produced between those who have land to spare, and want other necessaries, and those who have such necessaries to spare, and want lands. This commerce, then, will be for the good of both, and those who are friends to both ought to encourage it . . . In truth, the ultimate point of rest and happiness for them is to let our settlements and theirs meet and blend together, to intermix, and become one people.

Incorporating themselves with us as citizens of the United States, this is what the natural progress of things will, of course, bring on, and it will be better to promote than to retard it. Surely it will be better for them to be identified with us, and preserved in the occupation of their lands, than be exposed to the many casualties which may endanger them while a separate people. I have little doubt, but that your reflections must have led you to view the various ways in which their history may terminate, and to see that this is the one most for their happiness. And we have already had an application from a settlement of Indians to become citizens of the United States. It is possible, perhaps probable, that this idea may be so novel as that it might shock the Indians, were it even hinted to them. Of course, you will keep it for your own reflection; but, convinced of its soundness, I feel it consistent with pure morality to lead them towards it, to familiarize them to the idea that it is for their interest to cede lands at times to the United States, and for us thus to procure gratifications to our citizens, from time to time, by new acquisitions of land.

expression of presidential policy than was possible in the official correspondence of the secretary of war. His instructions to Harrison included the suggestion that influential men be induced to "run in debt" in order to encourage cessions of land and that any tribe be driven across the Mississippi if it were "foolhardy enough to take up the hatchet." And he went on to explain in detail how he wished Harrison to proceed in the quest of Indian lands along the banks of the Mississippi.[31]

These considerations, including the desirability of removing uncooperative tribes west of the Mississippi, were written at a time when Jefferson's emissaries in Paris were negotiating with France for the purchase of the New Orleans region in order to provide free navigation for United States shipping all the way down the Mississippi into the Gulf of Mexico. The unexpected windfall of the Louisiana Purchase brought within the bounds of the United States a whole new world of Indian tribes, with whom could be opened a lucrative trade in furs and across whose lands could be found the long-sought passage by river to the Pacific. But it also made more feasible the removal of those eastern tribesmen who wished to continue the old way of the huntsman on the western prairies. In his third annual message to Congress, requesting from the Senate a confirmation of the treaty with France, he suggested the wisdom of "confirming to the Indian inhabitants [of Louisiana] their occupancy and self-government, [and] establishing friendly and commercial relation with them."[32]

In view of the uncertain legality of the Louisiana Purchase, Jefferson also drafted constitutional amendments, one of which included the proviso that lands purchased by the United States on the west side of the Mississippi could be exchanged by act of Congress for Indian lands wanted by the United States on the east side of the river, and that whites on the west side might be removed to the thus-acquired lands on the east side.[33] In private correspondence he was even more explicit, suggesting that the part of Louisiana north of New Orleans "will probably be locked up from American settlement, and under the self-government of the native occupants."[34] To the economist DuPont de Nemours, a friend from his days in Paris, he suggested that "our policy will be to form New Orleans, and the country on both sides of it to the Gulf of Mexico, into a State; and, as to all above that, to transplant our Indians into it, constituting them a Marechausee to prevent emigrants crossing the river, until we have filled up all the vacant country on this side" (a process he estimated to require fifty years).[35]

This proposal for a wholesale exchange of populations, and the other provisions of the amendment, were not accepted by Congress or the general population, but they indicate clearly that with the acquisition of Louisiana, Jefferson's Indian policy had by July 1803 reached its mature form as a plan for obtaining Indian land for the expansion of the white population of the United States. The plan, reduced to simplest forms, had seven elements:

1. Maintain peace with the Indians, using a limited system of forts garrisoned by regular army troops to try to prevent white encroachment and other abuses, which might provoke border warfare, and to suppress incipient Indian uprisings.
2. Use a nonprofit, whiskey-free chain of publicly supported fur trade factories to counter the influence of foreign (primarily British) traders and to get leading Indians so far into debt that they would be willing to sell land to pay off their obligations.
3. Employ the Indian superintendents and agents under the direction of the War Department to keep the tribes from alliances with encircling, hostile foreign powers (at one time and in one place or another, Britain, Spain, and France) and to persuade them to sell land.
4. Encircle the eastern tribes by first acquiring the land on the east bank of the Mississippi, compressing them into a vast but ever-shrinking enclave between the Mississippi and the Appalachian mountains.
5. As game diminishes in the eastern enclave, offer the tribes the capital goods and education needed for survival as European-style agriculturists and citizens of the republic in exchange for their lands.
6. For those who reject the offer of "civilization" as the sole alternative to their extinction, removal into the Louisiana Purchase, which will become the next native enclave, where refugees and aboriginal residents can freely hunt for skins and furs and trade to mutual profit with the United States and her citizens, until such time as the land is needed for white settlement.
7. When border trouble escalates to the point of threatened or actual war, obtain Indian lands as the price of peace.

The legal authority and administrative mechanisms necessary to carry out this plan were, by 1803, already in place, in the form of two constitutional provisions; one that gave Congress the right to supervise commerce with the Indian tribes, now expressed through the Trade and Intercourse

Act of 1802, and a second that gave the President the power to enter into treaties, with the advice and consent of the Senate, including treaties with Indian tribes for the purchase of their lands.

Jefferson was certainly sincere in his belief that Indian people must ultimately adopt the white man's ways in order to survive. He and his contemporaries were determined to carry out the intentions of their Federalist predecessors in providing them with the tools and education necessary to ascend from the communalistic hunting stage to the level of agricultural society with private property. This governmental philanthropy was extremely moralistic, especially as it allied itself with missionary evangelism. It was also (at least to us, by hindsight) patently self-serving, the missionary and the plow justifying the relentless pursuit of Indian lands. And it was psychologically and culturally extremely naive, expecting rational calculations of economic self-interest to induce a total transformation of Indian society in a very brief period of a few years, not really paying any attention to the impossibility of persuading many Native Americans to suddenly abandon cherished values of communal responsibility, mutual aid, and kinship obligation, and demanding the relinquishment to strangers of the graves of their ancestors.

Furthermore, it ignored the simple economic fact that the cash crop on which Indians had traditionally depended for the purchase of European goods—including, in some cases, agricultural tools—was the harvest of skins and furs that they secured from the very hunting grounds Jeffersonian philanthropy demanded that they sell. White folks in many frontier communities, such as Redstone and Greenbrier, were having a very hard time getting their farm surpluses to market and were consequently cash poor. There was no guarantee that Indian farmers in the backcountry of Georgia or Tennessee would fare any better. From the rational point of view of many a Native American, it would in principle have been perfectly possible to combine fur-trade hunting, communal property, and the perpetuation of traditional social organization and religion with selected elements of white technology. Recent history records a number of very successful hybrids of European technology and non-Western social and religious culture.

Cessions North of the Ohio

In the letters to Dearborn and Harrison, Jefferson had suggested that the process of land acquisition north of the Ohio begin with the owners of the territory fronting on the Mississippi: the Cahokias (now extinct), the Peorias, and the Kaskaskias. All were members of the old Illinois Confederacy whose tribes were now reduced to a few dozen surviving families by disease, dissipation, and the long wars with the Iroquois, the Sac and Fox, and other northern Indians. Over a century earlier the Illinois tribes had converted to Christianity under the influence of French Jesuit missionaries and had remained loyal to the French and to the United States, France's ally, during the Revolution and the subsequent wars in the Ohio valley. In so doing they earned the hatred of the pro-British, anti-American tribes around them.

In 1790 the Kaskaskias, reputedly the largest surviving group, having absorbed the others, suffered heavy losses in a battle with the Potawatomis; in 1802 they were attacked by a Shawnee war party and again endured serious casualties. They lived in a village at the mouth of the Kaskaskia River, along the Mississippi about sixty miles south of St. Louis, and numbered between 100 and 200 individuals.[36] Their chief was the same Jean Baptiste du Coigne whom Jefferson had met twenty years earlier at Charlottesville and who had named his infant son in honor of the French-speaking governor of Virginia. Harrison in his memoirs recalled du Coigne as "a gentlemanly man, by no means addicted to drink, and possessing a very strong inclination to live like a white man; indeed has done so as far as his means could allow."[37]

In his instructions to Harrison, Jefferson suggested that a spy be introduced into his friend du Coigne's village to sound him out and subtly suggest the idea of a cession. Harrison went about the business promptly and on August 13, 1803, by a treaty held at the territorial capital, Vincennes, secured a cession from the Kaskaskia chiefs and warriors, on behalf of "the several tribes of Illinois Indians," of all their land in the Illinois country except for a reservation of 350 acres near the town of Kaskaskia (the site of the ancient village) and an additional 1,280 acres, to be located later. In return, the United States undertook to protect the Kaskaskias from other Indian tribes, granted them an annuity of $1,000, and promised to erect a church for the Catholic congregation and pay the expenses of a priest (who would also teach the three Rs) for seven years. These emoluments, it was asserted, would procure them "the means of improvement in the arts of civilized life." For du Coigne, the United States undertook to build a house "suitable for the accommodation of the chief of the said tribe" and to enclose for his family's use 100 acres with "a good and sufficient fence."[38] Chief du Coigne continued to live at Kaskaskia and died there some time before the tribe was removed in 1832 to the Indian territory west of the Mississippi.

By the 1803 treaty with the Illinois tribes, the United States obtained a large tract of land in what is now the state of Illinois between the Mississippi and Illinois rivers on the west and the ridge bounding the eastern watershed of the Wabash River. Along the Mississippi the frontage, as Jefferson desired, was extensive, running from the mouth of the Ohio River north to the mouth of the Illinois River, just above St. Louis, a distance of nearly 200 miles. The next year, Harrison extended the United States frontage along the Mississippi by a cession extorted from the Sac and Fox which extended from the Illinois River north to the mouth of the Wisconsin River, near the site of the great trading post at Prairie du Chien.[39]

These two acquisitions of Indian lands along the Mississippi north of the Ohio effectively achieved Jefferson's purpose of pinching the tribes of the Western Confederacy between American holdings. The strategy now was to secure the territory on the north bank of the Ohio, between the Kaskaskia line in Illinois (on the eastern boundary of the future state) and the Greenville line in eastern Indiana. Only one tract within this stretch on the north bank (all of it in the future state of Indiana) had yet been secured, the so-called Clark's Grant at the falls of the Ohio, containing 150,000 acres promised by Virginia to General George Rogers Clark and the officers and men who served with him in the conquest of the Ohio country during the Revolution. The south bank of the river lay in the state of Kentucky; the Indian title there had been extinguished long ago by the Iroquois and Cherokee quit-claims on several occasions, most recently in the 1780s, and by the Shawnee relinquishment after Lord Dunmore's War in 1774.

The lower part of this tract, from the Wabash to Clark's Grant, was in the possession of the Delawares, to whom it had been granted by the Miamis and Piankeshaws as an asylum for members of that tribe displaced by the Greenville Treaty. On June 27, 1804, the secretary of war wrote to Harrison that it would be advisable "to obtain the tract between the southern line of the Vincennes territory and the Ohio."[40] The Vincennes territory was a large block of land around the town of Vincennes reserved at Greenville in 1795 and reconfirmed to the United States by a treaty at Fort Wayne in 1803. Harrison acted promptly, at Vincennes on August 18, 1804, obtaining from the Delaware tribe the rights to the land between the

Vincennes tract and road and the Ohio, from the Wabash to Clark's Grant; ten days later the Piankeshaws, who as the original occupants were co-claimants to the region, confirmed the cession.

Harrison's hasty arrangement of these cessions, however, left a legacy of bitterness, recriminations, and resentment that would culminate in the War of 1812. Protests against the Delaware cession of 1804 were communicated to Harrison as early as March 1805, when the three principal chiefs of the White River Delawares—Tetapachsit, Buckongehelas, and Hockingpomska— who had signed the agreement of cession, sent Tetapachsit's nephew, Billy Patterson, to William Wells, the agent at Fort Wayne, with a message denouncing the treaty. They claimed that it was "unlegal" because the Delawares did not have the right to sell the land. They accused Harrison of fraudulently converting a simple treaty of peace and friendship into a land sale, and they asked that the President be advised and that he "take measures" to prevent the land from being settled. Billy Patterson verbally explained the Delaware chiefs' views in a speech translated by John Connor, a respected white trader in Indiana, and it was witnessed by Johnston, the U.S. factor at Fort Wayne. The Patterson speech was very specific on the charge that Harrison had tricked the Indians into putting their marks on a paper that they could not read and that he had described as being merely a testimonial of mutual good will (see next page).[41]

But the information had already been communicated to Harrison by Wells that not only the Delawares but also the Miamis (through their famous war leader Little Turtle), the Potawatomis, and in fact, the whole body of the Western Confederacy protested the Vincennes treaties. And Little Turtle had sent an address to Jefferson himself, and agent Wells had sent an accompanying letter, so that Harrison had to conclude that "the matter will be fully before the President." Harrison in early March 1805 therefore wrote a long letter to the secretary of war, whose contents no doubt also reached the President, denying the charge of fraud, asserting the right of the Delawares and the Piankeshaws to sell the disputed land, and accusing Wells and Little Turtle of a conspiracy to subvert Harrison's plans and to revive the old Western Confederacy under Little Turtle's command. He regarded as "improper" the suggestion that a special conference be held with the Delawares and Piankeshaws, Miamis, and Potawatomis to negotiate the issue and demanded that Wells be advised that he was to report directly to Harrison as his superior, not directly to the President or the secretary of war—an administrative reform which Dear-

Billy Patterson's Message to the President

Friend and Brother, my Chiefs inform you that their minds are troubled concerning the visit they made Governor Harrison. Last summer at Vincennes they were invited to that place . . . [and] was told by the Governor that he wish them to become more civilized and that he would give them an addition to their annuity of Five hundred Dollars a year to enable them to procure the necessary articles for the purpose of enabling them to cultivate their lands and that he was present when the Miamies gave all White River to the Delawares and that he would give them an instrument of writing that would show that the country on White River belonged to the Delawares . . .

Friend and Brother! When these words was spoke to our chiefs by the governor they were much pleased with what he said, the Governor then wrote two papers which he told our chiefs contained the words he had just spoken to them and he wished them to sign them both that he would send one to the President of the United States and one they could keep themselves in order that the good words he had spoke might be kept in remembrance by the white and red people. Our chiefs cheerfully signed these papers.

Friend and Brother! You may judge how our chiefs felt when they returned home and found that the Governor had been shutting up their eyes and stopping their Ears with his good words and got them to sign a Deed for their lands without their knowledge.

Friend and Brother! The Chiefs of my nation now declare to you from the bottom of their hearts in the presence of God that they never sold Governor Harrison or the United States any land at Vincennes last summer to their knowledge.

Friend and Brother! My chiefs declare to you that they are not willing to sell the lands on the Ohio from the mouth of the Wabash to Clarks Grant at the Falls and that they consider it out of their power to do any such thing without the consent of the other nations in this country.

Friend and Brother! My chiefs wishes you to prevent this land being settled by the white people.

Friend and Brother! These are the words that was put in my mouth by the chiefs of my nation, in order that I might deliver them to you.

born duly instituted by requiring that Indian agents be responsible to the governors of their respective territories.[42]

Jefferson and Dearborn discussed the problem, and then in May 1805 Dearborn reported to Harrison the President's decisions on the subject: first, that a conference should be held, as soon as possible, with the chiefs of the Delawares, Miamis, and Potawatomis "for the purpose of such an explanation of the doings, so much complained of, as will satisfy the chiefs, generally, that the transaction was not only open and fair, but such as they have no right to object to." And the offending chiefs should be "severely reprimanded" in front of the other chiefs and told that in the future "no chief, who so far degrade themselves as to deny their own doings, will be considered as deserving of the confidence of their father, the President of the United States, or admitted to any conference with him, or any of his principal officers or agents."[43] At about the same time Jefferson was writing directly to Harrison, mostly about the latter's administration of Indian relations in Louisiana, but he mentioned the affair of the Delaware treaty in passing: "The Little Turtle is indisposed. Ambition will account in some degree for his effort to produce a great confederacy; but perhaps we also may have been defective in our kindnesses to him. A liberality towards him which would not be felt by us, might prevent great embarrassment & expence."[44]

Although still convinced that Wells and Little Turtle were plotting against him, Harrison obediently convened the tribes at Vincennes in August 1805 in order to settle the Delaware treaty affair "to the satisfaction of the President" (and he vowed to the secretary of war "that I will answer with my head to execute every wish of the President relative to the Indians in this quarter"). And the treaty at Vincennes did indeed turn out, on the surface, to be a love feast. Harrison was reconciled with Little Turtle and Captain Wells (with whom he agreed to "a general amnesty and act of oblivion for the past"). The Delaware chiefs "explicitly acknowledge[d] the Treaty," and the Miamis and Potawatomis agreed that the Delawares had a right to sell because the land had been given them by the Piankeshaws years ago. The land claims of the various tribes on the Wabash and White rivers were settled to mutual satisfaction. "In pursuance of the President's directions," Harrison promised Little Turtle an annuity of $50 and ordered Captain Wells to go to Kentucky and there "purchase a negro man for him."[45] And, as a final coup to earn the President's approval, Harrison was able to secure from the Miamis, Eel Rivers, and Weas their land on the Ohio east of Clark's Grant.

This cession, and the cession from the Piankeshaws a few months later of land in Illinois that included a stretch of a few miles on the Ohio just below the Wabash, completed the acquisition of all the lands on the north bank of the Ohio.[46] In his annual message to Congress on December 3, 1805, Jefferson congratulated himself on his accomplishment of his goal: "it completes our possession of the whole of both banks of the Ohio from its source to near its mouth, and the navigation of that river is thereby forever rendered safe to our citizens settled and settling on its extended waters."[47]

But the aftermath of the Delaware treaty affair was not happy for everyone, particularly not for the Delaware chiefs principally involved in it: Buckongehelas, Tetapachsit, and Hockingpomska, and their spokesman, Billy Patterson. Buckongehelas was already an old man at the time of the treaty at Vincennes. He had been for many years a principal war chief of the Delawares, leading the warriors during the Revolution (when he laid siege to Wheeling, West Virginia), at the defeat of St. Clair by Little Turtle, and at the battle of Fallen Timbers. Buckongehelas distrusted whites in general, having heard John Heckewelder's warning back in 1781 that the Delaware converts on the Tuscarawas, who were friendly to the Americans, were in danger of being attacked by frontier whites: "I admit that there are good white men, but they bear no proportion to the bad; the bad must be the strongest, for they rule. They do what they please. They enslave those who are not of their colour, although created by the same Great Spirit who created us. They would make slaves of us if they could, but as they cannot do it, they kill us. There is no faith to be placed in their words. They are not like the Indians, who are only enemies while at war, and are friends in peace. They will say to an Indian; 'My friend, my brother.' They will take him by the hand, and at the same moment destroy him. And so you [addressing himself to the Christian Indians] will also be treated by them before long. Remember that this day I have warned you to beware of such friends as these. I know the long knives; they are not to be trusted."[48] These Christian Indians were indeed massacred a year later at Gnadenhütten.

Buckongehelas's distrust of white promises was renewed in 1794 when the British, after having encouraged the western confederates to resist the Americans, then refused to give the fleeing Indian survivors of Fallen Timbers asylum in the British fort nearby. Buckongehelas signed the Treaty of Greenville to end the war, and he signed the Vincennes treaty in

1804, but he remained a conservative to the end, refusing to trust the Americans and urging the Delawares not to forsake their religion and other customs. He was chief of the largest Delaware town on the west fork of the White River, Wapecomekoke, near present Muncie, Indiana, until his death, supposedly of natural causes, in 1805. Colonel John Gibson informed Harrison of the death of "the Great Chief and Warrior Bokongehulas."[49]

Gibson at the same time referred to Tetapachsit as "the other Chief of the Delawares." Tetapachsit presided over the so-called Munsee Town (on the actual site of Muncie, Indiana). He too was an old man, a former fighter against the Americans, but now somewhat more friendly. He had invited the Moravian missionaries to establish themselves near the Delaware towns on the White River. Although he publicly opposed the traffic in whiskey, he himself was a whiskey trader, bringing barrels of whiskey into his own village. He confessed his sin in a public ceremony: "My children you see how old I am, how gray my hair is; I am still not on the right road as God desires it of us. We have also often admonished you not to drink, nor to commit any evil, but nothing came of it. We remained as we were. We chiefs have now discovered why you have not changed either, because we ourselves do not do what we tell you to do."[50]

In March Tetapachsit was seized by Delaware followers of the famous Shawnee Prophet Tenskwatawa, who had accused him of causing the death of Buckongehelas by witchcraft. Under torture, he confessed to witchcraft and implicated a Delaware Moravian convert, Joshua. Although he later repudiated his confession, Tetapachsit and Joshua were brought before the Shawnee Prophet, who claimed to have special powers to identify witches. Tenskwatawa condemned them to death. Tetapachsit was tomahawked by his own son and thrown alive into a great fire, which burned up part of the nearby woods. Tetapachsit's nephew, Billy Patterson, a converted Christian, was also seized and burned at the stake as a witch. Tetapachsit's widow, a young woman who had replaced the murderous son's mother in the old chief's affections, nearly suffered the same fate but was saved by her brother. And finally, Hockingpomska, also prominent in the Vincennes treaty affair, was accused of witchcraft but rescued by friends.[51]

The Delaware witch hunt singled out as victims or practitioners of witchcraft precisely the four men who were most closely involved in the sale of the Delaware lands along the Ohio River. It hardly would seem to be a mere coincidence. When Harrison learned of the Delaware witch hunt, he sent a passionate speech to them, condemning the recent murders and urging them not to follow the "dark, crooked and thorny" path down which the Shawnee Prophet was leading them. "My heart is filled with grief, and my eyes are dissolved in tears, at the news which has reached me . . . He ['this pretended prophet'] tells you that the Great Spirit commands you to punish with death those who deal in magic, and that he is authorized to point them out . . . Let your poor old men and women stay in quietness, and banish from their minds the dreadful idea of being burnt alive by their own friends and countrymen. I charge you to stop your bloody career . . . if you wish the friendship of your great father the President."[52] But Harrison would not be able to check the career of the Prophet and his brother Tecumseh; and eventually Jefferson would be drawn deeply into the problem.

Jefferson's other accomplishments in obtaining land in the old Northwest Territory were in northern Ohio and southern Michigan. South of Lake Erie, between Sandusky and Cleveland, and west of the Greenville Line lay country occupied by remnants of various Indian nations but claimed by Connecticut on the basis of colonial charter. This was the Connecticut Western Reserve, which Connecticut ceded to Congress in 1800 with the hope that it would go to the Connecticut Land Company and the company of Connecticut "sufferers" of British depredations during the Revolution. The directors of the Connecticut Land Company and the Sufferers' Company petitioned Jefferson directly, asking him to appoint commissioners to treat with the Indian proprietors. Jefferson complied, and the commissioners duly met with the representatives of the interested tribes, a motley collection of Wyandots, Ottawas, Chippewas, Potawatomis, Munsees, Delawares, and Shawnees. On July 4, 1805, they ceded the Western Reserve, amounting to about 1,200,000 acres, for a price of about one cent per acre in annuities payable by the United States and about one and a half cents per acre payable by the land companies in a combination of cash and annuities, the total amounting to $32,666.67.[53]

Jefferson also took personal initiative in obtaining a cession of the lands surrounding Detroit, in extreme northern Ohio and southern Michigan. In 1803 the old Northwest Territory had been split in two, one half becoming the new State of Ohio. In 1805 Jefferson had created the new territories of Michigan and Indiana out of the other half. General William Hull, the first governor of Michigan Territory, was instructed to call together the chief men of the tribes in the Detroit area, mostly Ottawas, Potawatomis, and Chippewas, the "Three Fires." Jefferson, anticipating war with Britain, desired the neutrality of the Indians in that quarter.

His message, as relayed by Hull, was threatening in tone: "we have learnt that some tribes are already expressing intentions hostile to the United States, we think it proper to apprise them of the ground on which they now stand, and that on which they will stand; for which purpose we make to them this solemn declaration of our unalterable determination, that we wish them to live in peace with all nations, as well as with us; and we have no intention ever to strike them or to do them an injury of any sort, unless first attacked or threatened; but, that, learning that some of them meditate war on us, we, too, are preparing for war against those, and those only, who shall seek it: and that, if ever we are constrained to lift the hatchet against any tribe, we will never lay it down till that tribe is exterminated, or driven beyond the Mississippi. He adjures them, therefore, if they wish to remain on the land which covers the bones of their father, to keep the peace with a people who ask their friendship without needing it; who wish to avoid war without fearing it: in war they will kill some of us; we shall destroy all of them. Let them then continue quiet at home; take care of their women and children, and remove from among them the agents of any nations, persuading them to war, and let them declare to us explicitly, and categorically, that they will do this; in which case they will have nothing to fear from the preparations we are now unwillingly making, to secure our own safety."[54]

He also ordered Hull to acquire the land about Detroit, from the Western Reserve on the south and east to Saginaw Bay on the north, comprehending the eastern half of the peninsula. The Indians were compliant, being suspicious of British promises and not eager to offend the President, and Hull treated the 700 to 800 native visitors "kindly" and gave them "what they want to eat." They proposed to live under the protection of the United States, vowed neutrality in the coming conflict, and in November 1807 agreed to a cession of land. It was somewhat smaller than Jefferson desired, extending south only to the Maumee River and north far short of Saginaw Bay, with a number of reservations for their villages, but the price was only $10,000—not more than two cents an acre for land worth $2.50 at public auction.[55]

These transactions completed Jefferson's program of land acquisitions north of the Ohio. By 1807 he was preoccupied by the prospect of war with

Great Britain, which would inevitably bring at least some of the tribal factions of the northwest into the fray on the side of the British and their Indian allies in Canada.

Cessions South of the Ohio

Persuading Indian tribes to sell land south of the Ohio River proved more difficult. Almost all of Kentucky was clear of Native American title, except for small tracts owned by the Chickasaws along the Mississippi and by the Cherokees south of the Cumberland. But most of Tennessee remained in Cherokee and Chickasaw hands, and most of Georgia was occupied by Creeks and Cherokees. Choctaws, Chickasaws, and Creeks held nearly all of present Mississippi and Alabama, and Florida, still under Spanish sovereignty, was largely taken up by the displaced bands of Creeks known as Seminoles. These were all large tribes, still capable of putting thousands of warriors into the field despite their internal factional disputes, and many of them were warmly attached to Spanish, French, or British interests. It was prudent to move warily among them.

Furthermore, there was no one in the southern department comparable to the aggressive Harrison, who was governor, military commander, and Indian superintendent all at once. William Claiborne was governor of Mississippi Territory, but Benjamin Hawkins and General James Wilkinson led the negotiations with the Chickasaws, Choctaws, and Creeks. Hawkins was, of course, principal agent among the Creeks; among the Cherokees, the agent responsible for land negotiations was Return Jonathan Meigs. Both of these men, domiciled in the states of Georgia and Tennessee, reported to the secretary of war.

Georgia authorities were unhappy that Hawkins had obtained only part of the lands in the Oconee–Ocmulgee fork during his negotiations at Fort Wilkinson in 1802. In 1803 Dearborn ordered him and General James Wilkinson to run the 1802 boundary and to negotiate another treaty with the Creeks to secure the remainder of the lands around the fork. Hawkins again commenced difficult and protracted negotiations with the Creeks, whose split between the Upper and the Lower factions, general resentment against frontier outrages, and irritation at incessant demands by the state of Georgia for the return of slaves, horses, and other property seized in the course of many years made reaching a generally acceptable agreement difficult. Dearborn consulted with Jefferson about the problem and was advised that the United States government did not wish to intervene in factional disputes, even if it led to a nation splitting into two or more tribes.[56]

Hawkins was able to secure the cession, but the Senate rejected it on the grounds of improper financial arrangements. Eventually in 1805 a compliant Creek delegation led by William McIntosh visited Washington and negotiated directly with Jefferson. Jefferson insisted on the grant of the entire Oconee–Ocmulgee fork and also the right to build a road across Creek territory from Fort Hawkins on the Ocmulgee to Fort Stoddart on the Mobile River at the edge of the Choctaw cession of 1802. The Creek delegates in November 1805 were persuaded to sign the treaty of cession on Jefferson's terms, receiving in return a tribal annuity of $12,000 a year for eight years and $11,000 a year for ten more. This was the last of the Creek treaties during Jefferson's presidency.[57] Thereafter a rising tide of native nationalism, partly home-based and partly inspired by the Shawnee Prophet's emissaries from the north, stiffened Indian resistance to further cessions of land in the south.

Jefferson had wanted to secure the banks of the Mississippi, and on November 16, 1805, two days after the Creek Treaty of Washington, his agents among the Choctaws, James Robertson and Silas Dinsmoor, obtained a cession of land from the chiefs of that nation. This cession, however, was for land on the Florida border, between the Natchez Trace and the Creek boundary. This location was contrary to the agents' instructions, and Jefferson in disgust refused to submit it to the Senate for ratification. This was a curious act on the part of a President who publicly asserted that the United States would buy Indian land whenever the proprietors wished to settle their debts and secure capital for civilization. In this case, the Choctaws wished the largest part, $55,500, of the purchase money to be paid to British merchants and traders to whom they were in debt; beyond that, $3,000 annually was to be paid as a tribal annuity, plus a personal bonus of $500 and a $150 annuity to the three principal chiefs.

Jefferson did finally submit the treaty to the Senate for ratification in 1808, when deteriorating relations with Great Britain and Spain suddenly made the despised cession militarily valuable. His message of transmittal to the Senate was candid: "Progressive difficulties, however, in our foreign relations, have brought into view considerations, other than those which then prevailed. It is now, perhaps, become as interesting to obtain footing for a strong settlement of militia along our southern frontier, eastward of the Mississippi, as on the west of that river; and more so than high up the river itself. The consolidation of the Mississippi Territory, and the establishing a barrier of separation between the Indians and our southern neighbors, are also important objects. The cession is supposed to contain about five millions of acres, of which the greater part is said to be fit for cultivation, and no inconsiderable proportion of the first quality, on the various waters it includes; and the Choctaws and their creditors are still anxious for the sale."[58]

Not only was Jefferson concerned about invasion from the south by Spaniards and their Indian allies; he was also worried, on the basis of advice from General Wilkinson, about Aaron Burr and other American adventurers' plans (in which Wilkinson himself was implicated) to invade Mexico or possibly Florida. Sealing the border through the Choctaw cession was now imperative.

The other major goal of Jefferson's southern policy was to obtain more land from the Cherokees. The last Cherokee cessions of land, on the Clinch and Holston Rivers in Tennessee, had been made in the 1790s. The settlers were now pressuring the government to persuade the Cherokees to give up land north of the Tennessee River. There was already a federal store at Tellico, whose secret purpose was to get the Cherokee hunters to run so deeply in debt that the chiefs would feel the need to sell lands to pay off their obligations. The factor at Tellico, J. W. Hooker, described his personal indoctrination by Jefferson in March 1801 in colorful language: "when he was at the Norard in conversation with Mr. Jefferson he [Jefferson] asked him if he could get the Cherokee to run in debt to the amount of ten or twelve thousand dollars in the public store. Mr. Hockker told him for answer fifty thousand. Well, says he, that is the way I intend to git there countrey for to git them to run in debt to the publick store and they will have to give there lands for payment. Mr. Hockker's answer was if that is your Deturmeanation you must git sum other pursun to keep the store."[59] Hooker did, however, accept the position, and under his guidance the store consistently advanced more credit to the Cherokees than it received in skins and furs.[60]

Another gambit to secure the desired lands was to approach the Chickasaws, who were perfectly willing to sell their overlapping claims to Cherokee territory. In October 1805 agent Meigs at Tellico secured from certain Cherokee chiefs, by means of bribes of annuities and private reservations (promptly leased to white men), the sale of a tract immediately south of the old Hopewell Treaty line, including Colonel Wofford's settlement. In addition, the treaty provided the right-of-way for a road from Tellico to the Tombigbee River.[61] Shortly after this cession, the same chiefs obediently made their way to Washington and, with Benjamin Hawkins as a witness, on January 7, 1806, agreed to sell all Cherokee lands north of the Tennessee River. Jefferson delivered an unctuous farewell address to the departing delegation, congratulating them on their progress toward civilization and urging them to make even more strides forward.[62]

This transaction ended Jefferson's program of acquisition of the lands of the southern Indians.[63] It merely exacerbated, however, the tensions within the Cherokee nation over the question of land sales, removal, and civilization.

The Land that Jefferson Obtained

Jefferson's policy of "obtaining lands" resulted in the acquisition of close to 200,000 square miles of Indian territory in nine states of the present Union, mostly in Indiana, Illinois, Tennessee, Georgia, Alabama, Mississippi, Arkansas, and Missouri. His agents, under his general mandate, conducted approximately thirty-two treaties with about a dozen tribes or tribal groups, including the Osage treaty, which was not ratified by the Senate until after he left office, and the treaty at Fort Wayne with the Ohio tribes, completed by Harrison in September 1809.

The land thus acquired far exceeded the immediate needs of the expanding white population or the desires of the Native Americans to divest themselves of hunting grounds in order to take advantage of the civilization program. When one looks at the location of the tracts secured, one realizes that for the most part they were chosen primarily to clear Indians from the banks of the great rivers, the Ohio and the Mississippi, and to compress the eastern tribes into an interior region west of the Appalachians and east of the Mississippi, where they would be easier to dominate. It was essentially a military strategy: secure the supply lines and encircle the enemy.

As he left office, the banks of the Ohio were safe, much but not all of the Mississippi shoreline was in the government's hands, and public roads traversed Indian territory in a number of directions, connecting American forts, frontier settlements, and centers of commerce. Jefferson had seen to the national security and the future expansion of the growing white population into the remaining Indian territory east of the Mississippi, a task which Andrew Jackson would nearly complete a few years after Jefferson's death.[64]

CHAPTER EIGHT

The Louisiana Territory

THE LOUISIANA PURCHASE confronted Jefferson with a new and little-known population of Indians. For years he had sought to acquire for the United States more information about the inhabitants of the vast domain west of the Mississippi. Part of the interest, as always with Jefferson, was strategic: to draw the tribes on America's borders away from menacing alliances with her real or potential enemies, particularly the British. One means for countering foreign influence was to open up trade with these Indians, hopefully weaning them away from English traders working out of Canada and Florida.

Plans for the Lewis and Clark expedition, which would advance American commerce with the Indians of the west, were being made well before news of the purchase reached Washington in the summer of 1803. Jefferson had for many years sought to encourage the exploration of these territories in order to find a direct water route to the Pacific Ocean for American traders. This had been a plan of his father and other associates in the Loyal Company as far back as the 1750s, when they projected an expedition up the Missouri to the Rocky Mountains and then down the rivers flowing westward into the South Sea.

Jefferson made a number of efforts to promote the Missouri transit scheme. As early as 1786, while minister in Paris, he proposed to the American adventurer John Ledyard, a survivor of the late Captain Cook's voyage to the South Seas, that he undertake to cross North America, approaching the New World either by traversing Russia to Kamchatka, or from the Atlantic westward. Apprehended by emissaries of the Empress Catharine, Ledyard was prevented in his object and died soon after in Egypt.[1] A few years later, in 1792, hearing of the discovery of the Columbia River, Jefferson persuaded the American Philosophical Society in Philadelphia to establish a fund to finance an expedition to locate the Northwest Passage. The eminent French naturalist André Michaux was selected to head the party, and Jefferson wrote him a letter of instruction on behalf of the Society: "The chief objects of your journey are to find the shortest and most convenient route of communication between the U. S. and the Pacific Ocean, within the temperate latitudes, and to learn such particulars as can be obtained of the country through which it passes, it's productions, inhabitants and other interesting circumstances." He went on to specify that the chosen route was to be up the Missouri to its headwaters and thence across by land "to some principal river of the Pacific Ocean—perhaps the Oregon."[2]

But Michaux's journey was canceled when Jefferson learned that the intriguing Citizen Genet was using Michaux as a secret agent to provoke Kentucky irregulars into an armed assault on Spanish Louisiana, hoping to embroil the United States in France's war with Great Britain and her ally Spain.[3] A few years later, in 1799, when Jefferson's Albemarle County neighbor Captain Meriwether Lewis was stationed in Charlottesville as a recruiting officer, he applied to Jefferson for the Northwest Passage assignment but was turned down. (In his biographical sketch of Lewis, written many years later, Jefferson misremembered the event, placing "Captain Lewis" as a recruiting officer in Charlottesville in 1792, seven years prematurely, when he was only eighteen and not yet even a volunteer militiaman let alone a captain in the regular army.)[4]

Lewis's chance would come soon, however. Shortly after taking office as President in 1801, Jefferson chose Lewis as his private secretary, domiciled in the White House. By 1802, the two were making plans for the expedition to the Pacific, notifying Spanish and British authorities of their intentions to mount a "literary pursuit" and putting together estimates of cost. Lewis was sent off to Philadelphia and the American Philosophical Society for a crash course in science with the most eminent professors (Benjamin Smith Barton, Caspar Wistar, Benjamin Rush, Robert Patterson, and, in Lancaster, Andrew Ellicott) to prepare him to make observations in natural history, medicine, and navigation.[5]

In January 1803, Jefferson delivered a secret message to Congress, describing the plan and requesting the necessary appropriation of funds ($2,500). He characterized the purpose of the expedition as being primarily commercial, to divert the immense fur trade of the Missouri tribes from Canada to the United States, and incidentally to find a "continued navigation . . . possibly with a single portage, from the western ocean, and finding to the Atlantic a choice of channels through the Illinois or

Wabash, the Lakes and Hudson, through the Ohio and Susquehanna or Potomac or James rivers, and through the Tennessee and Savannah rivers."[6] Congress approved the plan, and Captain Lewis was appointed to lead the exploring party, with his friend Captain William Clark as second in command.

The Corps of Discovery

Jefferson wrote Lewis a formal letter of instructions dated June 20, 1803. On the subject of Indians, he was ordered to learn and record as much as he could about the tribes they would meet along the way and to invite the tribes to peace, friendship, and mutually profitable relations with American fur traders (see next page).[7] The Indians of the lower Missouri watershed were reasonably well known to the Chouteau brothers and their trading organization in St. Louis, and to various other French, Spanish, and British traders, but they were an unknown quantity to Jefferson and to other Americans of the eastern seaboard. They were, in fact, occupants of several different culture areas, ranging from the village-dwelling, corn-growing Osages, Mandans, and Omahas along the lower Missouri to the more mobile hunting bands of Yankton and Teton Sioux now encroaching on the Plains, to the traditional horse-stealing and buffalo-hunting "wild Indians" like the Pawnees, to the hunters and gatherers of the Great Basin and Plateau. These people were not like the relatively sedentary, and by now harried and depopulated, village dwellers of the east. Whites of the eastern seaboard, who had dealt with eastern Indians for two centuries, were not familiar with the customs of the western tribes, their politics, or their intertribal alliances and hostilities.

There is no need to describe here the adventures of Lewis and Clark in their three-year journey to the Pacific Ocean and back. The experiences of the Corps of Discovery have been recounted many times, most recently by Stephen Ambrose in *Undaunted Courage.* James Ronda has carefully chronicled their relations with the Indians, and in an earlier chapter we reviewed the ethnographic significance of their observations.[8]

Jefferson's plans for the exploration and mapping of the Louisiana Purchase envisaged expeditions to the southwest and to the north in addition to the Lewis and Clark drive up the Missouri. To the southwest lay the Spanish possessions in Texas and New Mexico. The boundaries between Spain and the United States were uncertain, awaiting diplomatic negotia-

Further Instructions from Jefferson to Lewis and Clark

In all your intercourse with the natives, treat them in the most friendly & conciliatory manner which their own conduct will admit; allay all jealousies as to the object of your journey, satisfy them of its innocence, make them acquainted with the position, extent, character, peaceable & commercial dispositions of the U.S., of our wish to be neighborly, friendly & useful to them, & of our dispositions to a commercial intercourse with them; confer with them on the points most convenient as mutual emporiums, and the articles of most desirable interchange for them & us. If a few of their influential chiefs, within practicable distance, wish to visit us, arrange such a visit with them, and furnish them with authority to call on our officers, on their entering the U.S. to have them conveyed to this place at the public expence. If any of them should wish to have some of their young people brought up with us, & taught such arts as may be useful to them, we will receive, instruct & take care of them.

Such a mission, whether of influential chiefs or of young people, would give some security to your own party. Carry with you some matter of the kine-pox; inform those of them with whom you may be, of its efficacy as a preservative from the smallpox; & instruct & encourage them in the use of it. This may be especially done wherever you winter.

tion, but Jefferson wanted as much knowledge as could be obtained from observations on the ground, and he wanted to establish friendly relations with the Indian nations in that quarter who now were joined by old alliances and commercial ties with Spain and whose neutrality, in the event of war with Spain, would be important to secure.

Plans were set in motion for a "grand expedition" to the southwest even before Lewis and Clark had set out from St. Louis. Jefferson wrote to William Dunbar, in March 1804 with a request to organize two coordinated expeditions to the westward, one up and down the branches of the Platte River and the other up the Arkansas to its source and then along the height of land to the source of the Red River, and down that river to

Captain Meriwether Lewis. Watercolor on paper by C. B. J. Févret de Saint Mémin, 1807.

the Mississippi, near Fort Adams south of Natchez. Dunbar was a good choice as director of these enterprises. Owner of a plantation just below Natchez, he was an experienced surveyor who with Andrew Ellicott had laid out the southern boundary of the nation at the 31st parallel, maintained an active interest in natural history, and built his own astronomical and meteorological observatory. He became a member of the American Philosophical Society and published the results of his geographical and meteorological researches in the society's *Transactions.*

But Dunbar expressed misgivings about the plan to ascend the Arkansas; an anti-American faction of the Osages had recently moved onto the Arkansas and might disrupt or even attack any expedition. And so the venture was called off. Instead, Dunbar and his scientist-colleague, a physician from Philadelphia, led a small party up the Ouachita River, a tributary of the Red River, into southern Arkansas, to the Hot Springs.[9]

The plan for the major southwestern expedition now shifted to a foray up the Red River, to be led by the surveyor Thomas Freeman, with Peter Custis, a medical student of Benjamin Smith Barton's, as expedition scientist. Jefferson's instructions to Freeman were virtually the same as those to Lewis a year before, including specification of the information to be obtained about the Indian nations.[10] The Red River expedition, however, did not get under way until 1806 and was turned back by a Spanish military detachment at the Texas border; the published and unpublished records of the expedition were sparse. The venture was a failure, but that fact was obscured by threats of war with Spain and the unrest accompanying the activities of Aaron Burr and General James Wilkinson, commanding general of the U.S. Army and governor of the Territory of Louisiana.

At about this time, General Wilkinson was launching two governmental expeditions, both led by a young lieutenant, Zebulon Montgomery Pike, who had been recommended by Lewis.[11] Wilkinson sent Pike and a detachment of twenty men up the Mississippi as far as practicable during the summer of 1805. His mission was to establish relations with the northern Indians, to buy sites for army posts if possible, to announce to the Indians and to the British traders the sovereignty of the United States, and to escort an Indian delegation back to St. Louis for a treaty. Pike's party spent the winter in Minnesota, part of the time searching for the source of the Mississippi, and returned to St. Louis in the spring. In no sense was this a scientific research enterprise, but Jefferson was pleased by the extension of geographical knowledge contained in Pike's surveys and journals and had a professional cartographer redraw the map, as he had Clark's, to submit to Congress and the public.

In the summer of 1806 Pike set out on a second exploring expedition, under orders from Wilkinson to ascend the Arkansas to its source, cross over to the head of the Red River, and descend it to Natchitoches—all in one summer, with summer uniforms and equipment. Along the way he was to return some Osage prisoners, make peace between the Kansas and the Pawnee Indians, and establish friendly relations between the Comanches and the United States. After discovering, but not climbing, what came to be called Pike's Peak, he and his men wandered off onto the headwaters of the Rio Grande, where they were arrested and temporarily detained by the Spanish.

With the return of Pike's expedition to American soil in the summer of 1807, Jefferson's own plans for the exploration and mapping of the Louisiana Purchase came to an end. The task, of course, was not finished, and a decade later Major Stephen Long would commence a series of ventures into the wilderness, expanding geographical knowledge of the Rocky Mountains and locating the sources of the Mississippi River. Long's expeditions included a naturalist from Philadelphia, Thomas Say, who brought back more systematic information about Indian tribes than had been possible for Lewis and Clark, Dunbar, and Pike in the turbulent times of Jefferson's presidency. The purposes of the expeditions sponsored by Jefferson and Wilkinson were largely practical: to define the boundaries of the new territory, to map its rivers and mountains, to establish friendly contact with the Indian nations while making them sensible of the power and authority of the United States, to identify locations for trading posts and forts, and to counter the influence of foreign traders. If scientific, including ethnological and linguistic, information could be garnered along the way, that would be very welcome, but the diplomatic, military, and commercial aspects of the missions were preeminent.

Jefferson could not help but look to the future of the western Indians. Even while he was preparing to open an extensive trade in skins and furs—a proceeding that would effectively bind them to the hunter state for years to come—he was also planning to introduce implements of husbandry and recognizing the need for gathering "knowledge . . . of the state of morality, religion and information among them, as it may better enable those who may endeavor to civilize and instruct them to adapt their measures to the existing notions and practices of those on whom they are to operate." The prescription is rather coldly put, but it is an exact-enough definition of some kinds of applied anthropology in our own time.

The Treaty with the Sac and Fox

Jefferson's initial policy toward western Indians was very different from his policy toward his eastern neighbors. The thought here was less of obtaining land and more of obtaining trade. Although in the future, some day, western Indians too would have to give up their lands, abandon the hunt, and become civilized, for now the new Louisiana Territory would be, as Merrill Peterson expressed it, "a great Indian reserve," closed to all settlers and governed by the military.[12] But traders, both well-established firms like the Chouteau family of St. Louis and new ones such as John Jacob Astor's American Fur Company in the Great Lakes region, were strongly encouraged to establish trading posts at suitable locations along the Missouri. As Jefferson wrote to Astor in 1808: "You may be assured that in order to get the whole of this business passed into the hands of our own citizens, and to oust foreign traders, who so much abuse their privilege by endeavoring to excite the Indians to war on us, every reasonable patronage and facility in the power of the Executive will be afforded."[13] Astor's company eventually dominated the fur trade in the west.

Despite this interest in trade, one of the first transactions with the Indians of Louisiana Territory was to purchase land. On October 1, 1804, the Territory of Louisiana was united for administrative purposes with Indiana Territory, and William Henry Harrison, Indiana's territorial governor, became the governor of Louisiana also.[14] Harrison himself arrived in St. Louis in the middle of October, bearing instructions from Jefferson, via the secretary of war, "to procure from the Sacs" cessions of land on the east side of the Mississippi both north and south of the Illinois River.[15] Most of the Sac villages were situated on the west side of the Mississippi, beginning about 100 miles north of the settlements about St. Louis.

Harrison was not personally acquainted with the tribes in the new territory of which he had just become governor, but he had found the Sacs in the east to be pro-British troublemakers. Furthermore, his principal adviser on Indian affairs was the trader Auguste Chouteau, who was well informed about Indian matters but was perhaps biased against the Sac Indians because of their chronic war against the Osage nation, among whom the Chouteau family were the principal traders.[16] On his arrival in

St. Louis, Harrison found what he took to be a golden opportunity to obtain a cession of land from the Sac and their allies the Fox, not only on the east side of the Mississippi but on the west as well. In his interpretation of the situation he was no doubt advised by Chouteau and his half-brother Pierre, both of whom witnessed the treaty that was signed on November 3, 1804, only two weeks after Harrison's arrival in St. Louis. Jefferson lost no time in sending the treaty to the Senate for ratification by the end of December.[17]

The circumstances leading up to this impromptu treaty deserve some scrutiny. In September of 1804, relations between the Sac and Fox and the whites in Illinois and Missouri were becoming tense. United States officials were uneasy because the Sacs were a large group not bound by any treaty with the United States, and they were refusing to give up prisoners or stolen horses.[18] There were rumors of impending war. Into this uneasy situation four Sac hunters tossed a bombshell in 1804 by murdering some of the white settlers who were trespassing on Indian hunting lands on the Cuivre River north of St. Louis.

The Sac chiefs who heard of the murders were greatly alarmed. They denounced the killings and sent a delegation to St. Louis to adjust the matter peaceably. These Sac deputies found the white settlements in great alarm, some fleeing, some repairing to a stockaded fort being built on the Cuivre River, some preparing for war, and generally harboring the conviction that the Sac also were preparing for war. These chiefs were given a message in "strong language" to take back to their nation, demanding that the murderers be given up under the implicit threat of war, and inviting "a large proportion of them" to a council with Governor Harrison, at which "measures may be taken that will produce those warriors." The Sac deputation hastened back, and on October 27 another small deputation arrived in St. Louis. They brought with them one of the murderers for trial and possible punishment by the Americans.

Harrison, who had arrived in St. Louis only two weeks earlier and had been busy organizing the territorial government, met the Sac deputation promptly. He entered upon negotiation with the desire to buy land, as had been suggested in his general instructions from the War Department of June 27, 1804, which mentioned the desirability of a cession from the Sacs on both sides of the Illinois River. The Sac delegation had not been given authority to sell any land, only to settle the issue of the recent murder on the Cuivre River and by so doing to remove the threat of war and invasion, thus paving the way to friendly trading and political relations with the United States. Five Indians signed a treaty which effected several things. It (1) established the Sac and Fox as allies of the United States, under the federal government's friendship and protection; (2) guaranteed the Sac and Fox secure possession of their lands; (3) made an explicit agreement providing for an orderly and just settlement of complaints by individuals of one nation against those of another; (4) provided for the regular conduct of the Indian trade; (5) provided for a peace treaty (duly held later) between the Sac and Fox and the Osage; (6) ceded to the United States a vast territory in present-day Illinois, Wisconsin, and Missouri; (7) gave to the Sac and Fox the sum of $2,234.50 and an annuity of $1,000. The Indian

"Discovery Dance, Sauk and Fox." Oil on canvas by George Catlin, 1835–1837. The simultaneous patting of the dancers' feet on the ground, in perfect time, mimicked the sound of approaching game or enemies. Courtesy of the National Museum of American Art, Washington, DC / Art Resource, NY.

murderer, who gave himself up, was pardoned, but the pardon arrived after the Indian had been shot "when attempting to make his escape."

The coup achieved by Harrison did not, however, prove to be of immediate benefit to the white population of Louisiana; it led, instead, to continued frontier incidents that plagued the subsequent administrations of Governor Wilkinson and Governor Lewis and provided the grievances that precipitated the Black Hawk War of 1832. The 1804 cession by the Sac and Fox also exemplifies perfectly the process of obtaining land by the pragmatic procedure of allowing whites to encroach, as hunters and settlers, on unceded Indian land until violent retaliation by the Indians brought the threat of open frontier warfare, at which point a cession was demanded by federal authorities as the price of peace.[19]

The Plan for Population Exchange

In 1805 the Territory of Louisiana (north of the 33rd parallel) was formally created by Congress. The following January, Jefferson appointed General Wilkinson as governor for a three-year term, replacing Harrison, who had served while upper Louisiana was temporarily annexed to Indiana Territory. Wilkinson actually arrived in St. Louis as acting governor in July of 1805, however, pending the confirmation of his appointment by the Senate, and immediately was confronted with the problems of Indian affairs left over by his predecessor, particularly the dispute generated by the treaty with the Sac and Fox. A deputation of 150 Sac and Fox was awaiting him on his arrival in St. Louis to protest the killing of the accused murderer of the whites on the Cuivre River. Wilkinson explained that the prisoner had been shot by a sentinel "when attempting to make his escape," and then he "produced the President's pardon which arrived soon after the catastrophe." The governor somewhat unctuously observed that God must have over-ruled the President: "It had been the will of the Great Spirit that he [the warrior] should Suffer for Spilling the Blood of his White Brethren, without Provocation." The pardon was presented to the brother of the dead Indian, who through an orator expressed satisfaction, and next day the deputation departed up the river, apparently with good will.[20]

Unfortunately, whatever good will this incident generated was soon dissipated. By December Wilkinson was reporting to the secretary of war that the Sac and Fox and their neighbors the Iowa were "disposed for war," instigated by traders from both Canada and St. Louis. He recommended

James Wilkinson. Oil on canvas by Charles Willson Peale, c. 1797. Courtesy of Independence National Historical Park Collection.

that the best way to humble "those Refractory nations" would be to "interdict all trade the next season" and clap the offending traders in irons pending deportation. At the same time, he sent an admonitory address to the Sac chiefs, complaining about murders and depredations on the frontier and threatening them with the same destruction that had been visited upon the tribes in the Ohio country, who had "roused the anger of your Father beyond forgiveness, and then he turned loose his Warriors upon them as numerous as the trees in the woods, who destroyed their towns, their Fields and their Stock, Carried their women & children in Captivity, humbled those nations into the Dust and took their Country from them."[21]

These strong words did not have the chastening effect the governor had hoped for (nor did similar threats from his successor, Meriwether Lewis). In general, the governor's philosophy of Indian affairs seems to have been one of heavy-handed confrontation, hoping to extort Native American submission to United States sovereignty by banning foreign traders and threatening to cut off U.S. trade supplies, and proposing to build an extensive network of military posts in Indian country. Jefferson seems to have understood and supported in principle Wilkinson's militaristic stance. As he observed in refuting certain congressional objections to the general's appointment on the grounds of the unconstitutionality of combining civil and military authority in one person, he regarded the administration of Louisiana "not as a civil government, but as a military station."[22] In effect, the governor's mission was to defend the territory against Spanish and British encroachment, whether commercial or military, to subdue and pacify the Native American tribes, and to prepare the territory for the immigration of Indians to be removed from the east.

Pacification was indeed an important element of Jefferson's Indian policy for Louisiana. The salient problem was a traditional enmity between the Osage nation, aboriginal proprietors of the west bank of the Mississippi from the Arkansas River north to the Missouri, and the several tribes of the Ohio valley. Between them, generations of old scores always remained to be settled, and the bitterness had been exacerbated by the recent increase in the number of hunting expeditions across the river by Ohio valley Indians dispossessed of much of their land and game. Jefferson was concerned lest the continued hostilities make the Mississippi a "river of blood," and through the secretary of war directed the governors of the Indiana and Louisiana territories to bend their efforts toward making peace among the tribes.[23]

Accordingly, the tribes were assembled at St. Louis by the two governors, and on October 22, 1805, a peace treaty was signed by representatives of the Great and Little Osages on the one part, and of the Delawares, Miamis, Potawatomis, Kickapoos, Sacs, Foxes, Kaskaskias, Sioux of the Des Moines River, and the Iowas on the other. The two groups agreed to end all hostilities, and if isolated individual injuries were done, to take no private revenge (the traditional excuse for war) but rather to complain to the offender's tribe and, failing satisfaction there, to the governors as superintendents of Indian affairs.[24]

This peaceable accommodation, alas, was short-lived. Within months a party of Potawatomis and Kickapoos fell upon a hunting encampment of the Osages while most of the men were absent and killed a large number of women and children; others were taken captive, and some of them were left with the Sac nation.[25] Jefferson was deeply disturbed by this deterioration in Indian affairs and wrote directly to Harrison explaining his personal sentiments (to be communicated later, he suggested, by the secretary of war as "official" policy).

Jefferson wrote: "The British have clearly no right to trade with the

Indians in Louisiana. It is therefore decided to keep that trade to ourselves as the only means of governing those Indians peaceably. This will render it important to be particularly friendly to the Sacs, Foxes, Kickapoos, Sioux, & other Indians residing on the borders between the British & us; and by taking their pelts & furs at higher prices, & selling them goods at lower prices than the trade will bear without loss, to let them see their own interest in an exclusive adhesion to us. What we lose with them, we must make up from other quarters, our principle being neither to gain nor lose on the whole Indian trade taken together. The late stroke of the Poutewatamis on the Osages must be strongly reprimanded, and no exertion spared to recover & restore the prisoners & make satisfaction for the killed. The Indians on this side of the Missisipi must understand that that river is now ours, & is not to be a river of blood. If we permit those on this side to cross it to war against the other side, we must permit the other side to come over to this for revenge. The safety of our settlements will not admit of this."[26]

The secretary of war wrote to Wilkinson on the same subject, after receiving the delegation of chiefs who visited Washington following the peace treaty, with instructions to give sufficient presents to the Osages to forestall a new cycle of revenge killings—but also to warn the Osages of the President's displeasure at their attacks on the Caddoes of Red River.[27]

In addition to his desire to see peace among the Indian tribes and profitable commercial relations between the Indians and American fur traders, Jefferson had another less public agenda: to replace the white population of upper Louisiana, amounting to about 8,000 whites and their 1,500 black slaves, with Indians from east of the Mississippi. In the proposed constitutional amendment he drafted in July 1803 to legalize the purchase of Louisiana and arrange for its administration, he provided for an exchange of lands and movement of populations (see opposite).[28] To effect this goal, of course, the eastern Indians and the Louisiana whites would have to cede their lands to the United States. The amendment was not approved by Congress.

But Jefferson did not abandon the plan, and attempted to carry it out covertly (just as the whole Louisiana Purchase procedure had to be carried off, as he advised his Cabinet, "*sub silentio*"). When Meriwether Lewis reached St. Louis in December 1803, he brought with him instructions from Jefferson to inquire into the possibility of persuading the French inhabitants of the area to exchange their lands and property for new

Jefferson's Proposed Constitutional Amendment

The province of Louisiana is incorporated with the United States and made part thereof. The rights of occupancy in the soil, and of self-government are confirmed to the Indian inhabitants, as they now exist. Preemption only of the portions rightfully occupied by them, and a succession to the occupancy of such as they may abandon, with the full rights of possession as well as of property and sovereignty in whatever is not or shall cease to be so rightfully occupied by them shall belong to the United States. The Legislature of the Union shall have authority to exchange the right of occupancy in portions where the United States have full right for lands possessed by Indians within the United States on the east side of the Mississippi; to exchange lands on the east side of the river for those of the white inhabitants on the west side thereof and above the latitude of 31 degrees: to maintain in any part of the province such military posts as may be requisite for peace or safety: to exercise police over all persons therein, not being Indian inhabitants: to work salt springs, or mines of coal, metals and other minerals within the possession of the United States or in any others with the consent of the possessors; to regulate trade and intercourse between the Indian inhabitants and all other persons; to explore and ascertain the geography of the province, its productions and other interesting circumstances; to open roads and navigation therein where necessary for beneficial communication; and to establish agencies and factories therein for the cultivation of commerce, peace and good understanding with the Indians residing there.

homes east of the Mississippi. Lewis responded politely to his commander-in-chief, averring that the "advantages of such a policy has ever struck me as being of primary importance to the future prosperity of the Union . . . I gave it my earliest and best attention." But he went on to warn the President of difficulties ahead arising from the fear of both French and American slaveholders that once they arrived on the east side of the Mississippi, the government would immediately emancipate their slaves.[29]

Some of the negative reaction to Lewis's inquiries evidently arose from rumors of Jefferson's opposition to slavery and the prohibition against slavery in the Northwest Territory (although his proposed amendment assured the white inhabitants of their security in pre-existing property rights, presumably including the ownership of slaves). Other obvious objections could have been anticipated: the reluctance of powerful fur traders, upon whose commerce the city of St. Louis was founded, to abandon their capital and its network of suppliers and customers; the unwillingness of proprietors of valuable properties like hotels, saloons, and mills of all kinds to sell; the attachment of prosperous landowners to their thousands of acres. Such opposition was communicated to Jefferson's close associates, including Secretary of the Treasury Albert Gallatin.

It is not apparent that Jefferson charged Harrison with the duty of carrying out the transfer policy when he temporarily assumed the governorship of northern Louisiana. When Harrison retired from that office in July 1805, in his address to the General Assembly of Indiana he expressed satisfaction at the prospect to be beheld by the "astonished traveller" upon the waters of the Mississippi: "Upon either bank, a people governed by the same laws, pursuing the same objects, and warmed with the same love of liberty and science."[30] But to Harrison's successor as governor of Louisiana Territory, General Wilkinson, Jefferson privately issued instructions to carry out the population transfer policy.

In November 1805, after Wilkinson had had a few months to assess the situation in his district, he wrote a letter directly to the President, to be delivered by private courier (thus bypassing the secretary of war, to whom he ordinarily reported). After enthusiastically describing the merits of timber sawed from the cottonwood tree and the immense wealth to be obtained from the lead ore so abundant in the territory, he got to the central duties of his mission: trade, peace, and population transfer (see opposite).[31] The secrecy with which Wilkinson felt obliged to work toward "depopulation" was no doubt responsible for the dearth of written documentation of how Wilkinson went about imposing his "discouragements to the present Establishments" and preparing something other than "Beds of down" in order to "get rid of unwelcome guests." Jefferson must have cringed at his agent's flamboyant language ensconced in a less than secure communication; but he did not destroy the letter, which remained among his papers eventually delivered to the Library of Congress, and he does not seem ever to have disavowed what proved to be a fruitless scheme.

How Wilkinson went about discouraging the local establishments is

James Wilkinson's Views on Removal

The three great Objects to which you directed my attention, are in my Judgement all attainable, viz: the prevention of the Trade from Canada to the West of the Mississippi—the depopulation of our loose settlements below this on the Mississippi & its branches—and the transfer of the Southern Indians to this Territory—But for their accomplishment, decisive Legislative sanctions, a zealous faithful & cordial cooperation among the public functionaries in this quarter, and some money will be found indispensable.—

The first Object may be accomplished, by a strong Military post at the Ouisconsin, to make necessary Detachments, and a law prohibiting the Intercourse under severe & heavy penalties—the second by discouragements to the present Establishments, & allurements to a change of position—and the Third, by a permanent peace between the Osage[s] & the Tribes to be moved, a partition & distribution of the vacant territory, national annuities [&] bounties to great Warriors, & pensions to leading Chiefs—Depopulation must precede the transfer of the Indians, and this will never be accomplished whilst high official Characters within the Territory encourage the expectation of our speedy admission into the Union, and treat your Ideas as the speculations of an Individual, which are not to have effect—It is not by preparing Beds of down, that we are able to get rid of unwelcome Guests—On this subject I have been obliged to Act with much caution & reserve because the extent of my utility, will be measured in some degree, by my influence with the People, & to preserve this I must avoid saying or doing unpalatable things—Col. Jn B. Scott, who has returned to Virginia for his family, and who is the soundest & ablest officer of the Territory; will wait on you, & can give you correct information on this point—

not clear. Apparently he was not eager to dislodge the local fur traders; indeed, with the Chouteaus as partners, he himself invested in fur trading expeditions, and on his own he bought land (ostensibly for the purpose of erecting a military post)—activities that brought criticism of his administration. One administrative office that does seem to have operated to the disadvantage of the local land claimants was the Land Commission, established to evaluate titles derived from previous French and Spanish administrations. The operations of the commission, composed of presidential appointees, aroused enormous controversy. It imposed impossible deadlines for the filing of claims, met in St. Louis, which was inaccessible during much of the year to outlying settlements, and had to deal with a maze of legal intricacies left over from the chaotic tangle of earlier laws and regulations. Whether Wilkinson hoped, or was able, to use this commission's slow and cumbersome procedures as a lever to pry loose local landowners and force them to emigrate to the eastern side is not clear.[32]

Another device of discouragement was an absolute silence as to when any of the public lands in the territory, including those acquired from the Sac and Fox, were ever to be put up for sale. This denied settlers the prospect of obtaining desirable lands at a low price and signaled an indefinite postponement of the creation of any new states within the northern part of the territory. The first of these, Missouri, was not admitted to the Union until 1821.[33]

The other half of the population transfer problem was, as Wilkinson noted, the reluctance of the southern Indians to sell their lands. Wilkinson was well-informed on this subject, for he had been for three years Jefferson's personal representative as commissioner to treat with the southern Indians to secure permission for building roads and military posts, to survey boundary lines, and to obtain cessions of land in strategic locations. Although with the help of Benjamin Hawkins and other Indian agents resident in the region he had been able to obtain relatively small and, in the case of the Choctaws, ill-located grants of land, he seemed more engaged with running boundary lines, cutting roads to connect military posts and towns, and establishing forts. His effort to persuade the Choctaws and Chickasaws to cede lands along the east bank of the Mississippi date back to 1802, well before the Louisiana Purchase made population transfer an issue. And during his tenure in St. Louis as governor, he was not involved in either of the west bank land cessions that were accomplished during Jefferson's presidency. The Sac and Fox purchase was made in 1804 by Governor Harrison, and the Osage purchase was accomplished in 1808 by Governor Lewis.

How to draw southern Indians across the river perplexed Wilkinson. He complained to the secretary of war that he had "received no specific Instructions, relatively to the measures to be pursued, to attract the Southern Indians to their Territory" but promised to develop a plan, and he noted with satisfaction the presence of a Delaware and Shawnee population in the territory that could muster 600 warriors.[34] These emigres had been brought over by the Spanish beginning in 1789, during the wave of disgust with the postwar treaties that swept through the tribes in the Ohio country. The Delawares and Shawnees were concentrated about Cape Girardeau. A settlement of Cherokees, true southeastern Indians, numbering 1,000 according to information received by Wilkinson in September 1805, was located on the St. Francis River in what is now northeastern Arkansas. But Wilkinson properly observed that the prevalence of warfare was a powerful deterrent to the westward movement of the southern tribes. He recommended diplomatic efforts to establish a general peace—and, failing that, a war of conquest: "I have said before I believe, and I beg leave to repeat, that an indispensable preliminary to the transfer of the Southern Nations, to the West of the Mississippi is a solid peace between those nations and the Osages particularly, and a general Peace among the whole, excepting always a plan of settlement founded on Conquest, which is I believe most natural and agreeable to Savages."[35]

It was not clear whether the "conquest" should be made by Indian migrants or the Army of the United States; but probably Wilkinson did entertain fantasies of a kind of *pax Romana* to be imposed by U.S. military force, with attendant seizure of Indian land, for he advised the secretary of war that he needed more "strength, of men . . . [and] means, to meet the occasion and profit by the favourable circumstances of the moment." Among the challenges and opportunities he mentioned the powerful Indian nations "who if not made our friends . . . [will] become our enemies" and the vastness of the territory "to be occupied or controlled." Soon, he warned the secretary of war, these savage tribes, instigated by the British and Spanish, would make war upon the United States.[36]

Wilkinson did succeed, in collaboration with Harrison, in bringing the tribes together for a short-lived treaty of reconciliation, but neither he nor his successor, Meriwether Lewis, could impose a peace. The policy of the government, guided by Jefferson, was one of frugality in military expenditures, and Wilkinson constantly chafed at the financial constraints that frustrated his grandiose plans to build forts, recruit soldiers, and send large Indian delegations to Washington to visit their "Father," the President. Wilkinson's own increasing unpopularity among the people of upper Louisiana and his confrontational style of Indian diplomacy made the prospect dim for an early transfer of populations. By the summer of 1806 it would seem that Jefferson's plan to exchange populations had fallen into abeyance, and the governor's function changed to establishing a *modus vivendi* with Spain on the Mexican frontier and to dealing with the Burr conspiracy from his new station in New Orleans.

Why Did Jefferson Choose Wilkinson?

It is not immediately apparent why Jefferson chose Wilkinson as commissioner to treat with the southern Indians and then as governor and ex officio superintendent of Indian affairs of Louisiana Territory. For four years, from 1802 to 1806, he was in a position to execute Jefferson's agenda. But his experience in Indian matters prior to 1798 had been exclusively gained north of the Ohio and primarily at the point of a gun. In 1791 he led a raid against the northern Indians, and he later served under General Anthony Wayne, whose campaign he sought to obstruct and discredit (as he had earlier sought to thwart and discredit the leadership of George Rogers Clark in Kentucky). In 1798 Wilkinson was transferred to the southern frontier, ostensibly to pacify the Indians and keep relations with the Spaniards in Florida and Louisiana on a friendly basis. Tiring of military life, he lobbied to be appointed governor of Mississippi Territory or at least surveyor general. Failing in this, he built fortifications on the Tombigbee River just north of Mobile, near the boundary of Spanish West Florida. In 1803, he shared with Governor Claiborne the honor of formally taking possession in New Orleans of the Louisiana Purchase.

All the while Wilkinson remained in the pay of Spain, as he had been since 1787, when he had taken an oath of allegiance to the Spanish Crown and promised to detach Kentucky from the Union and even to place it under Spanish dominion. He was handsomely paid for his presumed services to Spain, but he actually seems to have done little more than feather his own nest and provide the Spaniards with intelligence when western discontent prompted plans for filibustering expeditions against Spanish possessions. Since such attacks upon a friendly power by U.S. citizens were not only illegal but contrary to the national policy, Washington, Adams, and Jefferson probably were happy to use him as an informal channel of communication. Furthermore, his connections in New Orleans opened that port, sporadically, to commerce with Kentucky and Tennessee. Wilkinson was ostensibly acting in his capacity as border guard when he revealed Aaron Burr's conspiracy to persuade the west to secede and invade Mexico. He was exonerated of his own complicity in this scheme. Jefferson never wavered in his support of the general and afterward appointed him as an emissary to Spanish officials in Cuba. Eventually Wilkinson retired to Mexico and died there in 1825.[37]

Jefferson's stonewall defense of Wilkinson in the face of abundant evidence, which he must have known, of his financial misconduct and "secret" understanding with Spanish officials has intrigued many historians. Most recently, David Chandler in *The Jefferson Conspiracies* attempts to implicate Wilkinson in the supposed murder of Meriwether Lewis and to convict Jefferson (who described the death as suicide) of a cover-up of the crime. This accusation appears to be a little far-fetched, but there does seem to be something more in Jefferson's steadfast support of the scandal-tainted general, who all historians seem to agree was a thorough scoundrel, than the need to have the commander-in-chief of the U.S. Army personally guard Spanish frontiers from American invasion.

The Jefferson–Wilkinson connection probably goes back to the critical days of the 1790s when the Federalists attempted to muzzle the nascent Republican party, with its "democratic societies" and anti-Federalist free press, by passing the Alien and Sedition Acts. This action, coming on top of what Jefferson regarded as the betrayal of the Revolution and the negation of the Declaration of Independence by the increasingly "monarchical" style of government under Washington and Adams, prompted Jefferson to persuade the Kentucky legislature in 1798 to pass the so-called Kentucky Resolutions declaring the acts unconstitutional. Virginia, spurred on by Jefferson's friend James Madison, followed suit with her own resolutions. These resolutions did not go so far as to explicitly mention secession from the Union as the ultimate recourse of a dissatisfied state. But in Kentucky, the notion of defiance of federal policy had a strong following. Wilkinson himself had been an early advocate of Kentucky's separation from Virginia and at one time had persuaded Spanish authorities that he favored secession of the states and territories west of the Appalachians.

Jefferson himself was a political associate of Republican Senator William Blount of Tennessee, formerly governor of that state, when in 1797 Blount was accused of conspiring with British agents to attack and seize New Orleans and establish an independent western federation. The Federalist Secretary of State Timothy Pickering denounced Jefferson as a fellow conspirator and, over Jefferson's objections, the Senate expelled Blount while Jefferson was absent at Monticello. Blount was later impeached and charged with treason, but the Senate demurred and Jefferson dismissed the federal charges on the basis of legal advice that the proper venue was Blount's home state of Tennessee. Jefferson was also a friend and correspondent of Blount's colleague William Tatham of North Carolina, a zealous Wataugan with whom Jefferson may have been associated in his North Carolina real estate investment.[38]

Another of Jefferson's political allies, John Breckenridge of Kentucky, was tarred by the same brush. Before the Burr conspiracy was openly revealed by Wilkinson, Jefferson was advised by the U.S. attorney for Kentucky, Joseph H. Davies, that the Burr conspiracy involved many prominent western politicians—all Jeffersonian Republicans—including Breckenridge of Kentucky and Harrison of Indiana Territory. Breckenridge happened to be Jefferson's attorney general and was an old associate in the political wars with the Federalists. It was he who had pushed through the Kentucky Resolutions in 1798. He had been a member of the U.S. Senate until Jefferson appointed him to his cabinet post. Breckenridge was a radical Westerner who wanted the federal government to act more forcefully to open the Mississippi to American shipping; he went so far as to support George Rogers Clark's own intrigue with the French ambassador, Citizen Genet, and his agent in Kentucky, André Michaux, to raise a volunteer American army to seize Louisiana and perhaps separate the western states.

So what exactly were Jefferson's views on the possible secession of the western states? A candid letter from the President to Breckenridge, written from Monticello in August 1803, makes it clear that he could contemplate such an event with equanimity (see opposite).[39] Commenting on the recent flurry of opposition to the Louisiana Purchase from the eastern Federalists, he stated his willingness to see a new nation in the west, and he revealed the germ of his plan for the transfer of populations.

He repeated his sentiments about a new nation in a letter to Joseph Priestley in January 1804: "I confess I look to this duplication of area for the extending a government so free and economical as ours, as a great achievement to the mass of happiness which is to ensue. Whether we remain in one confederacy, or form into Atlantic and Mississippi confederacies, I believe not very important to the happiness of either part. Those of the western confederacy will be as much our children & descendants as

Jefferson on Western Secession

Objections are raising to the Eastward against the vast extent of our boundaries, and propositions are made to exchange Louisiana, or a part of it, for the Floridas. But, as I have said, we shall get the Floridas without, and I would not give one inch of the waters of the Mississippi to any nation, because I see in a light very important to our peace the exclusive right to its navigation, & the admission of no nation into it, but as into the Potomak or Delaware, with our consent & under our police. These federalists see in this acquisition the formation of a new confederacy, embracing all the waters of the Missipi, on both sides of it, and a separation of its Eastern waters from us. If it should become the great interest of those nations to separate from this, if their happiness should depend on it so strongly as to induce them to go through that convulsion, why should the Atlantic States dread it? . . . The future inhabitants of the Atlantic & Missipi States will be our sons. We leave them in distinct but bordering establishments. We think we see their happiness in their union, & we wish it. Events may prove it otherwise; and if they see their interest in separation, why should we take side with our Atlantic rather than our Missipi descendants? It is the elder and the younger son differing. God bless them both, & keep them in union, if it be for their good, but separate them, if it be better.

those of the eastern, and I feel myself as much identified with that country, in future time, as with this; and did I now foresee a separation at some future day, yet I should feel the duty & the desire to promote the western interests as zealously as the eastern, doing all the good for both portions of our future family which should fall within my power."[40]

In the political climate of the period from the passage of the Alien and Sedition Laws to the end of his second presidential term, Jefferson was continually haunted by the fear of a Federalist seizure of power and the creation of a monarchy as despotic as any in Europe. It is not unreasonable to speculate that he may have thought, in the event of such a catastrophe, of creating a new, free, western nation built upon Republican principles, and he may have looked upon Wilkinson, with all his faults, indeed precisely because of his faults, as the potential commander of the military force needed to defend the independence of the trans-Appalachian Republic from the Federalist army that would inevitably be sent to suppress it. It would be the Whiskey Rebellion all over again but with a difference: this time the rebels—not just the oppressors—would have a general and an army.

The Return of Shahaka, the Mandan Chief

Lewis and Clark's expedition returned to St. Louis on September 23, 1806, and in November the two leaders were on their way to a triumphal reception in Washington. They brought with them a Mandan Indian, Shahaka, and his family. Shahaka was a principal chief of the village where the expedition had wintered in 1804–1805, and Shahaka had been friendly and helpful. The Mandan visit was most successful.[41] The President greeted the party personally with a welcoming address, and Shahaka attended the President's New Year's Day reception, along with an Osage delegation brought to the capital by Pierre Chouteau.[42] He spent the winter in Philadelphia and was invited by Jefferson to visit Monticello.

While Shahaka and the Osage chiefs were in the east, enjoying Jeffersonian hospitality, the President was moved to reward his illustrious explorers with official appointments in the administration of the new Territory of Louisiana. Meriwether Lewis was made governor, replacing Wilkinson, who had become mired as usual in political intrigues, and William Clark was made the brigadier-general of militia and superintendent of Indian affairs. The lives of Shahaka, Clark, Chouteau, and Jefferson himself were to become even more closely, and tragically, entwined.

Shahaka returned to St. Louis in the spring of 1807 and in May set forth for his home village far up the Missouri. The Shahaka party consisted of himself, wife, and child; his interpreter, also with wife and child; and a fourteen-man military escort under the command of an ensign who had been one of Lewis and Clark's men. Traveling with this group were twenty-four Sioux, with their own escort, and two parties of fur traders, one of them consisting of thirty-two men under the command of Pierre Chouteau, which was planning to visit the Mandans. But at an Arikara village in September the Arikaras, who were now at war with the Mandans, attempted to seize Shahaka. A fight commenced, and as the flotilla retreated downstream they were fired on from the shore; two men were

Shahaka, "Mandan King." Black and white chalk on paper by C. B. J. Févret de Saint Mémin, 1807.

Yellow Corn, "Mandan Queen," wife of Shahaka. Black and white chalk on paper by C. B. J. Févret de Saint Mémin, 1807.

killed and several wounded, including Shahaka's interpreter. Shahaka was returned to St. Louis.

Governor Lewis remained in Washington until the end of summer, trying to administer Louisiana from a distance. He finally left for St. Louis in September 1807. Jefferson learned of the disaster to the Shahaka expedition from other sources, and Lewis in fact never did communicate directly with the President on this or any other matter until the following year, after Jefferson gently upbraided him in July 1808 for his failure to write, especially about the problem with the Mandan chief's return (see opposite).[43] A month later Lewis had still not communicated any news about the Mandan chief, and Jefferson wrote again on August 24: "I am uneasy hearing nothing from you about the Mandan chief, nor the measures for restoring him to his country. That is an object which presses on our justice and our honor, and further than that I suppose a severe punishment of the Ricaras indispensable, taking for it our own time and convenience. My letter from Washington asked your opinions on this subject. I repeat my salutations of affection and respect."[44]

What Lewis apparently did not tell Jefferson was that arrangements had already been made, in the spring of 1808, for the Mandan chief's return. Lewis persuaded the War Department to pay $7,000 to a newly organized company of traders, the Missouri Fur Company, for the safe return of Shahaka. The financial commitment was large, considering that the entire cost of the Lewis and Clark expedition had been about $38,000. The members of the Missouri Fur Company turned out to be none other than William Clark, superintendent of Indian affairs; Reuben Lewis, the brother of Meriwether Lewis and subagent to the Osages; Pierre Chouteau, who hoped to do business with the Mandans; Auguste Chouteau, Pierre's half-brother, who traded with the Arkansas band of Osages and was also a principal advisor on Indian matters; Manuel Lisa, the Chouteaus' chief rival in the fur trade; three other traders, Benjamin Wilkinson, Pierre Menard, and William Morrison; Sylvestre Labbadie, a prominent landowner; and Andrew Henry, a mining entrepreneur. This group of well-placed men in May 1809 put together a combined military and commercial expedition of 350 men, under the command of Colonel Pierre Chouteau, in boats well loaded with presents and trade goods and delivered Shahaka and family at last to his village in September of that year.[45]

Lewis apparently never did write to Jefferson about the return of the

Jefferson on Meriwether Lewis's Failure to Write

Since I parted with you in Albemarle in September last, I have never had a line from you nor I believe has the Secretary of War with whom you have much connection through the Indian department. The misfortune which attended the effort to send the Mandan chief home, became known to us before you had reached St. Louis. We took no step on the occasion, counting on receiving your advice so soon as you should be in place, and knowing that your knowledge of the whole subject and presence on the spot would enable you to judge better than we could what ought to be done. The constant persuasion that something from you must be on its way to us, has as constantly prevented our writing to you on the subject. The present letter, however, is written to put an end at length to this mutual silence, and to ask from you a communication of what you think best to be done to get the chief and his family back. We consider the good faith, and the reputation of the nation, as pledged to accomplish this. We would wish indeed, not to be obliged to undertake any considerable military expedition in the present uncertain state of our foreign concerns and especially not till the new body of troops shall be raised. But if it can be effected in any other away and at any reasonable expense, we are disposed to meet it.

Mandan chief, and the whole affair became increasingly embarrassing to him. It has been suggested by a biographer of Lewis that he was a silent partner in the company, and contemporary rumors that his loyalties lay more with the company than with the United States were being heard in St. Louis—allegations that he indignantly denied in a letter to Secretary of War Dearborn. The expedition to return Shahaka, it was being said, was really intended to set up a country independent of the United States, perhaps even to invade the British domain. All this was untrue, he told Dearborn.[46] The expedition was entirely peaceable, bent only on returning Shahaka and doing a little commerce with the tribes on the Missouri and Columbia rivers. No invasion of another country was being contemplated. "Be assured Sir, that my Country can never make 'A Burr' of me—She may reduce me to Poverty; but she can never sever my Attachment from her."[47]

The Osage Cession

But Lewis had other difficulties as well that, by the summer of 1808, made the Shahaka problem and the Missouri Fur Company appear unimportant. In true Jeffersonian fashion, he saw Indian affairs in a geopolitical frame, the Indians potentially playing the role of the enemy within the gates, incited by evil foreign powers without. But he wrote of his concerns not to Jefferson, as other territorial governors did, but to the secretary of war, within whose department lay responsibility for Indian affairs and for any necessary military intervention, in case negotiation failed to accomplish the national purpose. Perhaps also, as a former army officer, he felt more comfortable with a military than a civilian commander. On July first, 1808, he wrote Dearborn at length on the increasing difficulties he perceived in Indian affairs in the territory. It was a long and ominous letter, but it was not received in Washington until six weeks later; as Dearborn was absent from the city, it was forwarded to Jefferson, who responded promptly and not entirely favorably.

The gist of Governor Lewis's letter was that an Indian war was imminent, instigated by the Spaniards, who were holding a council in the west with a disaffected portion of the Great Osages, and with the Kansas and Pawnees. Lewis requested authority to organize and equip three companies of rangers and about a thousand militiamen "for the defence of the country." And he announced that he had already held councils with the eastern Indians now resident in the territory—Shawnees, Delawares, and Kickapoos—and with the Iowas and Sioux to the north, notifying them that the Great Osages, on the Osage River, were "no longer under the protection of the United States" and that the friendly tribes who acknowledged their allegiance to the United States "were at liberty to wage war against them . . . to cut them off completely or drive them from their country." And he urged the establishment of a fortified trading post at Fire Prairie near the Great Osage villages and not far from the hunting grounds of the Kansas, Iowas, and Sacs.

Northward along the Mississippi, things were not much better. The Sacs had refused to deliver the murderer of an American citizen, had stolen about forty horses, and had killed several Sioux and Iowa families on the Des Moines River. Worse still, a large body of Sac and Fox, including 800 "well-armed" warriors, had set up a new village at the mouth of the Rock River (in northern Illinois). This band, Lewis believed, had been tampered with by "British agents" and were about to forge "a close alliance with the British." Lewis proposed new trading posts at the mouth of the Des Moines River and at Prairie du Chien at the mouth of the Wisconsin, and recommended sending up troops to keep out British traders and cut off supplies to the hostile band of Sac and Fox. In general, he proposed to control the Indian tribes by controlling the traders so that the United States would have "the power of withholding merchandise from them at pleasure."[48]

Jefferson, replying directly to Lewis on August 21, expressed his approval of the measures that Lewis proposed with respect to the Osages. He even went a bit farther than Lewis, telling him that he had already instructed the secretary of war to provide the friendly Indian war parties with logistical support. He had evidently observed in previous wars the failure of Indian armies in the field as a result of inadequate resources. "As the principal obstacle to the Indians acting in large bodies is the want of provisions, we might supply that want, of ammunition also if they need it."

But he was not so well pleased with Lewis's position on the Sac and Fox issue. Lewis's tone seemed to him to be unnecessarily belligerent, and he lectured him on the importance of "the preservation of peace," which, as he had advised General Jackson a few years before, was the first half of the nation's Indian policy (the other half, of course, was "obtaining lands"): "With the Sacs & the Foxes I hope you will be able to settle amicably, as nothing ought more to be avoided than the embarking ourselves in a system of military coercion on the Indians. if we do this, we shall have general & perpetual war. when a murder has been committed on one of our stragglers, the murderer should be demanded. if not delivered, give time & still press the demand. we find it difficult, with our regular government, to take & punish a murderer of an Indian—indeed I believe we have never been able to do it in a single instance. they have their difficulties also, & require time—in fact it is a case where indulgence on both sides is just & necessary to prevent the two nations from being perpetually committed in war by the acts of the most vagabond & ungovernable of their members. when the refusal to deliver the murderer is permanent & proceeds from the want of will & not of ability, we should then interdict all trade and intercourse with them till they give us complete satisfaction, commerce is the great engine by which we are to coerce them, & not war." And he went on to articulate a general policy toward the western tribes that centered on replacing itinerant British traders with a network of American trading posts and on continuing on the western side of the Mississippi that course of "forbearing conduct" that over the past seven years, in his opinion, had endeared the United States to the "Cis-Mississippian Indians."[49]

But forbearance, for Jefferson, had its limits. The proposal to "interdict all trade and commerce" with recalcitrant Indian nations, written in 1808, echoed his sponsorship of the infamous Embargo Act of 1807, which interdicted all trade and commerce with disrespectful European naval powers. Or perhaps the Embargo Act itself was suggested by the policy, older than Jefferson's application of it, of colonies restricting trade to uncompliant Indian tribes. Unfortunately, neither embargo turned out well: the Indians were driven back into the arms of British and Spanish traders, and Americans suffered more than the British and the French from the interruption of transatlantic commerce.

Jefferson sent his own letter to Dearborn for transmittal to Lewis, along with Lewis's letter and a covering letter to the secretary of war—actions which suggest that the President thought Mr. Lewis might be somewhat of a loose cannon. Lewis's letter, he said, "presents a *full,* and not a pleasant view of our Indian affairs west of the Mississippi." He instructed the secretary to facilitate the governor's suggestions about the measures to be taken toward the Osages and approved the establishment of the trading posts on the Missouri and the Mississippi. But he was alarmed at Lewis's belligerence toward the Sac and Fox and repeated for Dearborn the policy he had outlined to Lewis: "I hope the Governor will be able to settle with the Sacs and Foxes without war, to which, however, he seems too much committed. If we had gone to war for every hunter or trader killed, and murderer refused, we should have had general and constant war." Governor Lewis should be enjoined to "pursue our principles" of forbearance and the manipulation of trade, not war, to induce the tribes to adhere to the American interest.[50]

Lewis's fears of a war with the Osages proved to be groundless. Neither the Great Osages nor any other of the tribes supposedly seduced by the Spaniards dispatched war parties to raid the frontier. And the league of friendly tribes did not launch an all-out attack on the Osages. What did happen was a cession of land by the Osages that seems not to have been anticipated by Jefferson. The Osage cession was precipitated by the decision to establish a fort and trading post at Fire Prairie, a site on the southwest side of the Missouri about 300 miles from its mouth, and 50 or 60 miles east of the Osage villages. Lewis proceeded with the plan outlined in his July 1 letter to Dearborn, instructing William Clark to proceed up the Missouri with eighty mounted dragoons and riflemen from the militia under his command, ordered out by the governor himself.[51] At Fire Prairie, Clark immediately fixed on a site for a fort, store, and trading establishment. He then summoned the Osages to council on September 12. The Great and Little Osages had been made aware of the government's displeasure at certain incidents of horse stealing by the retaliatory curtailment of trade and no doubt knew of Lewis's threat to set loose the eastern tribes in a war of extermination. They had collected and were turning over as many of the stolen horses as they could find and begged to be forgiven and taken under the protection of the United States.

Clark took advantage of the situation to extort a cession of lands. He asserted the necessity of "a line to be established between them and the United States." According to Clark, they "cheerfully" agreed and even "appeared anxious to give up then a portion of their country the bounds of which had been mentioned by me." Clark reduced his language to writing, and on September 14 the chiefs signed an agreement to give up all the Osage lands between the Arkansas and Missouri Rivers east of a line running due south from the fort at Fire Prairie. The area was estimated by Clark to amount to "near 50,000 square miles of excellent country." The Osages in return were promised protection under the guns of the fort and freedom to trade at the store there. Clark also promised that the government would provide them with $1,200 in merchandise (to be delivered a year hence, if the Osages behaved themselves), a blacksmith, a mill, plows, and two log houses. After the treaty, Clark handed over "a present" of guns, powder, ball, and blankets, worth $317.74. Clark then went on to implement his plans for the fort and trading post. The militia and regular soldiers proceeded to construct the fort and store, and when the construction was nearly done, Clark returned to St. Louis.

In his letter to Dearborn, Clark was at pains to convince him that "no unfair means had been taken on my part to induce the Osage to seed to the United States such an extensive Country for what is conceived here to be so small a compensation." He argued that it was "fully adequate" if one considered the value of the stolen horses (somewhat less than $4,000 in all since 1803) and "the expense of the troops and the fort." If one counts the expenses of the military as proper compensation for lands, and the provision of blacksmithing and saw mill tools and two log houses as part of the "civilization" program, already funded, the actual compensation to the Indians comes to about $5,000—by Clark's reckoning, about ten cents per square mile of land, saleable by the government at $1.25 to $2.00 per acre.[52]

But Governor Lewis was not satisfied with this treaty. A party of Osage chiefs and warriors had reached St. Louis even before the return of General Clark, complaining that they had been deceived by the interpreter, that they had not intended to sell lands but only to convey hunting rights, and that anyway the few chiefs who signed the treaty were not authorized to do so without obtaining the consent of the whole nation "in council." Then Lewis sent Pierre Chouteau, as the Osage agent, back to Fire Prairie to negotiate a revised treaty more favorable to the interests of the United States. The treaty was signed on November 10, 1808.

The operative change was to have the cession include not only all lands east of the north-south meridian from Fire Prairie between the Arkansas and Missouri rivers but also "all lands northwardly of the river Missouri," plus "a tract of two leagues square, to embrace Fort Clark." The compensation was adjusted upward, too: $1,000 in merchandise was delivered on the spot, and an annuity of $1,000 in merchandise was to be delivered at Fire Prairie each year. Other articles provided for the peaceful adjustment of disputes between the Osages and citizens of the United States, for the supplying of such devices of civilization as a water mill, a gunsmith with tools, and other "utensils of husbandry," and for the continuance of trade at Fort Clark. And the treaty placed the Osages under the protection of the United States troops garrisoned at Fort Clark. It was later also approved by chiefs and warriors of the Osage bands living on the Arkansas River on August 31, 1909, after Jefferson left office.[53]

Lewis sent the new treaty off to the President on December 15, 1808, but Jefferson did not approve it before the end of his term in March 1809. It was not sent to the Senate for ratification until January 1810, and the Senate refused to act until it could be explained under what authority a private citizen (Pierre Chouteau) could make and conclude such a treaty. By this time Lewis was dead, but Clark was able to find a copy of the governor's commission to Chouteau for the negotiation of the treaty with the Osages. The treaty was eventually ratified in March 1810.[54]

The aftermath of the Osage treaty, and his other transactions with the

Native Americans as governor of Louisiana Territory, were personally catastrophic for Meriwether Lewis. He had gradually lost the confidence of his patron, Thomas Jefferson, who complained of his failure to write and, when he did, disapproved of his readiness to embroil the United States in perpetual Indian wars. Jefferson seems not to have responded personally with praise for Lewis's (and Clark's) negotiation of the Osage treaty, leaving it to James Madison and the new secretary of war, William Eustis, to deal with Lewis. Eustis, displeased with the way Lewis was handling his office, refused to honor Lewis's claim for $500 additional expenses in the return of the Mandan chief and questioned his authority to call on regular army troops to serve at his command in what Lewis defined as frontier emergencies. The questioning of his accounts prompted Lewis's creditors to demand payment. With his financial affairs in disorder, his alcoholism out of control, his patron Jefferson cool and now retired, and Clark and Chouteau at loggerheads over Osage policy, a deeply depressed Lewis took himself off toward Washington to straighten things out with the government. He never arrived: his suicide at a rude wayside inn in Tennessee suddenly ended what had been a bright and promising career.[55]

For the Mandans, the future was tragic also. Shahaka lost reputation among his people as a result of endless boasting about his travels among the white people and his warm reception by the President of the United States. A few years later he was killed during a battle with the Sioux in which he apparently was a passive spectator. The Mandans, who by Lewis and Clark's count numbered 1,250 in 1805, suffered a smallpox epidemic about 1837 and were reduced to between 125 and 150 souls.[56]

Jefferson's Removal Policy

Jefferson had begun to contemplate the removal of the eastern Indians months if not years before the Louisiana Purchase made such a plan seem feasible. In his letter to Governor Harrison of February 27, 1803, he had anticipated removal as an alternative to incorporation, predicting that the Indians "will in time either incorporate with us as citizens of the United States, or remove beyond the Mississippi." Indeed, if any tribe were so "fool hardy" as to make war on the United States, he proposed "the seizing of the whole country of that tribe, and driving them across the Mississippi, as the only condition of peace."[57] In May 1803—before news of the purchase had reached Washington—he instructed Governor Claiborne of Mississippi Territory to make presents of trade goods to the southern tribes in order to encourage advance parties to cross the Mississippi "and thus prepare in time an eligible retreat for the whole."[58] And he proposed a constitutional amendment to permit and facilitate removal; when that method was rejected by Congress, he proceeded to try to implement the policy by executive action. His instructions to Governor Wilkinson of Louisiana Territory included the exchange of populations—a plan that, as far as the white settlers in Louisiana were concerned, died aborning.

Jefferson himself directly suggested removal to some of the Indian delegations that visited Washington, proposing that they sell some of their lands in the east in return for either money and goods or "land unoccupied by any red men . . . beyond the Mississippi." Such an offer of western lands was made to a Chickasaw delegation in March 1805 and to Choctaw and Cherokee representatives in 1808. The Cherokees, indeed, were asking to be made citizens; instead of welcoming this movement toward incorporation, Jefferson put them off, shifting the responsibility for naturalization of Native Americans to Congress.[59]

After Jefferson left the White House in 1809, the pressure for removal temporarily waned. The rise of the Shawnee prophet's nativistic movement after 1805, the ascendancy of his brother Tecumseh, and finally the War of 1812 stiffened Indian resistance to both incorporation and removal. But before these events, some emigration by factions of several tribes had already occurred: some Delawares and Shawnees moved to the region around Cape Girardeau, and some Illinois and Kickapoos had also gone to Missouri, in the period 1763–1765. Choctaws had begun emigrating to lower Louisiana as early as 1763, and by 1820 there were as many as 1,200 on the Sabine River in Texas. The Sac and Fox had almost all moved out of Illinois and Wisconsin, beginning in the eighteenth century and completing the exodus after the 1804 treaty. Large numbers of conservative Cherokees voluntarily removed to Arkansas in the period from 1800 to 1820.

In 1818, at the Treaty of St. Mary's in Ohio, as part of the postwar settlement, the tribes north of the Ohio River, including Delawares, Miamis, Weas, and Potawatomis, made large land cessions. The Delawares in particular ceded all their land in the state of Indiana, where almost all of them lived, and in return the United States agreed to provide them with new homes west of the Mississippi and to protect them in their occupancy. By

1822 the Delawares of Indiana had moved to the White River in Missouri, and then after eight years to Kansas and eventually to Oklahoma. The Treaty of St. Mary's also inspired many remaining Kickapoos, Kaskaskias, Weas, and a few Miamis to move west. By the mid 1820s, therefore, the only major Ohio valley tribes still resisting emigration were the Miamis and Potawatomis. South of the Ohio, the Chickasaws began to emigrate as early as 1822, but the majority of the Five Civilized Tribes' population (the Cherokees, Creeks, Choctaws, Chickasaws, and Seminoles) remained until they were forced to emigrate under the provisions of the Removal Act of 1830.[60]

Clearly, when Jefferson first articulated his own removal policy in 1803, there were already Indian communities west of the Mississippi who had emigrated by choice as a result of factional dispute within tribes, opposition to the federal "civilization" program, desire for better hunting grounds, or fear of the chaos of the "middle ground" between savagery and civilization. This process of voluntary emigration continued during Jefferson's and later presidents' administrations, independent of any official removal policy. But the federal policy of removal—involuntary or voluntary—as the solution for dealing with Indians who rejected "civilization" or waged war on the United States was established by Thomas Jefferson.

CHAPTER NINE

Confrontation with the Old Way

THE TITLE of Bernard Sheehan's book on Jefferson's civilization policy, *Seeds of Extinction,* is taken from a letter James Wilkinson wrote in 1797 in which he extolled the philanthropic impulse to save the Indian from an extinction that was inevitable if he did not accept the white man's way: "When we contemplate the Fortunes of the Aborigines of our Country, the Bosom of Philanthropy must heave with sorrow, and our sympathy be strongly excited—what would not that man, or that Community merit, who reclaims the untutored Indian—opens his mind to sources of happiness unknown, and makes him useful to society? since it would be in effect to save a whole race from extinction, for surely—if this People are not brought to depend for subsistence on their fields instead of their forests, and to realize Ideas of distinct property, it will be found impossible to correct their present habits, and the seeds of their extinction, already sown, must be matured."[1]

But the "seeds of extinction" which Sheehan intends by his title were contained not in the savage way of life, as Wilkinson thought, but in the civilizing process itself, which promised a kind of cultural genocide by replacing an ethnic group's way of life and incorporating its people by intermarriage. In the Jeffersonian program, there was no interest in preserving the existing cultures of the aborigines. Jefferson saw no future for savage society—by which he meant the "hunter state"—in a world where game animals were rapidly becoming extinct and the tribes themselves were being demoralized and decimated by war, liquor, and disease. Only those who adapted by selling their lands, adopting white ways, intermarrying with whites, and eventually becoming robust yeoman farmers and U.S. citizens, could survive in the long run.

Establishing a secure proclamation line beyond which the Indians could maintain indefinitely the old hybrid fur-trade culture, as suggested by the British and the old Western Confederacy, had been tried before and had failed. All that a humane, educated, and politically powerful white man could do in the social milieu of the time was save as many brands as possible from the burning. And many responsible Native American leaders of the day also believed that the Indian's only hope for survival was to adopt the white man's ways.[2]

Jefferson's Civilization Program

As early as 1781, at the end of his term as governor of Virginia, Jefferson took the opportunity of the Kaskaskia chief du Coigne's visit to Charlottesville to declare his desire to spread civilization among the Indians. In his reply to the chief's address, he fulsomely asserted, "We desire above all things, brother, to instruct you in whatever we know ourselves. We wish to learn you all our arts," and he promised to send out "the best of schoolmasters" as soon as the war ended.[3]

In *Notes on the State of Virginia,* Jefferson returned to the schoolmaster theme in his proposals for the reform of the Brafferton Institution at the College of William and Mary. The Brafferton Institution was an Indian school founded in the 1690s and supported by part of the income from a bequest left by the English chemist Robert Boyle. (The other part of the income was used to educate natives at Harvard and to establish Christian missions among the New England Indians.) The original goal of the Brafferton was to become a seminary for Indian youths, who would eventually be sufficiently educated to take holy orders and go forth to convert their heathen brethren. The school's heyday came during the period 1710 to 1722, when Alexander Spotswood was governor and the Virginia Indians, now tributary to the colony, were sending as many as twenty-four students a year to William and Mary.

A second school was established at Fort Christanna, near the large Saponi village, where for a time a Quaker schoolmaster taught as many as one hundred students. When the school at Fort Christanna was closed, the schoolmaster—universally praised by Indians and colonials alike—was transferred to William and Mary. There a handsome Georgian-style two-story brick house was built in 1723 for the Indian students. Efforts were made to attract pupils from beyond Virginia's borders. The Iroquois at Lancaster declined the invitation in 1744 but kindly offered to raise some white boys in the Indian manner instead. Some Cherokees sent their children in the 1750s. But as the years went by, the Brafferton came to serve as the school's library, and its doors were opened to white lads from the neighborhood who entered as paying students.

Eventually, in 1777, the school closed for lack of funds, and when the reorganized college was again opened, the Brafferton was not characterized as an Indian school, although in the *Notes* Jefferson proposed that the Brafferton become a kind of missionary and ethnological research institute.[4] The Brafferton in its prime was one of the most successful of the early Indian boarding schools. It survived for about eighty years. Its pupils dressed like white students, ate the same food, and were taught, in English, reading, writing, and common arithmetic, and perhaps Latin and Greek. Some died, some fled, and some, like the well-known John Montour, went on to become bilingual interpreters and culture-brokers.[5]

The education of selected Indian youths in white schools, separate from their own people, was an experiment that had been tried for more than a century. Despite a few spectacular successes—notably, Joseph Brant and Alexander McGillivray—the outcomes seem often to have been unhappy. On returning to his village, the "educated" Indian frequently found it difficult to re-establish good relations with his peers or to find any use for the learning he had acquired.

The civilization policy of Jefferson's time, by contrast, aimed to teach Indians in their own villages the technical skills needed to use the Americans' tools and equipment to operate white-style family farms. Conversion to Christianity was desirable but not essential; fluency in Latin and Greek was not required, but some ability to speak English and to master the rudiments of the three Rs was deemed desirable, even essential, for at least some, to facilitate interaction with white men on a more or less equal basis. When in 1789 the elements of such a plan were proposed to President Washington by Secretary of War Knox, Jefferson as secretary of state concurred. And in 1801, when he became President, he accepted responsibility for continuing the implementation of the civilization program.[6]

His first administrative act in this regard was to report to the Congress, in his message on December 8, 1801, on the success of his predecessors in the "continued efforts to introduce among our Indian neighbors the implements and practice of husbandry," with the happy result that some tribes were now increasing in population and were becoming aware of the superiority of white farming methods "over the precarious resources of hunting and fishing."[7] He delivered along with his message a report by Benjamin Hawkins on the progress of civilization among the Creeks.[8]

Next month he reported to Congress on the beneficial effects of the government trading houses and recommended that the legislature renew the acts authorizing the factory system and regulating trade and intercourse with the Indians.[9] Two months later, on March 30, 1802, Congress passed "An Act to Regulate Trade and Intercourse with the Indian Tribes, and to Preserve Peace on the Frontiers," with no time limit on its extension; it remained the basic law governing Indian affairs until the revisions designed by William Clark and Lewis Cass were enacted during Jackson's administration in 1834.

Jefferson's law essentially preserved the provisions that had been enacted in the temporary acts of 1796 and 1799, with one major addition: a specific description of a boundary line "between the . . . Indian tribes and the United States," running from Lake Erie to Florida. As before, penalties were prescribed for various injuries perpetrated by one side or the other, but particularly by whites on Indians, such as encroachment, murder and other felonies, and unlicensed trade. Exceptions permitted trade and travel on Indian lands surrounded by white settlements, subject to the jurisdiction of individual states, and on certain roads and traces. The President was authorized, as he saw fit, "to prevent or restrain the vending or distributing of spirituous liquors" among the Indian tribes.

There was a special section XIII that provided for the continuance of the civilization policy, with an annual federal budget of $15,000 (although this amount was later reduced to $10,000): "And be it further enacted, That in order to promote civilization among the friendly Indian tribes, and to secure the continuance of their friendship, it shall be lawful for the President of the United States, to cause them to be furnished with useful domestic animals, and implements of husbandry, and with goods or money, as he shall judge proper; and to appoint such persons, from time to time, as temporary agents, to reside among the Indians, as he shall think fit."[10]

In his annual messages to Congress as well as in occasional communications recommending legislation Jefferson continued to devote considerable attention to the civilization program. On January 18, 1803—at about the time he was composing his letters to Dearborn, Jackson, Hawkins, and Harrison—Jefferson wrote to Congress outlining his Indian policy in very similar terms, as the justification for a renewal of the Trading House Act. He noted the stubborn refusal of many tribes to make any further sale of lands, even though they were living on lands no longer well stocked with game, and argued that only the abandonment of hunting for agriculture would lead them to a more accommodating disposition.[11]

In his third annual message of October 1803 he expressed satisfaction with the "improvements in agriculture and household manufacture" being made by many tribes.[12] In the second inaugural address, in 1805, he saluted the Delawares, whose recent sale of lands along the Wabash and Ohio, he claimed, was motivated by a desire "to extinguish in their people the spirit of hunting and to convert superfluous lands into the means of improving what they retain."[13] Jefferson may have believed this to be true, but many Delawares did not approve, and, as we have seen, the consequences were fatal for some of the people who signed the treaty.

During his second term, despite threats of war with Britain and Spain and his doubts about the loyalty of Indians generally, Jefferson continued to maintain an optimistic tone about the progress of civilization in his annual messages to Congress. In the fifth annual message in December 1805 he cheerfully reported: "Our Indian neighbors are advancing many of them with spirit, and others beginning to engage in the pursuits of agriculture and household manufacture. They are becoming sensible that the earth yields subsistence with less labor and more certainty than the forest, and find it their interest from time to time to dispose of parts of their surplus and waste lands for the means of improving those they occupy and of subsisting their families while they are preparing their farms."[14] In the sixth, the following year, he did not mention the progress of the civilization program, contenting himself with noting a "growing attachment of our Indian neighbors . . . inspired by their confidence in our justice and in the sincere concern we feel for their welfare."[15]

In the next year's message, delivered early in October 1807, he acknowledged "some fermentation" among "our Indian neighbors" but claimed that the tribes "most advanced in the pursuits of industry," especially those in the south, who were "much advanced beyond the others in agriculture and household arts," were remaining friendly and peaceable.[16] The final message of November 1808 applauded the progress toward civilization among the southern tribes, especially among the Cherokees. One of the two great divisions of the Cherokees were, he declared, even now considering whether "to solicit the citizenship of the United States, and to be identified with us in laws and government in such progressive manner as we shall think best."[17]

In the practical administration of the civilization program, the President had available several tools. One of these, of course, was the old and traditional corps of missionaries of various denominations, some of them—Episcopalians, Baptists, Congregationalists, and Presbyterians—aiming primarily at religious conversion and some, like Quakers and Moravians, hoping first to teach arts, crafts, and moral principles. Jefferson regarded himself as a Christian, in the secular sense of advocating the moral teachings of Jesus, and, despite his anticlericalism, was not averse to missionary efforts, even of the more evangelical kind, as evidenced by his proposals for reform of the Brafferton Institution. He also prepared a privately circulated syllabus of the teachings of Jesus and during his first term as President began his *Life and Morals of Jesus,* a compilation of extracts from the New Testament (excluding miracles) that Jefferson regarded as authentic statements on morality by the great teacher, whom he regarded as superior in his social gospel to all the philosophers of antiquity. This work was intended "for the use of the Indians" (and no doubt others in need of instruction in genuine morality), but it was not completed until late in his retirement at Monticello and was not published during his lifetime.[18]

Even those missionaries most zealously devoted to saving souls recognized the need to provide their charges with a minimal education in English in order to read the Bible and understand sermons and prayers. Few missionaries were as fluent in an Indian tongue as the Moravian John Heckewelder or were prepared to translate Biblical text into a written native language. And Christian charity required the saving of bodies, even if only as a necessary measure pending the saving of souls. Thus mission stations commonly were centers for technical education by example and for the distribution of hardware, dry goods, and livestock needed in an agricultural economy that was, in fact, becoming an essential component of Native American subsistence.

Jefferson's acceptance of limited missionary assistance in forwarding the civilization program did not extend so far, however, as an endorsement of missionary organizations of a size comparable to the federal apparatus. In 1822 the Reverend Jedidiah Morse, an ardent New England Calvinist with Federalist political sympathies, published a general survey of the Indian tribes commissioned by President Monroe and made recommendations for the best means of accomplishing Indian reform. Morse enthusiastically called for the formation of a society for the civilization and improvement of the Indian tribes, and proposed Jefferson and other luminaries as patrons.[19] Although Jefferson approved the benevolent intention, he declined the honor. The plan as offered threatened to cross "the line of demarcation between private associations of laudable views and unimposing numbers, and those whose magnitude may revitalize and jeopardize the march of regular government."[20]

The proposed machine of charity did indeed have a "gigantic stature," including *ex officio* all ex-Presidents, all current federal and state officials, all the members of both houses of Congress, all military and naval officers, all presidents and professors of all colleges and theological seminaries, and all the clergy of the United States (by Jefferson's estimate eight thousand). Jefferson pointed out that the clergy would dominate this association by sheer weight of numbers and that it would set a dangerous precedent of creating private combinations to undertake the work of government. In effect, when faced with the prospect of nongovernmental control of a state function—the conduct of Indian affairs—Jefferson transformed himself into a staunch Federalist.

Another device for the introduction of the new husbandry were treaties of land cession, whose terms often included the provision of tools and equipment as well as money and protection. At the infamous treaty with the Delawares at Vincennes in August 1804, the compensation was to be largely in the form of assistance in civilization. Four hundred dollars would be spent to deliver draft horses, cattle, hogs, and farm implements, and resident teachers would show them how to make fences, cultivate the earth, practice animal husbandry, and perform various domestic arts.[21] Similar provision for the work of civilization was inserted, sometimes at the request of the native negotiators, into other treaties and conferences as well.

Thus in October 1801, in their report to Dearborn on the success of their mission to the Chickasaws to gain permission for a road to Nashville across their territory, commissioners Wilkinson, Hawkins, and Perkins revealed that the Chickasaws had been making "considerable progress in agriculture, and in stocking their farms, and are desirous to increase their domestic manufactures." One of the chiefs even said, "We are about to raise cotton; we shall want [dugout] canoes to carry it to market; and adzes are necessary to build them." The commissioners urged the secretary to honor this request, and went on to "earnestly recommend to the councils of our country, a steady perseverance in that humane and beneficent system, which has for its object the civilization, and consequent salvation, of a devoted race of human beings."[22]

Next year the same commissioners made similar observations with regard to the Choctaws, the southern neighbors of the Chickasaws. Their report emphasized the desire of these Indians (or at least some of their chiefs) to mount the ladder of progress. A few of their families also had begun the culture of cotton. "At this conference, for the first time, the bounty of the United States has been implored, and we were supplicated for materials, tools, implements, and instructors, to aid their exertions, and to direct their labors. These circumstances induce us to cherish the hope, that, by the liberal and well directed attention of Government, these people may be made happy and useful; and that the United States may be saved the pain and expense of expelling or destroying them. It is a singular fact, perhaps, it is without example, and therefore it is worthy of record, that this council should not only reject a quantity of whiskey intended as a present to them, but should have requested that none might be issued before, during, or after, the conference." During the negotiations, the chiefs asked for a blacksmith and for his tools and a stock of iron and steel, in case he left, to make spinning wheels "for our young women, and half breeds" and "somebody . . . to teach them to spin," and a cotton gin. And they said they were "glad to hear it is the wish of our father, the President, to teach us to do such things as the whites can do."[23]

The treaty of October 1805 with the Cherokees likewise was the occasion for advancing the cause of civilization; part of the cash payment was to be used to provide "machines for agriculture and manufactures."[24] Again in the treaty at Washington in January 1806, the Cherokees were promised as part of the compensation for the ceding of lands north of the Tennessee River (including a tract on Elk River on which 200 white families had made illegal settlements) a grist mill and a cotton gin. And in March 1808 Jefferson explained to the Senate why a tract of land six miles square at the mouth of the Chickamauga on the Tennessee had lately been bought of the Cherokees; the tribe wanted to acquire convenient access to an iron works.[25] The Senate, however, refused to ratify the agreement. The President's comments revealed both his philosophy of the civilizing process as benefiting both the United States and the Indians and his impatience with, and discounting of, those natives who opposed his plans for their improvement.

North of the Ohio also, land purchase negotiations were an occasion for pushing the Indians toward civilization. Here, however, some had already been substantially converted by missionaries—Catholic among the Illinois tribes, and Moravian among the Delawares. In 1806 a small band of pro-civilization Delawares, dwelling on land ceded by the 1805 treaty, petitioned Congress for a grant of land to permit them to stay where they were. Montgomery Montour, the memorialist, explained that they feared "to go to the Missouri, to settle among strange and warlike tribes" lest they be "cut off, or lose what advances they have already made in the arts and manners of the white people." Montour assured Congress that his people loved the white people, wanted to be settled near them, wanted to learn all about "agriculture and other improvements of life and manners," and, "in short, as soon as convenient, to become willingly one people with them."[26] Congress compassionately acceded to Dearborn's recommendation that this request be granted, and set apart thirteen sections of public lands for the use of these Delawares. But the United States got the 8,320 acres back ten years later in a special cession, and by the 1820s Montour's little band was on its way west.[27]

The Treaty of August 1803, with du Coigne's Kaskaskia band, representing the remnants of the Illinois tribes, was officially rationalized as providing "the means of improvement in the arts of civilized life, and a more certain and effectual support for their women and children."[28] The Piankeshaw cession of 1804 specified payment in "money, merchandise, provisions, or domestic animals, and implements of husbandry."[29] But the Shawnees, Kickapoos, Miamis, and the more northerly tribes of Ohio and the Michigan peninsula—the Ottawas, Chippewas, Potawatomis, and Wyandots—evinced less interest in obtaining the apparatus of civilization. It was not until the 1808 cession that the northern tribes accepted the option of receiving part of the payment in "implements of husbandry or domestic animals."[30]

Jefferson's stated policy of keeping the major part of the Louisiana Territory as a game preserve for exploitation by Indian hunters and American traders did not prevent his agents from holding forth civilization as an inducement to sell land. The Sac and Fox treaty specified that the $1,000 annuity might in the future, if the tribes so wished it, in part be furnished in the form of "domestic animals, implements of husbandry and other utensils convenient to them, or in compensation to useful artificers who may reside with or near them and be employed for their benefit."[31] The Osage treaty was even more explicit. The United States agreed, among other things, to build a fort and trading post at Fire Prairie, along the Missouri, a place convenient of access from the Osage towns, and further "to furnish at this place, for the use of the Osage nations, blacksmith and tools, to mend their arms, and utensils of husbandry, and . . . to build them a horse mill or water mill, also to furnish them with ploughs, and to build for the great chief of the Great Osages, and for the great chief of the Little Osages, a strong block house in each of their towns, which are to be established near that Fort."[32] Presumably civilization would promote pacification.

The Creeks and Cherokees

Jefferson's principal agents in carrying out the civilization policy embodied in the Trade and Intercourse Acts and the various treaties were, to the south, Benjamin Hawkins and, to the north of the Ohio, William Henry Harrison, both appointees of the previous administration. Hawkins' agency on the Flint River in western Georgia was first established in 1801 after Jefferson renewed his appointment as "principal agent." It was about five miles square and was a fine southern plantation, a manor in the wilderness maintained by Hawkins in virtually baronial style. Hawkins already owned a plantation in North Carolina, and he brought some of his slaves to the agency to care for the stock of horses and cattle and to work the fields of corn, wheat, hay, tobacco, and cotton, cherry and quince orchards, and various vegetable gardens, including cabbages, potatoes, peas, cucumbers, and "other" garden stuff. He cultivated a vineyard for wine, planted additional peach and apple orchards, and specialized in the raising of berries, especially raspberries and strawberries. His fields were plowed and fenced.

Hawkins was an advocate of scientific farming and eagerly experimented with the use of manure, deep spading, and the growth of Sea Island cotton. The agency became a center for the manufacturing of tinware. Leather was tanned and fashioned into hats, shoes, boots, and saddles. Cotton was spun and woven; Hawkins boasted, "My family of eighty persons are all clothed in homespun." He corresponded with Jefferson on matters of mutual interest as farmers. By the end of Jefferson's second term, Hawkins had earned a wide reputation as a successful and innovative farmer.[33] The Flint River agency also served as a demonstration farm, school, and distribution point for capital goods like plows, spinning wheels, and cotton gins. Creeks came there to visit and to learn. A Georgia newspaper offered effusive praise for "the enlightened and indefatigable exertions of Colonel Hawkins to ameliorate the conditions of the aborigines of the Country, by introducing among them the blessings of civilization. The success with which these efforts have been attended in the short period of ten years is without parallel in the history of savage nations."[34]

Part of Hawkins's success among the Creeks was certainly owing to his genuine concern for their survival and welfare. Although he loyally carried out orders to undermine the influence of anti-American factions and to arrange, if he could, cessions of land, he was perennially criticized by land-hungry southerners for being excessively devoted to the Indians, to the detriment of white interests. He survived the criticism and was continued in his post by James Madison, for whom he named his son; a daughter was named Jeffersonia. Hundreds of his Creeks were killed by the troops of Andrew Jackson in the War of 1812, and much of their land was taken in the postwar treaties. Hawkins died in 1816 at the age of sixty-two; less than a month later, his house burned down and his widow and children barely escaped with their lives.[35]

The Cherokees, whose country lay to the north of the Creeks in Georgia and Tennessee, for the most part pursued an independent course of relations with the federal government. In regard to the federal civilization program, they anticipated it by several years. At the Treaty of Holston in July 1791, which substantially ended a decade of frontier warfare between the Cherokee and the Wataugans/Franklinites, they secured from the United States a promise to provide the tribe with "useful implements of husbandry" in order that "the Cherokee Nation may be led to a greater degree of civilization, and to become herdsmen and cultivators, instead of remaining in a state of hunters." The treaty also provided for a number of resident white "interpreters" to assist in communication and training.[36] On a visit to Philadelphia a few month later the Cherokee delegation pointedly reminded Secretary of War Henry Knox of this promise: "The treaty mentions ploughs, hoes, cattle, and other things for a farm, this is what we want, game is going fast away among us. We must plant corn and raise cattle, and we desire you to assist us . . . In former times we bought goods of our traders cheap; we could then clothe our women and children; but now game is scarce and goods dear, we cannot live comfortably."[37]

In the fall of 1796 Hawkins, on the way to the Creeks, visited the Cherokee towns and found that the Cherokees had already made notable advances in civilization, raising cattle and selling them to white settlers, planting cotton and pleading for spinning wheels and cards. Here and there he observed farms with fenced fields, orchards, cattle, chickens, hogs, and horses, and crops of corn, peas, and potatoes. Much of this progress was owing to the influence and example of the many Scottish and Irish traders who had married Cherokee women and raised their children to speak English and practice farming in the manner of whites.[38]

In 1797 President Adams appointed Silas Dinsmoor agent to the Cherokees, with orders to instruct them in animal husbandry, the use of the plow, and the mechanical arts. In 1801 Dinsmoor was transferred to the Chickasaw agency, and Return Jonathan Meigs took his place; he was confirmed in his post among the Cherokees by Jefferson. Meigs was a redoubtable figure, comparable to Hawkins: a retired military officer with a spectacular and heroic Revolutionary War record, a member of Symmes's Ohio Company and in 1788 one of the founders of Marietta, Ohio. He was sixty years old when he entered upon his duties as Cherokee agent, and he remained their agent until his death in 1823 at the age of eighty-two, allegedly of pneumonia contracted when he gave up his house to a visiting Cherokee chief and slept outdoors in a tent. Although Meigs, sometimes with the aid of a little bribery, persuaded the Cherokees to sell parts of their domain at a long succession of treaties, he retained their affection, largely because of the remarkable success of the civilization program under his benevolent supervision.[39]

Meigs was assisted in his efforts by the religious missions which were eventually admitted into the Cherokee country. In 1801 the Moravians, who had been invited by the council several years earlier, established a school at Springplace in Georgia where Indian children were taught the three Rs. Again in 1803 the chiefs authorized a Presbyterian minister from Tennessee, Gideon Blackburn, to set up a school at Tellico, near Meigs's agency and near the federal trading post, Tellico Factory, where implements of farming and manufacture were being distributed. Blackburn's ambition was to convert the Cherokees to civilization and Christianity by educating their children. In 1804 he constructed a boarding school and in 1805 proudly presented his first class at a kind of graduation ceremony, where little Cherokees, dressed in white clothing, demonstrated their ability to read from books and sing hymns in English. This drew a tear from the eye of the grizzled old Indian fighter John Sevier, now governor of Tennessee.

Blackburn sought to instill not just skills but the Protestant ethic in these children—good study habits, nice table manners, personal hygiene, obedience to strict time schedules, and marching in orderly columns of twos. By 1815 he is said to have taught five hundred Cherokee youngsters to read English. The Tellico complex—agency, factory, and school—was a powerful influence among the mountain-dwelling Overhills Cherokees. In 1808 Blackburn boasted that the Cherokees had advanced "further I believe than any other nation of Indians in America."[40]

Jefferson could not have been more pleased. He addressed the complaisant Cherokee delegation who visited him in Washington in January 1806 in complimentary terms: "I cannot take leave of you without expressing the satisfaction I have received from your visit. I see with my own eyes that the endeavors we have been making to encourage and lead you in the way of improving your situation have not been unsuccessful; it has been like grain sown in good ground, producing abundantly. You are becoming farmers, learning the use of the plough and the hoe, enclosing your grounds and employing that labor in their cultivation which you formerly employed in hunting and in war; and I see handsome specimens of cotton cloth raised, spun and wove by yourselves. You are also raising cattle and hogs for your food, and horses to assist your labors. Go on, my children, in the same way and be assured the further you advance in it the happier and more respectable you will be." In the same speech, Jefferson took the opportunity to contrast the Cherokee success with the far slower progress being made by the tribes north of the Ohio.[41]

The Iroquois and Delawares

Actually, some of the Indians north of the Ohio were comparable in civilization to the Cherokees. The most recent and perhaps the most spectacular success in the civilization program was among the Iroquois of New York, Pennsylvania, and Ontario. Particularly advanced were a portion of the Mohawks along the Grand River in Canada, led by Joseph Brant, a zealous follower of the Church of England, and the Oneidas in New York state under the leadership of Sturgeon and Captain Hendrick, who were influenced by Samuel Kirkland, their devoted missionary.

The Seneca chief Cornplanter, or Ki-on-twog-ky.
Oil on canvas by F. Bartoli, c. 1796.

These missionaries and their followers favored extensive adoption of white customs.

Also making progress were the Senecas, who occupied the lands along the Genesee and upper Allegheny rivers. The initial leader of the civilization faction among the Senecas was Cornplanter. As early as the winter of 1790–1791, on a visit to George Washington, he had appealed eloquently for aid in his civilization program on the Cornplanter Grant: "The Game which the Great Spirit sent into our Country for us to eat is going from among us. We thought that he intended that we should till the ground with the Plow, as the White People do, and we talked to one another about it . . . We ask you to teach us to plow and to grind Corn; to assist us in building Saw Mills, and supply us with Broad Axes, Saws, Augers, and other Tools, so as that we may make our Houses more comfortable and more durable; that you will send Smiths among us, and above all that you will teach our Children to read and write, and our Women to spin and weave . . . We hope that our Nation will determine to spill all the Rum which shall hereafter be brought to our Towns."[42]

About a year later Cornplanter sent two of his sons to be educated by Quakers in the Philadelphia area, in part for the purpose of having them manage the sawmill that he had installed about 1795. In response to Cornplanter's plea, Washington promised to provide a set of carpenter's tools to each Iroquois village, schoolmasters, and a blacksmith for both the Oneidas and the Senecas. Timothy Pickering (who had served briefly as superintendent of Indian affairs for the Iroquois before becoming secretary of war) did not approve the practice of educating Indian youth in white schools, believing correctly that they were apt to be marginalized when they returned to their home communities. But he did support Knox's and Washington's plans to introduce the arts of husbandry directly to the villages. He negotiated the Treaty of Canandaigua with the Iroquois in 1794, which included among other things the provision of funds for civilization.

The federal funds and administrative apparatus were inadequate for the effective dispatch of substantial aid to the Iroquois. When in 1795 the Philadelphia Yearly Meeting of the Society of Friends, who knew Cornplanter and his solicitation of aid, formed a committee "for the civilization and real welfare of the Indian nations," Pickering wrote to the resident agents among the Iroquois enthusiastically recommending the Quaker plan to introduce "the most necessary arts of civil life . . . useful practices: to instruct the Indians in husbandry and of the plain mechanical arts & manufactures directly connected with it." The Indian Committee soon was sending supplies not only to the Iroquois reservations but also to the Creeks (via Benjamin Hawkins), the tribes of the Northwest Territory, including Wyandot, Delaware, Shawnee, Miami, Ottawa, Chippewa, and Potawatomi, and to the other tribes of the south, the Cherokees, Choctaws, and Chickasaws—virtually all of the tribes east of the Mississippi.

The most successful Quaker mission, however, was directed to the Senecas of the Cornplanter Grant and the adjacent Allegheny Reservation. Five young Quakers arrived at the grant in May 1798; the mission they established there endured for generations, not as a center for religious proselytizing but as a demonstration farm, school, and distribution point for supplies and capital goods. In 1799 a religious prophet—Cornplanter's half-brother, Handsome Lake—began to experience a series of visions that simultaneously endorsed the Quaker program of secular reform in the economy, which emphasized plow agriculture and animal husbandry conducted by men, spinning and weaving by women, the integrity of the nuclear family, and the revival of native religious belief and ceremonies, which were now being challenged by Christian evangelists less interested in the survival of Indian bodies than in the salvation of Indian souls. He also most emphatically banned liquor, persecuted alleged witches, and prohibited further sales of land.

By 1801 the revitalization movement of Handsome Lake was inspiring many demoralized Senecas and other Iroquois to undertake new lives and to organize themselves politically to cope with the continuing threats to their welfare posed by the loss of their land base, the disappearance of game, and deaths attributable to alcohol-related accidents and mayhem. Handsome Lake agreed to lead a delegation to Washington to acquaint President Jefferson with recent events among the Iroquois and appeal to him for assurances of Iroquois title to their remaining lands, for prohibition of the liquor trade, and for more technical aid in the form of plows, livestock, spinning wheels, and other equipment.

On his arrival, the Seneca prophet advised the President that if he heeded his words, the Great Spirit would "take care of him" and his United States, too. Handsome Lake addressed Jefferson as "Dear Brother," not "Father," and claimed his own superiority as the "the fifth angel," deputized by the Great Spirit to be director of mankind. Jefferson, replying through the voice of Secretary of War Dearborn, agreed about the evils of the liquor trade and noted that Congress was considering a law banning the sale of liquor to Indians. He also agreed to put in writing a pledge not to permit anyone to take the tribe's land without its consent. Despite these agreements, the Iroquois party left Washington unhappy about recent land purchases from the several tribes still resident in New York.

In response to a communication from the prophet repeating these complaints, Jefferson wrote a personal letter to his "Dear Brother" Handsome Lake endorsing his divine mission to reform the Iroquois and particularly praising his crusade against "the abuse of spirituous liquors." He defended the past cessions as being perfectly open and legal but promised again that no more land would be purchased without their free consent. And in fulsome rhetoric, he urged the Iroquois, now that game was becoming scarce, in contradiction to Handsome Lake's advice, to sell part of their "extensive forests . . . and lay out the money in stocks and implements of agriculture": "Go on then, brother, in the great reformation you have undertaken. Persuade our red brethren then to be sober, and to cultivate their lands; and their women to spin and weave for their families. You will soon see your women and children well fed and clothed, your men living happily in peace and plenty, and your numbers increasing from year to year. It will be a great glory to you to have been the instrument of so happy a change, and your children's children, from generation to generation, will repeat your name with love and gratitude forever. In all your enterprises for the good of your people, you may count with confidence on the aid and protection of the United States, and on the sincerity and zeal with which I am myself animated in the furthering of this humane work. You are our brethren of the same land; we wish your prosperity as brethren should do. Farewell!"[43] This was precisely the theme that he was to reiterate, and elaborate, in his messages to Congress, the secretary of war, and his Indian superintendents a few months later.

For Handsome Lake and his followers, Jefferson's letter was an inspiration, despite its disagreement with the prophet's position on land sales. It was treasured as an endorsement of the prophet and his holy message by the President of the United States, and the framed text hangs today on the walls of the council houses where the rituals and the recitations of the code of the Old Way of Handsome Lake are still performed. It also reinforced the civilization program of the Quakers. Quaker advice and the prophet's urging soon worked a remarkable secular transformation among the Senecas and other Iroquois communities. The Iroquois reservations in New York state became settlements of sober farmers whose families resided in log houses, with fenced fields, plow agriculture, livestock, and spinning wheels. These rural communities, admired by visitors both white and Indian, differed dramatically from the slums in the wilderness they had been before. The Quakers, the prophet, and President Jefferson combined to make "civilization" respectable to erstwhile hunters and warriors and their womenfolk.[44]

The other partial success of the civilization program north of the Ohio was with the Delaware Indians (and the refugee Mahicans they had taken under their wing). The Delawares (also known as Lenni Lenape) had been resident in New Jersey and eastern Pennsylvania before the sale of their land. The French and Indian War, during which many had sided with the French, resulted in their exodus first to the upper Susquehanna valley at Wyoming, then westward to Ohio during the Revolution and the subsequent war for the Northwest Territory, and after the Treaty of Greenville to Indiana.

Beginning in the 1740s the Moravians at Bethlehem in Pennsylvania had sought to convert the Delawares to Christianity and to organize native cooperative communities similar to their own communal settlements at Bethlehem, Nazareth nearby, and elsewhere in North America. The Moravian converts, with their resident missionaries, occupied separate villages but moved westward with the rest of the tribe during the half century of migration. The Moravian Indians periodically endured violent assaults, particularly a massacre by pro-French Delawares near Bethlehem in 1756, the massacre by white militia at Gnadenhütten in Ohio in 1782, and the final witchcraft persecution by the Shawnee prophet in 1806. Some of the Moravian Delawares eventually chose to live in the more tolerant atmosphere of Canada; others, a kind of leavening, remained with the tribe.[45]

Only a fraction of the Delawares were ever converted by the Moravians and came to live in their utopian communities. Those who remained "pagans" were not unaware of the advantages of white technology but preferred to obtain the guns, traps, blankets, and other necessaries through the fur trade rather than from evangelical Christians. From the middle of the eighteenth century, the Delaware towns kept a variety of livestock—horses for riding, pigs for meat, and a few cattle for milk and butter—but made no use of the plow, spinning wheel, or loom.[46] The Treaty of Vincennes in 1804 provided an annuity of $300 per year for ten years for the sole purpose of "introducing among them the arts of civilized life." In addition, agents were to be sent to them to teach them how to build fences, plow fields, and use the implements of husbandry, which were to be supplied at the expense of the United States, along with plow horses, cattle, and pigs.[47] Livestock, capital goods, and teachers were brought to the Delaware towns, but apart from the Moravian communities, the men refused to assume the role of dirt farmers. The advent of the Shawnee prophet in 1805 and the War of 1812 combined to block further progress.

Harrison and his subagents, John Johnston and William Wells, were persistent in pressing the Indians under their jurisdiction to accept the white man's way. At treaty after treaty during Jefferson's presidency, Harrison offered to introduce technology and the arts of civilization—at the Kaskaskia treaty in October 1803, the Delaware and Piankeshaw treaties in 1804, the Sac and Fox treaty in 1804, the treaty with the Wyandots, Ottawas, Chippewas, and Potawatomis in 1808. But less effort seems to have been made toward converting the Miamis, the Shawnees, and the Kickapoos, who insistently relied on the hunt for obtaining trade goods. The Indians on the Wabash in 1807, mostly Miamis and Shawnees, refused to accept a Quaker mission that had received $6,000 from the government at Jefferson's direction to copy the Friends' success with the Senecas.[48] The treaty with the Miamis and their dependents in September 1804 did not mention the advantages of civilization but did promise part payment in the form of cattle and hogs, the raising of which, Harrison assured them, "required little labor and would be the surest resource as a substitute for the wild animals which they had so unfortunately destroyed for the sake of their skins."[49]

Of all the tribes in Indiana, the Shawnees were probably most in need of the blessings of civilization, and least likely to receive them. After being driven from their homeland in the lower Ohio valley, they had for generations been guests—often, unwelcome guests—on the lands of others, wending their way through Pennsylvania and Ohio, almost perpetually at war. By the first decade of the nineteenth century they were reduced in population to perhaps 2,000 individuals, divided among several settlement areas—about Cape Girardeau in Missouri, among the Miami on the Wabash, on the upper Miami River and the Auglaize in central Ohio, a few to the south among the Creeks. They had no land to sell in return for the implements of husbandry showered on other tribes and clung desperately to what was left of the old way of life.[50]

Alcohol as an Impediment to Civilization

Jefferson was acutely aware that one of the principal impediments to the progress of civilization among the Indians was the abuse of alcohol. Drunken Indians, both male and female, were a familiar sight in frontier towns as well as in native villages. Deaths and injuries from drunken brawls were common; intoxicated men and women fell down, went to sleep, and froze to death on cold nights. Even the most responsible men, dedicated to the advancement of civilization among their people, were not immune to the liquor-borne plague of social disorganization and death. Joseph Brant, for instance, was attacked with a knife by his drunken son Isaac when they were visiting a tavern together; both were wounded, and the son died of his injuries three days later.[51]

On visits to Washington and Philadelphia, all too often the chiefs celebrated the occasion by tours of nearby bars and brothels, sometimes contracting venereal diseases. The President, who himself enjoyed a glass of wine but did not drink to excess, was distressed by the dissipation of many of his Indian visitors. But liquor was a part of the way of life in many native communities, just as it was among whites. Liquor traditionally accompanied the conclusion of treaties; it even lubricated the spirits of participants in native ceremonies.

Among the first matters to engage the attention of Harrison after he was appointed governor were the dire consequences of the liquor trade, particularly among the same Indians on the Wabash whom Constantin Volney had met a few years earlier and whose drunkenness he had described so vividly.[52] Writing to Secretary of War Dearborn in July 1801, complaining about the rapid decline of the Indian population, he predicted the complete "exterpation" of these "unhappy people" and formally requested the secretary to convey to the President the need to do "something." Harrison's description of the condition of the Wabash Indians and their behavior at Vincennes echoes Volney's account (see next page).[53] Harrison followed up his observations with action, immediately issuing a proclamation forbidding traders from selling liquor to Indians in and around Vincennes; later in the summer another proclamation forbade licensed traders from following the Indians to their hunting grounds, in compliance with a directive directly from the President.[54] At Jefferson's urging, the Trade and Intercourse Act of 1802 contained provisions to prohibit the sale of liquor to Indians, and to that end Harrison and other

William Henry Harrison on Selling Alcohol to Indians

The Indian Chiefs complain heavily of the mischiefs produced by the enormous quantity of Whiskey which the Traders introduce into their Country. I do not believe there are more than six Hundred Warriors upon this River (the Wabash) and yet the quantity of whiskey brought here annually for their use is said to amount to at least six thousand Gallons. This poisonous liquor not only incapacitates them from obtaining a living by Hunting but it leads to the most atrocious crimes—killing each other has become so customary amongst them that it is no longer a crime to murder those whom they have been most accustomed to esteem and regard. Their Chiefs and their nearest relatives fall under the strokes of their Tomahawks & Knives. This has been so much the case with the three Tribes nearest us—The Peankashaws, Weas, & Eel River Miamis that there is scarcely a Chief to be found amongst them . . . All these Horrors are produced to these Unhappy people by their too frequent intercourse with the White people. This is so certain that I can at once tell by looking at an Indian whom I chance to meet whether he belong to a Neighbouring or a more distant Tribe. The latter is generally well Clothed healthy and vigorous the former half naked, filthy and enfeebled with Intoxication, and many of them without arms except a Knife which they carry for the most villanous purposes.

state and territorial governors and their legislatures took steps along the same lines. But federal efforts to stop the traffic were ineffective.[55]

Native American leaders were well aware of the evils of alcohol abuse and for generations had appealed to colonial and then federal authorities to halt, or at least control, the liquor trade. The negative impact of alcoholism on the civilization process was pointed out by Little Turtle in his speech to the secretary of war in 1802: "Your [red] children are not wanting in industry, but it is the introduction of this fatal poison which keeps them poor. Your children have not that command over themselves you have, therefore before anything can be done to advantage this evil must be remedied."[56] Little Turtle was making the point that many Indians would sell *anything*—not only skins and furs but also clothes, horses and other livestock, implements of husbandry, land—to get money to buy liquor. Annuity money, if it was doled out per capita, would go for liquor, not plows or spinning wheels or sawmill irons. Furthermore, liquor sold for incredibly high prices among Indians, as much as two dollars a pint, at a time when farmland could be purchased for twenty-five cents an acre.

Jefferson and Harrison were in fact confronted by a black market in a highly addicting drug. Whether the addiction was psychological or physiological, or in some measure both, it was as destructive to the addict as more recent drugs like heroin and cocaine have proved to be. And traffic in the drug was no easier to block, for the financial rewards were sufficient to encourage the purveyor, whether Indian or white, to invent new and devious ways to evade the law.

Furthermore, those who wanted to obtain Indian land had an interest—whether consciously recognized or not—in Indian alcoholism. Skins and furs were the cash crop that Indian men depended on to buy what had become, over hundreds of years, necessary imports of hardware and dry goods: knives, guns, traps, kettles, cloth, beads, cosmetics, and so forth. If they sold the capital equipment, such as traps and guns, needed to harvest this crop, or spent the money paid them for skins and furs, on whiskey, they were depriving themselves and their communities of necessities. A substitute cash crop, so to speak, was land, which could be sold for "gifts" (sometimes hundreds of gallons of liquor) and for annuities that could be spent either on traditional trade goods or alcohol—or to pay the traders to whom improvident, drunken Indians had run up huge debts.

Indian Objections to Changing Values

Other impediments to the civilization program were economic and social. The advantage of retaining extensive hunting grounds in order to ensure the cash crop of skins and furs was obvious to sober Indians, particularly in the south, where the ravages of alcohol seem to have been less manifest. Dependence on hunting and reluctance to become "civilized" were not entirely the result of a romantic attachment to the old way of life that men of the Enlightenment, like Jefferson, imagined. "Civilization" meant making dirt farmers out of professional huntsmen who were used to traveling hundreds of miles in search of the game needed in the trade; it was not a matter of killing local rabbits and deer for meat. If the hunters abandoned the chase, what would be the cash crop needed for the purchase of these necessaries? Subsistence agriculture by men would merely replace subsistence agriculture by women; horses would pull plows, and cattle, pigs, and chickens would provide meat, milk, butter, and eggs, supplemented by local small game and fish. But skins and furs were the traditional cash crop that procured hardware, cloth, and other necessaries for Indian families.

Another source of cash was sawed lumber, but that required a sawmill. The southern Indians hoped to raise cotton, but that required a gin, a baling press, and, again, wagons and boats to get the product to market. In effect, conversion to a rural white economy implied more than minimal subsistence agriculture and animal husbandry; it required large, centralized, expensive capital equipment operated and maintained, and if possible built, by trained Indian mechanics. This, in turn, implied changes in education and social organization. And after all this, what would be gained? Small wonder that many Indians concluded that their interests lay in staying sober, hunting for the fur trade, and protecting the land base from white encroachment or purchase.

Among the changes in social organization proposed by white missionaries and agents, two aroused particular resistance: altering the economic roles of the sexes and creating a new type of leadership based on wealth. These changes were especially repugnant to the northern Indians, among whom, traditionally, women were the gardeners, raising their crops of corn, squash, and beans with minimal help from the men, who occupied themselves with hunting, war, and diplomacy and whose leaders were chosen on other bases than wealth—normally kinship and prowess in hunting, warfare, and council rhetoric. The fur trade had only added emphasis to the distinction between the female world of village and cornfields and the male world of travel through the forests to distant places for purposes of hunting, war, and diplomacy. Marriage between white men and Indian women produced a class of leaders whose familiarity with Europeans and whose fluency in French or English (and, elsewhere, Spanish) made them useful, even indispensable, but not necessarily rich, spokesmen. Furthermore, the incessant wars and the ravages of disease tended to produce a demographic turbulence marked by frequent flights of villages and even of whole tribes to refuge among alien peoples and to necessitate the formation of "republican" communities of multiple ethnicities where leadership went to those who were bilingual. But these leaders too, while not necessarily qualified by lineage to represent the clans and moieties in traditional council, were not chosen because of their economic power.[57]

The core proposal of the civilization program, whether advanced by federal agents or Christian missionaries, was that men take over agriculture from the women, raising livestock and plowing the fields like white men. To many northern Indians, both male and female, this was tantamount to castration, making women of warriors; to sow seed and to walk behind the plow would be a disgraceful end to a masculine career. Among the Senecas, reported one of the Quaker missionaries in 1809, in the old days "If a man took hold of a hoe to use it the women would get down his gun by way of derision & would laugh to say such a Warrior is a timid woman."[58]

Volney, basing his opinion on a number of interviews with the Miami chief Little Turtle and his interpreter William Wells, who had been raised among the Miamis, also emphasized the influence of conservative opinion in impeding the acceptance of male farming: "in all these tribes there is a generation of old warriors, who, when they see a man handling the hoe, are incessantly exclaiming against the degeneracy from ancient manners, and who pretend, that the decline of the savages is entirely owing to these *innovations,* and that to recover their ancient strength and ancient glory, nothing is necessary but a return to their primitive manners."[59]

The white notion of private property was also anathema to these communitarian savages, among whom it was honorable to share. Among the Iroquois, Handsome Lake's half-brother Cornplanter was an exemplar of the native capitalist. Unlike Handsome Lake, who was one of the lineage chiefs appointed by the clan mothers to represent the tribes at the great council of the Iroquois Confederacy at Onondaga, Cornplanter was only a "pine tree chief" who had achieved influence and respect among the Senecas by his service as a warrior during the Revolution and by his wisdom in council. But he had acquired economic power by receiving as a reward from the state (some might have said a bribe) for his services on behalf of Pennsylvania at the treaty of Fort Harmar three private grants of land totaling 1,500 acres, location to be chosen by himself.

One of these fiefdoms was on the upper Allegheny; it consisted of 750 acres of fertile bottom lands and ancient hillside forests adjacent to the Seneca reservation across the line in New York. He held this land in fee simple, to be passed on to his descendants generation after generation. It was near the location chosen by the Quaker mission to establish their farm and school; and when the Quakers erected a sawmill here, Cornplanter promptly considered it to be his own because it lay on his property. Timbers sawed from this mill were floated down in rafts to Pittsburgh and sold for cash by the white millwright to whom Cornplanter leased the facility; the rental of tens of thousands of board feet yearly was appropriated by Cornplanter and his family. When Cornplanter demanded that the Allegheny Senecas allow him to relocate his sawmill to a better location on communally held land, and still take the rental, a dispute erupted. Cornplanter ordered the whole band (some 400 people) off his private reservation; they moved upstream, deposed Cornplanter as chief, and set up a competing sawmill at a better location, leased to one of Cornplanter's own millwrights![60]

Similar anecdotes could be told of other northern chiefs (of various degrees of legitimacy, both traditional and innovative) whose rewards (read bribes) from the United States gave them major economic advantages. Du Coigne, Jefferson's friend, received special financial attention, a house, and a fenced field; but this largesse "gained him the hatred of the other chiefs"; his brother-in-law was murdered, and the army had to guard him and his village.[61] Little Turtle, the pro-American Miami leader for whom Jefferson had purchased a slave, lived in a house built for him by the government and affected white clothes and cuisine, but when he acquired a cow for his wife to make butter, a jealous warrior killed it; traditional chiefs did not live more richly than their fellow tribesmen.[62] Harrison was dismayed at the carnage among the chiefs of the Piankeshaws, Weas, and Miamis who favored the assimilation of white ways: "There is scarcely a chief to be found among them," he lamented; "all these Horrors are produced to these unhappy people by their too frequent intercourse with the White people."[63]

Class and Politics among the Southern Tribes

The situation was somewhat more favorable to the acceptance of civilization among the southern Indians. They were, for one thing, far more numerous and still possessed of major portions of their domain. Furthermore, they were heirs to a cultural tradition which required a major male role in the intensive agriculture that regularly produced surpluses for emergencies and trade and which gave chiefs a degree of rank, privilege, and social control that made the entrepreneurial role far less offensive than it was to the north. For generations, white fur traders in the south had lived in Indian villages, married Indian women, raised their sons and daughters to speak English, and in some instances sent them away to white academies for education.

The so-called half-breeds among these tribes constituted virtually a special class that commanded both personal fortunes and political leadership. Among the Creeks was Alexander McGillivray, the wealthy half-breed fur trader and negotiator of treaties with the whites. Among the Cherokees, a Chickamauga chief named James Vann was one of the promoters of civilization; he encouraged the Moravians to establish their school at Springplace in northern Georgia on land obtained from him. Vann was one of the chiefs who were bribed in 1806 to sign the large cession of lands north of the Tennessee River, in northern Georgia and Tennessee. He prospered mightily from his transactions, owning a plantation on the Federal Road from Augusta, Georgia, to Nashville, that was worked by Negro slaves, plus a mill and a ferry. One of Vann's associates in the Washington treaty was assassinated and the execution of others was discussed in council; eventually Vann too was killed. But these disputes had less to do with resistance to civilization than factional divisions over land policy and political power, and the rise of a Cherokee class of elite plantation owners continued unabated until the forced removal of 1838.[64]

Political integration was also regarded by federal agents and missionaries alike as necessary to the success of the three goals of American Indian policy: maintain the peace, obtain the land, and civilize the savages. Among the Cherokees, in the middle of the eighteenth century, a high degree of political centralization had been achieved under the leadership of priestly leaders like Old Hop and his successor Old Tassel. The dozens of villages and several regional divisions had a national council, and national consensus was orchestrated by the amiable old men who were recognized as principal chiefs. This nascent Cherokee state was ripped apart, however, by the schism between the fiercely anti-American Dragging Canoe and his warriors, who became known as the Chickamaugas, and the rest of the tribe led by Old Tassel. The Chickamaugan villages separated themselves geographically from the mountain Cherokees, and their villages were ruled by warrior captains rather than priestly chiefs. The tribal council ceased to control even the mountain villages, and opposition to the civilization program appeared quickly.[65] Even Old Tassel, a "friendly" chief, was opposed to the early federal policy of land acquisition and civilization. Copies of a highly edited English translation of his protest (or at least a protest attributed to him) against the land cession and civilization policy of the whites circulated widely on the frontier (see opposite).[66]

The division between the Chickamaugas and the Upper Cherokees was bitter during Jefferson's presidency, the two sides competing for favor in Washington. In the spring of 1808 the Upper Cherokees sent a delegation to Washington to complain about the bad behavior of the Lower Cherokees and to propose a formal division of the nation, with the Upper Cherokees becoming citizens of the United States. Jefferson hedged in responding, observing that agreement between the two parties as to a dividing line might be difficult to achieve but suggesting that the disappointed minority might wish to exchange their present lands for a new territory west of the Mississippi. Jefferson duly notified Congress of the Cherokee application, but no action was taken. These transactions eventually led to the departure of some Chickamaugans to new homes west of the Mississippi.[67]

To agent Meigs and the Reverend Blackburn, this political chaos appeared to be an obstacle to the orderly conduct of affairs, and they urged the leading men to revitalize the Cherokee polity. In the fall of 1808, a tribal council was held to organize a national government. A written constitution was adopted that established a single council with both legislative and judicial powers; a police force was created to apprehend alleged criminals, to be tried before the council (private vengeance was prohibited); and taxes were levied. This council stood firmly for the civilization program.[68]

A similar situation existed among the Creeks, the Upper Creeks favoring accommodation with the Americans and the Lower Creeks leaning toward the Spanish in Florida (where their kinsmen the Seminoles had taken refuge over the years). The individual towns had their own chiefs and were so independent that in 1799 Hawkins declared, "The Creeks never had, till this year, a national Government and law."[69] To be sure, there had been a Creek Confederation, a loose assemblage of chiefdoms, each of which had a ceremonial center where religious rituals were conducted; each chiefdom had a council of chiefs, and each had an executive chief or *miko* (sometimes called "king" by white men) who distributed food from a public granary and performed various ceremonial duties. This

Old Tassel's Protest of Land Cessions and Civilization

It is a little surprising that when we entered into treaties with our brothers, the whites, their whole cry is more land! Indeed, formerly it seemed to be a matter of formality with them to demand what they knew we durst not refuse. But on the principles of fairness, of which we have received assurances during the conducting of the present treaty, and in the name of free will and equality, I must reject your demand.

Indeed, much has been advanced on the want of what you term civilization among the Indians; and many proposals have been made to us to adopt your laws, your religion, your manners and your customs. But, we confess that we do not yet see the propriety, or practicability of such a reformation, and should be better pleased with beholding the good effect of these doctrines in your own practices than with hearing you talk about them, or reading your papers to us upon such subjects.

You say: Why do not the Indians till the ground and live as we do? May we not, with equal propriety, ask, Why the white people do not hunt and live as we do? . . .

The great God of Nature has placed us in different situations. It is true that he has endowed you with many superior advantages; but he has not created us to be your slaves. We are a separate people! He has given each their lands, under distinct considerations and circumstances; he has stocked yours with corn, ours with buffaloe, yours with hog, ours with bear; yours with sheep, ours with deer. He has, indeed, given you an advantage in this, that your cattle are tame and domestic while ours are wild and demand not only a larger space for range, but art to hunt and kill them; they are, nevertheless, as much our property as other animals are yours, and ought not to be taken away without our consent, or for something equivalent.

loose state of affairs was not satisfactory to Hawkins, however, and he set about to change it.

In the fall of 1799 he convened a national council of chiefs from the various major towns and advised them to develop a plan of government for a new political entity, the Creek Nation. Hawkins wrote a glowing description of the newly organized government which so impressed Jefferson that he included it in his message to Congress in December 1801. At the heart of the plan was a national legislature *cum* supreme court that was to meet annually, with Hawkins providing logistical support, at a town on the Tallapoosa River in eastern Alabama. Hawkins took it upon himself to act as a kind of prime minister, setting the agenda for debate and putting its important decisions in writing as "the will of the nation."[70]

Obviously, having such a central institution to which to take matters involving Indian–white relations, from land cessions to murders to complaints about stolen horses, was extremely helpful to the agent. Furthermore, it provided a forum where pro-civilization propaganda could be introduced and support for the program solicited. Both the Cherokee and Creek national councils did in fact cooperate with the civilization program by allocating annuity monies to educational programs and to capital enterprises. Among the Indians north of the Ohio, however, no such administratively effective national councils existed. There were so-called tribal councils, but they tended to be arenas of factional debate among delegates from autonomous villages. There was no central tribal institution to promote and administer the civilization program that many Indians, as well as benevolent Jeffersonians, desired.

But even the native proponents of civilization were generally in disagreement with the Jeffersonian policy of "obtaining lands." They saw no reason why hunting for the fur trade should be incompatible with a white-style farm economy. Hunting brought cash for hardware and dry goods, dirt farming and animal husbandry yielded subsistence. After 1806, Jefferson's agents were able to make only a few more purchases of land, none of them in the south.

Nativistic Movements and the Shawnee Prophet

Although in most of the tribes an influential body of chiefs were advocates of civilization, there was always a conservative faction that maintained a nativistic stance. Jefferson was annoyed by any resistance to his plans and complained to Congress in 1805 that despite the benevolent efforts his administration had made to save the Native Americans from extinction by giving them the tools of civilization, some persisted in stubborn opposition to progress (as did by implication the benighted Federalists).[71] Among the southern Indians, the Creek nativistic faction centered in, but was not confined to, the Lower Towns and was led by Tame King, the town chief of Tallasie. Tame King had been pro-American during and after the Revolution, opposing even the redoubtable McGillivray, and seems to have been a willing friend of Georgia and the United States until he was taken hostage by the Georgians in 1786 after having complaisantly signed a treaty with the state confirming previous land cessions. He and his followers became ardent opponents of Benjamin Hawkins from the start and supported the adventurer Bowles in his efforts to create the new nation of Muscogee, allied with the British. When Tame King and his followers harassed Andrew Ellicott's party surveying the line between Spanish Florida and the United States, Hawkins persuaded the new Creek national council to punish Tame King by a public flogging. One of Tame King's followers was brutally executed, as the executioner reported to Hawkins: "We pulled down and set fire to his house, we beat him with sticks until he was on the ground as a dead man, we cut off one of his ears with a part of his cheek and put a sharp stick up his fundament."[72]

Hawkins applauded the incidents of punishment, which he reported to the secretary of war, and assured the Creek national council that because it was "the Law" that had killed the dead man, his relatives ought not to take revenge. But the council was offended and Tame King and his followers became more deeply inflamed against the United States, its agents, and its civilization policy. Mad Dog, the speaker of Hawkins's new national council, who had personally led the party of seventy-two warriors who bound and whipped Tame King, resigned his office a few years later. Tame King survived to become one of the leaders of the nativistic faction in the Creek War in 1812, incited by another Hawkins-inspired public execution, and a follower of the Shawnee Prophet. Hawkins's (and Jefferson's) policy of pushing Creeks to punish their own malefactors deserves some credit, however; it was a strategy for the prevention of escalating exchanges of revenge raids by white frontiersmen and native warriors and for thus aborting the need for military intervention by the U.S. army.[73]

The trouble among the Creeks was temporarily tapering off, with the capture and extradition of Bowles in 1803 (by Hawkins's order, again), when a new difficulty with the civilization program began to rise north of the Ohio, among the Shawnees. The displaced Shawnees had divided, both ideologically and geographically, into two factions. A pro-American faction, led by an aging war chief named Black Hoof, established the village of Wapakoneta on the Auglaize River in central Ohio, on land claimed by the Ottawas and others. Black Hoof believed that to survive, his people had to adopt the ways of the white man, and in the winter of 1802–1803 he visited Washington requesting technical assistance in the form of farm equipment, livestock, and log cabins. He also requested a deed from the government to the land they now occupied on the Auglaize—a request that could not be granted, for the land did not yet belong to the United States. Dearborn did, however, promise that "Your Father the President" would send them plows and other implements, and cattle. But little in the way of supplies arrived from the distribution point at Fort Wayne, most of it going to the Miamis under Little Turtle and to the Potawatomis.

In the meantime, the conservative faction of the Shawnees, settled in villages farther to the west, tried to continue the traditional mode of subsistence, the women planting corn and the men hunting the ever-dwindling supply of fur-bearers and trading with British merchants from Canada. Their villages were poverty-stricken, disease-ridden, populated by frustrated, angry, drunken men and women who blamed their plight in part on the Americans and in part on witches among themselves.[74]

In the spring of 1805 in one of these villages a failed hunter, failed medicine man, notorious drunkard, and loud-mouthed ne'er-do-well named Lalawethiker or "The Rattle" fell into a trance and had a vision. It was remarkably like Handsome Lake's vision of his tour through the next world and may have been influenced by reports of the Seneca prophet's preaching. Guided by angels sent by the Master of Life, he was shown a heaven where the virtuous enjoyed the traditional Shawnee way of life and a hell where the evil were punished and destroyed.

Some of the tortures of the damned he articulated were similar to those described by Handsome Lake, in particular the sufferings of the drunkard, whom both prophets saw being forced to swallow molten metal. The fate of the unrepentant abuser of alcohol was an especially meaningful threat to both Handsome Lake and the Shawnee Prophet, for both were drunkards soon to become teetotalers who demanded abstinence from their converts. Another category of sinners doomed to burn to ashes were the

"The Open Door, known as The Prophet, Brother of Tecumseh." Shown with his sacred string of beads and fire stick, which he acquired through a vision. The Prophet was approximately sixty years old, and blind in one eye, when this portrait was painted. Oil on canvas by George Catlin, 1830. National Museum of American Art, Washington, DC / Art Resource, NY.

witches, whom Lalawethiker (soon to be renamed Tenskwatawa) blamed for the moral decay he saw around him; like Handsome Lake, he tried to abolish certain rituals and shamanistic practices that he considered corrupt.[75]

At first the Shawnee Prophet seemed to preach only repentance, demanding that his followers abstain from alcohol and abandon the practice of witchcraft. Through the summer and fall of 1805 he made many converts among the Shawnees and Delawares, and by the fall was attracting delegations from Ottawas, Wyandots, Kickapoos, and even Senecas. As time went on, the Prophet had additional visions and formulated a new social gospel for the Indians. Handsome Lake's early apocalyptic message had also been amplified by a social gospel, but the two prophets' images of reform were radically dissimilar. Handsome Lake recommended the Quakers' program of civilization, whereas Tenskwatawa demanded a return to aboriginal customs. He condemned wealth in private property and banned domestic animals—sheep, cattle, hogs—as unclean; meat must come from wild animals, hunted with bows and arrows. Tools were to be made from wood, stone, and bone, as their ancestors had fashioned them. Contact with whites was to be minimized: no sexual relations, minimal trade, no conversion to Christianity. And Americans were especially to be avoided, as a demonic race spawned by the Evil Spirit (in distinction from the British, French, and Spanish, who were created, like Indians, by the Master of Life). The Master of Life, he said, wanted Indians to live lives of sobriety, simplicity, and virtue, as good hunters, faithful spouses, and peaceful villagers, no longer warring with other tribes. And if they obeyed him, the Master of Life would bring back the game, restore the dead to life, and drive the Americans into the sea from which they came.[76]

These strange doings among the savages do not seem to have been of interest to American officials at first. But during the spring of 1806, Tenskwatawa visited the Delawares on the White River and assisted some of his converts in identifying the guilty among a dozen suspected witches, most of them Christian converts. Several were subsequently executed, including Tetapachsit, who had signed the controversial treaty of cession at Vincennes. After conducting his purge of witches among the Delawares, the Prophet moved on to the Wyandots and condemned four women to death; they were saved by the intervention a pro-American chief, Tarhe "The Crane."

The murder of Tetapachsit and another Delaware accused of witchcraft attracted Harrison's attention, and he wrote an impassioned letter to the Delawares denouncing the Prophet as an imposter and demanding that they drive him from their towns, lest they forfeit the friendship of their Father the President. In a fine rhetorical flourish, Harrison told the Delawares to test the truth of the Prophet's claim that he was the messenger of the Great Creator by asking him to perform some miracles. "If he is really a prophet, ask of him to cause the sun to stand still."[77] Unfortunately, an eclipse of the sun was just then impending, and the Prophet had learned of it from white astronomers who were setting up observation stations in Indiana. He called his followers to assemble at his new town near Greenville, Ohio, on June 16, to witness how he could blacken the sun. The eclipse occurred on schedule, and the prophet claimed credit for the event. The Delawares rejected Harrison's appeal, refusing to apologize for the executions. "You white people also try your criminals, and when they are found guilty, you hang them or kill them, and we do the same among ourselves."[78]

The Prophet's next challenge to American authority occurred among the Kickapoos in Illinois. During the summer of 1806, a Kickapoo delegation from the Sangamon River visited the Prophet and brought back the new religion to their towns. Late in June he received word "through a trader of unquestionable veracity" that the Kickapoos and the Sacs were planning a war against the United States and were inviting the Weas and other tribes to join them. He promptly sent a message to the Kickapoos warning them not to "follow the advice of those who would lead you to destruction" and about the same time wrote directly to Jefferson informing him of the enmity of the Sacs and the Kickapoos and the likelihood of an outbreak of hostilities. Although Harrison assured the President that the tribes in Ohio and Indiana remained loyal to the United States, he was sufficiently concerned to convene a conference with the neighboring tribes that same summer and to plead with the legislature to take steps to ensure that when white men injured or killed Indians they would receive the same punishment as that visited upon Indian offenders.[79]

Meanwhile, the Prophet continued to receive delegations from other northeastern tribes at his center at Greenville. Throughout the remainder of 1806 and into the summer of 1807 he harangued and converted representatives of the Potawatomis, Ottawas, Chippewas, Winnebagoes, and Sacs. The new religion spread throughout the Great Lakes region to the shores of Lake Superior. The tide of pilgrims to the Prophet's council house grew so great that William Wells, the agent at Fort Wayne, wrote to both Harrison and the secretary of war in the spring of 1807 warning that the Prophet was becoming a serious danger to American authority in the Old Northwest and advising that the Prophet and his followers be driven from Greenville.

White settlers too were becoming alarmed, and the governor called out the state militia. Wells demanded that the Prophet and his followers come to Fort Wayne and that they abandon the village at Greenville, which lay within the bounds of the Greenville treaty cession. But the Prophet haughtily refused, demanding instead that the President "send to us the greatest man in his nation" and threatening to blacken the sun again.[80]

Up to this point, the sound and fury aroused by the Prophet's preachings seem to have been regarded by Jefferson as a minor annoyance. In later years, in a letter to John Adams on April 20, 1812, he described his rather tepid initial reaction. Adams, writing at the outset of the War of 1812, had asked his old friend what were his views on the Prophet who had inspired so many Indians to ally themselves with the British and how he compared with a black prophet named Christopher Macpherson, whom Jefferson had known for a long time. Jefferson replied that the Prophet was a harmless visionary who sought only to persuade his people to forsake the ways of the white men and return to the simple customs of their forefathers. Jefferson doubted that many would want to give up the new comforts they had learned to enjoy (see opposite).[81]

Jefferson's attitude toward the Shawnee Prophet's movement underwent a sudden change, however, in the summer of 1807. The *Chesapeake* affair, in which an American naval vessel was attacked and boarded by a British warship searching for alleged deserters, some of them American citizens, brought the United States and Great Britain to the brink of war. Jefferson mobilized the army and navy and prepared to defend the country. In this crisis, the hostile mutterings of the Prophet and some of his followers took on a more ominous aspect, for in the event of war these Indians might join the British, defeat American armies, and lay waste the northwest frontier as they had done fifteen years before.

In July, Harrison wrote an alarming letter to the secretary of war; its contents were no doubt relayed to the President. There was bitter, and justified, resentment among all the tribes over the failure of the United

Jefferson on the Shawnee Prophet

The Wabash prophet is a very different character, more rogue than fool, if to be a rogue is not the greatest of all follies. He arose to notice while I was in the administration, and became, of course, a proper subject of inquiry for me. The inquiry was made with diligence. His declared object was the reformation of his red brethren, and their return to their pristine manner of living. He pretended to be in constant communication with the Great Spirit; that he was instructed by him to make known to the Indians that they were created by him distinct from the whites, of different natures, for different purposes, and placed under different circumstances, adapted to their nature and destinies; that they must return from all the ways of the whites to the habits and opinions of their forefathers; they must not eat the flesh of hogs, of bullocks, of sheep, etc., the deer and buffalo having been created for their food; they must not make bread of wheat, but of Indian corn; they must not wear linen nor woolen, but dress like their fathers in the skins and furs of animals; they must not drink ardent spirits, and I do not remember whether he extended his inhibitions to the gun and gunpowder, in favor of the bow and arrow. I concluded from all this, that he was a visionary, enveloped in the clouds of their antiquities, and vainly endeavoring to lead back his brethren to the fancied beatitudes of their golden age. I thought there was little danger of his making many proselytes from the habits and comfort they had learned from the whites, to the hardships and privations of savagism, and no great harm if he did. We let him go on, therefore, unmolested.

States to bring to justice the known murderers of inoffensive Indians, and the Prophet was bringing the Indian sense of injustice to a boil. He thought that the Prophet was a bad influence, "an engine set to work by the British for some bad purpose" but that he meant more mischief than he could accomplish.[82] In response to these warnings about American justice and the Prophet, Jefferson wrote to the secretary of war from Monticello on August 12, agreeing that justice must be done and suggesting a $1,000 reward for the capture of one suspect. He also intimated that he would not be upset if the Prophet were bribed into alliance, or even assassinated, preferably by Indians who opposed his teachings: "With respect to the prophet, if those who are in danger from him would settle it in their own way, it would be their affair. But we should do nothing towards it. That kind of policy is not in the character of our government, and still less of the paternal spirit we wish to show towards that people. But could not Harrison gain over the prophet, who no doubt is a scoundrel, and only needs his price?"[83]

The situation continued to deteriorate, however. In his message to the territorial legislature in Indiana on August 17, 1807, Harrison gave Indian affairs an ominous character. A combination of British intrigue and American neglect was pushing the Indians of the northwest toward war. "Although the agency of a foreign power is producing the discontents among the Indians cannot be questioned, I am persuaded that their utmost efforts to induce them to take up arms would be unavailing, if one only of the many persons who have committed murder on their people could be brought to punishment. Whilst we rigorously exact of them the deliver of every murderer of a white man, the neglect on our part to punish similar offences committed on them forms a strong and just ground of complaint, for which I can offer no excuse or palliation."[84] He assumed command of the militia himself and requested that the President authorize the arming of these troops from federal military arsenals.[85]

The warnings of Harrison and other correspondents now convinced Jefferson that his earlier laissez faire attitude toward the Indians could no longer be continued. He ordered that the governors of Ohio, Michigan, and Indiana mobilize their militia and that adequate arms, ammunition, and provisions be deposited in the proper locations for defending the posts and settlements. And he instructed the secretary of war to impress upon the Prophet's followers the fact that the United States was prepared to destroy them if they took sides in the coming war. In the preceding couple of years, he observed, the Prophet had seemed an innocuous figure; his nativistic movement had seemed to be only "a transient enthusiasm, which, if let alone, would evaporate innocently of itself, although visibly tinctured with a partiality against the United States."[86] But now the tribes must be assembled and warned in the strongest terms of the disastrous consequences of following the Prophet's bellicose advice.

"We have learnt that some tribes are already expressing intentions hostile to the United States, we think it proper to apprise them of the ground on which they now stand; for which purpose we make to them this solemn declaration of our unalterable determination, that we wish them to live in peace with all nations as well as with us, and we have no intention ever to strike them or to do them an injury of any sort, unless first attacked or threatened; but that learning that some of them meditate war on us, we too are preparing for war against those, and those only who shall seek it; and that if ever we are constrained to lift the hatchet against any tribe, we will never lay it down till that tribe is exterminated, or driven beyond the Mississippi. Adjuring them, therefore, if they wish to remain on the land which covers the bones of their fathers, to keep the peace with a people who ask their friendship without needing it, who wish to avoid war without fearing it. In war, they will kill some of us; we shall destroy all of them," Jefferson wrote.[87] At the same time, all negotiations for the purchase of Indian lands, particularly around Detroit, must be suspended, lest the Indians "think that these preparations are meant to intimidate them into a sale of their lands."[88]

The crisis gradually eased without the armed conflict for which Jefferson was preparing. The national enthusiasm for war with England ebbed; although plans for an invasion of Canada were pending and British warships were barred from American waters, Jefferson still preferred a peaceful settlement. Finally, in December 1807, having failed to obtain satisfaction from the British (or the French) for interference with American shipping, Congress, at the President's request, passed the infamous Embargo Act prohibiting seaborne commerce in American goods. Alarms and excursions continued in the Indiana and Michigan territories, but no general outbreak occurred. In November Governor Hull of Michigan was even able to negotiate the land purchase that Jefferson had warned against.

By May the Prophet, still professing peaceful intentions in conferences with both American and British agents, was preparing to remove, with his multitribal following, to Tippecanoe, alias Prophetstown, on the upper Wabash. This removal caused consternation among the Miamis and Delawares, most of whom still resisted his pretensions to divine authority but feared his temporal power, and led Harrison to complain to the secretary of war: "The Shawnese imposter has acquired such an ascendancy over the minds of the Indians that there can be little doubt of their pursuing any course which he may dictate to them, and that his views are decidedly hostile to the United States is but too evident . . . I most sincerely wish the President would think himself authorized to have him seized and conveyed to the interior of the United States until the present appearance of war is removed."[89]

But during the summer of 1808 the Prophet and Harrison exchanged a number of messages, and finally the Prophet and his entourage visited Harrison at Vincennes, where over a period of two weeks they harangued each other repeatedly. Harrison's opinion of the Prophet changed as a result of these meetings, and he advised the secretary of war of his new, more favorable impression. The Prophet now appeared to Harrison to be an able man, a man of principle, not necessarily a British puppet, who sincerely aimed to reclaim the Indians from their bad habits, particularly their passion for war and whiskey.[90] His professions of friendship led Harrison to provide the Prophet's starving followers with life-saving food in the winter of 1808–1809 and led Hull at Detroit to prevent an attack by Ottawa and Chippewa warriors, who now believed the Prophet had bewitched their starving relatives at Prophetstown.

By this time Jefferson was winding up the affairs of his presidency and apparently was not following closely the Prophet's career between the war crisis of 1807 and the actual outbreak of hostilities in 1811, when Harrison's troops attacked the Prophet's camp at Tippecanoe. As he blandly put it to Adams in 1812: "But his followers increased till the English thought him worth corruption and found him corruptible. I suppose his views were then changed; but his proceedings in consequence of them were after I left the administration, and are, therefore, unknown to me; nor have I ever been informed what were the particular acts on his part, which produced an actual commencement of hostilities on ours. I have no doubt, however, that his subsequent proceedings are but a chapter apart, like that of Henry and Lord Liverpool, in the Book of the Kings of England."[91] The comparison of the Prophet to "Henry" is revealing of the thought processes of Jefferson when it came to Indians. Henry was a New England Federalist allegedly seduced by Lord Liverpool, the British foreign secretary at the time of the Embargo, into an intrigue to have the New England states declare their neutrality in the expected war in return for peace and free trade.

Jefferson's bland denial of knowledge of the Prophet's later career also implicitly denies knowledge of the career of the Prophet's brother, the famous war leader Tecumseh. The Prophet never seems to have organized his following in the various tribes into a unified political and military force, but Tecumseh attempted to do just that. At first working in the shadow of his brother, he came to the fore after the failure of the Prophet's

Shawnee war chief Tecumseh. Engraving by Benson J. Lossing, c. 1848, after a drawing from life by Pierre Le Dru, c. 1808. Lossing replaced the Indian costume with regimentals, on the mistaken belief that Tecumseh was a brigadier-general in the British army. No fully authenticated portrait of Tecumseh is known to exist. From John Sugden, *Tecumseh: A Life* (Henry Holt, 1998).

preachings to prevent the 1809 land cession. Tecumseh promulgated a more secular doctrine, asserting that Indian land properly belonged in common to all the tribes and therefore individual parcels could not be alienated by those who now, temporarily, were settled upon them. He planned to put together a confederacy that would embrace not only the members of the old Western Confederacy that had fought the Americans for the Northwest Territory but also the powerful tribes of the south. He intrigued with the British for supplies of arms and apparently hoped to drive the Americans out of the territory north of the Ohio and establish an Indian buffer state, whose security would be guaranteed by both the United States and Great Britain—an old dream of British agents.

Harrison came to respect—and fear—Tecumseh, whom he considered capable of founding "an Empire that would rival in glory that of Mexico or Peru."[92] Tecumseh traveled tirelessly among the tribes, attracting many adherents, particularly among the Creeks, with whom bands of Shawnees often lived (perhaps giving rise to the story that his and Tenskwatawa's mother was Creek). While Tecumseh was absent among the Creeks, Harrison launched his pre-emptive strike, destroying the Indian force gath-

A campaign poster, c. 1840, illustrating William Henry Harrison's qualifications for the presidency. Fittingly, the Battle of Tippecanoe forms its base. Courtesy of the Library of Congress.

ered at Prophetstown in the Battle of Tippecanoe on November 7, 1811, and effectively aborting Tecumseh's plans for a military confederacy. Several years earlier Jefferson himself had suggested such an attack as a last resort.

When the long-anticipated war broke out in 1812, the Creek "Red Sticks" and the Prophet's followers to the north joined the British. Tecumseh was killed fighting to protect the British retreat from Detroit, and Andrew Jackson crushed the Creeks in a series of battles in 1814.

Farewell to the Indians

To the Miamis and Delawares, led by chiefs favoring civilization over the hunter state and the American alliance over the British, Jefferson delivered a fond farewell in December 1808. A delegation of the two tribes was visiting the capital just as Jefferson was preparing to step down from office. He took this opportunity to make a final recommendation for peace, sobriety, agriculture, and private property in land. And he looked forward to an ultimate union of the races: "You will wish to live under . . . [our laws]; you will unite yourselves with us, join in our great councils, and form one people with us, and we shall all be Americans. You will mix with us by marriage. Your blood will run in our veins, and will spread with us over this great island."[93]

But political priorities came first. At the same time that he was exhorting the Miamis and Delawares to amalgamate with the whites, Jefferson was instructing Harrison to meet with the Kickapoos in order to ascertain their boundaries and if possible to secure a cession of part of their lands, in order to "close our possessions on the hither bank of the Mississippi, from the Ohio to the Ouisconsine." The purpose here was to block off British traders from access to Louisiana.[94] No question had to be raised about making the progress of civilization among the Kickapoos an object or condition of the sale; they were "very much under the influence of the prophet." And Jefferson was also directing Harrison to acquire the lands on the Wabash, from the Miamis, Delawares, and Potawatomis, even though the United States "had no immediate use for them."[95]

Harrison waited for a few months and made a purchase of 3,000,000 acres at the Treaty of Fort Wayne after Jefferson left office. In the last analysis, "obtaining lands" needed for defense against invasion by British troops or traders took precedence over the policy of peace and civilization.

CHAPTER TEN

Return to Philosophical Hall

UPON LEAVING the White House in March 1809, Jefferson returned to Monticello and to the philosophical pursuits he so much enjoyed. Although public life had sometimes made it difficult for him to join the gatherings of the society in Philosophical Hall, he frequently attended meetings while he was resident in Philadelphia from 1790 to 1794 and presided over twenty meetings from 1797 to 1800. He had also vigorously encouraged research and publication by the members and urged them to support investigations in natural history. In particular he had labored to expand the scope of the society's interests to include the sort of historical, archaeological, linguistic, and ethnological questions that he had advanced in *Notes on the State of Virginia.*

In retirement, Jefferson found it even more difficult to make the trip to Philadelphia, and in 1814 he resigned the presidency of the society. But Monticello itself was a second Philosophical Hall for him, and there he continued to gather information and to correspond with his peers on his accustomed variety of subjects, including the American Indians. As he did so, some of the projects that he had nurtured took on lives of their own.[1]

The Historical and Literary Committee

The Philosophical Society's Historical and Literary Committee, and especially its program of research in American Indian linguistics, is an outstanding example of a Jeffersonian project becoming an independent enterprise.

Although the comparison of standardized vocabularies ultimately proved to be an unproductive method for discovering the origin of Native Americans, it would remain a valuable tool for the classification of languages into families or stocks. But American linguistics would soon move on from the largely taxonomic and historical and into a more analytical mode, and Jefferson's protégé, Peter Stephen DuPonceau, member of the American Philosophical Society and corresponding Secretary of the Historical and Literary Committee, was the early architect of this transformation. After giving up the priesthood and supporting himself in Paris as a translator, Peter Stephen DuPonceau emigrated from France during the American Revolution. He was versed in a number of languages—French, of course, Latin, Greek, German, Italian, and English. During the Revolution he served as Baron Von Steuben's interpreter and aide-de-camp at Valley Forge. After the war he studied law, was admitted to the bar in Philadelphia, and on account of his familiarity with European matters and constitutional issues became an authority on international and constitutional law, a subject on which he published several books. He was elected to membership in the American Philosophical Society in 1791, and later as the leading member of the Historical and Literary Committee he was able to indulge his principal intellectual passion, the study of American Indian languages.

The Historical and Literary Committee was first suggested in 1811 by DuPonceau while Jefferson was still President of the society, and was officially established in 1815 as the seventh of the standing committees of the society, with all society members invited to join.[2] It was essentially a re-creation of the informal and abortive 1797 enterprise and like its predecessor sought to collect materials on the history and literary productions of the state of Pennsylvania and the nation. Although the committee did assemble a valuable collection of books and manuscripts and laid the basis for the expansion of the society's library into the domain of the humanities, it soon had as competitors several other institutions, including the Historical Society of Pennsylvania (founded in Philadelphia by, among others, members of the Philosophical Society disappointed by the increasingly linguistic focus of the committee's plans), the New-York Historical Society, the Massachusetts Historical Society, and the American Antiquarian Society (of which also Jefferson became a member).

The officers of the committee—Judge William Tilghman, chairman; John Vaughan, the society's librarian since 1803, recording secretary; and Peter S. DuPonceau, corresponding secretary—concentrated less on history than on the acquisition and analysis of American Indian language materials. As corresponding secretary, DuPonceau in effect managed the committee from 1815 until its gradual demise in the 1830s, depending not on the issuance of printed advertisements, which elicited minimal response, but on an aggressive program of personal solicitation and scientific correspondence. He and Vaughan personally purchased and deposited in the society's library most of the available European and American publications on linguistics; and he wrote and published path-breaking works of his own that profoundly influenced the development of linguistic science in America.

DuPonceau at the outset wrote to Jefferson notifying him of the formation of the committee and asking, in the most respectful terms, for Jefferson's help in discovering the authorship of a document describing the survey in 1728 of the boundary line between Virginia and North Carolina. Jefferson in reply testified to his satisfaction at learning of the society's "enlargement of the scope of their institution. I have," he went on to say, "always thought that we were too much confined in practice to the Natural and Mathematical departments." He offered to give or procure documents of relevance, and as an earnest of his intentions, enclosed his copy of Benjamin Hawkins's account of the Creek Indians, written in the years 1798 and 1799. He also added information about the boundary survey question, to whit, that "Doctor Byrd," one of the surveyors, was the author of the narrative.[3]

DuPonceau by this time was busy working out his ideas about "polysynthesis"—the combining of "many ideas together into one word"—as a grammatical characteristic of all American Indian languages. In February 1817 he wrote to Jefferson about the new direction taken by the Historical and Literary Committee. "You will be pleased to hear, that our committee have particularly turned their attention to the languages of our Indian nations." He explained to Jefferson his own discovery (which was indeed a salient event in the history of American linguistics) and asked for any comments on this line of thought.[4] Jefferson does not seem to have responded at all to DuPonceau's ideas about polysynthesis or about the superiority of grammatical comparisons as opposed to what DuPonceau disparagingly called "mere 'word-hunting' for the sake of finding affinities of sound" (which was, of course, Jefferson's own avocation). And in a letter in June following, Jefferson declined to offer anything for publication in the forthcoming issue of the society's *Transactions.* It was rather a sad letter, almost a farewell to scholarship. "In earlier life when I should from inclination have devoted myself to pursuits analogous to those of our society, my time was all engrossed by public duties, and now without either books or memory I could offer nothing which would do credit either to the society or myself."[5]

The Native American Language Project

In January 1819, DuPonceau read to the society his "Report . . . of his Progress in the Investigation committed to him of the General Character and forms of the Languages of the American Indians." The thirty-four-page report was duly published in the *Transactions.* In it he presented his argument that the languages of the Indians of both North and South America are all polysynthetic in grammatical form: that words are constructed by joining root forms so as to make a single word convey what in Indo-European languages requires a number of words related to one another in phrases, clauses, or whole sentences. The concept of polysynthesis as a characteristic of American Indian languages generally was not entirely new, having been broached by Professor Vater in the *Mithridates,* where he raised the question whether there were any languages of the Old World that fell into the same class as the American Indian languages. Vater considered Basque, Tschuktschi (Chuckchee), and the African language of the Congo to be comparable.

DuPonceau went to some pains to discount this assertion. The whole essay was footnoted with reference to European scholarship and citations of sources of information on particular languages from Araucanian in South America to Eskimo in the North. He insisted that he had worked only from critically examined primary sources. And—most significantly for the course that linguistic research would take—he abjured the historical goals that motivated men like Jefferson and Benjamin Smith Barton to collect vocabularies: "Whether the Indian population of this country took its origin from the Tartars, or from any other race of men; whether America was peopled from any of the countries of the old hemisphere, or those from America, are questions upon which I have never yet employed my mind. I have purposely left it free, that I might pursue my philological enquiries in an abstract point of view, unmixed and unconnected with those more important subjects on which their results, when fully ascertained, may, perhaps, ultimately throw light."[6]

DuPonceau illustrated his points about polysynthesis from Delaware examples supplied him by the Moravian missionary John Heckewelder, with whom he corresponded. He also entered into an exciting correspondence with the notable European and American linguists of the day: Frederick Adelung, John Severin Vater, Alexander and Wilhelm Humboldt, John Pickering, and Albert Gallatin. DuPonceau went on to collect more vocabularies, grammars, and printed works for the society and to collate the harvest, including Jefferson's contributions, in a systematic way. DuPonceau was (to use a later generation's phrase) conducting a state-of-the-art program of linguistic research at the American Philosophical Society during the early nineteenth century.

Jefferson was out of his depth in this new world of linguistic studies. In 1817 he conveyed to the society his few vocabularies and the fragments of the comparative tabulation that remained after the theft and vandalism of 1809. In 1820 Jefferson sent DuPonceau a vocabulary of the Nottoway Indians taken by John Wood, a professor of mathematics at William and Mary, which, Jefferson thought, revealed that the Nottoway spoke a language akin to Powhatan, an Algonkian tongue. DuPonceau quickly corrected his mentor, notifying him that, to his own astonishment, Nottoway was clearly Iroquoian and that the venerable Heckewelder agreed.[7]

Thereafter communications between Jefferson and DuPonceau on the subject of language ceased. But Jefferson's interest in linguistics continued and indeed was piqued a few years later by a correspondence with John Pickering, the eminent Massachusetts lawyer and philologist who had helped to establish a program in linguistic studies at the American Academy of Arts and Sciences. Pickering's father, Timothy, had led the Federalist opposition in Congress to Jefferson throughout his presidency. John Pickering corresponded regularly with DuPonceau and when in 1820 his academy published his *Essay on a Uniform Orthography for the Indian Languages of North America,* he sent copies to both DuPonceau and Jefferson.

Jefferson, of course, like other collectors of vocabularies, had been plagued by the absence of a standard phonetic alphabet, which made much more difficult the recognition of those "affinities of sound" on which his own research depended. Jefferson wrote a thank-you note, welcoming Pickering's proposal and expressing the hope that it would become the basis for "an uniform orthography for the world." A year later Pickering sent him a copy of his analysis of Jonathan Edwards's observations on the Mohegan language, eliciting from Jefferson another note approving Pickering's comparison of Mohegan to Delaware and his use of "collation" as the only true method for "tracing the affiliations of those numerous tribes,

Sequoya (also known as George Guess), holding the Cherokee syllabary he invented. Lithograph by I. T. Bowen, 1836, after a portrait by Charles Bird King, 1828. Courtesy of the Archives and Manuscripts Division of the Oklahoma Historical Society.

and of remounting thro' the gloom of ages toward their origin." He also noted that it was "not without curiosity" that linguistic analysis should "unfold to us structures of speech so radically different from those of the whole European families," of which both he and Pickering were learned scholars.

In 1823 Pickering met David Brown, a young Cherokee preacher then studying at Andover, and agreed to help him prepare a grammar of Cherokee, written in his standard orthography. The project as a whole was, according to Pickering, aborted in 1827 because of the invention and rapid spread of a Cherokee "alphabet" of eighty characters (Sequoyah's famous syllabary). But Pickering did send Jefferson some initial sheets of the Cherokee grammar, and these intrigued the aging sage of Monticello sufficiently to earn from him, on February 25, 1825, an extended reply (see next page).

But the last exchange, in October 1825, less than a year before Jefferson's death, dealt not with American Indian but Greek syntax, and Jefferson here revealed—not for the first time—his impatience with grammarians:

Jefferson's Remarks on the Cherokee Grammar

I thank you for the copy of your Cherokee grammar, which I have gone over with attention and satisfaction. We generally learn languages for the benefit of reading the books written in them. But here our reward must be the addition made to the philosophy of language. In this point of view your analysis of the Cherokee adds valuable matter for reflection and strengthens our desire to see more of these languages as scientifically elucidated. Their grammatical devices for the modification of their words by a syllable prefixed, to, or inserted in the middle, or added to its end, and by other combinations so different from ours, prove that if man came from one stock, his languages did not. A late grammarian has said that all words were originally monosyllables. The Indian languages disprove this. I should conjecture that the Cherokees, for example, have formed their language not by single words, but by phrases. I have known some children learn to speak, not by word at a time, but by whole phrases. Thus the Cherokee has no name for "father" in the abstract, but only as combined with some one of his relations. A complex idea being a fasciculus of simple ideas bundled together, it is rare that different languages make up their bundles alike, and hence the difficulty of translating from one language to another. European nations have so long had intercourse with one another, to have approximated their complex expressions much towards one another. But I believe we shall find it impossible to translate our language into any of the Indian, or any of theirs into ours. I hope you will pursue your undertaking, and that others will follow your example with other of their languages. It will open a wide field for reflection on the grammatical organization of languages, their structure and character.

"Grammar, in fact, unconnected from it's use in teaching us languages, is not a science of itself. It is a branch of Metaphysics, a region of fog, like that, in which we have neither star nor compass to guide us, nor a harbor of usefulness, in which to expect remuneration for the time and labor of our misty pursuit of it." It would seem that Jefferson's prejudice in favor of lexicon over grammar, and the historical world view over the analytical, persisted to the end.[8]

It was Albert Gallatin who most directly continued the Jeffersonian program of linguistic and ethnological research. Gallatin had maintained a quiet interest in Native American studies ever since he encountered Abenaki Indians in Maine in 1781, and early on he made himself a master of the geography of western and northern North America, advising George Washington on portages from the Potomac to the Ohio and supplying Lewis and Clark with maps of their anticipated route to the Pacific. After he left the Treasury in 1817, at the end of Madison's administration, he concentrated his energies on the study of Indian languages, using the vocabularies stored at the American Philosophical Society and sending out inquiries to well-informed persons.

In 1826, at Gallatin's suggestion, the secretary of war issued a circular requesting officers and agents in Indian country to collect vocabularies and translations of sentences (for the purpose of studying grammar). Enclosed with the order were a standard vocabulary form (expanded from Jefferson's earlier list), a sketch of John Pickering's system for a uniform orthography to represent speech sounds, a standard set of English sentences, and a preliminary paper by Gallatin presenting a classification of the languages and dialects of the Indian tribes east of the Rocky Mountains.[9] Gallatin's paper was based on an earlier effort, made in 1823 in response to a request from Alexander Humboldt, to compose a classification of the Indian languages.

This paper had been published in Europe, unbeknownst at first to Gallatin.[10] When in 1831 the American Antiquarian Society asked Gallatin for a copy of the paper, he found that he had not kept one, but he proceeded to prepare a fuller treatise, incorporating the set of vocabularies (including Jefferson's) from the American Philosophical Society, as collated by DuPonceau, along with the answers he had received from his own correspondents, a set of vocabularies of seven southern Indian languages he had personally obtained from a delegation visiting Washington in the winter of 1825–1826, and the lone Cherokee vocabulary received in response to the War Department circular. The resulting monograph earned him a reputation as "the father of American ethnology." Entitled *A Synopsis of the Indian Tribes within the United States East of the Rocky Mountains, and in the British and Russian Possessions,* it was published, in 1836, as had been Caleb Atwater's earlier pioneering study of the mound-builders, in

Archaeologia Americana, the Transactions and Collections of the American Antiquarian Society.[11]

Although Gallatin had surveyed the existing literature thoroughly and judiciously and summarized much of the reliable information on tribal locations, history, and customs, along with a valuable map, the heart of the book is its classification of the Indian languages, based on both grammar and lexicon. He recognized twenty-seven families; eight of these constituted "great families," each of which embraced a number of distinct languages, and the remaining nineteen had each only a single known representative (although some would, he predicted, later be found to belong with other families). His great families were Eskimo, Athapaskan, Blackfoot, Sioux, Algonkian, Iroquois, Cherokee, and Muskogean. Since Gallatin's time, Cherokee has been definitely recognized as Iroquoian, and Blackfoot as Algonkian. The remaining six great families have continued to be recognized as independent stocks by linguists to this day.

John Wesley Powell, Director of the Smithsonian's Bureau of American Ethnology, in his authoritative 1886 monograph *Indian Languages of America North of Mexico,* compared Gallatin's linguistic classification system to the taxonomy of Linnaeus. He paid tribute to Gallatin—and indirectly to his mentors Jefferson, Barton, DuPonceau, and Pickering—for having "thoroughly introduced comparative methods, and . . . circumscribed the boundaries of many [language] families, so that a large part of his work remains and is still considered sound."[12]

The Politicizing of Jeffersonian Ethnology

In the summer of 1820 Jedidiah Morse—at the request of President Monroe—made a tour of the United States in order to ascertain "the actual state" of the Indian tribes. This was a horseback survey, not the intimate ethnographic field work of a Volney or a Heckewelder, but it was Jeffersonian in its philosophy and, to a degree, in its recommendations. In his 1822 *Report to the Secretary of War of the United States on Indian Affairs* Morse concluded that the Native Americans, at least in the south, could be "educated where they are, raised to the rank and privileges of citizens, and merged in the mass of the nation," and he urged the government to undertake "a complete civilization of the Indians," with the aid of a benevolent consortium of clergy and government officials. Morse was a prominent New England clergyman, a national leader of the Protestant evangelical movement, and an eager proponent of Christian missions to the Indians. However sympathetic Jefferson might be with the idea of civilization, he did not approve of Morse's proposed merger of church and state in a matter of national interest—and he may have preferred removal of the Indians to reform, if "being educated where they are" implied interference with "the obtaining lands."[13]

Post-Jeffersonian ethnology rapidly became politicized by the controversy generated by Jefferson's policy of purchase, removal, and civilization, which, as Andrew Jackson later pointed out, was self-contradictory: "Professing a desire to civilize and settle them, we have, at the same time, lost no opportunity to purchase their lands, and thrust them further into the wilderness . . . The Indians, in general, receding further and further to the West, have retained their savage habits. A portion, however, of the Southern tribes, having mingled much with the whites, [have] made some progress in the arts of civilized life."[14]

The issue of the extent to which the Indians were adopting "civilization," and how rapidly they could be expected to do so in the future, tended to dominate the discussion of their current state of society. Missionary types tended to perceive Native Americans as well on the path to conversion to both Christ and the culture of Christians. In addition to Morse's *Report* advocating a crash program of "civilization," Heckewelder's *History, Manners, and Customs* ended with the cautious prediction that if the white people would obey the golden rule, peace would prevail and the Indians "might easily be brought to a state of civilization."[15]

But the kind of sympathetic image of the Indians implicit in Morse's, Heckewelder's, and Jefferson's works, and in the writings of those inspired by them, were anathema to a new breed of frontier intellectuals. Jeffersonians they might be in their professions of respect for reason and in their enthusiastic support of the settler families of the trans-Appalachian wilderness. But they were definitely not Jeffersonian in their negative attitude toward the Indians.

A leading critic of Indian sympathizers was Lewis Cass, governor of Michigan Territory from 1813 to 1831, dubbed by his biographer "the last Jeffersonian." As ex-officio territorial superintendent of Indian affairs, he was in frequent personal contact with the Indian peoples of the Ohio valley and the upper Great Lakes. From the agents whom he appointed from time to time to deal with the various tribes, he systematically collected answers to a printed questionnaire that he prepared, inquiring about

Indian languages, behavior, and beliefs. He wrote influential articles on Indian matters for the highly respected *North American Review* and, on nomination by DuPonceau and Jared Ingersoll, was elected to membership in the American Philosophical Society in 1826 in recognition of his "considerable knowledge of the habits, manners, customs, and languages of the Aborigines of this Country . . . He has collected ample materials of information on these subjects, which he is preparing for publication."[16] Although Cass never published his major work on the Indians, grateful twentieth-century anthropologists have used some of the surviving responses to his questionnaire in ethnohistorical research.

Cass's protégé Henry Rowe Schoolcraft did, however, turn out scholarly works, in spectacular fashion. Stationed as Indian agent at the remote outpost of Sault Ste. Marie in northern Michigan, Schoolcraft married a bilingual Chippewa woman, the daughter of the wealthy trading post factor John Johnston, lived with the Johnston family, and quickly undertook to learn something of the language and customs of the surrounding Chippewa community. Schoolcraft had been trained as a geologist and believed that the scientist should base his observations on an intimate "acquaintance with the country," not on "assumed premises," an attitude that Jefferson would have applauded. Although he had practical duties to perform, he came close to being the resident philosophical observer that Jefferson believed, in principle, should carry out linguistic and ethnological studies.

Schoolcraft began circulating English translations of Algonkian myths and legends as early as 1826, culminating in the celebrated *Algic Researches* in 1839. From renderings of Indian mythology, Schoolcraft went on to the collection of historical and statistical facts about the Indian tribes of the east, beginning with *Notes on the Iroquois* in 1847 and producing from 1851 to 1857, with governmental support, the elephantine six-volume *Historical and Statistical Information Respecting the History, Condition, and Prospects of the Indian Tribes of the United States.*

In the course of this career in the Indian Service and in Indian studies, Schoolcraft underwent a transformation from friendly admirer of Indian folklore and mythology to severe critic of the mentality that Indian languages and religious beliefs revealed to him. In 1831 Schoolcraft underwent a conversion experience during a religious revival that swept over northern Michigan, and thereafter resolved to dedicate his life and his ethnological work to the reclamation of the Indians from the pagan superstitions that were responsible for their slothful indifference to progress. The civilization program was doomed, a mere casting of pearls before swine, unless the Native Americans could be saved spiritually. Not surprisingly, his marriage to Jane, his Chippewa wife, deteriorated into mutual estrangement as Schoolcraft's opinions of Indians evolved into contempt. Like Cass, he concluded that removal was the proper final solution.

Cass and Schoolcraft were to a degree justified in their rebuttal of Jefferson, Morse, Heckewelder, and other eastern admirers of Indian character and language. Some of those men had not observed personally the actual conditions of life on the Indian frontier, and none of them were interested in making the study of "acculturated" Indians and the processes of ongoing, present-day culture change a part of ethnology. They wanted to preserve a record of the "authentic" native culture uncontaminated by post-contact changes. In fairness to the Jeffersonians, it must be pointed out that the study of acculturation and nativistic movements was not given academic recognition or acceptance by the American Anthropological Association until the 1930s and 40s.

But the underlying debate was about civilization versus removal, and because this was a political issue, it inevitably led the protagonists on each side to select opposing ethnological arguments to rationalize their positions. Jefferson and his peers were progressivists who thought Indians were capable of taking an upward path toward civilization; both Cass and Schoolcraft were degenerationists who saw Indians as the fallen descendants of more worthy forebears. Cass emphasized the destructive effects of the fur trade and association with the lower element of frontiersmen. Schoolcraft went further and sought to trace the course of degeneration back to the destruction of the cultures of the mound-builders, and indeed back to the Biblical deluge.[17]

The University of Virginia and Rafinesque

After committing the remains of his projects on Native American ethnology and linguistics to the American Philosophical Society, Jefferson turned his attention to the task of establishing the University of Virginia at Charlottesville. He had been designing and proposing systems of primary, secondary, and university education ever since his unsuccessful "bill for the more general diffusion of knowledge" was turned down by the Virginia legislature in 1778. As the keystone of a future three-tiered system of education in the state, the legislature in 1817 approved Jefferson's proposal for a state university, and the University of Virginia received its charter in January 1819. Jefferson served as rector and proceeded to design the celebrated architecture of the institution, based on classical models. He also started the search for faculty, hoping to attract "supereminent professors" in the various branches of learning, preferably from the United States but if necessary from European institutions such as Oxford, Cambridge, and Edinburgh.[18]

Word of the plans for the new superuniversity in Virginia traveled fast. At Transylvania University in Lexington, Kentucky (founded as early as 1783), the news inspired the professor of natural history there, Constantine Samuel Rafinesque, to write to Jefferson submitting his resume and offering his services. Rafinesque was born in Constantinople of French and German heritage, and being a seasoned, well-traveled, profusely published scholar, he was already known to Jefferson. He had originally arrived in the United States in 1802 at the age of nineteen, with a reputation as a botanist, and was introduced to the President, the secretary of war, Mr.

"The University of Virginia, at Charlottesville." Wood engraving by Henry Howe, c. 1845. Courtesy of the Prints File, Special Collections Department, University of Virginia Library.

Madison, and other worthies. He for a time had hopes of being appointed to serve as botanist on the Lewis and Clark expedition, but it and other scientific posts were never filled. He did, however, apply to Jefferson in 1804 for a position as botanist with the expedition being planned to explore the Arkansas and Red River country. Jefferson replied promptly, offering him the post, if he would be willing to serve without salary, but Rafinesque suddenly departed for Europe, without following through on an invitation to visit Monticello. After failing to receive an application from ornithologist Alexander Wilson and being turned down by the aging William Bartram, Jefferson gave the place of naturalist to a medical student of Dr. Barton's.[19]

Jefferson put off Rafinesque's application in 1819 and later ones as well on the grounds that the university, for reason of financial constraint, was not prepared to appoint faculty; such funds as were available had to go for construction. In 1822 Rafinesque wrote again, offering to donate his own library and collections (some 27,000 specimens) to the university and to create a botanical garden. Again in February 1824, hearing that the university was about to open, he put his name forward, now offering to teach, in addition to natural history, "The Ancient History of America, Archeology, Universal phonology and Philology, & c."

By this time Rafinesque was linked with Jefferson in another quest—the search for Indian origins. As far back as 1802, Rafinesque had met some American Indians and had formed the opinion that they were "of Tartar or Siberian origin." In the summer of 1804, he was introduced to the Osage delegation visiting Washington and, perhaps encouraged by Jefferson, obtained "a good vocabulary" of the Osage language from "*Pauska* or White Head their chief." If Rafinesque turned over his Osage vocabulary to Jefferson in Washington, as well he might, it apparently did not survive the loss of the western vocabularies in the accident of 1809.[20]

Some time in 1820 Rafinesque sent Jefferson "three letters on American or rather Alleghanee Antiquities." By 1821, according to his own account, he had begun to study "earnestly" the American Indians and, in order to advance his researches, had decided to master "the whole of comparative philology." By 1823 he had a large number of manuscripts in various stages of preparation for publication, which he listed as part of the bibliography sent to Jefferson in 1824 in support of his application for a chair at the University of Virginia.

In his accompanying letter Rafinesque spoke of his interest in languages and the search for origins, and promised to send Jefferson an offprint of his first extended publication on the subject, originally published in Frankfort in 1824 as the introductory chapter to H. Marshall's *History of Kentucky.*[21] The forty-three page chapter bore a modest title and a pretentious subtitle: "Ancient History, or Annals of Kentucky; with a Survey of the Ancient Monuments of North America, and a Tabular View of the Principal languages and Primitive Nations of the Whole Earth." His goal, he stated, was to understand "the filiations, migrations, and annals" of the Indian tribes, based on several kinds of evidence: physique, languages, monuments, religions, manners, histories, and traditions.

The challenging part of the paper was the catastrophic interpretation of the peopling of the Americas. Rafinesque asserted that there had been two waves of migration. First came the highly civilized Atalans from Europe and Africa westward across the Atlantic; they created the towns and fortifications whose grass-covered remains constituted the great mounds being discovered in the Mississippi and Ohio valleys and in the noble constructions of the Aztecs and Incas. Then came the Iztacans and Oghusians across the Pacific and the Bering Strait about 2,000 years ago; the Oghusians in particular included the Lenapians or Eastern Algonkians, the Iroquoians, and the Muskogheans. These savage tribes destroyed the great civilization of the Atalans and inherited their territories; the Shawnees, in particular, occupied Kentucky, whence in 1774 they were driven by the Virginians, after twenty years of resistance, their "best claim having never been attended to" in the treaties with the Iroquois and Cherokees.

Rafinesque probably based his theory of the destruction of the mound-builders' civilization on a similar account in Heckewelder's *History, Manners and Customs of the Indian Nations,* published in 1819.[22] Whether Jefferson ever read Rafinesque's "Ancient History" is uncertain, but if he did he was not likely to have been pleased with it.

Jefferson died in 1826 and would not see the flowering of investigation into the culture of the mound-builders, the political use of the catastrophic theory of their destruction by President Jackson to justify Indian removal, the sacralization of the catastrophic history by Joseph Smith and the Mormons, or the passage of Rafinesque's papers—including his notes on the Walam Olum, the supposed legend of migration across the Bering Strait fabricated by Rafinesque himself—into the hands of Jefferson's enemy, Brantz Mayer, the critic of Jefferson's account in the *Notes* of the murder of Logan by Michael Cresap. But Jefferson would probably have been amused by the curious twists of scholarship set in motion by Rafinesque's abuse of linguistic and archaeological evidence in fabricating his story of the Walam Olum and the demise of the mound-builders.

Debate continued over the identity of the mound-builders, their fate, and their relationship to the Indians occupying the land when the Europeans arrived. Some resolution was achieved in 1894 with the publication of Cyrus Thomas's 730-page *Report on the Mound Explorations of the Bureau of Ethnology,* based on exhaustive review of the literature and examination of the mounds. Thomas was a respected scientist, head of the Bureau of American Ethnology, and a former believer in the theory that the mound-builders were a people of higher culture and of an origin different from the historic tribes. His conclusion, as expressed in a brief summary article in the *Handbook of American Indians North of Mexico* (1912), was that romantic theories of lost civilizations were erroneous.

Thomas wrote: "The articles found in the mounds and the character of the various monuments indicate a culture stage much the same as that of the more advanced tribes found inhabiting the region at the advent of the whites . . . The conclusion, reached chiefly through the investigations of the Bureau of American Ethnology, and now generally accepted, is that the Mound builders were the ancestors of the Indians found inhabiting the same region by the first European explorers."[23] Specifically, he attributed the mounds of the Ohio valley to the Cherokees and Shawnees and pointed out that some of the southern Indians were still actively building mounds and using them for ceremonial purposes when DeSoto marched through the southeast in the middle of the sixteenth century. Jefferson would have been glad to see the mound-builders' technology recognized as compatible with that of the Indian nations known to him, and he would have been pleased to see his methods of patient, methodical, cross-sectional analysis employed so productively a hundred years after his own dissection of a small Virginia burial mound.

There has, of course, been much research since Thomas's time. The time-span during which mounds were build has been extended back to about 3000 B.C.; periods of decline and renascence have been identified; different stylistic traditions have been recognized. And awareness has grown that the building and support of these great earthworks required a larger and more secure agricultural population than that found by the early explorers, a population that maintained, for hundreds of years at a time, a stable, complex social order. As Jefferson came to realize in his philosophical years of retirement, there had indeed been a classical antiquity in Virginia before Jamestown, an antiquity now being discovered by archaeologists. Not only would Logan be remembered, but so would his more civilized forebears.

Jefferson expressed his satisfaction with this realization in a letter to Isaiah Thomas, president of the American Antiquarian Society, in 1820. Thanking him for sending a copy of Atwater's *Archaeologia Americana,* which first provided exact measurements of mounds and other earthworks, Jefferson wrote: "It is truly pleasing to hope that, by [the American Antiquarian Society's] attention, the monuments of the character and condition of the people who preceded us in the occupation of this great country will be rescued from oblivion before they will have entirely disappeared."[24]

To the end, Jefferson retained his vision of the tragic fate of the First Americans, as a scattered remnant retreating westward, leaving behind the graves of their ancestors and the monumental remains of their former civilizations—and vacant lands.

CONCLUSION

Jefferson's Troubled Legacy

After Jefferson left office in 1809, his immediate successors in the presidency kept in place not only most of the values and administrative apparatus that he had helped to create but also several of the original executors of his policies. North of the Ohio River, William Henry Harrison continued as governor of Indiana Territory and superintendent of Indian Affairs. In 1811 his militia launched a pre-emptive strike against the Shawnee Prophet's village at Tippecanoe while Tecumseh was absent in the south recruiting followers among the Creeks. In the ensuing war, Harrison, as commanding general of American forces in the northwest, was responsible for driving the British army and their Indian allies from Detroit and killing Tecumseh during the British retreat.

Following the war, Harrison negotiated several cessions of land in Indiana and Illinois. Thereafter, he rose rapidly in the political world, serving several terms in Congress and eventually being nominated for the presidency. His successful campaign in 1840 with John Tyler under the banner "Tippecanoe and Tyler Too" appealed to the expansionist sentiments of the frontier. He was elected President, only to die after a month in office.

Also north of the Ohio, in Michigan Territory, Lewis Cass held sway after the War of 1812 as governor and Indian superintendent for eighteen years. After Congress passed the Removal Act in 1830, then-President Andrew Jackson appointed Cass secretary of war, and in that capacity he arranged coercive treaties of cession and supervised the transport of tens of thousands of unwilling Indians, mostly of the southern states' Five Civilized Tribes, west of the Mississippi. Thousands died on what came to be called the Trail of Tears. His administration also saw the onset of the bloody Seminole War, a long and frustrating tropical conflict comparable to the American experience in Vietnam.

In the South, Andrew Jackson—Jefferson's old correspondent on Indian affairs—gained his initial fame as a hero of the War of 1812 by defeating the Creeks in a bloody campaign. After the war, as treaty commissioner, he extorted from the Creeks the large tracts of land that Jefferson's agent, Benjamin Hawkins, had been unable (or, as Jackson charged, unwilling) to obtain. He accepted the Jeffersonian premise of the doom of the red race, and indeed considered it inevitable—and morally justifiable, in view of his belief that the ancestors of the present-day Indians had slaughtered the mound-builders.

West of the Mississippi, Jefferson's old ally from Albemarle County, William Clark, remained in place as superintendent of Indian affairs of Louisiana Territory until he was appointed governor in 1813. He served as

"Prairie Meadows Burning." Oil on canvas by George Catlin, 1832. Courtesy of the National Museum of American Art, Washington, DC / Art Resource, NY.

governor until 1821, when he returned to the office of Indian superintendent, which he filled until his death in 1838. He amassed the best collection of Indian artifacts west of Monticello. Clark and Cass were the principal advisors in designing the new federal Bureau of Indian Affairs, which Congress established in 1834. And both Clark and Cass were involved in the suppression of a small band of Sac Indians in the Black Hawk War of 1832, which grew out of grievances created by the Sac and Fox Treaty of 1804. Black Hawk's band, attacked by militia while trespassing on ceded land in Wisconsin and then trying to escape across the Mississippi, were massacred by federal troops firing from steamboats. Following the Black Hawk War, the Sac and Fox were required to cede a substantial territory as indemnity for the expenses of the U.S. military, even though the Sac nation as a whole had not supported Black Hawk. The long shadow of Jefferson's policy of "obtaining lands" after "exterminating" the hostiles moved ever westward.

But despite the Jeffersonians' funereal vision of the inevitable demise of the First American cultures and the assimilation of the survivors into a pan-continental Anglo-Saxon civilization, native resistance has never ceased. While many Native Americans have indeed entered the mainstream, at least insofar as education and occupation are concerned, the old ways have been preserved in many reservation communities, where some of the traditional values, patterns of kinship and social relations, religion, and language still flourish. Politically adroit native leaders have for generations managed to negotiate accommodation with white authorities in a style reminiscent of the Indian chiefs whose eloquence and wisdom Jefferson so much admired.

Nevertheless, much has been lost. The Indian population of the Americas has been reduced, according to some authorities, to 5 percent of what it was in pre-Columbian times, and in the United States the Indian reservations are notorious for high levels of unemployment, alcohol and drug abuse, and other social problems. The reservation world is the direct consequence of a general policy, maintained throughout the nineteenth century, of relentlessly removing Indians to ever-shrinking isolated enclaves, often far from their ancestral homelands. Jefferson was not alone in formulating this policy, but he made it central to the federal system and, by mourning the passing of the Indians into oblivion or civilized invisibility, gave moral justification to the seizure of lands he said they no longer needed.

Could the United States have undertaken another policy? Could there have been indefinitely maintained a vast reserve, protected from encroachment, where Indians could perpetuate a kind of middle ground, a cultural mix of fur trade, agriculture, and syncretic institutions and values? This was the proposal of the Western Confederacy of the Ohio valley and Great Lakes tribes in the 1780s and 90s. Jefferson himself envisioned such a future, temporary to be sure, in his original plan for Louisiana Territory. Andrew Jackson's conception of an Indian Territory west of the Mississippi had elements of such an idea. But the process of encroachment, followed by war, followed by land cession, never ceased. Politically, given the state of public sentiment among whites and the reluctance of government to spend money or shed blood to police the boundaries, a policy of Indian land preservation was impossible. And as justification of the United States' commitment to expansionism, Jefferson and Madison helped to establish the belief in the redeemer nation's manifest destiny to move westward.

This problem is not just an American one. The sharing of spaces among different ethnic groups is a difficult value to instill in a national ethos. The holocausts, the ethnic cleansing, the pushing aside of native populations, the racial and religious wars of the twentieth century are the global product of the same kind of moral dilemma that bedeviled white Americans in Jefferson's time: in their case, what ultimately to do about the presence of black slaves and free Indians. Jefferson resolved this problem, in his own mind, by favoring the separation, or elimination, of disparate ethnic groups—Indians and blacks—who refused to disappear through civilization and assimilation, or were, in his view, incapable of participating as citizens in the republic. Too many national leaders of the twentieth century have also sought such final solutions.

But in building a nation, the challenge is not to enforce uniformity but to orchestrate diversity. In the Federalist Papers, James Madison and colleagues, with Jefferson's support, recommended a constitution that provided for institutions capable of combining the varied economic and political interests of the several states into a federal union. Would that Jefferson and Madison had also applied their considerable intellectual powers to the writing of a second set of Federalist Papers, one that devised institutions capable of weaving together the strands of ethnic diversity in the republic, instead of pulling them apart.

Notes

Acknowledgments

List of Illustrations

List of Documents

Index

Notes

A Note on Principal Sources

Much of the research for this book was done at the Library of the American Philosophical Society, which owns a collection of Jefferson manuscripts and holds microfilm copies of the major Jefferson collections at the Library of Congress, the University of Virginia, the Massachusetts Historical Society, and the Huntington Library. The American Philosophical Society also maintains an excellent collection of works by Jefferson's contemporaries and many of the more recent secondary sources about Jefferson and his time.

Published primary documents that have been indispensable in this research and have been repeatedly cited in the references include: *American State Papers, Indian Affairs,* vol. 1 (Washington: Gales and Seaton, 1832), hereafter cited as ASPIA; Albert E. Bergh, ed., *The Writings of Thomas Jefferson* (Washington: Thomas Jefferson Memorial Association, 1907–), hereafter cited as Bergh, *Writings;* Julian P. Boyd et al., eds., *The Papers of Thomas Jefferson* (Princeton: Princeton University Press, 1950–), hereafter cited as Boyd, *Papers;* William Peden, ed., *Notes on the State of Virginia, by Thomas Jefferson* (New York: Norton, 1972), hereafter cited as Peden, *Notes*; Merrill Peterson, ed., *Thomas Jefferson: Writings* (New York: Library of America, 1984), hereafter cited as Peterson, *Writings;* James Richardson, ed., *A Compilation of the Messages and Papers of the Presidents,* vol. 1 (New York: Bureau of National Literature, 1897), hereafter cited as Richardson, *Messages.*

Of special value in discussions of Native American history and culture are three secondary sources: Frederick W. Hodge, ed., *Handbook of American Indians North of Mexico,* Bulletin 30, Bureau of American Ethnology (Washington: Government Printing Office, 1912), hereafter cited as Bulletin 30; Charles C. Royce, *Indian Land Cessions in the United States,* 18th Annual Report of the Bureau of American Ethnology, 1896–97 (Washington: Government Printing Office, 1899), hereafter cited as Royce, *Land Cessions;* William C. Sturtevant, ed., *Handbook of North American Indians,* vol. 15, *Northeast,* ed. Bruce Trigger (Washington: Smithsonian Institution, 1878), hereafter cited as Sturtevant, *Handbook.*

The most useful biographies of Jefferson have been Fawn M. Brodie, *Thomas Jefferson: An Intimate Biography* (New York: Norton, 1974), hereafter cited as Brodie, *Jefferson;* Dumas Malone, *Jefferson and His Time,* 6 vols. (Boston: Little, Brown, 1948–1977), hereafter cited as Malone, *Jefferson;* Merrill Peterson, *Thomas Jefferson & the New Nation* (New York: Oxford University Press, 1970), hereafter cited as Peterson, *Jefferson;* and Joseph Ellis, *American Sphinx: The Character of Thomas Jefferson* (New York: Knopf, 1997), hereafter cited as Ellis, *American Sphinx.*

Abbreviations

APS:	American Philosophical Society
ASPIA:	*American State Papers, Indian Affairs*
DAB:	*Dictionary of American Biography*
LOC:	Library of Congress
TJ:	Thomas Jefferson

Introduction: Logan's Mourner

1. Peden, *Notes,* p. 63.
2. Ibid., p. 62.
3. I am indebted to Robert Grumet for advising me of the existence of this monument.
4. Brantz Mayer, *Tah-gah-jute; or Logan and Cresap: An Historical Essay* (Albany: Munsell, 1867), p. iii.
5. The literary tradition of celebrating the noble but doomed savage, so well represented by Jefferson's story of Logan, has been described in Harvey Pearce, *The Savages of America: A Study of the Indian and the Idea of Civilization* (Baltimore: Johns Hopkins Press, 1953), and Alfred I. Hallowell, "The Impact of the American Indian in American Culture," in *Contributions to Anthropology: Selected Papers of A. Irving Hallowell* (Chicago: University of Chicago Press, 1957), pp. 481–497.
6. The anthropologist Raymond Fogelson introduced and discussed the concept of the "epitomizing event" in his paper "The Ethnohistory of Events and Non-Events," *Ethnohistory* 36 (1989): 135–137. He suggests restricting the use

of the phrase "epitomizing event" to fictional or mythical narratives. I have chosen to use this useful expression to refer as well to real events that have assumed importance to a community.

7. Peden, *Notes,* pp. 62–63.
8. I. D. Rupp, *Early History of Western Pennsylvania* (Lewisburg, Pa.: Wennawoods Publishing, 1995), Appendix, pp. 213–217.
9. The *Virginia Gazette* version of Logan's speech appeared in the February 4, 1775, issue (on microfilm at APS). Jefferson's account of how he became aware of the speech is found in Peden, *Notes,* pp. 226–229, and Peden discusses Jefferson's somewhat confused account of its provenance in a series of footnotes. James Madison seems to have been the first to record the speech in manuscript and to see to its publication in Bradford's *Pennsylvania Gazette* in the issue of Janurary 20, 1775. See Irving Brant, *James Madison: Virginia Revolutionist* (New York: Bobbs Merrill, 1941), pp. 281–291, and William T. Hutchinson and William M. E. Rachal, *The Papers of James Madison*, vol. 1 (Chicago: University of Chicago Press, 1962), p. 136, for the text of the Madison version. There are substantial differences in language between the Jefferson version and the *Virginia Gazette* version; Jefferson clearly was using the *Pennsylvania Gazette* text. How Madison acquired his text and how Jefferson, some time before writing the *Notes,* came into possession of a copy of it may never be known. Although they were not personal friends in 1774–75, Madison came to be close to Jefferson when he served on the Governor's Council in 1779–1781 and may have given him a copy then.
10. Peden, *Notes,* p. 253.
11. Ibid., p. 232.
12. Which of Shikellamy's sons was Logan the orator has been a matter of dispute. Logan and Shikellamy are subjects in DAB and Bulletin 30. For further biographical information see also: Paul A. W. Wallace, *Conrad Weiser, Friend of Colonist and Mohawk* (Philadelphia: University of Pennsylvania Press, 1945); Paul A. W. Wallace, *Indians in Pennsylvania* (Harrisburg: Pennsylvania Historical and Museum Commission, 1961); and James Merrell, "Shikellamy, A Person of Consequence," in Robert Grumet, ed., *Northeastern Indian Lives, 1632–1816* (Amherst: University of Massachusetts Press, 1996), pp. 227–257. Mayer, *Tah-gah-jute*, confuses James with John Logan (Tachnedorus). I am indebted to Ronald Wenning for sharing with me his essay, "Logan: Chief of the Mingoes." Logan is refered to in numerous secondary works on the history of central and western Pennsylvania.
13. Mayer, *Tah-gah-jute.* Brant, *James Madison,* discusses Mayer's handling of Clark's letter. See also Peden's comments in *Notes,* pp. 298–301.
14. Paul A. W. Wallace, ed., *Travels of John Heckewelder in Frontier America* (Pittsburgh: University of Pittsburgh Press, 1985), pp. 118–119.

15. Clark's letter was published in Mayer, *Tah-gah-jute,* pp. 149–156.
16. See Thomas P. Abernethy, *Western Lands and the American Revolution* (New York: Russell & Russell, 1959), pp. 113–115.
17. TJ, "A Summary View," in Peterson, *Writings,* p. 106.
18. Brant, *Madison,* p. 288.
19. Lord Dunmore's War and its antecedents and consequences have been dealt with in a number of sources. Primary documents from the Draper Collection at the Wisconsin Historical Society are available in Reuben G. Thwaites and Louise P. Kellogg, eds., *A Documentary History of Lord Dunmore's War, 1774* (Madison: Wisconsin Historical Society, 1905). Excellent secondary accounts are given in Randolph C. Downes, *Council Fires on the Upper Ohio* (Pittsburgh: University of Pittsburgh Press, 1940), Abernethy, *Western Lands,* and Richard White, *The Middle Ground: Indians, Empires, and Republics in the Great Lakes Region, 1650–1815* (Cambridge: Cambridge University Press, 1991).
20. J. Todd to TJ, January 24, 1781, in Boyd, *Papers,* vol. 1, p. 442.
21. Heckewelder's "Declaration" in Peden, *Notes,* pp. 249–250.
22. Donald H. Kent and Merle H. Deardorf, eds., "John Adlum on the Allegheny: Memoir for the Year 1794," *Pennsylvania Magazine of History and Biography,* vol. 84 (1960), pp. 471–472.
23. Jefferson's biographers, particularly Brodie, have described various aspects of his style of domestic and official behavior. Margaret Smith, *The First Forty Years of Washington Society* (New York: Scribner's, 1906), sketches Jefferson's social manner, his dinner parties, his purging of Federalists, and quotes his comment on the cabinet as "one family." Harold Levy, *Jefferson and Civil Liberties* (Cambridge: Harvard University Press, 1963), examines the "dark side" of Jefferson's urge to control.
24. Smith, *First Forty Years,* pp. 10–12
25. Levy, *Jefferson and Civil Liberties.*
26. TJ to Short, January 3, 1793, in Peterson, *Writings,* p. 1004.
27. TJ to William Smith, November 13, 1787, ibid., p. 911.
28. Robert W. Tucker and David C. Hendrickson, *Empire of Liberty: The Statecraft of Thomas Jefferson* (New York: Oxford University Press, 1990), p. 250.
29. TJ to James Monroe, November 24, 1801, ibid., p. 1097.
30. Wilcomb E. Washburn, *The American Indian and the United States: A Documentary History* (New York: Random House, 1973), vol. 4, p. 2556 (in Cherokee Nation vs. the State of Georgia, 1831).

1. The Land Companies

1. See Malone, *Jefferson,* vol. 1, Appendix 2, for a review of the bequests of land from Peter Jefferson. John Alden, "Imaging the West," in James Ronda, ed., *Thomas Jefferson and the Changing West: From Conquest to Conservation* (St.

Louis and Albuquerque: Missouri Historical Society and University of New Mexico Press, 1997), p. 21 fn.9, mentions a bequest to Jefferson by his father of some land "on the Mississippi," size and location unspecified; this tract is not refered to in other Jefferson papers. His own western investments are recorded in James A. Bear, Jr., and Lucia C. Stanton, eds., *Jefferson's Memorandum Books: Accounts, with Legal Records and Miscellany, 1767–1826,* in Boyd, *Papers.* None of his western lands are listed in the Land Roll for 1794; see Henry S. Randall, *The Life of Thomas Jefferson* (New York: 1858), vol. 2, pp. 237–238.

2. Peterson, *Writings,* p. 106.
3. Ibid., pp. 119–120.
4. Ibid., p. 343.
5. Ibid., p. 96.
6. Ibid., p. 281.
7. Ibid., pp. 135–136.
8. See, Helen C. Rountree, *Pocahontas's People: The Powhatan Indians of Virginia through Four Centuries* (Norman: University of Oklahoma Press, 1990), for an analysis of the changing methods by which Virginia colony acquired Indian land.
9. Evans, "Analysis of a General Map of the British Colonies," in Lawrence Henry Gipson, *Lewis Evans* (Philadelphia: Historical Society of Pennsylvania, 1939), p. 156.
10. E. B. O'Callaghan, ed., *Documents Relating to the Colonial History of the State of New York,* vol. 5 (Albany: Weed, Parsons, 1855), pp. 669–677.
11. Wallace, *Weiser,* p. 167.
12. There were several closely similar versions of the minutes of the Lancaster Treaty published shortly after the event. The first was Benjamin Franklin's; it has been reprinted in facsimile along with other Indian treaties printed by Franklin 1736–1762 with a valuable introduction by Boyd in Julian P. Boyd, ed., *Indian Treaties Printed by Benjamin Franklin* (Philadelphia: Historical Society of Pennsylvania, 1938), pp. 41–79. A virtually identical version was issued in Williamsburg, together with an ethnographic essay by Weiser on the Six Nations and other corollary documents (including a specification of the route of the Warriors' Road and the form of the passes to be issued to Indian travelers); see APS microfilm. The minutes were also printed in *Minutes of the Provincial Council of Pennsylvania,* vol. 4, pp. 698–737. Wallace, *Weiser,* gives an account of the proceedings.
13. Excerpts from this correspondence are published in Wallace, *Weiser,* pp. 197–205.
14. Peden, *Notes,* p. 195.
15. Wallace, *Weiser,* p. 350.
16. The affairs of the Ohio Company have long been a subject of scholarly

interest. Two standard works are Kenneth P. Bailey, *The Ohio Company of Virginia and the Westward Movement 1748–1792* (Glendale: Arthur H. Clark, 1939), and Alfred P. James, *The Ohio Company: Its Inner History* (Pittsburgh: University of Pittsburgh Press, 1959). Lois Mulkearn, ed., *George Mercer Papers Relating to the Ohio Company of Virginia* (Pittsburgh: University of Pittsburgh Press, 1954), publishes much primary material and supplies an excellent commentary and annotations.

17. Mulkearn, *George Mercer Papers,* pp. 250–251.
18. The list of Loyal Company members is in Mulkearn, *George Mercer Papers,* pp. 250–251. Archibald Henderson, "Dr. Thomas Walker and the Loyal Company of Virginia," *Proceedings of the American Antiquarian Society,* n.s. 41 (1932): 177–178, provides a general history of the company and its members. See also Susan De Alba, *Albemarle County, Virginia* (Natural Bridge Station, Va.: Rockbridge, 1993).
19. Fry's life is chronicled in Phillip Slaughter, *Memoir of Col. Joshua Fry,* n.p., 1880.
20. Fry and Jefferson's map has been reproduced in facsimile by the University of Virginia Press.
21. James Maury's letter is quoted in Ann Maury, ed., *Memoirs of a Huguenot Family* (New York: Putnam, 1907), p. 391. The ambitions of the Albemarle group are discussed in John Allen's classic *Lewis and Clark and the Image of the American Northwest* (New York: Dover, 1991, a republication of the 1975 *Passage through the Garden*).
22. For the interaction between attempts at settlement in the Ohio valley and the French and Indian War, see Bailey, *Ohio Company,* and especially Randolph C. Downes, *Council Fires on the Upper Ohio* (Pittsburgh: University of Pittsburgh Press, 1940).
23. See Clarence E. Alvord, *The Mississippi Valley in British Politics* (New York: Russell and Russell, 1959), for a review of the English situation, and Thomas P. Abernethy, *Western Lands and the American Revolution* (New York: Russell & Russell, 1959), for a complementary analysis of the American scene.
24. The text of the Proclamation of 1763 is printed in Wilcomb E. Washburn, ed., *The American Indian and the United States: A Documentary History,* vol. 3 (New York: Random House, 1973), pp. 2135–2139.
25. The 1768 Fort Stanwix treaty and the events leading up to it are analyzed in Downes, *Council Fires,* and Abernethy, *Western Lands.*
26. Bear and Stanton, *Memorandum Books,* entry of February 18, 1769; Palmer, *Calendar of Virginia State Papers,* vol. 1, p. 262.
27. Peden, *Notes,* pp. 14–14.
28. Bear and Stanton, *Memorandum Books,* entries of March 22 and June 23, 1769. Robert D. Meade, *Patrick Henry: Patriot in the Making* (Philadelphia: Lippincott, 1957), p. 236, mentions the Kanawha petition.

29. Hugh Cleland, *George Washington in the Ohio Valley* (Pittsburgh: University of Pittsburgh Press, 1955), pp. 233–269.
30. The 1745 grant of Lewis et al. is listed in Mulkearn, *George Mercer Papers,* p. 248.
31. Bear and Stanton, *Memorandum Books,* December 29, 1771.
32. These transactions with Dr. Walker are recorded in the Huntington Library's copy of Jefferson's Account Book, "Personal Stock for Lands and Slaves sold," undated, following an entry of January 29, 1778. The information was kindly provided by Lucia Stanton.
33. Bear and Stanton, *Memorandum Books,* entry of November 29, 1773. See also Malone, *Jefferson,* vol. 1, pp. 430–431, for pertinent genealogical information.
34. *Memorandum Books,* entry of February 22, 1777.
35. Boyd, *Papers,* vol. 7, p. 503.
36. See Huntington Library, Jefferson's Account Book, Land and Slaves sold.
37. The Watauga settlements are described in William S. Lester, *The Transylvania Colony* (Spencer, Ind.: Samuel R. Guard, 1935), Samuel Cole Williams, *The Lost State of Franklin* (Philadelphia: Porcupine Press, 1974), and Abernethy, *Western Lands.*
38. Abernethy, *Western Lands,* pp. 44–46 and passim. For detailed descriptions of the various major land company schemes, see Mulkearn, *George Mercer Papers,* pp. 668–670.
39. For an account of the Transylvania Company's rise and fall see Lester, *The Transylvania Company.*
40. Jefferson, "Draft Constitution for Virginia," in Peterson, *Writings,* p. 343.
41. E. Woods, *Albemarle County in Virginia* (Charlottesville: Michi Company, 1901), pp. 224–225, identifies Jefferson's appointee as John Harvie, probably a relative of his old guardian.
42. Peterson, *Jefferson,* pp. 120–122, reviews Jefferson's efforts in the Assembly from 1776–1779 to clear up the land grant chaos and to settle the Transylvania claim.
43. Lester, *Transylvania Company,* p. 47, quoting from the Draper MSS.
44. Alvord, *Mississippi Valley,* vol. 2, pp. 109, 115.
45. Peterson, *Writings,* pp. 786–789.
46. Boyd, *Papers,* vol. 7, pp. 503–504.

2. The Indian Wars

1. Louis K. Koontz, *The Virginia Frontier, 1754–1763* (Baltimore: Johns Hopkins Press, 1925), contains much detail on the forts built to protect the colony, and their fate, and on the war with the Cherokees, in the French and Indian War and Pontiac's Rebellion. See also James Mooney, *Myths of the Cherokees,* Nineteenth Annual Report, Bureau of American Ethnography, part I (Washing-

ton, 1900); R. S. Cotterill, *The Southern Indians: The Story of the Civilized Tribes before Removal* (Norman: University of Oklahoma Press, 1954); Randolph C. Downes, *Council Fires on the Upper Ohio* (Pittsburgh: University of Pittsburgh Press, 1940); Fred Gearing, *Priests and Warriors: Social Structures for Cherokee Politics in the 18th Century* (American Anthropological Association, Memoir 93, 1962); and Grace S. Woodward, *The Cherokees* (Norman: University of Oklahoma Press, 1963), for accounts of Virginia's military engagements with the Indians in the 1750's and 1760's.

2. Ann Maury, ed., *Memoirs of a Huguenot Family* (New York: Putnam, 1907), pp. 434–436
3. Peterson, *Writings,* p. 14.
4. Bergh, *Writings,* vol. 13, p. 160 (TJ to Adams, June 11, 1812). General biographical information on Outacite ("Outacity") may be found in DAB.
5. There are numerous accounts of Lord Dunmore's War in secondary sources, including Thomas P. Abernethy, *Western Lands and the American Revolution* (New York: Russell & Russell, 1959), pp. 105–115, and Downes, *Council Fires,* pp. 152–178. Reuben G. Thwaites and Louise P. Kellogg, eds., *Documentary History of Dunmore's War, 1774* (Madison: Wisconsin Historical Society, 1905), presents a collection of primary documents from the Draper Collection.
6. Abernethy, *Western Lands,* pp. 114–115; Woody Holton, "The Ohio Indians and the Coming of the American Revolution in Virginia," *Journal of Southern History* 60 (1994): 453–478.
7. APS, microfilm of Purdie's *Virginia Gazette,* August 4, 1775.
8. P. M. Hamer, "John Stuart's Indian Policy during the Early Months of the American Revolution," *Mississippi Valley Historical Review* 17 (1930): 351–367, gives details on Stuart's actual conduct in 1775–76. See also John R. Alden, *John Stuart and the Southern Colonial Frontier* (Ann Arbor: University of Michigan Press, 1944), for a general study of Stuart's career.
9. Boyd, *Papers,* vol. 1, pp. 210–211, 217.
10. Hamer, "John Stuart's Indian Policy," p. 365.
11. Peterson, *Writings,* pp. 21–22.
12. Ibid., p. 337.
13. Eric Foner, ed., *Thomas Paine: Collected Writings* (New York: Library of America, 1995), p. 35, and Alfred O. Aldridge, *Thomas Paine's American Ideology* (Newark: University of Delaware Press, 1984), p. 222.
14. Anthony M. Lewis, "Jefferson and Virginia's Pioneers," *Mississippi Valley Historical Review* 34 (1948): 569.
15. See Mooney, *Myths of the Cherokees,* and Woodward, *Cherokees,* pp. 90–97, for general accounts (the latter occasionally marred by inaccuracies) of the early days of the second Cherokee War.
16. Bergh, *Writings,* vol. 18, p. 141.
17. Quoted in Woodward, *Cherokees,* p. 99.

18. Mooney, *Myths of the Cherokees,* and Woodward, *Cherokees,* pp. 97–102, provide general accounts of the struggle between the Chickamauga Cherokees and the states of Virginia and North Carolina. See also Cotterill, *Southern Indians,* pp. 47–53.
19. Peterson, *Thomas Jefferson,* p. 193.
20. Boyd, *Papers,* vol. 3, pp. 447–449.
21. Ibid., vol. 4, pp. 447–449.
22. Ibid., vol. 5, pp. 359–363.
23. Ibid., vol. 5, pp. 436–439, 534–537.
24. Downes, *Council Fires,* p. 182.
25. Boyd, *Papers,* vol. 1, pp. 244–245.
26. See accounts of the treaty of Fort Pitt in Downes, *Council Fires,* pp. 183–186, and Abernethy, *Western Lands,* pp. 141–143.
27. See Downes, *Council Fires,* pp. 191–207, for an account of border warfare between Virginia and the Ohio Indians in 1777.
28. Clark's successful Illinois campaign in 1777 and 1778 has been described in detail by many historians. See Downes, *Council Fires,* chap. 10, pp. 228–250, and Abernethy, *Western Lands,* chap. 15, pp. 193–204.
29. Boyd, *Papers,* vol. 2, pp. 132–133.
30. See C. A. Weslager, *The Delaware Indians: A History* (New Brunswick: Rutgers University Press, 1972), pp. 313–317, for an account of the massacre at Gnadenhuütten.
31. Cotterill, *Southern Indians,* pp. 49–50.
32. John D. Barnhart, *Henry Hamilton and George Rogers Clark in the American Revolution* (Crawfordsville, Ind.: 1951), p. 189; Lewis, "Jefferson and Virginia's Pioneers," pp. 577–578; Holton, "The Ohio Indians." Richard S. White, *The Middle Ground* (Cambridge: Cambridge University Press, 1991), also discusses the atrocities perpetrated during Clark's campaign.
33. White, *The Middle Ground,* p. 384.
34. Ibid., p. 407.
35. Quoted in White, *The Middle Ground,* pp. 376–377.
36. Malone, *Jefferson,* vol. 1, pp. 308–312, provides an extended account of Jefferson's treatment of Hamilton.
37. Quoted in Malone, *Jefferson,* vol. 1, p. 293.
38. Boyd, *Papers,* vol. 3, pp. 44–49.
39. Ibid., vol. 3, p. 46.
40. Ibid., vol. 3, pp. 46–47.
41. Quoted in Peterson, *Thomas Jefferson,* p. 179.
42. APS, Readex Microprint edition of Early American Imprints.
43. John Filson, *The Discovery, Settlement and Present State of Kentucky* (Wilmington, Del.: James Adams, 1784), p. 64.
44. Downes, *Council Fires,* p. 191, and Peterson, *Thomas Jefferson,* p. 179.

45. Peden, *Notes,* pp. 104–106.
46. Boyd, *Papers,* vol. 4, pp. 413–414.
47. Peterson, *Thomas Jefferson,* p. 219.
48. Ibid., p. 238.
49. Jefferson's reply to du Coigne, along with useful editorial commentary, is in Boyd, *Papers,* vol. 6, pp. 60–64.

3. Notes on the Vanishing Aborigines

1. Boyd, *Papers,* vol. 6, pp. 139, 159–170.
2. Peden, *Notes,* p. 43.
3. Jefferson's celebrated defense of the Native Americans, and his notorious denigration of blacks, are to be found in Peden's edition of *Notes,* pp. 58–64, 138–143.
4. Peterson, *Writings,* p. 801, TJ to Chastellux, June 7, 1785.
5. Bergh, *Writings,* vol. 9, p. 363.
6. Peden, *Notes,* pp. 138–143.
7. Ibid., pp. 138–143, 162–163.
8. Ibid., p. 101.
9. Peden, *Notes,* pp. 96–97.
10. Smith's writings and his map, first published in 1612, have been republished in several editions. A one-volume edition is Karen O. Kupperman, ed., *Captain John Smith: A Select Edition of His Writings* (Chapel Hill: University of North Carolina Press, 1988). Jefferson knew at least one of Smith's works, *The Generall Historie* of *Virginia, New-England, and the Summer Isles* (London, 1624), and refered to it as a principal source in the *Notes,* p. 177. The watercolors of John White, one of the earlier settlers at Raleigh's colony of Roanoke, were presented as woodcuts in Theodore DeBry's *Report* (Frankfurt, 1590) but were not reproduced in color until 1964. Jefferson does not mention DeBry in the bibliography in *Notes,* and it is not listed as part of his library in E. Millicent Sowerby, *Catalogue of the Library of Thomas Jefferson* (Washington: Library of Congress, 1952–1958).
11. Ibid., p. 93.
12. Ibid., p. 95.
13. Louis B. Wright, ed., *History and Present State of Virginia, by Robert Beverly* (Chapel Hill: University of North Carolina Press, 1947), p. 232.
14. William K. Boyd, ed., *William Byrd's Histories of the Dividing Line Betwixt Virginia and North Carolina* (Raleigh: North Carolina Historical Commission, 1929), p. 4.
15. Peden, *Notes,* p. 96.
16. James Mooney, "Powhatan," in Bulletin 30.

17. Christian T. Feast, "Virginia Algonquians," in Sturtevant, *Handbook,* vol. 15, pp. 253–270.
18. The most comprehensive and detailed accounts of Powhatan culture and history are Helen C. Rountree, *Pocahontas's People: The Powhatan Indians of Virginia Through Four Centuries* and *The Powhatan Indians of Virginia* (Norman: University of Oklahoma Press, 1989). See also Robert S. Grumet, *Historic Contact: Indian People and Colonists in Today's Northeastern United States in the Seventeenth Through Eighteenth Centuries* (Norman: University of Oklahoma Press, 1995).
19. For surveys of the ethnohistory of the Piedmont, see Jeffrey L. Hantman, "Between Powhatan and Quirank: Reconstructing Monacan Culture and History in the Context of Jamestown," *American Anthropologist* 92 (1990): 684; Jeffrey L. Hantman, "Powhatan's Relations with the Piedmont Monacans," in Helen C. Rountree, ed., *Powhatan's Foreign Relations 1500–1772* (Charlottesville: University Press of Virginia, 1993), pp. 94–111; Jeffrey L. Hantman and Gary Dunham, "The Enlightened Archaeologist," *Archaeology,* May/June 1993, pp. 44–49; and David J. Bushnell, Jr., "Virginia before Jamestown," in *Essays in Historical Anthropology in North America* (Washington: Smithsonian Miscellaneous Collections, vol. 100, 1940), p. 144.
20. Boyd, *William Byrd's Histories of the Dividing Line,* pp. 98–102, 308–310. See also Hantman's forthcoming book on the Monacans.
21. APS, Records of the Historical and Literary Committee, TJ to DuPonceau, November 7, 1817.
22. See, for example, Knights and Cummings' edition of the *Discoveries* of John Lederer, a late seventeenth-century traveler through Piedmont Siouan country. Douglas L. Knights and William P. Cummings, eds., *The Discoveries of John Lederer* (Charlottesville: University Press of Virginia, 1958).
23. Peden, *Notes,* pp. 94–95.
24. Ibid., pp. 92, 97, 101.
25. Horatio Hale, "The Tutelo Tribe and Language," *Proceedings of the American Philosophical Society* 21 (1883): 9–11.
26. Peden, *Notes,* p. 101.
27. Ibid., p. 100.
28. Ibid., pp. 98–100.
29. Mooney in *Siouan Tribes of the East* took up Hale's suggestion of an eastern origin for the western Siouans. Frank Speck, *The Tutelo Spirit Adoption Ceremony,* (Harrisburg: Pennsylvania Historical Commission, 1942), p. 9, laments the demise of the Tutelo "idiom."
30. Peden, *Notes,* p. 96.
31. The list is in Peden, *Notes,* pp. 103–107.
32. Ibid., pp. 96–97. Jefferson's identification of the Monacans with the Tus-

caroras was perhaps derived from Lewis Evans's 1755 "Analysis of a General Map of the Middle British Colonies," in Lawrence Henry Gipson, *Lewis Evans* (Philadelphia: Historical Society of Pennsylvania, 1939), pp. 12, 156.

33. Peden, *Notes,* p. 177.
34. William Stith, The *History of the First Discovery and Settlement of Virginia* (Williamsburgh: W. Parks, 1747), p. 67.
35. James F. Pendergast, "The Massawomeck: Raiders and Traders into Chesapeake Bay," *Transactions of the American Philosophical Society* 81, pt. 2 (1991): 68–73.
36. Karl Lehman-Hartleben, "Thomas Jefferson, Archaeologist," *American Journal of Archaeology* 47 (1943): 161–163, credits Jefferson with anticipating the fundamental approach and methods of modern archaeology by a full century, and Hantman (1993) praises his excavation strategy and research design as "extraordinary" for its time.
37. Peden, *Notes,* pp. 58–62.
38. Peden, *Notes,* p. 59.
39. For Thomson's career see Lewis R. Harley, *Life of Charles Thomson, Secretary of the Continental Congress and Translator of the Bible from the Greek* (Philadelphia: Jacobs, 1900), and the scholarly review by Whitfield J. Bell, Jr., in *Patriot Improvers: Biographical Sketches of Members of the American Philosophical Society,* vol. 1 (Phildelphia: APS, 1997). His role as secretary to Teedyuscung and protagonist of the Delawares is recounted, from various perspectives, by Paul A. W. Wallace, *Conrad Weiser, Friend of Colonist and Mohawk* (Philadelphia: University of Pennsylvania Press, 1945, rpt. Wennawoods Publishing of Lewisburg, Pa.); Anthony F. C. Wallace, *Teedyuscung, King of the Delawares* (Philadelphia: University of Pennsylvania Press, 1949, rpt. Syracuse University Press); and in several works of Francis Jennings, most recently *Benjamin Franklin—Politician: The Mask and the Man* (New York: Norton, 1996).
40. Harley, *Thomson,* p. 50.
41. Peden, *Notes,* pp. 197–208.
42. Roy Harvey Pearce, *The Savages of America: A Study of the Indian and the Idea of Civilization* (Baltimore: Johns Hopkins Press, 1953), pp. 91–96.
43. Ibid.
44. For reviews of currents of thought in the early development of anthropology, see Marvin Harris, *The Rise of Anthropological Theory* (New York: Crowell, 1968), and A. I. Hallowell, "The Beginnings of Anthropology in America," pp. 36–125, in *Contributions to Anthropology: Selected Papers of A. Irving Hallowell* (Chicago: University of Chicago Press, 1976). The role of Philadelphia and the APS is described in A. I. Hallowell, "Anthropology in Philadelphia," ibid. See also Freeman, "The American Philosophical Society in American Anthropology," in Jacob W. Gruber, *The Philadelphia Anthropological Society* (New York: Temple University Publications, 1967), pp. 32–46, and Clark

Wissler, "The American Indian and the American Philosophical Society," *Proceedings of the American Philosophical Society* 86 (1942): 108–122.
45. ASPIA 1, p. 53.
46. TJ to William Ludlow, September 6, 1824, quoted in Pearce, *Savages,* p. 155.
47. Peden, *Notes,* p. 143.
48. Ibid., p. 151.
49. Donald Jackson, *Letters of the Lewis and Clark Expedition, with Related Documents, 1783–1854* (Urbana: University of Illinois Press, 1978), vol. 2, pp. 669–673.
50. APS, *Transactions* 4 (1799): xxxviii.
51. Jackson, *Letters,* vol. 1, pp. 62–63.
52. Ibid., pp. 50–51.
53. Ibid., pp. 157–161.
54. For a careful accounting of the fate of the Lewis and Clark journals and other scientific "booty" of the expedition, see Paul R. Cutright, *A History of the Lewis and Clark Journals* (Norman: University of Oklahoma Press, 19XX), and *Lewis and Clark: Pioneering Naturalists* (Urbana: University of Illinois Press, 1969), and Gary Moulton, ed., *The Journals of the Lewis and Clark Expedition* (Lincoln: University of Nebraska Press, 1987–1996). There have been a number of versions and editions, beginning with Nicholas Biddle, *History of the Expedition under the Command of Captains Lewis and Clark* (Philadelphia: Bradford and Inskeep, 1814), and including most notably the 8-volume edition by R. G. Thwaites, *Original Journals of the Lewis and Clark Expedition, 1804–1806* (New York: 1904–1905), which for the first time published the journals in full from the manuscripts in the library of the APS. A new edition of the original journals, cited above, has been prepared by Gary Moulton from the original manuscripts. An invaluable supplement is Donald Jackson's two-volume edition of the letters and other papers of the Lewis and Clark expedition. For the value of their ethnographic observations, see Verne Ray and Nancy Lurie, "The Contributions of Lewis and Clark to Ethnography," *Journal of the Washington Academy of Sciences* 44 (1954): 358–370.
55. ASPIA, p. 707.
56. Ibid., p. 710.
57. Ibid., p. 708.
58. Peden, *Notes,* p. 140.
59. For the most complete account of Jefferson's Indian cabinet, I am idebted to Anne Lucas of Monticello for personal communications on the subject. See also Anne Lucas, "American Indian Artifacts," in Susan R. Stein, ed., *The Worlds of Thomas Jefferson at Monticello* (Charlottesville: Thomas Jefferson Memorial Foundation, 1993), pp. 404–440, and Silvio Bedini, "Man of Science," in Merrill D. Peterson, ed., *Thomas Jefferson: A Reference Biography* (New York: Scribner's, 1986), pp. 253–276.

60. APS, *Transactions* 4 (1799): xxx–xxxviii.
61. Donald Jackson, *Thomas Jefferson and the Stony Mountains: Exploring the West from Monticello* (Urbana: University of Illinois Press, 1981), pp. 94–96.

4. Native Americans through European Eyes

1. See the American publication edited by Albert E. Stone of Hector St. John de Crevecoeur, *Letters from an American Farmer,* which includes *Sketches of Eighteenth Century America,* first published in 1925 (New York: Penguin Books, 1986).
2. Peterson, *Life,* pp. 293–334.
3. Quoted in John P. Foley, ed., *The Jeffersonian Cyclopedia* (New York: Funk & Wagnalls, 1900), p. 475.
4. This work is available in a recent English translation edited by an anthropological specialist in Iroquois ethnohistory: Joseph F. Lafitau, *Customs of the American Indians Compared with the Customs of Primitive Times,* 1724, trans. and ed. William N. Fenton and Elizabeth L. Moore (Toronto: The Champlain Society, 1974–1977).
5. Peterson, *Writings,* p. 1261.
6. Lafitau, *Customs,* vol. 1, pp. 335–336.
7. Fenton, "Introduction" to Lafitau, *Customs.*
8. Peterson, *Writings,* pp. 1261–1262.
9. Ibid., pp. 1262–1263.
10. Constantin Volney's *Voyage en Syrie et en Egypt, pendant les annees 1783, 1784, et 1785* (Paris, 1792) and *Les ruines: ou, Meditation sur les revolutions des empires* (Paris, 1792), were early acquisitions of the APS library. Biographical sketches of Volney may be found in the *Nouvelle biographie generale* (Paris, 1866), and by Count Daru in the American edition of Volney's *Ruins,* but the major biography is Jean Gaulmier, *Volney: Un grand temoin de la revolution et de l'empire* (Paris: Hachette, 1959).
11. The event is recounted in Brodie, *Jefferson,* pp. 287–288, from a quotation from Volney's journal in Gaulmier, *Volney,* pp. 210–211.
12. The letter is quoted in Chinard, *Volney en L'Amerique,* p. 41.
13. Constantin Volney, *View of the Climate and Soil of the United States* (London: J. Johnson, 1804), pp. 396–397.
14. See Chinard, *Volney,* and Gaulmier, *Volney,* for accounts of Volney's American trip. Metchie Budka, *Under Their Vine and Fig Tree: Travels through America . . . by Julian Ursyn Niemcewicz* (Elizabeth, N.J.: Grassman, 1965), pp. 46–47, describes Volney's dinner with Jefferson.
15. Chinard, *Volney,* pp. 171–175.
16. There is a biography of Little Turtle by Harvey Carter, *The Life and Times of Little Turtle, First Sagamore of the Wabash* (Springfield: University of Illinois Press, 1987).

17. Volney's account of his meetings with Little Turtle was extensive, covering pp. 397–437 of the 1804 London edition. The Miami vocabulary occupies pp. 494–503.
18. TJ to A. von Humboldt, December 6, 1813, in Peterson, *Writings,* p. 1311.
19. A biographical sketch of Heckewelder may be found in DAB.
20. See George W. K. Stocking, Jr., "French Anthropology in 1800," in his *Race, Culture, and Evolution: Essays in the History of Anthropology* (New York: Free Press, 1968), for an extended account of the *Société.*
21. A sketch of the lives of Victor and Gabrielle du Pont may be found in Riggs's *Guide* to the collections at the Hagley Museum and Library, and there is a biography by Bessie Gardner du Pont, *Lives of Victor and Josephine du Pont* (Newark, Del., 1930).
22. See Wayne Andrews, "The Baroness Hyde de Neuville's Sketches of American Life, 1807–1822," and William N. Fenton, "The Hyde de Neuville Portraits of New York Savages in 1807–1808," *New-York Historical Society Quarterly* 38 (1954), for accounts of the drawings and their significance.
23. The manuscript of *La reserve Indienne,* with a partial English translation by Gabrielle du Pont's daughter Amelia, is at the Hagley Museum and Library, Winterthur MSS, Group 3, Series E (Mme. Victor du Pont), Box 33 ("Writings and Memoirs").
24. Augustus J. Foster, *Jeffersonian America* (San Marino: Huntington Library, 1954), pp. 192–193.
25. Ibid.
26. See William E. Foley and Charles D. Rice, "Visiting the President: An Exercise in Jeffersonian Indian Diplomacy," *The American West* 16 no. 6 (1979), for an overall account of Indian visits to Jefferson in Washington.
27. John Adams to TJ, June 28, 1813, in Bergh, *Writings,* vol. 13, p. 285.

5. In Search of Ancient Americans

1. The term "mounds" is commonly used to denote a variety of ancient American earthworks, including conical mounds, rectangular pyramids, square and circular walled enclosures with interior moats or ditches, and roads and causeways flanked by stone or earthen walls. A general summary of the archaeology of the mounds is provided in Roger Kennedy, *Hidden Cities: The Discovery and Loss of Ancient North American Civilization* (New York: Penguin Books, 1996), along with an extensive discussion of the reports of eighteenth- and nineteenth-century observers, and of the relative neglect shown by the general public.
2. Jones's *Journal* was reprinted for Joseph Sabin (New York, 1865).
3. Peden, *Notes,* p. 97.
4. Ibid., p. 13. Jefferson's investment in lands on the Ohio near the mouth of the New (Kanawha) River is noted in James A. Bear, Jr., and Lucia C. Stanton,

eds., "Jefferson's Memorandum Books," in Boyd, *Papers,* entry for March 22, 1769.

5. Bishop James Madison, "A Letter on the Supposed Fortifications of the Western Country," *Transactions of the American Philosophical Society* 6, pt. 1 (1804): 138–139.
6. Kenneth P. Bailey, *The Ohio Company of Virginia* (Glendale: Arthur H. Clark, 1939), pp. 154–155; map facing p. 210.
7. Quoted in Paul A. W. Wallace, *Indian Paths of Pennsylvania* (Harrisburg: Pennsylvania Historical and Museum Commission, 1961), p. 110.7. For other references to Indian antiquities at Redstone, see I. D. Rupp, *Early History of Western Pennsylvania* (Lewisburg: Wennawoods, 1995), p. 272; George P. Donehoo, *A History of Indian Villages and Place Names in Pennsylvania* (Lewisburg: Wennawooods, 1998), pp. 170–173; and Joseph E. Walker, ed., *Pleasure and Business in Western Pennsylvania: The Journal of Joshua Gilpin* (Harrisburg: Pennsylvania Historical and Museum Commission, 1975), pp. 46, 50.
8. Malone, *Jefferson,* vol. 1, pp. 242, 255.
9. Thomas P. Abernethy, *Western Lands and the American Revolution* (New York: Russell & Russell, 1959), gives valuable detail on all aspects of Virginia's interest in trans-Appalachian lands. For the Redstone squatters, see Abernethy, *Western Lands,* pp. 35, 77, and Randolph C. Downes, *Council Fires on the Upper Ohio* (Pittsburgh: University of Pittsburgh Press, 1940), p. 129.
10. TJ to Stiles, September 1, 1786, in Peterson, *Writings,* pp. 864–865.
11. TJ to Thomson, September 20, 1787, in Bergh, *Writings,* vol. 6, pp. 311–312.
12. Quoted in Kennedy, *Hidden Cities,* p. 85.
13. The discussion of Turnbull's theory is contained in TJ's correspondence with Edward Rutledge in Boyd, *Papers,* vols. 12, 13, and 15: Rutledge to TJ, October 23, 1787; TJ to Rutledge, July 18, 1788; Rutledge to TJ, April 1, 1789.
14. John Filson, *The Discovery, Settlement, and Present State of Kentucky* (Wilmington, Del.: Adams, 1784), pp. 87–91; see also the letter of Major Jonathan Heart to B. S. Barton in Gilbert Imlay, *Topograhical Description of the Western Territory of North America* (New York: Johnson Reprint, 1968), pp. 296–304.
15. Kennedy, *Hidden Cities,* pp. 73, 121, provides details of Jefferson's collection of Indian statuary.
16. Jonathan Heart, "A Letter . . . to Benjamin Smith Barton," *Transactions of the American Philosophical Society* 3 (1793): 214–222; Francis Harper, ed., *The Travels of William Bartram* (New Haven: Yale University Press, 1958); Peden, *Notes,* pp. xx, 42, 266; Kennedy, *Hidden Cities,* p. 24.
17. APS, *Transactions* 4 (1799): pp. xxxvii–xxxix.
18. Senator John Brown to William Lytle, Washington, November 22, 1803, in Library of the Cincinnati Historical Society, Cincinnati, Ohio.
19. Quoted in Kennedy, *Hidden Cities,* p. 134.

20. Madison, "Letter on the Supposed Fortifications."
21. Breckenridge's archaeological researches are described in Kennedy, *Hidden Cities,* pp. 183–185.
22. Caleb Atwater, "Description of the Antiquities Discovered in the State of Ohio and Other Western States," *Transactions of the American Antiquarian Society*, Archeologica Americana, 1820 (rpt. with introduction by Jeremy Sabloff, New York: AMS Press, 1973). Kennedy, *Hidden Cities,* pp. 239–240, gives the work high praise.
23. Albert Gallatin, "Synopsis of the Indian Tribes of North America," *Transactions and Collections of the American Antiquarian Society* 2 (1836): 1–422. He reiterated this view in 1845 in his work *On the Ancient Civilization of New Mexico and the Great Colorado of the West.* See Robert E. Bieder, *Science Encounters the Indian: The Early Years of American Ethnology* (Norman: University of Oklahoma Press, 1986), chap. 3, "Albert Gallatin and Enlightenment Ethnology," for a careful evaluation of Gallatin's scientific contributions. Gallatin's scientific contributions to the study of the mounds are praised by Kennedy in *Hidden Cities.*
24. Again, see Bieder and Kennedy for evaluations of Squier and Davis's contributions. Gordon R. Willey and Jeremy Sabloff, *A History of American Archaeology* (San Franciso: W. H. Freeman, 1980), review much of the early work on the mounds.
25. Peden, *Notes,* pp. 100–102.
26. W. Keith Percival, "Biological Analogy in the Study of Language before the Advent of Comparative Grammar," in Henry Hoenigswald and Linda F. Wiener, *Biological Metaphor and Cladistic Classification* (Philadelphia: University of Pennsylvania Press, 1987), p. 26.
27. Peden, *Notes,* pp. 100–101.
28. Peterson, *Writings,* p. 865.
29. John P. Foley, ed., *The Jeffersonian Cyclopedia* (New York: Funk & Wagnalls, 1907), pp. 1–2.
30. Ibid., p. 475.
31. E. Millicent Sowerby, *Catalogue of the Library of Thomas Jefferson* (Washington: Library of Congress, 1952–1958), vol. 5, pp. 59–63.
32. APS, "Vocabularies and Other MSS relating to Indian Languages," catalog number 497/v85; Boyd, *Papers,* vol. 20, pp. 467–470 ("The Northern Journey").
33. APS, "Vocabularies," 497/v85. The manuscript does not appear to be in Jefferson's hand, but an unidentified person's, possibly the one who collected the vocabulary, or DuPonceau's, who, while collating the APS vocabulary collection, inscribed the name "Mr. Thos. Jefferson" on the margin.
34. Peterson, *Writings,* p. 1083.
35. Bergh, *Writings,* vol. 5, p. 390; vol. 6, pp. 231, 244.
36. C. L. Grant, ed., *Letters, Journals, and Writings of Benjamin Hawkins,* vol. 1

(Savannah: Beehive Press, 1980), p. 340. Hawkins's career is described in the biography by Merritt B. Pound, *Benjamin Hawkins—Indian Agent* (Athens: University of Georgia Press, 1951).

37. APS, "Vocabularies," 497/v85.
38. The Jefferson vocabularies are part of the larger Collection of "Vocabularies and Other MSS relating to Indian Languages," APS 497/v85, and DuPonceau's digest 497/In 2.
39. Foley, *Cyclopedia*, p. 2.
40. Jefferson's comparative vocabulary at APS is 497/J35/.
41. See the detailed accounts of the Freeman and Pike expeditions in Dan L. Flores, ed., *Jefferson and Southwestern Exploration* (Norman: University of Oklahoma Press, 1984), and Donald Jackson, *Thomas Jefferson and the Stony Mountains: Exploring the West from Monticello* (Urbana: University of Illinois Press, 1981).
42. Jackson, *Thomas Jefferson and the Stony Mountains*, p. 172.
43. TJto B. Barton, September 12, 1809, in Peterson, Writings, pp. 1212–1213.
44. See Edward C. Carter II, *One Grand Pursuit: A Brief History of the American Philosophical Society's First 250 Years* (Philadelphia: APS, 1993), for a brief but authoritative history of the society, and Whitfield J. Bell, Jr., *Patriot Improvers* (Philadelphia: APS, 1997), for biographies of the early members.
45. APS, *Transactions* 4 (1799): xxxvii–xxxix. See also Roy Goodman and Pierre Swiggers, "John Vaughn and the Linguistic Collection in the Library of the American Philosophical Society," *Proceedings of the American Philosophical Society* 138 (1994): 251–271.
46. Barton's chequered career is reviewed in Whitfield J. Bell, Jr., "Benjamin Smith Barton, M.D. (Kiel)," *Journal of the History of Medicine and Allied Sciences* 26 (1971): 197–203; see also the biography in DAB.
47. Benjamin Smith Barton, *New Views on the Origin of the Tribes and Nations of America* (Philadelphia: Birren, 1797), pp. 186–188.
48. See Mary Haas's review of the 1968 reprint of Barton's *New Views* in *International Journal of American Linguistics* 36 (1970): 68–70; also see Mary Haas, "Grammar or Lexicon: The American Indian Side of the Question from Duponceau to Powell," *International Journal of American Linguistics*, 35 (1969): 239–255.
49. Barton, *New Views*.

6. Civilizing the Uncivilized Frontier

1. Thomas P. Abernethy, *Western Lands and the American Revolution* (New York: Russell & Russell, 1959), pp. 244–247, 270–273.
2. Peterson, *Writings*, p. 376.

3. Peter Onuf, *Statehood and Union: A History of the Northwest Ordinance* (Bloomington: Indiana University Press, 1992), p. 22.
4. Ibid., p. 63.
5. The Treaty of Fort Harmar is published in Wilcomb E. Washburn, *The American Indian and the United States: A Documentary History*, vol. 4 (New York: Random House, 1973), pp. 2278–2285. See Randolph C. Downes, *Council Fires on the Upper Ohio* (Pittsburgh: University of Pittsburgh Press, 1940), and R. S. Cotterill, *The Southern Indians: The Story of the Civilized Tribes before Removal* (Norman: University of Oklahoma Press, 1954), for careful reviews of these events.
6. *Constitution*, vol. 7 (Articles 6 and 9).
7. Quoted in Francis P. Prucha, *American Indian Policy in the Formative Years: The Indian Trade and Intercourse Acts, 1790–1834* (Cambridge: Harvard University Press, 1962), p. 30.
8. *Constitution*, vol. 7, pp. 31, 33 (Articles 1 and 2).
9. Boyd, *Papers*, vol. 9, pp. 640–642.
10. Bergh, *Writings*, vol. 5, p. 390.
11. ASPIA, pp. 53–54.
12. Ibid.
13. See John W. Caughey, *McGillivray of the Creeks* (Norman: University of Oklahoma Press, 1938).
14. Washburn, *The American Indian and the United States*, vol. 4, pp. 2286–2291.
15. Ibid., vol. 3, pp. 2151–53.
16. Quoted in Peterson, *Life*, p. 491.
17. See biography by North Callahan, *Henry Knox: General Washington's General* (New York: Rinehart, 1958).
18. For an account of these and other diplomatic and military events see Downes, *Council Fires*.
19. Peterson, *Writings*, p. 977.
20. Ibid., p. 982.
21. The diplomatic maneuverings and course of combat in the War for the Northwest Territory from 1789 to 1795 are carefully described in Downes, *Council Fires*, pp. 310–338.
22. Malone, *Life*, vol. 2, p. 412. Both Malone and Peterson provide accounts of Jefferson's inconclusive sparring with Hammond.
23. Ibid., vol. 2, p. 416.
24. This exchange is quoted in Drinnon, *Facing West*, pp. 81–82.
25. Quoted in Malone, *Life*, vol. 2, p. 413.
26. Brant's visit to Philadelphia is described in Isabel T. Kelsay, *Joseph Brant 1743–1807: Man of Two Worlds* (Syracuse: Syracuse University Press, 1984), pp. 478–482.

27. For an account of the reception at the Glaize of the American proposals see Downes, *Council Fires,* and Kelsay, *Joseph Brant.*
28. Richard White, *The Middle Ground: Indians, Empires, and Republics in the Great Lakes Region, 1650–1815* (Cambridge: Cambridge University Press, 1991), pp. 460–461; John G. Fitzpatrick, ed., *The Writings of George Washington* (Washington: Government Printing Office, 1939), vol. 8, p. 178.
29. Peterson, *Life,* pp. 546–547.
30. Ibid., pp. 456–458.
31. The most authoritative account of the Whiskey Rebellion is Thomas P. Slaughter, *The Whiskey Rebellion* (New York: Oxford University Press, 1986).
32. Peterson, *Writings,* pp. 1015–1017.
33. Jefferson's draft of the Kentucky Resolutions is included in Peterson, *Writings,* pp. 449–456. Both Peterson and Malone discuss Jefferson's reaction to the Alien and Sedition laws at some length.
34. The visit to Poosepatuck is described in Boyd's notes on Jefferson's itinerary for the northern tour (Boyd, *Papers,* vol. 20, pp. 449–452), along with a discussion of Jefferson's linguistic labors. The Unquachog vocabulary is printed in Boyd, *Papers,* vol. 20, pp. 467–470, and the original is at the APS.
35. Ethnohistorical accounts of the Unquachog community are to be found in Robert Grumet, *Historic Contact: Indian People and Colonists in Today's Northeastern United States in the Sixteenth through Eighteenth Centuries* (Norman: University of Oklahoma Press, 1995), pp. 159–163, and Ellice B. Gonzalez, "Tri-Racial Isolates in a Bi-Racial Society: Poosepatuck Ambiguity and Conflict," in Frank W. Porter, *Strategies for Survival: American Indians in the Eastern United States* (New York: Greenwood Press, 1986), pp. 113–137.
36. Henry R. Schoolcraft, *Historical and Statistical Information, Respecting the History, Condition, and Prospects of the Indian Tribes of the United States,* vol. 3 (Philadelphia: Lippincott, 1851–1857), p. 424, where the vocabulary was published and attributed to Madison; the original is at the APS.
37. An ethnohistorical account of Brotherton is provided in Edward M. Larrabee, *Recurrent Themes and Sequences in North American Indian-European Culture Contact* (Philadelphia: APS, 1976). A contemporary eye-witness account of a visit in 1795 is to be found in Henry Kammler, ed., *J. F. H. Autenrieth's Description of a Short Walking Tour in the Province of New Jersey* (Hamburg: C. E. Bohn, 1795). The site is now named Indian Mills, and a historical marker memorializes Brotherton.
38. Samuel S. Smith, *An Essay on the Causes of the Variety of Complexion and Figure in the Human Species* (Cambridge: Harvard University Press, 1965), p. 173.
39. Charles A. Weslager, *The Delaware Indians: A History* (New Brunswick: Rutgers University Press, 1972), pp. 306–310.
40. Larrabee, *Recurrent Themes,* p. 15.

41. See Kammler, *Autenrieth's Walking Tour,* and Larrabee, *Recurrent Themes and Sequences,* for the continuing story of Brotherton.
42. The history of the Goshen community has been carefully described in Earl P. Olmstead, *Blackcoats among the Delawares: David Zeisberger on the Ohio Frontier* (Kent: Kent State University Press, 1991), based on the original Moravian records.
43. Olmstead, *Blackcoats,* p. 125.
44. Charles A. Weslager, *The Delaware Indian Westward Migration* (Wallingford, Pa.: Middle Atlantic Press, 1978), p. 72.
45. See Merritt B. Pound, *Benjamin Hawkins* (Athens: University of Georgia Press, 1951), pp. 107–117, for some account of these southern traders.
46. Hawkins to TJ, June 14, 1786, in Boyd, *Papers,* vol. 9, p. 641; TJ to Hawkins, August 13, 1786, in Bergh, *Writings,* vol. 5, p. 390.
47. Hawkins's career is described in Pound's biography, *Benjamin Hawkins;* a selection of his correspondence and other papers has been edited by C. L Grant, *Letters, Journals, and Writings of Benjamin Hawkins* (Savannah: Beehive Press, 1980).
48. Pound, *Hawkins,* pp. 117, 168–172.
49. The Wetzels are memorialized in the DAB and in Clarence B. Allman, *The Life and Times of Lewis Wetzel* (Nappanee, Ind.: E. V. Publishing, 1932), and appear in Otis K. Rice, *Allegheny Frontier: West Virginia Beginnings 1730–1830* (Lexington: University of Kentucky Press, 1970), pp. 168–169, and in Downes, *Council Fires,* pp. 265–266.
50. I. D. Rupp, *Early History of Western Pennsylvania* (Lewisburg, Pa.: Wennawoods, 1995), pp. 180–181, and Appendix, p. 221.
51. Quoted in Downes, *Council Fires,* p. 138.
52. Logan Esarey, ed., *Messages and Letters of William Henry Harrison,* vol. 1 (Indianapolis: Indiana Historical Commission, 1922), pp. 224–225.; TJ to Dearborn, August 12, 1807, in Bergh, *Writings,* p. 324.
53. John Heckewelder, *History, Manners, and Customs of the Indian Nations Who Once Inhabited Pennsylvania and the Neighbouring States* (Philadelphia: Historical Society of Pennsylvania, 1876, originally published 1819), pp. 335–336.
54. Ibid., p. 336.
55. Peden, *Notes,* pp. 164–169.
56. J. Hector St. John de Crevecoeur, *Sketches of Eighteenth Century America,* ed. Albert E. Stone (New York: Penguin Books, 1986), pp. 319–320.
57. Slaughter, *Whiskey Rebellion,* p. 69.
58. TJ to Madison, December 28, 1794, in Peterson, *Writings,* pp. 1015–1017.
59. For an account of the early settlement of West Virginia see Rice, *Allegheny Frontier.*
60. James A. Bear, Jr., and Lucia C. Stanton, eds., "Jefferson's Memorandum Book," in Boyd, *Papers,* entries for December 29, 1771.

61. The early movement into Kentucky is discussed in Otis K. Rice, *Frontier Kentucky* (Lexington: University of Kentucky Press, 1993).
62. The Wataugans and the abortive state of Franklin are described in Samuel Cole Williams, *The Lost State of Franklin* (Philadelphia: Porcupine Press, 1974).
63. Ibid., p. 213.

7. President Jefferson's Indian Policy

1. James Richardson, ed., *A Compilation of Messages and Papers of the Presidents*, vol. 1 (New York: Bureau of National Literature, 1897), p. 314. John C. Miller, *Wolf by the Ears: Thomas Jefferson and Slavery* (New York: Free Press, 1977), notes TJ's early opposition to the Trade and Intercourse acts.
2. For an overview of the administration of Indian affairs in the early republic, see Francis P. Prucha, *American Indian Policy in the Formative Years: The Indian Trade and Intercourse Acts, 1790–1834* (Cambridge: Harvard University Press, 1970).
3. Malone, *Life*, vol. 4, p. 59.
4. Logan Esarey, ed., *Messages and Letters of William Henry Harrison*, vol. 1 (Indianapolis: Indiana Historical Commission, 1922), pp. 5–10.
5. See the biography of Hawkins by Merrit B. Pound, *Benjamin Hawkins—Indian Agent* (Athens: University of Georgia Press, 1951), and his writings edited by C. L. Grant, *Letters, Journals, and Writings of Benjamin Hawkins* (Savannah: Beehive Press, 1980).
6. Richard White, *The Middle Ground* (Cambridge: Cambridge University Press, 1991), pp. 500–501.
7. Pound, *Hawkins*, p. 160.
8. See Anthony F. C. Wallace, *The Long, Bitter Trail* (New York: Hill & Wang, 1993), for a discussion of the ideological and political issues involved in the Indian removal of the 1830s and 1840s.
9. Pound, *Hawkins*, pp. 166–167, 200.
10. Richardson, *Messages and Letters*, vol. 1, pp. 322–323.
11. Wilcomb E. Washburn, ed., *The American Indian and the United States: A Documentary History*, vol. 4 (New York: Random House, 1973), pp. 3162–3163.
12. Constantin Volney, *View of the Climate and Soil of the United States* (London: J. Johnson, 1804), pp. 393–397.
13. Prucha, *American Indian Policy*, chap. 6, describes in detail the efforts to control the whiskey trade.
14. Pound, *Hawkins*, pp. 174–189.
15. TJ to Hawkins, February 18, 1803, in Bergh, *Writings*, vol. 9, pp. 363–364.
16. Prucha, *American Indian Policy*, p. 159.
17. Ibid., p. 160.

18. Ibid., p. 162.
19. Ibid., p. 164.
20. Theodore J. Crackel, *Mr. Jefferson's Army: The Political and Social Reform of the Military Establishment, 1801–1809* (New York: New York University Press, 1987), contains an account of the military establishment during Jefferson's presidency.
21. ASPIA, p. 650.
22. Ibid., pp. 648–663.
23. Ibid., pp. 668–681.
24. The complications associated with the pretensions of Bowles and with Creek factionalism are detailed in R. S. Cotterill, *The Southern Indians* (Norman: University of Oklahoma Press, 1954), and Pound, *Hawkins.*
25. For the locations of factories, see Cotterill, *Southern Indians,* pp. 131–132, 139–140, and ASPIA, pp. 653–683.
26. TJ to Jackson, February 16, 1803, in Bergh, *Writings,* vol. 9, pp. 357–359.
27. TJ to Dearborn, December 29, 1802, Library of Congress microfilm 22110–22112 (copy at APS Library).
28. ASPIA, pp. 684–685; Richardson, *Messages,* vol. 1, pp. 340–342.
29. Bergh, *Writings,* vol. 9, pp. 357–360.
30. Ibid., pp. 361–363.
31. Ibid., pp. 369–371.
32. Richardson, *Messages,* p. 346.
33. John P. Foley, ed., *Jeffersonian Cyclopedia* (New York: Funk & Wagnalls, 1900), pp. 510–511.
34. Ibid., p. 515.
35. Ibid.
36. See Bulletin 30, "Kaskaskia" and "DuCoigne," and Sturtevant, *Handbook,* vol. 15, pp. 594–601 ("Illinois").
37. Harrison's *Memoirs,* quoted in Bulletin 30, vol. 1, p. 405
38. ASPIA, p. 687.
39. Maps and terms of the several land cessions mentioned in this and subsequent chapters are to be found in Charles C. Royce, *Indian Land Cessions in the United States,* Eighteenth Annual Report, Bureau of American Ethnology (Washington, 1899), the indispensable reference work on the subject.
40. Esarey, *Messages,* vol. 1, p. 101.
41. Ibid., pp. 121–123.
42. Ibid., pp. 80–81, 149.
43. Ibid., pp. 126–130.
44. Ibid., p. 128.
45. Ibid., pp. 147,149, 161, 164.
46. ASPIA, pp. 695–697; Royce, *Land Cessions.*
47. Richardson, *Messages,* vol. 1, p. 375.

48. C. Hale Sipe, *The Indian Wars of Pennsylvania* (Lewisburg, Pa.: Wennawoods, 1995), pp. 648–650.
49. Biographical details on Buckongehelas may be found in Bulletin 30; Charles A. Weslager, *Delaware Indian Westward Migration* (Wallingford, Pa.: Middle Atlantic Press, 1978), p. 62; Sipe, *Indian Wars,* pp. 715–716; and Esarey, *Messages,* vol. 1, p. 149.
50. Quoted in White, *Middle Ground,* p. 499.
51. The fate of the Delaware chiefs and others accused of witchcraft by the Shawnee Prophet is described in the White River Moravian misssion diaries edited by Lawrence Henry Gipson, *The Moravian Indian Mission on White River* (Indianapolis: Indiana Historical Bureau, 1938); see also White, *Middle Ground,* pp. 496–499; Weslager, *Delaware Indian Westward Migration,* p. 57; and R. David Edmunds, *The Shawnee Prophet* (Lincoln: University of Nebraska Press, 1983), pp. 44–46.
52. Esarey, *Messages,* vol. 1, pp. 182–184.
53. Royce, *Land Cessions,* pp. 53–54.
54. ASPIA, p. 745.
55. Ibid., pp. 745–748.
56. Pound, *Hawkins,* p. 184.
57. Cotterill, *Southern Indians,* pp. 152–153; ASPIA, pp. 698–699.
58. ASPIA, pp. 748–752.
59. Quoted in Cotterill, *Southern Indians,* p. 140.
60. Ibid., pp. 131–132.
61. ASPIA, p. 699.
62. Peterson, *Writings,* pp. 561–563; William G. McLoughlin, *Cherokee Renascence in the New Republic* (Princeton: Princeton University Press, 1968), pp. 92–108.
63. Cotterill, *Southern Indians,* pp. 157–159.
64. See Wallace, *Long, Bitter Trail,* for an account of Jackson and the Indian removal of the 1830s and 1840s.

8. The Louisiana Territory

1. From TJ's sketch of Meriwether Lewis, in Bergh, *Writings,* vol. 18, pp. 143–144.
2. Donald Jackson, ed., *Letters of the Lewis and Clark Expedition with Related Documents,* vol. 2 (Urbana: University of Illinois Press, 1962), pp. 669–672.
3. From TJ's autobiography in Peterson, *Writings,* pp. 61–62; see also TJ to Ezra Stiles, September 1, 1786, and to the Reverend James Madison, July 19, 1788, in Peterson, *Writings.*
4. TJ's sketch of Lewis in Bergh, *Writings,* vol. 18, pp. 144–145.
5. See Peterson, *Life,* pp. 763–764.
6. Jackson, *Letters of the Lewis and Clark Expedition*, vol. 1, p. 12.

7. Ibid., p. 64.
8. See James P. Ronda, *Lewis and Clark among the Indians* (Lincoln: University of Nebraska Press, 1984), for a detailed account of the interactions between the Corps of Discovery and the tribes they met along their way, and Stephen E. Ambrose, *Undaunted Courage: Meriwether Lewis, Thomas Jefferson, and the Opening of the American West* (New York: Simon and Schuster, 1995), for a stirring narrative of the expedition. The background of geographical knowledge (and fantasies) that inspired the quest for the Northwest Passage is provided in John Logan Allen's classic *Lewis and Clark and the Image of the American Northwest* (New York: Dover, 1991).
9. The following account of the Dunbar–Freeman expeditions in the southwest is drawn largely from Dan L. Flores, *Jefferson and Southwestern Exploration* (Norman: University of Oklahoma Press, 1984).
10. Ibid., p. 323.
11. Pike's involvement with Wilkinson and details of his two expeditions are described in Donald Jackson, *Thomas Jefferson and the Stony Mountains: Exploring the West from Monticello* (Urbana: University of Illinois Press, 1981), pp. 242–267.
12. Peterson, *Life*, pp. 771, 843.
13. Bergh, *Writings*, vol. 12, p. 28.
14. Harrison to TJ, June 27, 1804, in Logan Esarey, ed., *Messages and Letters of William Henry Harrison*, vol. 1 (Indianapolis: Indiana Historical Commission, 1922), pp. 96–100.
15. Ibid., pp. 100–101, Dearborn to Harrison, June 27, 1804.
16. Esarey, *Harrison's Messages*, vol. 1, pp. 110–111.
17. ASPIA, pp. 693–695. The area purchased is identified in Royce, *Land Cessions*, as "Cession 50."
18. Esarey, *Harrison's Messages*, vol. 1, p. 30.
19. The events leading to the treaty of 1804, and of the treaty itself, and to the Black Hawk War are documented in detail in Anthony F. C. Wallace, *Prelude to Disaster* (Springfield: Illinois State Historical Library, 1970).
20. Wilkinson to Dearborn, July 27, 1805, in, Clarence E. Carter, ed., *Territorial Papers of the United States, Louisiana-Missouri*, vol. 14 (Washington: Government Printing Office, 1949), p. 165.
21. Ibid., pp. 300–302.
22. Ibid., p. 504, TJ to Smith, May 4, 1806.
23. TJ to Harrison, January 16, 1806, in Esarey, *Harrison's Messages*, vol. 1, pp. 185–187.
24. Carter, *Territorial Papers, Louisiana*, vol. 14, pp. 245–247.
25. Ibid., p. 301.
26. TJ to Harrison, January 16, 1806, in Esarey, *Harrison's Messages*, vol. 1, pp. 185–187.

27. Dearborn to Wilkinson, April 9, 1806, in Carter, *Territorial Papers, Louisiana,* vol. 14, pp. 486–488.
28. John P. Foley, ed., *The Jeffersonian Cyclopedia* (New York: Funk & Wagnalls, 1900), pp. 510–511.
29. Lewis to TJ, December 8, 1803, quoted in Jackson, *Jefferson and the Stony Mountains,* pp. 147–148, from original in the Historical Society of Pennsylvania.
30. Esarey, *Harrison's Messages,* vol. 1, p. 153.
31. Ibid., p. 13.
32. Wilkinson to TJ, November 6, 1805, in Carter, *Territorial Papers, Louisiana,* vol. 14, pp. 266–267.
33. William E. Foley, "James A. Wilkinson, Territorial Governor," *Bulletin of the Missouri Historical Society* 65 (1968): 3–17, emphasizes that Wilkinson, already embroiled in controversies over the confirmation of Spanish land grants, was not sanguine about the chances for implementing the depopulation policy.
34. Wilkinson to Dearborn, August 10, 1805, in Carter, *Territorial Papers, Louisiana,* vol. 14, p. 183.
35. Ibid., p. 229, Wilkinson to Dearborn, September 22, 1805.
36. Ibid., pp. 230, 245.
37. Wilkinson has had several biographies, including James R. Jacobs, *Tarnished Warrior* (New York: Macmillan, 1938), which attests to the governor's remarkable combination of greed, duplicity, and political astuteness. David L. Chandler, *The Jefferson Conspiracies: A President's Role in the Assassination of Meriwether Lewis* (New York: Morrow, 1994), presents evidence to support the general thesis that Jefferson's involvement with Wilkinson was more complex than has been commonly supposed, although in my opinion it fails to prove that Lewis was murdered or that Jefferson was an accomplice after the fact by conspiring to conceal the general's involvement.
38. See Samuel C. Williams, "William Tatham, Wataugan," *Tennessee Historical Magazine* 7 (1921): 154–179.
39. Peterson, *Writings,* pp. 1137–1138.
40. Ibid., p. 1142.
41. Shahaka's visit to Washington and Philadelphia, and his return to the Mandan village, are chronicled in William E. Foley and Charles D. Rice, "The Return of the Mandan Chief," *Montana, The Magazine of Western History* 29 (Summer 1979). A brief biography of Shahaka may be found in Bulletin 30. One of the portraits of Shahaka allegedly painted by Saint-Mémin is actually that of a Delaware Indian; see Luke Lockwood, "The Saint-Mémin Indian Portraits," *New-York Historical Society Quarterly* 12 (1928), and Ellen G. Miles, "Saint-Mémin," *American Art Journal* 20 (1988): 3–33.
42. Peterson, *Writings,* pp. 564–566. 50.
43. TJ to Lewis, July 17, 1808, in Bergh, *Writings,* vol. 12, p. 99.

44. Ibid., p. 148, TJ to Lewis, August 24, 1808.
45. See Jerome O. Steffen, *William Clark: Jeffersonian Man on the Frontier* (Norman: University of Oklahoma Press, 1977), and Richard W. Dillon, *Meriwether Lewis* (New York: Coward McCann, 1965), pp. 63–86, for an account of the Missouri Fur Company.
46. Dillon, *Meriwether Lewis,* supports the allegation of Lewis's involvement with the Company.
47. Lewis to Dearborn, August 18, 1809, in Carter, *Territorial Papers, Louisiana,* vol. 14, pp. 290–293.
48. Ibid., pp. 196–203, Lewis to Dearborn, July 1, 1808.
49. Ibid., pp. 219–221, TJ to Lewis, August 21, 1808.
50. TJ to Dearborn, August 20, 1808, in Bergh, *Writings,* vol. 12, pp. 139–140.
51. Carter, *Territorial Papers, Louisiana,* pp. 196–203.
52. Ibid., pp. 224–228, Clark to Dearborn, September 23, 1808, containing the account of his treaty.
53. ASPIA, pp. 763–764.
54. Ibid., pp. 765–767.
55. For varying accounts of Lewis's death, see Dillon, *Meriwether Lewis;* Chandler, *Jefferson Conspiracies;* and Jefferson's own biographical sketch of Lewis.
56. Bulletin 30, "Mandan" and "Shahaka," and Foley and Rice, "Return of the Mandan Chief."
57. TJ to Harrison, February 27, 1803, in Bergh, *Writings,* vol. 9, pp. 370–371.
58. Ibid., vol. 10, pp. 390–396, TJ to Claiborne, May 24, 1803.
59. See Richard Drinnon, *Facing West: Indian Hating and Empire Building* (New York: Schocken Books, 1990), pp. 83–85, and Bergh, *Writings,* vol. 16, pp. 412, 431–435.
60. For the Delaware removal, see Charles A. Weslager, *Delaware Indian Westward Migration* (Wallingford, Pa.: Middle Atlantic Press, 1978). The movements of the Ohio Valley–Great Lakes tribes are detailed in the tribal histories in Sturtevant, *Handbook,* vol. 15.

9. Confrontation with the Old Way

1. Bernard Sheehan, *Seeds of Extinction: Jeffersonian Philanthropy and the American Indian* (Chapel Hill: University of North Carolina Press, 1973), p. 2.
2. The philosophical background of the civilization policy is discussed at length by Sheehan. More general treatments may be found in J. B. Bury, *The Idea of Progress* (New York: Dover, 1955), and Margaret T. Hodgen, *Early Anthropology in the Sixteenth and Seventeenth Centuries* (Philadelphia: University of Pennsylvania Press, 1964).
3. Peterson, *Writings,* p. 554.
4. Peden, *Notes,* p. 151.

5. The history of the Brafferton Institution is reviewed in chapter 3 of Margaret Szasz, *Indian Education in the American Colonies.* (Albuquerque: University of New Mexico Press, 1988).
6. For Knox's proposal, see ASPIA, pp. 53–54.
7. James Richardson, ed., *A Compilation of the Messages and Papers of the Presidents*, vol. 1, (New York: Bureau of National Literature, 1897), p. 314.
8. ASPIA, pp. 464–468.
9. Richardson, *Messages,* vol. 1, p. 322.
10. Wilcomb E. Washburn, ed., *The American Indian and the United States: A Documentary History,* vol. 3 (New York: Random House, 1973), pp. 2154–2168.
11. Richardson, *Messages,* vol. 1, p. 322.
12. Ibid., p. 347.
13. Ibid., pp. 359–360.
14. Ibid., pp. 374–375.
15. Ibid., pp. 395–396.
16. Ibid., pp. 415–416.
17. Ibid., pp. 441–442.
18. For discussions of Jefferson's religious views, see Peterson, *Life,* pp. 951–961; Brodie, *Jefferson,* pp. 372–373; and Malone, *Jefferson,* vol. 4, pp. 200–205. His extracts from the Gospels are printed in F. Forester Church, ed., *The Jefferson Bible: The Life and Morals of Jesus of Nazareth* (Boston: Beacon Press, 1989), which omits reference to miracles and the virgin birth.
19. Jedidiah Morse, *A Report to the Secretary of War of the United States on Indian Affairs* (New Haven: Converse, 1822).
20. TJ to Morse, March 6, 1822, in Bergh, *Writings,* vol. 15, pp. 35, 60–62.
21. ASPIA, p. 689.
22. Ibid., p. 651.
23. Ibid., pp. 659–662.
24. Ibid., p. 698.
25. Ibid., p. 704.
26. Ibid., p. 744.
27. Ibid., p. 674.
28. Ibid., p. 687.
29. Ibid., p. 690.
30. Ibid., p. 747.
31. Ibid., pp. 693–694; Washburn, *Documentary History,* vol. 3, p. 2313.
32. Ibid., pp. 763–764; Washburn, *Documentary History,* vol. 3, p. 2332.
33. Hawkins's agency is described in Merritt B. Pound, *Benjamin Hawkins* (Athens: University of Georgia Press, 1951), pp. 106–116, 142–147, and in Joel Martin, *Sacred Revolt: The Muskogees' Struggle for a New World* (Boston: Beacon Press, 1991), pp. 96–97.
34. Pound, *Hawkins,* p. 147.

35. For Hawkins's life, see the biography by Pound, and C. L. Grant, *Letters, Journals, and Writings of Benjamin Hawkins* (Savannah: Beehive Press, 1980).
36. The treaty provisions are summarized in Grace S. Woodward, *The Cherokees* (Norman: University of Oklahoma Press, 1963), pp. 121–123; see also Royce, *Land Cessions,* p. 652.
37. ASPIA, p. 205.
38. See Grant, *Letters,* and Pound, *Benjamin Hawkins,* pp. 102–106, for an account of the Cherokees in the 1790s.
39. See the biography of Meigs in DAB.
40. Blackburn's educational mission is described in Woodward, *The Cherokees,* pp. 123–127, and in Sheehan, *Seeds of Extinction,* p. 138.
41. Peterson, *Writings,* pp. 561–563.
42. Quoted in Anthony F. C. Wallace, *The Death and Rebirth of the Seneca* (New York: Knopf, 1970), pp. 203–204.
43. Peterson, *Writings,* pp. 556–557.
44. The story of the Quaker mission to the Senecas and the revitalization movement of Handsome Lake is told in detail in A. Wallace, *Death and Rebirth of the Seneca.*
45. See Anthony F. C. Wallace, *King of the Delawares: Teedyuscung, 1700–1763* (Syracuse: Syracuse University Press, 1990), and Charles A. Weslager, *The Delaware Indians* (New Brunswick: Rutgers University Press, 1972), for accounts of the Moravian missions among the Delawares. Primary sources on the Moravian missions are extensive, particularly in the Moravian Archives in Bethlehem, and a number of excellent secondary works are available that quote liberally from the manuscripts, such as Lawrence H. Gipson, *The Moravian Indian Mission on White River* (Indianapolis: Indiana Historical Bureau, 1938), Paul A. W. Wallace, *The Travels of John Heckewelder in Frontier America* (Pittsburgh: University of Pittsburgh Press, 1985), and Earl P. Olmstead, *Blackcoats among the Delawares: David Zeisberger on the Ohio Frontier* (Kent: Kent State University Press, 1991).
46. William W. Newcomb, Jr., *The Culture and Acculturation of the Delaware Indians* (Ann Arbor: University of Michigan, 1956), pp. 90–93.
47. ASPIA, p. 686.
48. Esarey, *Messages,* p. 218.
49. Ibid., pp. 259–265.
50. A. Wallace, *Death and Rebirth of the Seneca.*
51. Isabel T. Kelsay, *Joseph Brant 1743–1807: Man of Two Worlds* (Syracuse: Syracuse University Press, 1984), p. 564.
52. Constantin Volney, *View of the Climate and Soil of the United States* (London: J. Johnson, 1804), pp. 395–396.
53. Esarey, *Messages,* p. 29.
54. Ibid., pp. 31–32.

55. Richardson, *Messages,* vol. 1, pp. 322–323.
56. Quoted in Sheehan, *Seeds of Extinction,* p. 239.
57. Richard White, *The Middle Ground* (Cambridge: Cambridge University Press, 1991).
58. Quoted in A. Wallace, *Death and Rebirth,* p. 310.
59. Volney, *View,* pp. 434–435.
60. The episode of Cornplanter's sawmill is recounted in A. Wallace, *Death and Rebirth,* pp. 287–288.
61. Esarey, *Messages,* vol. 1, pp. 100, 115, 211–214.
62. White, *Middle Ground,* p. 496; see biography in DAB.
63. Esarey, *Messages,* vol. 1, p. 29; see also White's discussion of the Ohio–Great Lakes chiefs in *Middle Ground,* pp. 493–502.
64. Vann's career is reviewed in Woodward, *The Cherokees,* pp. 122–123, 129.
65. The demise of the Cherokee "state" is discussed in detail in Fred Gearing, *Priests and Warriors,* American Anthropological Association, Memoir 93, 1962.
66. Samuel Cole Williams, "William Tatham, Wataugan," *Tennessee Historical Magazine* 73 (1921): 154–179.
67. R. S. Cotterill, *The Southern Indians: The Story of the Civilized Tribes before Removal* (Norman: University of Oklahoma Press, 1954), pp. 158–160.
68. Woodward, *Cherokees,* pp. 126–127.
69. Quoted in Pound, *Benjamin Hawkins,* p. 162.
70. Hawkins's creation of a Creek national council is described in Pound, *Benjamin Hawkins,* pp. 162–164, and ASPIA, p. 647. Martin, *Sacred Revolt,* paints an unflattering portrait of Hawkins as a patriarchal, culturally chauvinist proponent of "Indian reform."
71. Richardson, *Messages,* p. 368.
72. Pound, *Benjamin Hawkins,* p. 136.
73. The career of Tame King is followed by Cotterill in *Southern Indians,* pp. 58, 61, 66, 72, 128–129, 135, 145.
74. R. David Edmunds, *The Shawnee Prophet* (Lincoln: University of Nebraska Press, 1983), pp. 17–19, describes the efforts of Black Hoof to get aid for his pro-civilization faction.
75. Ibid., pp. 28–29.
76. The definitive study of the Shawnee Prophet and his revitalization movement is Edmunds's *Shawnee Prophet.*
77. Esarey, *Messages,* vol. 1, p. 183.
78. Quoted in Edmunds, *Shawnee Prophet,* p. 48.
79. Ibid., pp. 193–194.
80. Edmunds, *Shawnee Prophet,* p. 58.
81. Bergh, *Writings,* vol. 8, pp. 142–143.
82. Esarey, *Messages,* pp. 223–224.

83. Bergh, vol. 11, p. 325.
84. Esarey, *Messages,* pp. 235–236.
85. Ibid., pp. 243–244.
86. Bergh, *Writings,* vol. 11, pp. 342–343.
87. Ibid., pp. 344–345.
88. Ibid., pp. 354–355.
89. Esarey, *Messages,* pp. 290–291.
90. Ibid., p. 202.
91. Bergh, *Writings,* vol. 13, p. 143.
92. Esarey, *Messsages,* p. 549.
93. Ibid., p. 334.
94. Ibid., pp. 322–323.
95. Ibid., pp. 387–391.

10. Return to Philosophical Hall

1. Edward C. Carter, II, *"One Grand Pursuit": A Brief History of the American Philosophical Society's First 250 Years, 1743–1993* (Philadelphia: APS, 1993).
2. The records of the Historical and Literary Committee (hereafter RHLC) are preserved in the library of the APS and include committee minutes and correspondence, chiefly of DuPonceau's on linguistic subjects.
3. HSP, RHLC, TJ to DuPonceau, January 22, 1816.
4. HSP, RHLC, DuPonceau to TJ, February 17, 1817.
5. HSP, RHLC, TJ to DuPonceau, June 28, 1817.
6. *Transactions of the American Philosophical Society,* n.s. 1 (1819): xvii–l.
7. HSP, RHLC, TJ to DuPonceau, July 7, 1820, DuPonceau to TJ, July 12, July 18, 1820.
8. See Thomas A. Kirby, "Jefferson's Letters to Pickering," in Thomas A. Kirby and Henry B. Woolf, eds., *Philologica: The Malone Anniversary Studies* (Baltimore: Johns Hopkins University Press, 1949), for the text of the Jefferson–Pickering correspondence, along with illuminating editorial comments and notes; also H. C. Montgomery, "Thomas Jefferson as a Philologist," *American Journal of Philology* 65 (1944): 367–371.
9. APS, "James Barbour Circular," May 15, 1826, among Vocabularies and other Manuscripts Relating to Indian Languages, 497/V85.
10. Roy Goodman and Pierre Swiggers, "Albert Gallatin's Table of North American Native Languages," *Bulletin internationale de documentation linguistique* 138 (1991–1993): 240–248.
11. Albert Gallatin, "A Synopsis of the Indian Tribes of North America," *Transactions and Collections of the American Antiquarian Society* 2 (1836): 1–422.
12. See Robert E. Bieder, *Science Encounters the Indian: The Early Years of American Ethnology* (Norman: University of Oklahoma Press, 1986), chap. 3 "Albert

Gallatin and Enlightenment Ethnology," for an evaluation of Gallatin's scientific contributions.

13. See the discussion of Morse's position in Anthony F. C. Wallace, *The Long, Bitter Trail* (New York: Hill & Wang, 1993), p. 61.
14. Andrew Jackson's message to Congress, December 8, 1829, rpt. in A. Wallace, *The Long, Bitter Trail,* p. 121.
15. John Heckewelder, *History, Manners, and Customs of the Indian Nations Who Once Inhabited Pennsylvania and the Neighbouring States* (Philadelphia: Historical Society of Pennsylvania, 1876), p. 345.
16. See the biography of Lewis Cass by Frank B. Woodford, *Lewis Cass: The Last Jeffersonian* (New Brunswick: Rutgers University Press, 1950). The nomination for membership in the APS is dated May 18, 1826. Cass's writings on the Indians and Indian removal are discussed in some detail in A. Wallace, *The Long, Bitter Trail,* pp. 41–49.
17. Franklin Edgerton, "Notes on Early American Work in Linguistics," *Proceedings of the American Philosophical Society* (1943): 25–34. The works of both Cass and Schoolcraft are reviewed by Bieder in *Science Encounters the Indian.*
18. See Peterson, *Life,* pp. 961–988, and Malone, *Life,* vol. 6 pp. 365–443, for accounts of Jefferson's role in creating the University of Virginia.
19. Edwin A. Betts, "The Correspondence between Constantine Samuel Rafinesque and Thomas Jefferson," *Proceedings of the American Philosophical Society* 87 (1944): 368–380, contains the correspondence between Rafinesque and Jefferson relating to the chair at Charlottesville and American Indian languages and history. His application for the post on the Red River expedition is described in Donald Jackson, *Thomas Jefferson and the Stony Mountains* (Urbana: University of Illinois Press, 1981), pp. 227–229, and Dan L. Flores, *Jefferson and Southwestern Exploration* (Norman: University of Oklahoma Press, 1984), p. 57.
20. Rafinesque's early meetings with American Indians are recounted in Constantine Rafinesque, *A Life of Travels in North America and South Europe* (Philadelphia, 1836). Jefferson's admiration for Pahuska and his Osage delegation is in TJ to Gallatin, July 12, 1804, in Donald Jackson, ed., *Letters of the Lewis and Clark Expedition,* vol. 1 (Urbana: University of Illinois Press, 1962), pp. 199–202.
21. Betts, "Correspondence," pp. 379–380.
22. Constantine S. Rafinesque, *Ancient History, or Annals of Kentucky; with a Survey of the Ancient Monuments of North America, And a Tabular View of the Present Languages and Primitive Nations of the Whole Earth* (Frankford, 1824), a 43-page pamphlet presented to the APS by the author. An edition by Eli Lilly, *Walam Olum or Red Score,* including a photographic reproduction of Rafinesque's original manuscript, his translation, and editorial essays by scholars, was published by the Indiana Historical Society in 1954. See David

Oestreicher, "Unmasking the Walam Olum: A 19th Century Hoax," and "Text Out of Context: The Arguments that Created and Sustained the Walam Olum," *Bulletin of the Archaeological Society of New Jersey,* nos. 49 and 50 (1995 and 1996), and "Unraveling the Walam Olum," *Natural History* 105 (1996): 14–20.

23. Bulletin 30, pp. 949–951.
24. TJ to Isaiah Thomas, October 14, 1820, MS in the Library of the American Antiquarian Society.

Acknowledgments

William N. Fenton, anthropologist and dean of Iroquoian studies, first suggested a book on Jefferson and the Indians at a conference we attended in 1952 at Williamsburg, Virginia, sponsored by the Institute of Early American History and Culture. His essay, with a bibliography, was later published by the Institute under the title *American Indian and White Relations to 1830* (Chapel Hill: University of North Carolina Press, 1957). The work contained the seminal phrase: "Jefferson's interest in and policy toward the Indians deserve a comprehensive study not yet written." As scholar, mentor, and friend, Bill Fenton has greatly benefited all of us who are concerned with the history of Indian–white relations.

This book began as a paper delivered at the Missouri Historical Society in St. Louis, at a conference on the subject of Thomas Jefferson and the West and published in the conference proceedings with the title "The Obtaining Lands: Thomas Jefferson and the Native Americans" in James P. Ronda, ed., *Thomas Jefferson and the Changing West* (Albuquerque: University of New Mexico Press, 1997, (pp. 25–41). To Merrill Peterson, then president of the Thomas Jefferson Memorial Foundation, I owe a debt of gratitude for the opportunity to seize a bear by the tail (or, to use Jefferson's phrase, a wolf by the ears) and enter the Jefferson industry.

Gratitude is also owing to many others. To the staff at Monticello, particularly to Daniel P. Jordan, president of the Thomas Jefferson Memorial Foundation, Douglas L. Wilson, former director of the International Center for Jeffersonian Studies, Lucia Stanton, director of research, and Anne Lucas, I want to express thanks for encouragement, hospitality, and assistance. The people at the Library of the American Philosophical Society were a constant and invaluable source of advice and aid, particularly Edward C. Carter, director of the library, Beth Carroll-Horrocks, manuscript librarian, and her successor, Robert Cox, Roy Goodman, curator of printed materials, and photographer Frank Margeson. The staff at the Alderman Library at the University of Virginia, particularly Robin D. Wear, were helpful in making their rich manuscript and microfilm resources available on short notice, and Marjorie McNinch at the Hagley Museum and Library has been of great assistance in this as in many other projects. J. Huston McCulloch of Ohio State University and Anne B. Shepard of The Cincinnati Historical Society generously provided me with information about Jefferson's interest in the earthworks at Milford, Ohio.

My friends Robert Grumet, Regna Darnell, and Raymond Fogelson read parts of the manuscript and provided indispensable critiques and bibliographical leads. To James Farrell I am indebted for preparing the excellent maps. And to Aida Donald and Susan Wallace Boehmer, my editors at Harvard University Press, I am grateful for insightful and supportive contributions. To my loyal typist, the late Judy Murray, I owe a large measure of gratitude for patiently deciphering my scrawl. And finally thanks go to my wife, Betty, who has been a constant source of encouragement and support, accompanying me on trips, looking up sources on Jefferson's friend James Madison, and making useful suggestions for rendering the book more readable.

List of Illustrations

List of Documents

Index